ENCYCLOPAEDIA OF COMPUTER SOFTWARE TECHNOLOGY

ENCYCLOPAEDIA
OF
COMPUTER SOFTWARE TECHNOLOGY

[Volume –Two]

Editor-in-Chief
Ajay Kumar

INSTITUTE FOR SUSTAINABLE DEVELOPMENT
LUCKNOW
&
ANMOL PUBLICATIONS PVT. LTD.
NEW DELHI - 110 002 (INDIA)

ANMOL PUBLICATIONS PVT. LTD.
4374/4B, Ansari Road, Daryaganj
New Delhi - 110 002
Ph.: 3261597, 3278000
Visit us at: www.anmolbooks.com

Encyclopaedia of Computer Software Technology

First Edition, 2003

ISBN 81-261-1385-5 (Set)

[Responsibility for the facts stated, opinions expressed, conclusions reached and plagiarism, if any, in these volumes is entirely that of the ISD, Lucknow. The Publisher bears no responsibility for them, whatsoever.]

PRINTED IN INDIA

Published by J.L. Kumar for Anmol Publications Pvt. Ltd., New Delhi and Printed at Mehra Offset Press, Delhi.

Contents

Vol. 3

Preface

Today, the term 'computer' is synonymous with digital computer, but until the 1960s, analog computers were popular. An analog computer relies on analogies between physical effects to make calculations. For example, the voltages in an analog computer may represent temperatures in a heat exchanger, capacitors may represent heat storage capacity, electrical currents may represent heat flow, and so forth. A digital computer, in contrast, deals with values as numerical digits. Because of their versatility, speed, and relatively low cost, digital computers have almost entirely replaced the analog variety.

Computer programs, the software that is becoming an ever-larger part of the computer system, are growing more and more complicated, requiring teams of programmes and years of effort to develop. As a consequence, a new subdiscipline, software engineering, has arisen. As the size and complexity of software has grown, the concept of reuse has become increasingly important in software engineering, since it is clear that extensive new software cannot be created cheaply and rapidly without incorporating existing program modules (subroutines, or pieces of computer code). Sophisticated techniques for testing software have therefore been designed. The need for better trained software engineers has led to the development of educational programs in separate program. The recommendation that software engineers, like other engineers, be licensed or certified is gaining increasing support, as is the momentum toward the accreditation of software engineering degree programs.

The lack of standardization and smooth interoperability in UNIX led Microsoft to develop Windows NT, an operating system that overcome these problems and also provided an integral GUI. From the outside, the system appears much the same as Windows 95 or a Macintosh system, with icons and a mouse. Internally it is quite different, structured so that it can serve in a hand-alone workstation or in a file server on a network, depending on the version of the product. The system also provides easy networking in a commercial environment; adding file servers or shared peripherals is a simple setup task that requires little more than physically interconnecting equipment and setting parameters in a menu.

Windows 95, MS-DOS, OS/2, and other common operating systems are then run as client processes under Windows NT, much in the same way CMS and MVS run under VM on IBM mainframes. A so-called hardware abstraction layer isolates the software from the details of the underlying hardware, giving Windows NT platform-independence. The operating system is therefore portable from one platform to another. Windows NT is used with the upper-end Intel microprocessors and DEC's Alpha chip, a microprocessor for the VAX computer, and will undoubtedly be transport to other platforms.

The present book in three volumes is welcome addition to the existing literature which is really encyclopaedic in nature. The entire information is gathered under twenty nine chapters followed by an exhaustive glossary and Index.

Finally, we will be failing in our duty if we do not acknowledge the kind of assistance we received from our colleagues at the Institute in completion of this volume. We are equally indebted to Shri J.L. Kumar, Managing Director, Anmol Publications Pvt. Ltd., New Delhi for publishing this manuscript in a very limited time.

—Editor-in-Chief

9

Software: System, Applications, Problem Solving and Algorithms

This chapter deals with an entirely different concept area from the first three chapters of the book. This chapter shall introduce the user to the concept of Software.

Software is a very widely and loosely used term to refer to various computer programs. In essence any program written in any language that will work on a given particular computer system can be classified as software. Hence, it can be said that "Software" is a logical and sequential series of instructions which are given to any computer system on the basis of which the system performs any given task.

A computer system may easily be called as a dumb heap of sand if it does not have any software. The system is called the hardware and will have other physical parts attached to itself.

The software available and necessary for the computer system to function at the most optimal level are numerous and varied. In fact, due to the tremendous variety of software available, it is necessary to classify software into diverse groups for a clearer understanding.

Though there is no universal classification of software, it can be divided into the following groups:

1. Processor Level Software
2. Systems Software
3. Applications Software
4. Custom Generated Software

Processor Level Software

This class of software is the kind which deals with designing and assembling of microprocessors. This will includes microprocessors used in equipment like washing machines, calculators etc.

This kind of software is usually developed in big concerns like Hewlett Packard, Intel etc., firms which are basically involved in designing microprocessors for various applications.

This software is usually written in machine code and is burnt onto the processor where it is stored in the form of magnetic patterns on transistors.

System Software

This software is programs which are written to look after and help in the management of computer systems. System software is used in almost any kind of computer system may it be a mainframe, mini or a microcomputer system.

The best example of a system software is the DOS or the Disk Operating System, also known only as the Operating System. Details of the operating system are dealt with later. System software is in fact a branch in itself. System programmers are hired by software development firms like Microsoft etc. to keep on writing better and improved systems software.

Systems software is usually written in either C or similar languages. Examples of some latest system software are DR-DOS, UNIX, OS-2, PC-MOS etc.

Applications Software

Applications software is software which is written for the user to develop further software of a certain kind. In fact, any programming language like BASIC, dBASE III, CLIPPER, PROLOG, PASCAL, ACAD etc. can be termed as an application software.

Applications packages are written in some or the other low level language like assembly language or in newer languages like C which allow the user to develop end user software of even application software. Applications software is usually sold by companies to either programmers who would develop custom packages for the end users or to end users who are able to use it directly without the help of an intermediary.

A good example of such a package is dBASE III Plus. We shall learn about dBASE III in detail, later on in this book. However, dBASE III is a package which can be used by the end user to maintain a lot of records as well as be used by a programmer as a developmental tool for making a computer program specific to the needs of the end user.

Besides such dual purpose packages, there also are other application software packages like LOTUS 1-2-3, Wordstar etc. which do not really allow any programming but facilitate certain specific tasks for the user.

Custom Generated Software

Custom Generated Software are programs written in any of the programming languages or applications software, which will carry out certain tasks, specific to the end user.

COBOL and BASIC were some of the most popular languages a few years back for writing such kind of software. However, with the advent of newer and more powerful languages like DBASE, FOXBASE, C, PROLOG, etc. these two languages have lost their popularity to a certain extent.

FUNDAMENTALS OF SOFTWARE DEVELOPMENT

In any situation which requires problem solving, the whole process can be divided into three phases. These are:

1. Analysis of the problem
2. Design of an algorithm for solving the problem
3. Computer implementation of the algorithm

Problem Analysis

Problem analysis can be further divided into the following separate steps.

1. Precisely define the problem
2. Determine whether or not a solution already exists for it
3. Identify the inputs and variables of the problem
4. Identify the outputs desired from the solution
5. Determine if a computer is required or not
6. Obtain all information required to develop a solution.

Definition of the problem is often considered to be a trivial step. Nothing could be further from the truth. In fact, a careful and precise definition of the problem is an absolute necessity. Several possible consequences of not developing a complete and precise definition may cause a number of difficulties.

This can be further explained by the following example. Suppose we had a problem of deciding which is the best route to follow in driving to and fro from work. We may spend a considerable amount of time in developing a method to solve this problem. But this may not be the problem which has to be really solved. Rather, the problem may be finding the best way of going to work (note, not route but way). In this case, several alternatives exist, like public transport, etc. Also, in choosing the best route to follow, the word best is ambiguous. This so because we do not know in what sense is the word 'best' used. The best route may be the shortest driving distance, or the shortest driving time, or one in which the least signals are encountered. Thus, an important criteria is that the problem should be defined in precise and clear terms.

Once a precise definition is obtained, we should attempt to find out if any solution already exists. If one does, it can save us the trouble of finding out a proper solution. Identification of the inputs to a problem and the variables involved, is a very important step. The inputs consist of the data to be processed. These have to be clearly defined beforehand.

The task of identifying problem outputs is closely related to the definition of the problem. A considerable amount of judgment is required in this step because producing more output than necessary is a waste of resources, while having less than needed is also wasteful.

After we have identified all the inputs, variables and outputs associated with a problem, our last step is to gather all the information of the problem. Once this is done, the programmer can get down to the task of solving the problem.

Algorithm Design

After a problem has been properly analysed, we are ready to develop a method for its solution. This method of solution is embodied in what we call an algorithm. An algorithm is simply a procedure consisting of a set of unambiguous rules which specify a sequence of operations that provides the solution to a problem in a finite number of steps. As we shall see, an algorithm can be represented in many different ways. Stated simply, however an algorithm represents the logic involved in arriving at the solution to a problem. The important points in the definition are:

1. An algorithm is a procedure made up of a set of rules
2. The rules must be unambiguous
3. The operations must be extended in a certain sequence
4. The procedure must give a solution to a specific class of problems
5. The solution must be obtained in a finite number of steps.

Whatever the rules for representing the algorithm, they must be unambiguous. This means that each time a particular rule is executed, it must carry the same meaning. Hence, great care has to be used in expressing an algorithm in a natural language, such as English. This because of single word can carry several different meanings in different contexts. Just specifying the set of rules is not sufficient to give the solution. We have to furnish the necessary sequence in which the rules have to be carried out. Once final requirement is that the solution must be obtained in finite number of steps. This requirement simply states that execution of the algorithm must produce a solution.

SUBALGORITHMS

The term subalgorithm is actually a short way of saying subordinate algorithm. It actually is an algorithm which is subordinate to another algorithm. There are three cases when we might have to use a subalgorithm. These are:

1. When the steps of an algorithm are to be performed in two or more places in an algorithm.
2. When the steps of the subalgorithm are to be performed in two or more algorithms.
3. When a very large algorithm has to be designed.

In the first case, we have a subproblem which needs to be solved in several places in an algorithm. In addition, this subproblem often involves different variables each time it requires solving. Another case is when the same steps have to be performed in several algorithms. An example can be found in many numerical algorithms, in which, there is need to find the logarithm in every algorithm whenever it is required. This solution is time consuming. A better approach is to develop a subalgorithm for finding the logarithm. Then, whenever an algorithm is written which requires the computing of a logarithm, all we need to do is to reference the logarithm subalgorithm.

Finally, a main algorithm can be developed which ties up all the subalgorithms. This approach is desirable because the subalgorithms are smaller and therefore easier to design and test than one giant algorithm. Another advantage to this approach is that we can have different people working at the same problem simultaneously. This would shorten the time required to develop the algorithm for solving the overall problem.

Rules for Subalgorithms

The algorithm which calls on the subalgorithm is known as the INVOKING ALGORITHM. The subalgorithm which is called upon is the INVOKED SUBALGORITHM. The points at which the subalgorithms are invoked are knows as the points of invocation. Note that an invoking algorithm may be a subalgorithm itself since subalgorithms can also call upon other subalgorithms.

All subalgorithms must have unique names which identify the points where execution of the subalgorithm may begin. The points where the subalgorithm may begin are knows as the ENTRY POINTS. Usually, there is only one entry point to a subalgorithm.

A subalgorithm may be invoked by two ways (a) Implicitly and (b) Explicitly. A subalgorithm invoked implicitly is called a function subalgorithm and is invoked by the appearance of the name of one of its entry points in an arithmetic or string expression. The action taken is to transfer control is transferred back to the point of invocation.

An explicitly invoked subalgorithm is knows as a general subalgorithm. It is invoked by the appearance of the name of its entry point in a pre-defined process. The action taken is to transfer control to the subalgorithm. Again, return of control takes place when the verb RETURN is encountered.

The three main differences between a general and a function subalgorithm are:

1. A function subalgorithm is invoked implicitly by giving the name of its entry point in an expression, whereas a general subalgorithm is invoked explicitly by using a pre-defined process box.
2. A function subalgorithm returns a string or numeric constant to the point at which it was involved.
3. A function subalgorithm return, causes control to be returned to the expression from which the subalgorithm was invoked. In a general subalgorithm the RETURN causes control to be returned to the step after the point of invocation.

P.S.: Students will find examples of these type of subalgorithms in the BASIC programming language and almost any other programming language also. The library function commands of BASIC are the built in subalgorithms. They are invoked implicitly by just typing in a command like SQR.

An explicit subalgorithm would have to be created by the programmer for a certain definite purpose. This kind of subalgorithm may be explicitly invoked by using the commands COSUB, CHAIN, etc.

COMPUTER LANGUAGES

Any computer language is essentially a set of codes used to write programs which, further, can be defined as a set of instructions given to the computer to perform specific tasks.

Computer languages can be broadly classified as follows:

1. High level languages
2. Low level languages

(a) Assembly level
(b) Machine level

High Level Languages

In this, the statements are written using English like words and mathematical notations e.g. BASIC, COBOL, PASCAL, FORTRAN PL/1, etc. A program written in a high level language can generally be run on many different computers with little or no modifications: Two very important advantages of high level languages are:

(a) Simplicity &
(b) Uniformity.

These languages are said to be relatively machine-independent i.e. it does not matter which computer is being programmed. The program written will remain the same.

In machine language, the program statements are written using binary codes and are then loaded directly into the main memory of the computer. Machine language is very cumbersome to work with. Since it consists only of a variety of 0 and 1, human errors become extensive. Checking out any mistakes becomes still more difficult. By itself, it is quite incomprehensible and a reference manual is required to understand what the various statements mean. Programs written in machine language are called object programs.

Assembly level languages are a type of go between of the machine language and high level languages. In this, statements are written using mnemonic codes (i.e. codes that suggest the meaning of functions) to represent operations and locations that relate to the main memory of the computer. These instructions correspond closely to the inbuilt functions and operations of a portion of a particular computer. Hence, a different computer make or model would use a different low level language; i.e. to say that these languages are machine dependent.

Programs may be written in either high or low language level languages. But they have to be translated into binary machine for the computer to understand them. This function of translating the high or low level language into binary machine code is performed by a program supplied with the computer. This may be a Compiler or an Interpreter. When an interpreter is used, each line of the program is read one at a time and translated into machine code and the instructions carried out. This task is done by the interpreter of the a particular language. Every high level language comes with its interpreter which translates the commands of the language into the appropriate codes for the particular microprocessor. If an interpreter or a complier of a certain language is not available for a particular system, it is not possible to program the particular system in that certain language.

When a compiler is used, the program is in fact, rewritten in machine language. Once this task is accomplished, the program can be directly run without the need of the compiler again. The program which is created is knows as the object code. The program from which the object code is created is knows as the source. It is the complier which converts the written program into a machine language program. As previously mentioned, once the compilation is completed, there is no further need of the compiler as far as that particular program is concerned. Compilers are usually available for most of the major programming languages.

OPERATING SYSTEMS

The hardware often provides an awkward or difficult to use interface to the world. In order to tame this "bare machine" operating systems have been developed that can manage the basic hardware resources and provide a more hospitable interface to users. Operating systems have become inseparable from hardware due to their immense utility.

The term Operating System denotes those program modules within a computer system that govern the control of equipment resources such as processors, main storage, secondary storage, I/O devices and files. The operating system resolves conflicts, attempts to optimize performance and simplify the effective use of the system. The operating system acts an interface between the user's program and the computer hardware.

The operating system is a program which when executed, controls the operating of the computer, eg. the operating system performs the task of scheduling the use of the computers. Sophisticated operating systems increase the efficiency and consequently decrease the cost of using a computer eg. it may provide for simultaneous operation by allowing one user's program to execute while the other user's program is being printed.

FRAMEWORK OF THE OPERATING SYSTEM

We will now present an overall framework of the operating system. We will base our discussion on the fact that the operating system is a manager of resources. The operating system is a collection of algorithms designed to manage the systems resources. These resources can be broadly divided into four types, namely, memory, processors, devices and information (programs and data). The operating system has to keep track of the status of each resource, decide which process is to get which resource, allocate it and eventually reclaim it.

The four resources can be divided into the following:

1. Memory Management Module
2. Processor Management Module
3. Device Management Module
4. Information Management Module

This computers a broad overview of the general working of an operating system and is component parts. Any of the available operating systems in the market have been built along-these lines. Some of the very common operating systems used for microprocessors are PC, DOS, MS-DOS, CP/M, UNIX, XENIX and now the latest one by IBM ie. the OS-2.

In 1981 when IBM, which is almost the kind in the computer industry launched its own microcomputer it also gave its own operating system along with the microcomputer it also gave its own operating system along with the microcomputer. They called it the PC-DOS ie. Personal Computer Disk Operating System. This was however meant only for their disk based personal computer. At that time, however, it had to give the user the option of using CP/M on its computers due to the tremendous popularity of CP/M at that stage.

However, today CP/M is hardly ever used by anybody. The latest launch by IBM is the Personal System -2 along with the Operating System called OS-2.

UNIX is another very powerful and popular operating system for the 16 bit systems. UNIX offers many more capabilities than most of the other systems. It is rising in popularity as more and more 16 and 32 bit systems are being put in the market.

DOS

DOS i.e. short for DISK OPERATING SYSTEM can be easily said to be the operating system with the largest user base in the world. It also one of the long standing and most popular operating systems for the last 10 years. Any DOS based system has a hardwired logic which will hunt for DOS on either a floppy disk or a hard disk in the system. It is assumed that DOS is located on a specific area of the floppy disk or the hard disk. DOS is read from the media and it takes over management of the computer resources. This process is knows as booting.

In case the computer was off the entire process is started from scratch and it is knows as a cold boot. In case the computer is on and for some specific reason DOS is to be reloaded it is knows as a warm boot. Once DOS takes over the user can execute any of the DOS commands or any other package created for DOS. The DOS commands are divided into two groups ie. Internal and External commands. The Internal commands are stored in the system memory when DOS is loaded. The external commands are actually small utility programs supplied along with DOS and are executed when required.

The following are a few of the Internal DOS commands which shall be covered in this chapter:

DATE
TIME
CLS
DIR
COPY
REN
TYPE

DATE

This DOS command is used for two purposes i.e. to display the system time and/or optionally set it to a new date if required. The syntax of the DOS command is very simple. The command DATE has to be typed at the prompt and immediately the current date will be displayed and the user is prompted to enter a new date to change the setting. If no change is required the Enter key can be pressed and the system date will remain the same. In case the date has to be altered then the new date can be keyed in and it will be saved as the system date.

TIME

This DOS command is very similar to the DATE command with the difference that it displays and sets the system time instead of the system date. The syntax and working is exactly similar to the DATE command.

CLS

This DOS command clears the screen and positions the cursor at the top left corner of the screen. The syntax of the command is just CLS.

DIR

This one of the most commonly used commands as also the most useful of the DOS commands. DIR is actually short of DIRECTORY and it essentially generates a list of all files stored on the current media. The manner in which the list is generated or displayed depends upon the options entered with the DIR command. The syntax of the DIR command in its simplest form is as follows

DIR followed by the ENTER key

This will generate a list of all files on the current media ie, hard disk or floppy disk. In case the number of files is greater than 24 the list will scroll on the screen continuously. The list will display the file name with extension, the file size and the date and time stamp of the file. In case the number of files is large the scrolling can be paused after each screen by issuing an optional parameter with the DIR command as follows

DIR/P followed by the ENTER key

This command will generate the same output as the previous command with the exception that the list will pause after each screen full of data. The next screen will be available on hitting any key. In case a selective list of files is desired it is possible to obtain the same by using wildcard after the DIR command for eg. in case all files with the extension "EXE" have to be listed then the wildcard can be used for the name followed by EXE for the actual extension. The actual syntax is as follows:

DIR*.EXE followed by the ENTER key.

The above will generate a list of all files with the extension as EXE. This may be combined the /P command to pause after each screen full of data. Another variation of the DIR command is the W parameter. This parameter is to be issued like the P parameter as follows

DIR/W followed by the ENTER key

The above will cause a horizontal output of the file names. There will be four file names on each line. However please not that with the "W" parameter only the file names are displayed without the size and data & time stamp.

Copy

This command is used to make of copy of any file on either the same media or another media. The general syntax of this command is as follows

COPY <Source> <Source File> <Target> <Target> <Target File>

The Source and Target represent the device from which the file will be read and the device on which the file will be copied. The two are usually represented by the letters A and Z. The source file name and the target file names are actual names of the files to be copied. Of the four values, the Source File name is compulsory while the others may be omitted under certain conditions. In case the Source Name is omitted the current drive is considered as the source and the target drive has to be mentioned in the command line. In case the Source device is keyed in and the Target Drive is not keyed in the current drive is assumed to be the Target drive. In case the Target File Name is not keyed in the copied file will have source File eg.

COPY C:ABC FIL D: CDE.FIL
COPY A: ABC. FIL
COPY ABC. FIL D:
COPY C: ABC.FIL D:

REN

This command will rename any particular DOS file. The syntax is as follows

REN <File Name> <New File Name>

In this command both the values are compulsory. Please note that in case a file already exists with the new file name, this command will not be executed and a relevant message will be displayed.

Type

This command displays the contents of any file in the screen. The syntax is as follows

TYPE <File Name>

The file name is compulsory and a file with the specified file name should exist. The contents of the file will be scrolled on the screen. In case the file does not exist the command will not be executed and a relevant message will be displayed on the screen.

10

Basic Program Organisation

What is a Program?

A Program is a set of logically organised instructions or statements written in a computer language for implementation by the machine for doing specific tasks. A program is analogous to a story in a spoken language. A story is a set of logically organised sentences which implement a plot on a theme. What does a computer program implement? A computer program implements an algorithm.

Structure of a BASIC Program

A BASIC Program consists of series of statements written on alone by line basis. This means a line (i.e., a line feed) terminates a Basic statement. We s aid that every Basic statement is given a number in the beginning and this is also called the line number. Line numbers musty be given only in the ascending sequence, say 5, 10, 15, 20 and so on. Of course one can give numbers as 1, 2, 3, 4 and so on. In this case, if we want to introduce a statement somewhere in between the numbers of the remaining statements have to be changed. In the former method, we can give some intervening numbers and avoid renumbering the remaining statements. The statement numbers are also used for referencing purposes. A statement can be as long as 255 characters. In the screen it will appear folded, since the screen width is only 80 characters. If the statements are small, more than one statement can be written in a line provided each pair is separated by a colon mark. The last statement in that line will have no punctuation mark, consistant with the notion that a line terminates a statement. However there are some restrictions in entering more than one statement in a line. DATA, DEF, DIM and END statements must be the only statements in a line. Then IF statement must be the first statement in a line. We can represent the structure of a Basic program as shown in the figure 1 Each one in the figure denotes a statement.

```
10 .............
15 .............
20 .............
30 .............
200 END
```

Fig. 1.

We say that statements are the building blocks of a program. A statement is not only the smallest meaningful unit to the computer but it is also the smallest syntactic unit to which any transfer of control can be referenced. Later we will see that we have to branch from one statement to another, which are not in sequence and in those cases, we have to use the statement numbers for referencing.

Example 1: A BASIC Program for finding the cost of 14 dozen oranges, given the rate per dozen, is shown in the figure 2.

```
10   rem program for finding the cost of oranges
20   read rate per dozen quantity
30   cost = rate per dozen quantity
40   print "cost of 14 dozen oranges is = Rs. ; cost
50   data 12.50, 14
60   end
```

Fig. 2.

When the above program is executed the result is displayed as below:

cost of 14 dozen oranges is = Rs. 175

A Note on BASIC Compiler and BASIC Interpreter:

The Computer cannot directly execute any high level language like BASIC. So the high level language program called the source program must be converted to the machine language program called the object program. Only the machine code program can be directly executed by the computer. Compilers and Interpreters are two types of programs which can translate the BASIC program to the machine language program. We have two types of BASIC, namely, the Interpreter BASIC and the Compiler BASIC depending on the type of the translator used.

The Interpreter BASIC translates the BASIC program line by line and executes them one after the other, when it is given the RUN command. If any syntax error occurs in any line, the Interpreter prints the error message and stops further translation and execution. The user has to correct the error and re-run the program. This must be repeated until the entire program runs correctly.

The Compiler Basic does the job in two stages. The first stage is called the compilation stage. The user gives what is called the compilation command. Then the computer reads the entire program and lists all the syntax errors in the program. The user has to correct all the syntax errors and give the compilation command once again. If there are no syntax errors in the entire program, the computer translates the BASIC program into machine language program and stops. Then comes the second stage called the execution stage. The user has to initiate the execution by giving what is called the execution command. The program is executed during this stage.

For developing programs one usually uses the Interpreter BASIC and for permanent use one uses the Compiler Basic. A great advantage with the Interpreter BASIC is that it has a Built-in Editor which can be used to quickly correct the program and run it immediately. Again it can be used in the calculator mode for computing any numeric expression instantaneously without writing any program. The general form for using the BASIC Interpreter in the Calculator Mode is

? numeric- expression

For example if one writes an arithmetic or numeric expression

?1255* (1 + 7.5/100)^5

The computed value of 1801.715 immediately appears in the next line. The disadvantage with Interpreter BASIC is that the translation of the source code to the object code has to be done every time the program is given the RUN command and this necessarily slows down the execution. In Compiler BASIC, once the object or the machine code is created, it is stored in separate file and when the program is to be executed for the second time only the execution command need be given. The execution time for an object code program is very small compared to the execution of a source code program. No such object code file is created in the Interpreter BASIC. This is the reason why for permanent use one uses compiler BASIC and for program development one uses Interpreter BASIC. In these lessons we will confine ourselves only to Interpreter BASIC.

How to Enter a Program in Interpreter BASIC?

The following are the commands used for invoking the Interpreter BASIC Editor and perform the different operations:

1. BASIC
2. NEW
3. AUTO
4. Break-Key (Control-ScrollLock Key)
5. SAVE
6. LIST
7. RUN
8. LOAD
9. LLIST
10. DELETE
11. SYSTEM
12. KILL
13. NAME
14. RENUM
15. FILES

Initially when the computer is booted you are in the system mode and the screen displays what is called the DOS prompt (A>). To enter the BASIC Editor mode key the word 'basic' and press the CR key. The screen gives some copyright message and finally displays a prompt 'Ok.' This prompt indicates that the system is ready to accept all BASIC system commands. Before giving any BASIC command the system must be at this command level, i.e. the prompt Ok must appear.

The NEW Command

It is advisable to start keying any fresh program after keying the command 'new' and pressing the CR key. This command will erase any old program that will reside in the main memory and clear it. If this command is not given it may happen that the lines keyed afresh may overlap with some program lines already residing in the main memory.

The AUTO Command

We have said that it is mandatory to enter line numbers to the statements in a BASIC program. Either you can key the line numbers yourself or you can ask the computer to enter the line numbers. Suppose you key the command 'auto' and press the carriage return the computer prints the first line number as 10 and waits for the user to key the first statement. When the user keys the first statements and presses the CR key the computer prints the number 20 in the second line and waits to enter the next statement. The line numbers are given automatically by the computer giving an increment of 10 every time. It is possible to instruct the computer to given any other increment instead of 10 and also start the number from any other value other than 10. The initial value of 10 and the increment value of 10 are called the default values which are assumed by the computer for a simple 'auto' command. The general form of the AUTO command is

AUTO [line-number [increment]]

where line number represents the beginning line number. Suppose one gives the command as

AUTO 25, 5

The computer gives the first line number as 25 and the subsequent numbers as 30, 35, 40, 45 etc. giving and increment of 5 every time.

How to End Keying the Program?

Suppose you have keyed the program containing say some 20 lines. The last line number under the simple auto command will be 200. After keying the last line you press the CR key. The next line number 210 is displayed and the cursor stops near it. Now press the control and the scrollock key together. The program entry is terminated and the screen prompt Ok appears. Now the program is stored only in the main memory. If at this stage the power goes off the entire program will be lost. So it is advisable to save the program in the disk as soon as it is keyed.

The SAVE Command

The general form of the SAVE command is
SAVE filename [A]

The filename must be given within quotes. The A option saves the program file in the disk in the ASCII format. In the absence of A option the program file is stored in compressed binary format and the same cannot be typed using the DOS command. Only ASCII filed can be typed using the DOS command. Suppose you want to give a name SAMPLE to the program you give the command as

SAVE "SAMPLE" or SAVE "SAMPLE" A

The system will automatically give the extension BAS and store the program file as SAMPLE.BAS in the Compressed Binary Format or the ASCII format as the case may be.

The LIST Command

Once you have saved the file in the disk you would like to see the listing on the screen. The general forms of the LIST command are

LIST [[line-number][-line-number]]

Suppose you give the command simply as LIST, the entire program which is currently in the main memory will be listed in the scrolling mode on the screen and stop with the last 24 lines. The command LIST 20 will display only the line 20 on the screen. The command LIST 20-100 will list all lines in the range 20 to 100. Please note that we cannot have two programs in the main memory simultaneously. If you want to get the listing on the printer, give the command LLIST after setting the printer on-line. If there is no program currently residing in the main memory nothing will be displayed excepting the prompt OK.

The LOAD Command

Suppose you want to select any one program from the program files stored in the disk, and bring it to the main memory for use. For this purpose the LOAD commands is used. The general form of the LOAD command is

LOAD file-name [R]

The file-name is the name with which you have saved the program in the disk. The R option will also run the program immediately after loading it in the main memory. Suppose you want to load the program SAMPLE.BAS in the main memory, you give the command as

LOAD "SAMPLE" or LOAD "SAMPLE.BAS" or LOAD "SAMPLE

Now if you give the list command the program will be listed on the screen.

The RUN Command

For executing the program which is already residing in the main memory you give the command as

RUN

When this command is given, the computer reads line by line, converts it into machine code and executes line by line one after the other. If at any line the computer detects a syntax error, it will display the error message on that lone and stop further execution. So one must know how to correct the errors and run again.

How to Correct the Errors in a Line?

One say to correct the errors in a line is to completely retype that line along with that line number and press the CR key. In that case the old line will be replaced by the new line. After typing the new line the program must be saved with the new line, otherwise the corrections will not be incorporated in the file. The other way is to invoke the EDIT command.

The EDIT Command

The general form of the EDIT command is

EDIT line-number

When you give the command, the particular line will be displayed below the command and the cursor will be on the first character. The curser can then be moved to any position using the left and the right arrow keys and any new characters can be overtyped or any new characters can be added in that line. Finally the CR key is pressed.

Insertion and Deletion of Statements

For deleting a statement simply key the line number of that statement and press the CR key. You can also give commands as follows:

DELETE 40 (deletes the statement in the line 40)

DELETE (40-80) (deletes all statements in the range 40 to 80)

If you want to insert a statement the line 20 and 30, you can give a line number 25, and type the new statement and finally press the CR key. If we had given the line numbers in the natural sequence as 1, 2, 3, 4, 5, etc., it will become difficult afterwards, if we want to introduce one or more lines in between. That is why, initially the line numbers are given with god intervals between them, say 5 or 10.

The command 'KILL-file-name' is used to erase unwanted files.

The command 'FILES' is used to list the files.

The command 'NAME old-file name AS new-file-name' is used to change the name of a file.

The RENUM Command

The general form of the RENUM command is

RENUM[[new-number][[old-number][increment]]

For example, the command RENUM renumbers the entire program with the beginning number as 10 and increment as 10. The command RENUM 200,20 renumbers the entire program starting with the number 200 and incrementing the line numbers by 20. The command RENUM 500,200,5 remembers the line 200 up, so that they start with line number 500 with increment of 5. When renumbering of the statement lines are done all line numbers referenced within the program by GOTO or GOSUM statements will also be appropriately changed.

The FILES Command

This is similar to the DIR command in DOS. When the command FILES is given the screen displays the list of files stored in the disk in the given drive.

The MERGE Command

The general form of the MERGE command is

MERGE filename

This command will insert any other program residing in the disk in the program currently in the main memory. If any lines in the disk file have the same line numbers as lines in the program in memory, the lines from the file on disk will replace the corresponding lines in memory. MERGEing may be thought of as 'inserting' the program lines into the program memory.

The SYSTEM Command

After finishing all the work within the BASIC Editor, one must come to the DOS mode before switching off the computer. The command SYSTEM enables the control to exit from BASIC editor and come to the DOS mode or DOS prompt.

One must familiarise with these BASIC editing commands to work comfortably with the Interpreter BASIC.

Explanation of the Program

There are six lines in the program. The first statement is the Comment statement not intended for processing and this is indicated by the key word REM. The second statement is the input statement. Here we have used the READ-DATA statement. If you want to use the INPUT statement, change the second line as follows:

20 input "enter values for rate and quantity", rate per dozen, quantity
Remove the DATA statement no. 50

The third statement is the computation statement. The fourth is the output statement which outputs the result on the screen. For outputting the result on the printer use the command LPRINT. The fifth statement is the DATA statement. The sixth and the last statement is the END statement which terminates the execution. After the execution of the END statement the computer will return to the Basic prompt 'OK'. If there is no OK prompt, it means that computer is hanging somewhere or doing some processing. The END statement, can be placed anywhere. This means that the END statement is not the physical end but only the logical end of the program. The physical end of the program end comes when the line numbers terminate. Consider the following program:

```
10 x = 10
20 if x>5 then end else go to 50
30 y = 20
50 print x, y
```

The end statement is in the line 20. Physically the program ends in the line 50. Though there is no END statement after 50 BASIC will assume that there is an END statement after 50 and display OK prompt after executing the line 50. There is also a STOP statement in BASIC. When the computer encounters the STOP statement, it will display BREAK in that line number. The STOP statement in BASIC simply pauses until the user types 'CONT' for continuing the processing of the statements, if there are any, after the STOP statement.

Concluding Note

The program which we have illustrated is a very small one. The number of data we have used is also very small. In real life situations the amount of data will be really voluminous and we will find that the above method of entering data will be impractical for various reasons.

Programs will contain several hundreds of lines. Of course one need not get frightened at this prospect. It is only the little drops of water that make up the mighty ocean. By gradually adding the required logics we can build any complex program. Please remember that nothing is born big in this world. Everything is born small, but grow big afterwards. We can also develop like this starting from a small program and finally going to big ones.

11

Word Processing

What is a Word Processor?

The introduction to the concepts of spreadsheets and databases already being done, we now come to the third most common and useful utility of a computer system, Word Processing. Word Processing is in fact, highly sophisticated electronic typing. Instead of typing on paper, the typed data is displayed on the screen of the computer and is stored in the computer's memory. The data can be transferred to a printer at any point of time. The advantage of word processing is that the data can be accessed, modified and printed at any point of time. The obvious advantage is that the mistakes in typing can be corrected without any waste of paper.

Who is it for?

However, one must not mistakenly assume that word processing is only meant for typists. It is used by writer, professionals, students, and many others. It is especially a boon to writers who have to write pages and pages and then they have to edit and revise relentlessly. This, manual re-copying and re-typing is very time consuming ad it can be totally relaxed by using a word processor. Word processing saves valuable time and increases their writing productivity by helping them to write and edit faster. Furthermore, printing becomes very easy, because a word processor is also used to layout the matter, design the margins, headers and footers of the pages, number them and select paragraph styles. Thus word processing has revolutionaised the publishing industry.

Which Word Processor?

A word processor is a programmed package which allows the user to enter his/her data through the keyboard, into distinct, files, view the data on the screen, save the data on the storage devices, recall it, edit it, format it, and print it on paper through the printer. There are many word processing systems and though all work on the same principle, they have their distinct and unique features. There are may companies in the market which sell word processing systems under various brand names like, Microsoft Word, WordPerfect, Wordstar, Peachtext, etc., Besides these exclusive word processors there are other "integrated packages" which provide the user with a spreadsheet, a D,M.M.S., as well as word processor like,

Symphony and Framework. One of the earliest exclusive word processors was "WordStar" marketed by Wordstar Incorporated International and even today it retains it's lead as one of the most popular word processing packages, especially with Indian users. Therefore we will learn elementary Wordstar commands in the following pages.

Starting Up Wordstar

Wordstar is a very easy to use and simple package. To start up an installed version of Wordstar, all that the user has to do after entering the Wordstar sub-directory, is to type the letters "WS" and hit the Enter key.

C:\WS>(Hit the Enter Key)

When this is done Wordstar is loaded into the computer memory and becomes operational. Wordstar is said to be a user friendly package in that even if the user does not know any of the commands, there is a permanent on-line help available on the top half of the screen. This help is in the form of a window in which the various commands are listed out and this help window is called a menu. The different processes which the user might wish to execute are initiated by these commands. This help is available by default but it can be shut off if the user is well versed with the commands and does not need the listed help.

What is the Opening Menu?

When Wordstar is loaded, the on-line help provides the first window of commands called the OPENING Menu. It laterally means that the choice of commands available in this menu allow the user open the files which to contain their respective data and manipulate those files. There are twenty commands in this window and all have to be executed by depressing just a single character. The first logical command that we must study over here is the one to open a new document file.

What is a Document File?

All the information that is typed and stored in the computer memory is stored in the form of a file exactly like the information in a book is stored in chapters. Like different chapters have different headings, different kinds of data is stored in different types of files which have exclusive names. The files which contain the data that is entered through Wordstar are called document files. The command for opening a new document file is available on the OPENING menu. The user simply has to type in the letter "D" and a slot appears which prompts the user to enter the name of the document file to opened. The name should not exceed eight characters. If a file of the same name as that entered by the user exists, then Wordstar opens that file. However, if there is no file of that name, the user is further prompted,

"File does not exist, Create new file? Y/N_"

and the user has to type "Y" for yes or "N" for no. Then the user types "Y" for yes, the new document file of the given filename will be opened and the user will be led from the

OPENING menu to the file screen. In this screen of information the lower half is blank space in which the user can key in the data. This part of the screen scrolls and provides unlimited space in which the user can enter the data. The upper half contain another help menu, the EDIT menu, which displays the commands to be used within the file in order to move the cursor around the file and to edit it.

Returning to the OPENING menu, we must mention some other commands to be studied from this menu. The "P" command is used to print, an existent document file on paper. The user simply has to type the letter "P" at the Opening menu and the program will prompt the user to enter the name of the file to be printed. Then it will prompt the user to enter a few basic print instructions like the number of pages to printed, the number of copies to be printed, whether the system is to pause for paper etc. Once this is done the user is prompted to get the printer ready and hit any key and then the document is printed on paper.

One of the many commands offered in the OPENING menu, the "E" commands is used to change the name of any existent file. The user simply has to press the "E" key and two slots will appear - in the first slot the user is prompted to enter the existent name of the file and press the Enter key. The user has to then enter the new name in the next slot and press the enter key and the name is changed.

In order to delete an existent file in Wordstar the user has to press the "Y" key and then enter name of the file to be deleted and press the enter key. In order to prevent accidental deletion, Wordstar does not delete the file immediately, instead it again prompts the user to confirm the deletion by asking "Conform deletion? Y/N — " and user has to type a "Y" for yes and the file will be deleted.

The OPENING menu also contains the command that will enable the user to exit Wordstar. One has to simply press the "X" key and Wordstar is shut down and the cursor comes back to the DOS prompt.

WITHIN THE DOCUMENT FILE

Once the user has pressed "D" and created a Wordstar document file, the user is led to a screen where in the top half contains the EDIT menu and the lower half is the typing space in which the user can enter his/her data. This space scrolls and the cursor is free to move around all over the document.

What are Function Commands?

At the bottom of the screen the "Function Commands" are displayed. In every keyboard there are ten Function keys, "F1" to "F10", and in Wordstar each of these function keys are assigned certain commands which are executed on pressing these different keys. Thus we have ten function commands assigned to these ten keys. When the function keys are depressed along with the Control key, then ten more commands are performed. Let us see some of these functions.

When the "F1" key is pressed the user gets the option to change the on-line help level. That is, the user can choose to remove the menus that are displayed on the screen if the user is familiar with commands and does not need the help. When the key is depressed five choices are given to the user. The help level in which all the menus are on, is help level "3" and is currently active.

When the "F2" key is pressed the user gets to see a page preview, that is, the user will be shown how the format of the current page will look when it is printed on paper. The user can press the "Esc" (Escape) key to get out of the page preview and return to the document.

The "F3" , "F4", "F5" and "F6" keys offer various formatting commands. The "F7" key is used to align the document, that is, when this key is pressed, the paragraph on which the cursor rests, is aligned as per the margins that have been set. "F8" key moves the cursor to the end of the current line.

The data that is being written on the screen has to be saved. That is it has to be written on to the storage device (the disks) and it's back up copy has to be created. In order to do this the user has to press the "F9". In order to prevent loss of data due to power failure or any other accident, the user must continually press "F9" and save the data. This is a quick automatic function and after the data is saved the user can continue to work in the file as earlier. When the user has finished keying in the data in a document file, the "F10" key should be pressed. This saves the data and shuts the document file, returning the control back to the Opening Menu.

The Function keys are used in combination with the Control key in order to execute more commands which are mostly concerned with the formatting of the data.

THE EDIT MENU

On the top half of the screen in the document file is the EDIT menu. It provides the user with commands which enable him/her to move the cursor and to make changes in the typed document. As in the Opening Menu, the commands are executed by pressing various characters. But in this case, the characters are pressed in combination with the "Ctrl" (Control)key.

Between the EDIT menu and the typing area there is a ruler line which displays the right and left margins. A line is divided into tab spaces which are set by default which are also displayed on the ruler line. Below the ruler line on the empty screen is a flashing block or a flashing line that takes the space of one character. This is the cursor and as the text is entered, the cursor moves forward. The cursor indicates the position where the next text character will appear on the screen. Now the user has to simply key in the data and it will appear on the screen. When the cursor comes to be end of the line, it will automatically move to the next line and the user can continue to type in the data without pausing.

There are other keys on the keyboard that are used to perform function in the Wordstar document file. The "Backspace" key is used to delete the character that comes before the cursor and the "Delete" key deletes the character on which the cursor rests currently. The "Shift" key is used exactly like it is in the manual typewriter; it is pressed in combination with the alphabet to type them in upper case and with other characters in order to type the character that is displayed on the upper half of the key. The "Caps Lock" is evidently used to print the alphabet in the upper case. The cursor that flashes on the screen can move back and forth, up and down, throughout the typed text. The cursor pad that shows four arrow keys is used tc move the cursor up or down, as per the arrow marking. The "Home" key is used to take the cursor to the top of screen and the "End" key is used to take the cursor key to the last character on the screen. The "PgUp" key takes the cursor to the previous screen that may have been typed and the "PgDn" key takes the cursor to the next screen of information. The "Enter" key is used to start a new line and go to the next paragraph.

The most powerful feature of a word processor is that it allows the user to add words, lines and indeed even pages, in between the data that has already been entered. For example, after typing a paragraph, the user can take the cursor back to any part of the text and add words or sentences. The user can thus insert text anywhere in between, shift the text and edit it.

The EDIT menu provides commands which aid and enhance the editing and deletion facilities. It also gives access to other menus which provide sophisticated features. All the commands from this menu are executed by pressing the specified keys along with the control key. The first six commands are the cursor commands in that they help to move the cursor around the document. The sign ^ is used to signify the control key which has to be pressed at the same time as the specified character and the command will be executed. For example when ^E is gives as the command, the Control key and the alphabet E have to be pressed at the same time. Let us see which are the six cursor commands and what function they perform.

Control + E	Takes the cursor one line up
Control + X	Takes the cursor one line down
Control + S	Takes the cursor one character left
Control + D	Takes the cursor one character right
Control + A	Takes the cursor one word left
Control + F	Takes the cursor one word right

The next set of commands in the EDIT menu enable the user to scroll the screen and they are as follows:

Control + W	Shifts the screen one line up
Control + Z	Shifts the screen one line down
Control + R	Shifts to the next screen
Control + C	Shifts to the previous screen

The EDIT menu also provides commands which enable the user to delete characters, words and lines.

Control + G	Deletes the character on which the cursor rests (Like the Delete key)
Control + T	Deletes the word on which the cursor rests
Control + Y	Deletes the one on which the cursor rests
Control + U	Undeletes the last deleted character/word/line

Besides these basic Edit commands there Other commands which perform functions very much like those performed the function keys.

Control + J	Enables the user to change the help level
Control + I	Enables the user to set tab spaces
Control + V	Turn the Insert facility on/off
Control + B	Aligns the paragraph on which the cursor rests
Control + N	Creates a new line

The EDIT men also gives the user access to four other submenus. These sub-menus branch into more commands that perform unique features. There are four sub-menus in Wordstar.

Control + O	This leads to the Onscreen Format menu which enables the user to set the lay out of the page as it will appear on paper.
Control + K	This leads to the Block and Save menu which enables the user to shift data in forms of blocks and to save the data.
Control + P	This is the Print Control menu which enables the user to set the fonts and style of the text according to the output required in the printer.
Control + Q	This is the Quick Functions menu which enables the user to perform the editing functions for large sections of the text, instantaneously.

Besides this, the Edit Menu also offers the user in option to create his/her own Shorthand which is accessed by pressing the "Esc" (Escape) key.

What are DOT Commands?

In the EDIT menu ^J provides a help level and it also gives a dictionary of DOT commands. DOT commands are codes which allow the user to insert commands within the text. These commands concern themselves with the format of the output on the paper. Before printing a document, the user will have to specify the length of the paper, it's width and the size of the margins. It is to be noted that the same commands can also be executed from the ONSCREEN FORMAT menu.

When the user presses ^J, that is the Control key gives help messages about the commands in EDIT menu. At the end of that window there is an option which allows the user to view the DOT commands by pressing a period, that is a full stop (.). The moment the period is pressed the user will be led to screens of information where the various DOT commands is listed along with the function they perform. In order to view the next screen of information, the user has to press the Enter key and in order to escape from this help, the user has to press the Escape key.

A DOT command is issued by pressing a period (.) at the first column on the screen. Immediately after this a code has to be typed in which consists of two or three letters. (All these codes are displayed in ^J help library.) Certain DOT commands require a numeric value at the end, for example if a DOT command is to be issued to specify the paper length, then the length has to be typed after the code, in inches. A typical DOT command looks like. Merely typing the command does not execute it and the user has to press the enter key after the command is type. ADOT commands are used to set the paper length, the width, headers, footers etc.

The monitor is divided into columns and each column can contain one character. If you look at the top of the screen in a document file you see that there is a ruler that marks out the page width and divides it into tabs and columns. The ruler line displays the left and the right margin. By default, there is 1 "left margin and 6.5" right margin. These margins can be changed with DOT commands. In order to specify the left margin, take the cursor to the first column of a new line and type a period, then type the code **lm** and leave a space, then specify the width of the required left margin, for example, 1" and press the enter key. The DOT command will be executed immediately and the change is reflected in the ruler line at the top of the screen. Below there is list of DOT commands. The variable in stands for a numeric value.

Period + lm + space + n" + Enter	Sets left margin
Period + rm + space + n" + Enter	Sets right margin
Period + pl + space + n" + Enter	Sets the page length

In order to delete a DOT command the user has to delete the entire line itself.

THE QUICK MENU

In order to access the Quick Menu the user has to press the Control key along with the "Q" key. On doing this, the EDIT menu is replaced by the QUICK menu and a new set of commands are displayed. This sub menu lasts on the screen only till the some command from this menu is chosen. You cannot continue keying in data while this menu is on. The user to select the command from the QUICK menu and return to the text. If the user does not wish to execute a command from the QUICK menu, then pressing any other key will take the user back to the text and the EDIT menu will appear again. Thus the QUICK menu is a temporary menu which stays on the screen only till a command is selected.

The first set of QUICK commands concern themselves with cursor movement. The cursor commands in the EDIT menu were used to move the cursor to the different characters. Through the QUICK menu, the cursor can be made to move all across the screen. In a sub-menu, the Control key has to be pressed in combination with two keys. Thus to execute any command in the QUICK menu, the user will have press the control key along with the "Q" key as well as another key of the valid character.

Control + Q + E	Takes the cursor to the top left of the screen (Like the Home key)
Control + Q + X	This takes cursor to bottom right of the screen. (Like the End key)
Control + Q + S	Takes the cursor to the beginning of the line
Control + Q + D	Takes the cursor to the end of the line

Thus you can see that the cursor moves over entire lines and throughout the page with the QUICK commands rather than moving across characters as it does in the EDIT menu. Even the scrolling command in the QUICK menu becomes rapid so as to allow the user to go directly to the first page of the text or the last page of the text.

Control + Q + R	Takes the cursor to the first page of the text
Control + Q + C	Takes the cursor to the last page of the text

There are many more commands in the QUICK sub-menu, and we will study some more commands. The QUICK commands also enable easier modes of deletion. Two of these commands are to delete all the words in a line to the left of the cursor position or to the right of the cursor position.

Control + Q + Del	Deletes the words in the line to the left of the cursor
Control + Q + Y	Deletes the words in the line to the right of the cursor position

This. Thesaurus can be accessed through the QUICK menu and the user can check the spelling and meaning of words and find synonyms when necessary.

Control + Q + N	Checks the spelling of the word on which the cursor rests
Control + Q + L	Checks the spelling of the rest of the document from the cursor position
Control + Q + J	Provides synonyms and definition of the word on which the cursor rests

The entire text can be aligned to fit in set margins and form by using ^QC command. One of the other features of Wordstar is a pop-up calculator which is accessed by the ^QM command. The calculator appears on the top half of the screen and user can carry out calculation and press the "Esc" key in order to return to the text.

Through the QUICK commands, the screen can be made to continually scroll upwards or downwards, line by line of the user wishes to scan the text.

Control + Q + W	Scrolls the screen upwards, one line at a time
Control + Q + Z	Scrolls the screen downwards, one line at a time

This scrolling can be stopped by pressing the "Esc" key. There are other QUICK commands which deal with scrolling and with finding and replacing text which are secondary features, not integral to the using of Wordstar.

THE ONSCREEN FORMAT MENU

The ^O function allows the user to enter the ONSCREEN FORMAT menu. This menu is very useful for publishing any document as it allows the user to set margins and paragraphs. Besides the user can also set typing and display controls from this menu. The user has to note that the ONSCREEN FORMAT men commands and the DOT menu commands from the EDIT menu perform similar functions.

When the user opens a file and starts entering the data, the left and right margins are set by default to be 1" and 6.5". However, the user has the option to change the margins to any desirable length. To set the left margin the user has to press ^OL. On doing this a screen appears which has various slots which contain the data on the margins, tabs, spacing etc. The first slot however, will be that of the width of the left margin and a default value will already exist. Now default value, the user has to press the F10 key so that this value is accepted by the wordprocessor. If the user merely presses the Enter key, the cursor will move to the next slot and if the Esc key is pressed, then the control will return to the text without changing the value. So, after entering the value the user must press F10. Similarly the right margin can be altered by pressing ^OR and the cursor will rest on the second slot which accepts the width for the right margin. The user has to enter a value in inches and press F10 in order to save that value.

Control + O + L + n" + F10 Sets left margin

Control + O + R + n" + F10 Sets right margin

The change in the margin widths will be seen when the user returns to the text on the ruler line at the top of the screen. Another useful command from the onscreen menu is the ^OC command. If the user has given a title or heading to the document, then this title can be made to appear in the centre of the line by using this command. On whichever line this command is executed, the data of that line will be shifted to the centre of the page.

Control + O + C Shifts line to the centre.

BLOCK AND SAVE MENU

In order to access the BLOCK & SAVE menu the user has to press the Control key along with the "K" key. On doing this the EDIT menu is replaced by the BLOCK & SAVE menu and a new set of commands are displayed. Like the QUICK menu this sub-menu lasts on the screen only till some command from this menu is chosen. You cannot key data in your text while this menu is on. The user has to select the command from the BLOCK & SAVE menu and return to the text. If the user does not wish to execute a command from this menu, then pressing any key will take the user back to the text and the EDIT menu will appear again.

The first set of BLOCK &SAVE commands concern themselves with saving the data on to the storage devices (Like the commands executed by the F9 and F10 key). Saving the data is done intermittently while entering the data and while closing the file when the complete text has been typed.

Control + K + S	Saves the data on the storage device and returns control back to the text
Control + K + D	Saves the data on the storage device and closes the file, returning the control to the Opening Menu.

The closed file can be opened again by using the "D" command from the Opening Menu. The user can also save a document file and at the same time step right outside wordstar, to the DOS prompt by the ^KX command.

Control + K + X	Saves the file and shuts down Wordstar

A third useful combination is ^KQ. If the user has opened a document file and has made changes, but would not like to maintain those changes, instead he/she would like to revert back to the original document as it was when the file was opened, then the user can abandon the changes by pressing ^KQ. This shuts the file and reverts the control back to the Opening Menu without saving any of the changes that have been made. Please not that ^KQ abandons the changes that have been made since the last time the document file was saved. Anything that has been saved earlier by the ^KS or ^KD commands, does not get abandoned. The ^KQ command must be exercised with great caution.

What is a Block?

While working on a data file the user has to often transfer, delete or copy, large sections of data while editing. However, rewriting or deleting large sections of data is a very tedious process. The BLOCK & SAVE menu allows you to group data into temporary sections called "blocks" and the entire block can be manipulated as one whole. It can be shifted, copied, deleted within the file and even copied on to any other document file.

In order to mark or define a block, the user must take the cursor to the start of the section that has to be manipulated and press ^KB and then take the cursor to the end of the section and press ^KK. On doing this the entire section is highlighted and is regarded as a block.

Control + K + B	Begins a block
Control + K + K	Ends a block

At any point of time, only one block can be marked. This block can be deleted by pressing ^KY. If this section of data has to be moved to another part of the text, then after defining the block, the cursor must be taken to the new position on which the block is to be placed and press ^KV and the entire block will be shifted automatically. If the block has to be copied on to another section of the text then after defining the block, the cursor must be taken to the position where the copy is required and press ^KC and a copy of a block will appear there

Control + K + Y	Deletes block
Control + K + V	Moves a block
Control + K + C	Makes a copy of the block

By pressing ^KH. Technically, this only hides the block and a block actually gets unmarked when a new block is created.

Control + K + H	Unmarks a block

The other manipulation that a user can do with a block is that it's case be changed from lower to upper and vice versa. If ^K' is pressed then text within the block will all change to lower case and if ^K" is pressed then the entire text within the block will change into capitals.

Control + K +'	Changes the text within the block to lower case
Control + K +'	Changes the text within the block to upper case

The BLOCK & SAVE menu allows the user to pull in external files into the document file which is currently open. Let us assume that the user is working in a file name DOCI and the user wishes to add in it the entire data of another document file. DOC2. Then the user has to position the cursor at the spot where the data from the second file has to be included and press ^KR. A slot will appear wherein the reader will be prompted to enter the name of the file that has to be pulled in and the user can type in the name DOC2. Then the entire data of the file DOC2 will be copied in to DOC1.

Control + K + R	Pulls in an external file at the cursor position in the currently open file.

Like the OPENING menu, the BLOCK & SAVE allows the user to maintain entire file. While working within a text the user can copy, delete, and rename files through the ^KO, ^KJ and ^KE commands respectively.

Exactly like a document file can be printed on paper through the OPENING menu the user can print a file while working within a document file through the BLOCK & SAVE menu. The user can even continue to key in data while the printing is going on. The ^KP command is used to print a file. On doing this the program will prompt the user to enter the name of the file to printed. Then, it will prompt the user to enter a few basic print instructions like the number of pages to be printed, the number of copies to be printed, whether the system is to pause for paper etc. Then the user is prompted to get the printer ready and hit any key. Once the printing is started, the control is returned to the document.

Control + K + P	Prints a document file

This completes our list of important Block & Save commands.

THE PRINT MENU

As we already know, a document file is printed either from the OPENING MENU or from the BLOCK & SAVE menu. The PRINT menu is not meant for the actual printing of the file on paper, but for setting printing instructions. Pressing ^P calls this menu to screen and the list of the commands is displayed. This menu is used to print things to bold, to underline, to use italics and to choose paragraph styles.

If a part of the text has to be highlighted, then it can be printed in bold by using the ^PB command. First, the user has to take the cursor to the position from where the text has to be highlighted and the user has to press the Ctrl key along with P and B. The marking of ^PB will appear on the screen. Then the cursor has to be moved to the position where in the bold printing has to end and the same command has to be pressed again. Here too, the ^PB marker will appear. All the text that comes with the two ^PB will be printed in bold. Similarly if a section of the text has to be printed in italics form ^PY has to pressed at the beginning of the text and at the end of the text. All the data that falls between the two ^PY markers will be in italics. If a section of the text has to underlined then the user has to press ^PS at the beginning and at the end of that section and the data within the two ^PS.

Control + P + B	Prints text in bold
Control + P + Y	Prints text in italics
Control + P + S	Underlines the text
Control + P + V	Subscripts the text
Control + P + T	Superscripts the text

It has to be noted that in these printing commands the same command has to always be pressed twice, at the beginning of the text and at the end. Then the entire portion that comes in between the two print commands is printed as desired. The other PRINT menu commands are not so relevant this stage. The PRINT menu is used to choose the type of printer, the paragraph styles and printing styles also.

12

Wordprocessing — An Overview

What is Wordprocessing for?

We know that high technology has led to high productivity in the industrial and the agricultural sectors. The increased materials production in turn has given rise to increased business handling which consists in the creation of meaningful documents. Wordprocessing is a new technology developed to increase the productivity in business handling by making the machine an obedient servant of man. Essentially Wordprocessing deals with creation, storage and printing of text matter or document matter with very high speed, very high quality and very high degree of accuracy. Wordprocessing is found to be very useful not only to typists, but also to every computer user, since it is required in many information processing jobs like creating and editing a data file, creating and editing a program file, editing a report file, creating and editing a new document file, printing a file in the desired format etc.

Need for a Scientific Approach to Learn Wordprocessing

It is found that due to some reasons, wordprocessing is left to be learnt by the users in some sort of trial and error method. This may work in some cases, but this method will tail more often than not. Trying to find out everytime, what each command will do, is time consuming, laborious and also frustrating. One must learn wordprocessing in a scientific way for achieving high productivity, high quality and accuracy. Scientific learning consists in knowing before hand the results of each wordprocessing command, so that one can use them with confidence to get the desired results without depending on the so called trial and error method.

Wordprocessor Versus Typewriter

Essentially a wordprocessor does the function of a typewriter, with the difference that the former does the job with a high degree of speed, accuracy and quality. In this sense a wordprocessor is only an improved typewriter and we would like to call it as a computer controlled type writer. This means that a wordprocessor will eliminate many of the disadvantages of a manual typewriter in the matter of document creation, editing and printing.

Before the advent of the computer all wordprocessing jobs were done by the typewriter. Initially we write the text in manuscript and then type the matter in the paper media. Very often, we would like to make many changes in the first draft. We make the necessary modifications and corrections and completely retype the whole matter. We must thank God if we had not made any typographical errors. If any such errors are present, the document may not be presentable and so we have to do the typing process over again. There is no means of doing this job without duplication. This results in loss of time, waste of stationery and very low productivity. In a computer we key the first draft not on the paper media, but on a magnetic media and we see the draft on the screen as we key it. Up to the preparation of the first draft, there is no difference between the typewriter and the computer as regards productivity and presentability. The essential difference between the typewriter and the computer starts from the second stage onwards when we revise and re-revise the text several times before we decide on the final draft. All revisions are made on the screen of the computer and the text is printed on paper only when it is found that there are no errors in the text as seen on the screen. Obviously such a facility is not available in the manual typewriter.

Typical Computer and Typewriter Keyboards

In a typewriter we have keys for alphabets, numbers and some special characters. In addition we have some keys like shift, backspace, space-bar etc., for doing some control operations, making a tally of about 60 keys. In a computer keyboard, we have all the typewriter keys and in addition we have some more, making the tally to about 84 to 101 keys. The extra keys are used mostly for control purposes. These additional controls lend to improved quality and productivity. Learning to use a wordprocessor consists only in learning the use of more control keys. Wordprocessors will definitely replace the manual typewriters in due course and so everybody must familiarise themselves with the use of wordprocessors. For good writing there is nothing to beat word processors.

F1	F2	~ `	! 1	@ 2	# 3	$ 4	% 5	^ 6	& 7	* 8	(9	) 0	_ -	+ =	| \	Esc	Num Lock	Scroll Lock	Sys Reg
F3	F4	|← →|	q	w	e	r	t	y	u	i	o	p	[{	] }		7 Home	8 ↑	9 PgUp	prtSc *
F5	F6	Ctrl	a	s	d	f	g	h	j	k	l	: ;	" '	← Enter		4 ←	5	6 →	-
F7	F8	Shift	z	x	c	v	b	n	m	< ,	> .	? /	Shift			1 End	2 ↓	3 PgDn	+
F9	F10	Alt	Space Bar										Caps Lock			0 Ins		Del	

Fig. 1.

The Fig. 1 shows the structure of a typical PC computer keyboard. There are 84 keys in this keyboard. In PC/AT machines there will be 101 keys.

The keys marked FI to F10 are called the Function Keys and they have important uses in wordprocessing. There are many other single keystroke and-multiple keystroke controls that are used in wordprocessing. We have to learn all of them one by one.

What are the Possible Wordprocessing Functions?

Wordprocessing involves one or more of the following operations :

1. Deleting a character.
2. Deleting a word.
3. Deleting a line.
4. Deleting a para.
5. Inserting a character.
6. Inserting a word.
7. Inserting a line.
8. Inserting a para.
9. Dividing a single para into one or more paras.
10. Combining two or more paras into a single para.
11. Indenting of some paragraphs.
12. Setting some paragraphs with different margins.
13. Setting a text matter in two or more columns.
14. Selling tabular reports.
15. Setting left, right, top and bottom margins.
16. Introducing page-breaks and numbering pages.
17. Setting single or double spacing and fixing lines per page.
18. Finding and replacing a word or a string.
19. Interchanging the positions of paras or what is called the cut and paste operations.
20. Duplicating a text matter at different places.
21. Joining two or more text files.
22. Highlighting certain portions of text by underlining.
23. Printing a file in the desired format with number of copies.
24. Mail Merge.
25. Saving the document in the final form for future use etc.

Any wordprocessing software provides keystroke commands to make all the above operations and one has to learn them by actual practising. Once you learn to use the wordprocessing commands with great facility, you will find that there is remarkable improvement in productivity as well as quality in document creation. Using a typewriter involves complete re-typing of the text after every revision. But by using a wordprocessor the text is typed only once and it is only the revisions and corrections that are re-typed. Any number of revisions and re-revisions can be made to the text until at last it appears perfectly alright on the screen. It is only at this stage that the text is transferred to the paper.

Wordprocessing Softwares

There are a number of Wordprocessing Softwares available in the market like Wordstar, Wordperfect, Displaywrite, Wordlord etc., with some minor differences in sophistication. We will presently deal with one of the most popular softwares, namely the WORDSTAR (Release 4).

Summary

In this lesson we have learnt why and what of wordprocessing and what are the operations involved in wordprocessing. We said that there are different wordprocessing softwares available with some minor differences. We will study about wordstar which has a large repertoire of commands for creating and editing text information. We say wordstar is a powerful text editor.

WORDPROCESSING — II

The main objective of WORDSTAR is to facilitate the creation of text files, edit them and print them in the desired format. Let us see how WORDSTAR does this job.

Getting Started

Take the floppy diskette containing the DOS system and put it in the A drive of the computer after switching on the power supply. When the CR key is pressed, the system is booted and the computer screen displays the system prompt (A>). If you are using a hard disk system no booting disk is required. When the system is switched on the system is booted and the prompt (C>) appears. For entering the WORDSTAR world, press the keys W, S and CR in succession. The screen displays the first menu called the OPENING MENU as in Fig. 2.

WORDSTAR PROFESSIONAL RELEASE 4

<<< OPENING MENU >>>

D	open a document	L	change logged drive
N	open a non-document	C	protect a file
P	print a file	E	rename a file
M	merge print a file	O	copy a file
I	index a document	Y	delete a file
T	table of contents	F	delete a file
X	exit wordstar	Esc	shorthand
J	help	R	run a DOS command

Fig. 2.

Setting the Help Level

WORDSTAR gives helpful menu screens while we create and edit our documents. There are four levels of help which are numbered as 0,1,2 and 3. In order to get the full benefit of all the help offered by WORDSTAR, it is suggested that the HELP level is set at 3. To set the Help level, press the key 'j' twice from the opening menu. The screen prompt appears as shown in the Fig. 3. Enter the number 3 and press the CR key. You are returned to the OPENING menu.

```
The four levels of help that can be in effect are :

    3   All menus are always on.
    2   Edit menu off, submenus (Block, Quick, etc.) on.
    1   Edit menu off, submenus off, confirmations off.
    0   No menus are on, status line off, confirmations off.

The current help level is 1.
What help level do you want?
```

Fig. 3.

About the OPENING Menu

The first line gives the title of the menu and in this case it is called the 'OPENING MENU'. The next 8 lines contain a list of 16 single letter commands for performing certain functions. Finally, the directory of the files residing in the currently logged drive is displayed. The current drive is A. We will be seeing the use of the different commands as and when we use them. One cannot appreciate the use of each command unless one feels the need for it while editing or creating a file.

Creating a Text File

From the OPENING MENU, we can proceed to create, edit and print text files. Text files can be created in two modes, namely the document mode und non-document mode. Non-document mode is used to create program files and data files. Document mode is used to create report files, where we want the printed matter to be justified in the right side as well. Special print effects can be given only in the document mode files. First of all we will create a non-document mode file, since it is easy to manage for the beginners. To create a non-document file press 'N'. WORDSTAR displays a message as in Fig. 4.

```
Type the file name of the non-document to create or change.
Include drive and directory if they are different from current.
The directory, if on, displays the names of existing files you may change.
To create a new document, type a new name and press Enter.
Non-document to open?
```

Fig. 4.

The screen prompt asks the user to type the name of the file to edit. Type a name for the file say, TEST.DOC and finally press the CR key. Immediately WORDSTAR does not open the file but it asks for confirmation by giving a message as shown below :

Can't find that file. Create a new one (Y/N)?

If you press Y, Wordstar unfolds its editing screen along with the editing menu at the top as shown in the Fig. 5.

C:TEST.DOC		100001 C01		Insert
		Non-Document Edit Menu		
CURSOR	SCROLL	ERASE	OTHER	MENUS
^E up	^w up	^G char	^J help	^K block & save
^X down	^Z down	^T word	^I tab	^P print controls
^S left	^R up screen	^Y line	^V insert off	^Q quick functions
^D right	^C down screen	Del char	^O set tab width	Esc shorthand
^A word left		^U unerase	^N split the line	
^F word right		^B top bit	^L find/replace again	

Fig. 5.

The first line is called the status line. It tells the name of the file that has been opened, the name of the drive in which it will be stored and the page, the line and the column number of the edit cursor. The edit cursor denotes the position on the screen where the keystroke will be captured at that instant. In the beginning, the edit cursor will be in the first column of the first line. As we type, the edit cursor will move and so also the column number and the line number in the status line. The second line gives the title of the menu. In this case, it is called the 'NON-DOCUMENT EDIT MENU'. The next 7 lines contain a list of commands for performing some functions. Then there is about half screen of blank space intended for the users to type their text matter. Now you can start typing any text matter as you do with ordinary typewriter. All matter keyed through the console will also appear on the screen. What if, one makes mistakes during typing and want to make corrections. To make any correction, the edit cursor must be brought to that position using the appropriate command keys and the new character is overtyped. In the ordinary typewriter, both the old and the new characters will appear in the same position. But in the computer, the old character will vanish and only the new character that is currently typed will remain.

The function of the different cursor control keystrokes as listed in the EDIT MENU are given as below. The appropriate keystrokes are used for moving the cursor or the text as the case may be.

1. ^S used for moving the cursor one position left. BS (<—) key can also be used. Left arrow key can also be used.

2. ^D used for moving the cursor one position right, (or right arrow key)
3. ^A used for moving the cursor one word left.
4. ^F used for moving the cursor one word right.
5. ^E used for moving the cursor one line up. (or up arrow key)
6. ^X used for moving the cursor one line down, (or down arrow key)
7. ^Z used for moving one line up along with the cursor.
8. ^W used for moving one line down along with the cursor.
9. ^C used for moving the screen up (next screen appears), [or Pg Dn)
10. ^R used for moving the screen down (previous screen appears), [or Pg Up]
11. ^G used for deleting the character below the cursor.
12. ^T used for deleting a word starting from the position of the cursor upto the start of the next word including the punctuation and space or carriage return if any.
13. ^Y used for deleting the line in which the cursor is present.
14. ^I used for giving tab settings.
15. ^B used for reformatting paragraphs.
16. ^V [or Ins key] used for changing the INSERT ON position to the off position and vice-versa. This acts like a toggle switch. When the EDIT MENU is displayed, you will see the words INSERT ON at the right hand top. In this position, when a character is overtyped, the old character moves one step right to give way to position the new character that is overtyped. In the INSERT OFF position, when a character is overtyped, the old character disappears and the new character appears in its position. The words INSERT ON will disappear on the screen, when you press ^V. If you again press ^V the words INSERT ON will reappear.
17. ^L used for Find and Replace commands.
18. ^N used for inserting a blank line to enable the user to key a new line in that position if required.
19. ^U used to stop a command.

Saving a Text Matter in a File

When you key the text matter, it is initially stored in the main memory. If by any chance, the power supply goes off during keying, then whatever you have keyed so far will disappear. Main memory is the working area and so it is used only during creation and editing operations. Once the editing is over, the text must be stored in the floppy diskette which is the permanent storage media for the computer. The floppy diskette is called the auxiliary memory or the secondary memory or simply the computer file. Just as the humans store the information in paper files, the computers use floppy diskettes or the computer files, for permanent storage of information. Much of the communication gap between the man and the machine can be reduced if the machines could decipher human files. That is, we would very much like the computers to store the information in paper and directly take the information from paper. Hopefully we will be shortly getting paper reading computers.

Till then we have to use the floppy diskettes. Suppose you have keyed a few lines of the text matter and now you want to save the file or abandon the file and exit. One can follow any one of the following procedures :

1. To return to the system prompt after saving the file TEST.DOC, press ^K and then X.
2. To return to the OPENING MENU after saving the file TEST.DOC, press the keys ^K and D. At the end of the OPENING MENU, you will see the listing of the file TEST.DOC in the directory.
3. To abandon the file TEST.DOC and return to the OPENING MENU, press the keys ^K and Q.
4. To save the file TEST.DOC keyed up to that time and return to the beginning of the same file, press the keys ^K and S.

Printing the Text File

Let us assume that you have successfully keyed the file TEST.DOC and saved it in the diskette. Now you want to take a hard copy of the file in the printer. What you see on the screen is called the soft copy and you cannot take home the soft copy. Hard copy is the one which is obtained on paper and you can take it home. When you are in the OPENING MENU, press the key P. WORDSTAR will display a message asking you the name of the file to be printed. Type the name of the file,TEST.DOC and press Esc key. WORDSTAR will print the file in its own built-in format and finally return to the OPENING MENU.

Retrieving an Old File

Suppose you want to retrieve the old file TEST.DOC and make further changes in it. Starting from the system mode key W S <CR> N and finally the file name TEST.DOC. The old file appears on the screen ready for any further editing. Thus we find that WORDSTAR safely stores the file in the auxiliary. memory and enables us to retrieve it whenever required. Remember that in the manual method files are stored on paper. Word processors tend to reduce paper usage in an office and make it clean and tidy. Paperless offices are indeed very fine.

Exercises

We said that non-document files are used for the following jobs :

1. Creating Program Files.
2. Creating Data Files.

We have given below 4 exercises for the user to practice and take one printed copy in each after making the necessary corrections. After completing the following exercises, one must be familiar with the N and the P commands from the OPENING MENU and the commands ^S, ^D, ^F, ^E, ^X, ^Z, ^W, ^C, ^R, ^G, ^T, ^Y, ^V, ^N and ^U from the MAIN MENU. The first exercise contains simple text matter. The second exercise contains a

COBOL program. The third exercise contains a COBOL Data File. The fourth example contains a BASIC Data File. Remember that in a COBOL program A margin starts from the 8th column and the B margin starts from the 12th column. The entries must not go beyond column 72. The output must look as below :

1. Wordprocessing has effected many changes in the business world, particularly in offices where the volume of paper work is high or where the quality and speed of work produced is an important factor. Documents can be edited, revised and reproduced easily and quickly. The output turns out to be of very good quality.

Complicated techniques such as filling, decimal tabulation and production of advanced mathematical formulas or personalised letters can all be carried out much less laboriously than when traditional methods are used. Again the finished results are of very high standard.

The advantages of the wordprocessor can be enjoyed both by the management and the staff. Management can expect increased productivity and improved quality, whereas the staff enjoy the benefits of easier work, relief from routine repetitive tasks such as continual retyping of draft reports and increased job satisfaction arising from the production of first-class work. Word processors can correct errors at the press of a button and will just as easily produce as many first copies as you require of the finished documents. The potential of the wordprocessor is in fact enormous.

2.

```
A B
IDENTIFICATION DIVISION.
PROGRAM-ID, sum-of-natural-numbers.
ENVIRONMENT DIVISION.
CONFIGURATION SECTION.
SOURCE-COMPUTER, siva p.c.
OBJECT-COMPUTER, siva p.c.
DATA DIVISION.
WORKING-STORAGE SECTION.
77 SUM PIC 9999 VALUE 0.
771 PIC 999.

PROCEDURE DIVISION.

PARA-1.

    PERFORM CALCULATION-PARA VARYING 1 FROM 1 BY 1
    UNTIL I > 100.
    DISPLAY 'SUM OF NATURAL NUMBERS UP TO 100 IS ' SUM.
    STOP RUN.
```

CALCULATION-PARA.

COMPUTE SUM-SUM + 1.

3

001 N.	MURUGANPROGRAMMER	120000000050000040000150000200
025B	GAYATRIPROGRAMMER	15000000040000020000150000100
100M	BALA MANAGER	50000000050000030000250000300
102R	MANI ENGINEER	40000000040000030000100000200
110R	RAJI LECTURER	30000000020000020000300000100
112B.	KARTHIKDIRECTOR	70000000030000020000400000500
122B.	ASHWIN PROFESSOR	90000000030000020000300000600
125B.	AVINASH PROFESSOR	85000000020000010000200000400
126B.	LAVANYA DOCTOR	95000000030000020000100000700

4.

1, N. MURUGAN, PROGRAMMER, 1200, 50, 40, 150, 200
25, B. GAYATRI,PROGRAMMER, 1500, 40, 20, 150, 100
100, M. BALA, MANAGER, 5000, 50, 30, 250, 300
102, R. MANI, ENGINEER, 4000, 40, 30, 100, 200
110, 4. RAJI,LECTURER, 3000, 20, 20, 300, 100
112, B. LAVANYA, DOCTOR, 9500, 30, 20, 100, 700

WORD PROCESSING - III

So far we have seen how to enter the WORDSTAR mode, create a non-document file, save it and print the same on paper. In this lesson, we will see how a document file is created, edited, saved and printed.

Creating a Document File

When the computer is first booted, it is in the system mode. To enter the WORDSTAR mode, press W, S and CR in succession. WORDSTAR unfolds its OPENING MENU. Set the help level to 3. To create a document file, press the key D. The screen displays a prompt asking for the document to be opened.

Suppose you key the name, TEST1.FIL and press CR, the screen displays the EDIT MENU, as shown in the Fig. 6. In the EDIT MENU you will find a ruler line at the bottom of the menu with the left end marked as 'L' and the right end marked as 'R'. The letters L and R denote the left and the right margins respectively. This is the default margin settings given by WORDSTAR and any text typed will be justified between these two margins. The edit cursor will stand at line 1 and column 1. Now we can start typing the text matter if we are satisfied with the margin set up, otherwise new set of margins can be set up as we will see now.

b:w33.fil	p01	130	c32	Insert	Align

Edit Menu

CURSOR	SCROLL	ERASE	OTHER	MENUS
^E up	^W up	^G char	^J help	^O onscreen format
^X down	^Z down	^T word	^I tab	^K block and save
^S left	^R up screen	^Y line	^V turn insert off	^P print controls
^D right	^C down screen	Del char	^B align paragraph	^Q quick functions
^A word left		^U unerase	^N split the line	Esc shorthand
^F word right	^L find/replace again			

Fig. 6.

Setting Margins

When the document file is opened, WORDSTAR gives the default margin settings as 1 on the left side and 70 on the right side. In creating document files, we will be interested in setting different margins on the left and the right. The left and the right margins are set by the Margin Set Commands. Suppose you want the left margin at the 5th column and the right margin at the 50th column, proceed as follows:

Give the keystroke command, ^OL

A screen prompt will appear asking for the new left margin. If a new margin is required type the number and press the CR key otherwise simply press the CR key for the default set up. For setting up the right margin give the keystroke commands ^OR. A screen prompt will appear asking for the new right margin. Type the new margin number and press the CR key. For default set up simply press the CR key. If you had set up the left and the right margins as 5 and 50 respectively, and 50th column respectively, you will find that the ruler line now extends between the 5th and the 50th columns and the letters L and R appear at the ends of the ruler line. In a similar fashion, you can set the left and the right margins to any desired values. One can give different margin settings for different paragraphs in the same document file. A particular margin setting has jurisdiction over only one paragraph. Of course the same margin setting can be used for any number of paragraphs.

Type the text matter shown in the Fig. 7 after setting the left and the right margins as 5 and 50 respectively. You will find that the typed matter appears from the 5th column. Continue typing without using any carriage return. You will find that when the matter tries to extend beyond the 50th column, there is an automatic readjustment of the spacing between the words and the first line terminates exactly at the 50th column and the next line starts at the 5th column. This is called WRAP. Once you set the margins, the text must be keyed continuously without giving any carriage return. Carriage return must be given only when you want to start another para. Within a para there must be no carriage returns. What if, you have inserted a carriage return by mistake within a para. It can be later on rectified during editing. It is this WRAP function that makes the text right justified as well. WRAP is really a marvellous operation. After keying the full text, start making corrections by bringing the cursor to the appropriate positions using the control keys. When you are editing, the appearance of the text will change. Don't get panicky about this, since we can reformat the whole stuff by a para reform command.

> Once you have become familiar with the operation of the WORDSTAR program, a new world opens up, especially if your typing output is of the kind that involves frequent re-typing of text and even more so if your typing is of the two-fingered variety! Your text is saved on a data disk and can be recalled at any time enabling you to print further copies, incorporate new material, delete unwanted material, print in a different format send the same letter to different persons, move text around to achieve the best effect and move copy pieces of text from one document to another. The more familiar you become with WORDSTAR, the more uses you will find for it to suit your particular needs and the higher your standards of presentation will become.

Fig. 7.

Paragraph Reform Command

This is one of the most important of the WORDSTAR commands which is used very frequently. Paragraph Reform or Reformatting as it is called is necessary, since during editing, the margins might have been shifted due to insertion or deletion of words, paras might have been wrongly given because of wrong insertion of carriage returns etc. All these things can be rectified using the Reformatting command. Move the cursor to the beginning of the first para or the para in which you have made alterations. Press ^B command. The para is now rearranged within the margins. During rearrangement, WORDSTAR will give option for hyphenation for long words. If you need hyphen, press the hyphen symbol (-), otherwise press ^B. The words will be automatically readjusted with perfect alignment on the right side. Sometimes unwanted carriage returns will appear. This will be indicated by the symbol (<) at the end of the line. To remove this bring the cursor to the position next to the last character in that line and press ^T. Words from the next line begin to come and join indicating that the carriage return has been removed. Now move the cursor above that line and press ^B. The para will be reformed. For removing every unwanted carriage return, the same sequence of operations have to be performed. Normally one ^B command given at the beginning of a para will reform that para completely. ^B command has to be given every time a change is made in that para. One will become familiar with this command only by practice.

Once you have become familiar with the operation of the WORDSTAR program, a new world opens up, especially if your typing output is of the kind that involves frequent re-typing of text and even more so if your typing is of the two-fingered variety !

The basic principle behind wordprocessing is that it allows you to type a text and then to correct and edit it without having to re-type the whole document. Your text is saved on a data disk and can be recalled at any time enabling you to print further copies, incorporate new material, delete unwanted material, print in a different format, send the same letter to different persons, move text around to achieve the best effect and move copy pieces of text from one document to another.

The more familiar you become with WORDSTAR, the more uses you will find for it to suit your particular needs and the higher your standards of presentation will become.

Some Flag Characters in WORDSTAR

We said that the text creation is done, when WORDSTAR is displaying its EDIT MENU. In the beginning, the portion reserved for typing the text matter will be blank excepting the last column which will display up arrows (^) on every line. These flags present at the end of every WORDSTAR edit line tells some information about the text matter in that line. Of course such flags will not appear when the text is printed on paper. These flags appear on the screen only for the use of the person keying the text using WORDSTAR. There are a number of flag characters, some of them even giving some warning to the users. Don't get panicky about them, but try to understand what WORDSTAR wants to tell you by referring to the manual or by seeking the help of the WORDSTAR HELP MENU screen.

When the flag is a up arrow (^), it means that you are either at the beginning of a file or at the end of a file.

When the flag is a blank (no flag character), it means that the current line has been terminated by a soft carriage return or under the word wrap command.

When the flag symbol is (<), it means that the current line has been terminated by a hard carriage return.

When the flag symbol is (+), it means that the text matter in the current line is extending beyond the right margin. Of course you can always bring your text matter within your stipulated margin settings using the para reform command (^B).

When the flag symbol is (?), it means that a wrong Wordstar command has been entered in the beginning of the current line. The user can check this and do the necessary corrections.

When the flag symbol is (P) appearing at end of a line of hyphens as shown below :

-- P

it means that a new page begins following this screen line. Of course this line will not be printed, but only appears on the screen for giving information to the user.

Thus we see that WORDSTAR tries to help the users by giving useful information on the screen without themselves getting into the text matter.

Now you have learnt the WORDSTAR commands to open a document file, set left and right margins, make corrections in the text matter like deleting characters, deleting words, deleting sentences, inserting characters, inserting words, inserting sentences and doing paragraph reform. You have also learnt to interpret some of the messages given by WORDSTAR on the screen. As an exercise you can key this complete lesson, make all the corrections and wait for printing the same on paper in the desired format. In the next lesson we will see some of the printing commands.

WORDPROCESSING - IV

In this lesson, we will see some of the items that are available in the three menus, namely the QUICK MENU, the ONSCREEN MENU and the BLOCK MENU, intended for-editing and formatting texts. We know that editing requires the quick movement of the edit cursor throughout the file. We have seen some keystroke commands in the EDIT MENU intended for moving the cursor only one step in the different directions. When we are dealing with large files, these slow moving commands may not be adequate. WORDSTAR provides some commands for quick searching of certain strings, locating and moving specified portions of the text from one place to another, setting margins and tabs etc. The ONSCREEN MENU and the BLOCK MENU provide commands for doing such operations. Again the PRINT MENU contains various items for formatting the text while printing. Please remember that the base for operating the different items in the different menus is the EDIT MENU. It is only from the EDIT MENU that you have to go to other menus. Each time you go to an item in another menu for doing a particular operation, you are immediately returned to the EDIT MENU as soon as that operation is over. This means that for every operation, you have to take instructions only from the items present in the EDIT MENU. There is a beautiful organisation, a beautiful structure and a beautiful coordination among the commands in the different menus. Once you are able to appreciate this beauty, you will become a WORDSTAR addict and you will not think of any other method for document creation.

QUICK MENU Items

When you press the keystroke ^Q from the EDIT MENU, you are taken to QUICK MENU screen as shown in the Fig. 8.

Q C:w44.file P01 L01 C01 Insert Align

QUICK MENU									
CURSOR		FIND		OTHER		SPELL			
E	upper left	P	previous	F	find text	U	align paragraphs	L	check rest
X	lower right	V	last find	A	find/replace	M	math Q repeat	N	check word
S	left side	B	beg block	G	char forward		ERASE	O	enter word
D	right side	K	end block	H	char back	Y	line to right		SCROLL
R	beg doc	0-9	marker	1	find page	Del	line to left	w	up, repeat
C	end doc	?	char count		(or line)	T	to character	Z	down

Fig. 8.

You will find that the keystroke commands ^S, ^D, ^E, ^X, ^Z, ^W, ^C and ^R which appear in the EDIT MENU can be speeded up when operated from the QUICK MENU. To invoke each of these commands you have to start from the EDIT MENU, which is our base of operations and so every one of these commands must be given as ^QS, ^QD, ^QX, ^QZ, ^QW, ^QC and ^QR respectively. The meanings of the above mentioned 16 commands when operated from the EDIT MENU are shown below :

^S	moves the cursor one position left	^QS	moves the curson left end of the line
^D	moves the cursor one position right	^Q	moves the cursor to the right end of the line
^E	moves the cursor one line up	^QE	moves the cursor to the to of the screen
^X	moves the curosor one line down	^QX	moves the cursor to the bottom of the screen
^C	moves the text up a screenful	^QC	moves the text to the end of the file
^R	moves the text down a screenful	^QR	moves the text to the beginning of the file
^Z	moves the text up one line	^QZ	moves the text up the screen continuously
^W	moves the text down one line	^QW	moves the text down the screen continuously

Scrolling

It may be noted that in the first four pairs of operations, the cursor moves, while the text remains stationery, whereas in the next four pairs of operations the cursor remains stationery, while the text moves. The operation performed by ^QZ and ^QW is called scrolling. WORDSTAR provides another facility for varying the speed of scrolling. When you enter the number 1 after keying ^QW or ^QZ the scrolling is fastest. When you enter the number 9, scrolling is slowest. The scrolling speed is intermediate for numbers in between 1 and 9. For stopping the scrolling press the space bar.

The Repeat Command

WORDSTAR allows you to repeat any keystroke function many times without having to keep pressing the key. The command ^QQ is called Repeat Command. After pressing ^QQ whatever command that you give will be repeatedly performed. Press the space bar for stopping the Repeat Command. To tell WORDSTAR to go on reformatting until you tell it to stop or until it reaches the end of the text, type the command ^QQ^B. If you inadvertantly type ^QQB, the letter B will repeat itself across your page. Suppose you want to draw a line of asterisks, give the command ^QQ*. The asterisks start filling up along the line and when you have enough of them in the line press the space bar to stop. ***************************************. The asterisk line shown is drawn using the ^QQ* command.

Making Quick Deletions

We know that ^Y deletes a complete line irrespective of the position of the cursor. In order to delete the portion of the line to the left or the right of the cursor, there are two commands, namely ^QDEL or ^QY. ^QDEL deletes the line starting from the character to the left of the current cursor position. This deletion will cause the line to shift left to fill up the spaces caused by this delete command. ^QY deletes the line to the right starting from the current cursor position.

Quick Commands Using Place Markers

Suppose you want to move to different locations in a file during the course of editing. WORDSTAR allows you to mark up to 10 locations by giving numbers from 0 to 9. In order to mark a particular location in the text, bring the cursor to that location and type ^K followed by the place marker number, say 1. You will find that the number 1, highlighted by reverse video gets inserted in the screen at the location. In a similar fashion you can mark up to 10 places in a file. Though those place marker numbers are seen in the screen and may also shift the lines out of the margins on the screen, they will not appear while printing. Once you have placed a place marker number in a file, you cannot remove them until you close the file with ^KD or ^KX commands. If you use ^KS, place markers will remain in the file. But you can hide the place marker by bringing the cursor to the position of the place marker and giving the command ^K followed by that particular place marker number. What is the use of these place marker numbers? Suppose you give a command ^Q followed by that place marker number, the cursor will immediately go to that location and stop, so as to enable you to make any editing operation at that place. You will notice that place markers behave in the same fashion as block markers. There can be only 2 block markers, whereas there can be 10 place markers in a file.

ONSCREEN MENU Items

Let us consider the function of some of the items in the ONSCREEN MENU. When you press ^O from the MAIN MENU, you get the display of the ONSCREEN MENU on the screen as shown in the Fig. 9.

Q C:w44.file P01 L01 C01 Insert Align

ONSCREEN MENU

MARGINS		TYPING		DISPLAY	
L	set left	W	turn word wrap off	D	turn print controls off
R	set right	J	turn right justify off	H	turn hyphen help on
X	release	E	enter soft hyphen	P	turn preview on
T	turn ruler off	G	temporary indent	B	turn soft space dots off
F	ruler from text	S	set line spacing		TABS
O	ruler to text	C	centre line	I	set tab stop N clear

Fig. 9.

In the ONSCREEN MENU, we have commands to set some settings like margins, tabs, word wrap, hyphen-help etc. We have seen, that to bet the left and the right margins, we have to use the commands ^OL and ^OR respectively. Please remember that all editing and setting commands are given only from the EDIT MENU. When you press ^O, you come to the ONSCREEN MENU. Once you make a setting in this menu, you are returned to the EDIT MENU. For example, by remaining in the ONSCREEN MENU itself you cannot set both the left and the right margins. Once you set the left margin, you are returned to the MAIN MENU and you have to again start from there to go to other menus. So whenever we give a command we always give it from the EDIT MENU. For centring a heading, bring the cursor to the heading line and give the command ^OC. You will see that the heading is centred to the margin settings at that time.

We have seen that when we use the ^B command for paragraph reform, WORDSTAR gives us an option for hyphenating long words at the end of a line. Sometimes this will slow down the reformatting process and so we can tell WORDSTAR to suppress the hyphen-help feature. If we give the command ^OH, the hyphen-help feature will be OFF. We say that ^OH command acts as a toggle switch. We give the same command for ON and OFF. We have seen that ^V used for INSERT ON and INSERT OFF also acts as a toggle. There are a number of toggle switches in WORDSTAR and we will explain them when we get the occasion to use them.

Adjusting Page Breaks

The places in a document where one page ends and the next page begins are called page breaks. Their positions can be critical; you don't want a chart or a table split between two pages, or the heading for a new section of text alone on the bottom of a page. The WORDSTAR screen display shows you where the page breaks will fall in your document with a line of hyphens across the screen and the letter P in the flag column. The default format settings are for standard paper, 8.5" by 11", with a .5" margin at the top and a 1.5" margin at the bottom. This leaves room for 61 lines of text on the page, and so, as you are entering the text, WORDSTAR displays a page break after each 61 lines of text. There are different ways to change the position of the page breaks in your file, depending on your needs for a particular document.

Suppose you are writing a report with several sections, and you would like each section to begin on a new page. One way to leave the rest of that page blank would be to insert blank lines with the return key, until the default page break displays appears on the screen. Then you could begin typing the second section at the top of the next page. However, there is a major problem with this approach, every time you make changes in that section, adding or deleting text, you have to go back and adjust the number of blank lines, so that the second section still begins at the top of the new page. This problem of introducing page breaks can be solved by making use of what are called Dot Commands. Move the cursor to the first blank line below the first section. Type the command '.pa' starting from the first column. Now you will find that the page divider jumps to the line below it. Now you have set an unconditional page break. The .pa command tells WORDSTAR to cause a page break on the very next line. The line containing the command .pa is not counted by WORDSTAR as a line of text.

The above unconditional page break command will work alright so long as you don't make any large scale editing after putting the page break command. For example, if during the editing operations, you add some text in the first section which just pushes the page break command to the very first line of the next page, you will find that the second page is left blank and the second section begins on page 3. You know that each break is displayed as a hyphen line across the screen with a P in the flag column. If you see two of these together with only the .PA command between them, you have a blank page inserted in your document, and you need to delete one .PA command.

Conditional Page Break Command

There are many times when it is important to avoid a page break to keep a list or table from being split between two pages, or to prevent pages from ending with a heading. The unconditional page break command will not be able to meet these situations. In such cases the conditional page break command must be used. The general form of the conditional page break command is

.CP <number>

The number tells WORDSTAR how many lines of text you want kept together on one page. For example, the command .CP5, tells WORDSTAR to start a new page in this location if there are less than 5 lines remaining on the current page. The number does not include the bottom margin, just lines of text on the page. Use the .CP command immediately before a table or a para or whatever it is you want to appear complete on one page. If you wish to apply a rule throughout a long document that at least two lines of a paragraph should be together at the bottom of a page, insert .CP2 on the line before every para. This will ensure that no matter how many times you edit your document, your para will stay looking good. It must be noted that this conditional page break command can be given in addition to the unconditional page break or the usual default page breaks.

BLOCK MENU Items

When you press the command ^K from the EDIT MENU, you get the display of the BLOCK MENU on the screen as shown in the Fig. 10.

Q C:w44.file P01 L01 C01 Insert Align

			BLOCK MENU SAVE MENU					
	SAVE		BLOCK				FILE	
S	save and resume edit	B	mark begin	C	copy	O	copy	P print
D	save document	K	mark end	V	move	E	rename	
X	save and exit Wordstar	H	turn display on	Y	delete	J	erase	
Q	quit without saving	W	write to disk	M	math	L.	logged drive/dir	
	CURSOR	N	turn column mode on			R	insert a file	
0-9	set/remove marker	I	column replace on			F	run a DOS command	

Fig. 10.

The BLOCK MENU contains commands for Block operations and File operations. In another lesson, we will be seeing all the block commands for marking blocks, copying blocks, moving blocks, deleting blocks, writing blocks in a file and so on. In the lesson 2 we have seen the commands for saving files, retrieving files, abandoning files etc. There are also two toggle commands in the BLOCK MENU, namely the Column and the File Directory. The file directory is initially OFF. If you press ^KF, the file directory becomes ON and you see the directory at the top of the screen. If you again press ^KF, the file directory becomes OFF. We will see the working of the column toggle in connection with moving and copying column blocks in a file.

It may be noticed that the commands L, F, E, O, P and Y which we give from the OPENING MENU produce the same result as the commands L, F, E, O, P and J which we give from the BLOCK MENU. For example, the command L from the OPENING MENU and the command L from the BLOCK MENU give rise to the same screen display.

The command F from the OPENING MENU change the File Directory toggle ON from OFF. The command from the BLOCK MENU makes the File Directory toggle OFF.

The command E from the OPENING MENU and the command E from the BLOCK MENU give the same screen display for renaming files.

The command O from the OPENING MENU and the command O from the BLOCK MENU give the same screen display for copying files.

The command P from the OPENING MENU and the command P from the BLOCK MENU give the same screen display for printing files.

The command Y from the OPENING MENU and the command J from the BLOCK MENU give the same screen display for deleting files.

In this lesson we have seen all the important items that are present in the QUICK MENU, the ONSCREEN MENU and the BLOCK MENU. We will see more about BLOCK MENU items again in a later lesson. In the next lesson we will see the items in the PRINT MENU. Whatever items you have in the other menus, it is only in the PRINT MENU you have the items which give all polish and beauty to your output.

WORDPROCESSING — V

In this lesson we will study the items in the PRINT MENU and their uses.

Print Menu

When you press ^P from the EDIT MENU you get the PRINT MENU displayed on the screen as shown in the Fig. 11. Most of the PRINT MENU items are concerned with giving some special effects like boldfacing, underlining etc., to the text matter that will appear on the printed paper. These special effect commands are usually toggles, which can be made OFF or ON by pressing the same command keys. For example, pressing ^PB produces printing of the text in boldface. This feature can be turned off by again pressing ^PB. These special effect commands must be turned OFF as soon as their use is over. The following table shows some of the toggle commands and the effects produced by them in the printed form.

^PB	gives boldface printing
^PS	produces underlining
^PD	produces double spacing
^PX	strikes out with hyphens
^PV	prints as subscripts
^PT	prints as superscripts

Q C:w55.file P01 L01 C01 Insert Align

PRINT CONTROLS MENU

BEGIN AND END				OTHER			
B	bold	X	strike out	H	overprint char	O	binding space
S	underline	D	double strike	DY	overprint line	C	print pause
V	subscript	Y	italics/color	F	phantom space	I	column tab
T	superscript	K	indexing	G	phantom rubout	@	fixed position
				Q W E R	custom	N	normal pitch
				L	form feed	A	alternate pitch

Fig. 11.

How to Enter the Toggle Commands in the Text?

The toggle commands are entered in the text itself as you type them. For example, you want to underline the word 'WORDSTAR' in the text. Type the word as ^PSWORDSTAR^PS. In the screen it will appear as 'WORDSTAR'. The other toggle commands can be entered in this fashion wherever their effects are required.

Hiding the Toggle Commands from the Screen

When the toggle commands are keyed in the text they appear to misalign the text on the screen, though they do not appear in the printed text. This gives us some inconvenience during screen editing since we are not able to visualise exactly what we will get in the actual print. So to visualise how the text will appear in the printed form, you can hide the print control toggle commands by pressing ^OD.

It may be noted that the ^OD command does not delete the toggle commands, but only hide them on the screen. After seeing the text without the toggle commands they can be restored again by pressing ^OD.

DOT Commands

We have seen some control character commands to give some special effects to the print characters. Now we will see another set of commands called the Dot commands used for page layout. Of course, WORDSTAR has default features for print characters, page layouts like top, bottom, left and right margins, number of lines per page etc., and they are quite good for normal use. But for the sake of adventurous people WORDSTAR provides extra commands to override the default features. Some of the Dot commands come under this category.

General Rules for Entering Dot Commands

A Dot Command always begins from the first column on a new line.

A Dot Command begins with a dot or period (.).

A Dot Command has a two letter code which is sometimes followed by a number.

A Dot Command is not printed although visible on the screen.

(This is an exception to the general philosophy of WORDSTAR which says, 'what you see is what you get').

The following are some Dot Commands available in WORDSTAR, with the effects shown on their right side.

.OP	Suppresses Page Numbering which WORDSTAR does by default.
.PN	Start Page Numbering again.
.PNn	Start Page Numbering at number n.
.PCn	Print the Page Number in column n instead of in the centre.
.LHn	(for "line height") controls line spacing on printers with microspacing. Line spacing is measured in 48ths of an inch, because this is the smallest vertical motion a printer with microspacing can make. The default is 8 (8/48ths of an inch), which equals 1 /6th of an inch, or 6 lines to the inch, n is a number obtained by dividing 48 by the number of lines per inch. For double spacing, i.e. 3 lines per inch, n will be 48/3 or 16. So you must give the command .LH16. For triple spacing, the command is .LH24. For normal spacing, i.e. default spacing, the command is .LH8.
.PLn	("page length") tells the length of page in terms of the number of lines. The standard page assumed by WORDSTAR is 66 lines long, calculated on the basis of an 11 inch page printed at 6 lines per inch. To calculate the number n to insert, measure the page in inches and multiply by 6. If the paper length is 18 inches you must give the command .PL108 to get correct pagination at single spacing.

.CWn ("character width") controls how many I20ths of an inch is allotted to each character (120ths of an inch is the smallest horizontal distance, a printer with microspacing can move). The default for standard pitch is 12 (12/120)ths of an inch or 10 characters to the inch-i.e., pica type. The default for the alternate pitch is 10 (10/120)ths of an inch, or 12 characters to the inch, i.e., elite type. .CW10 is default. Try with .CW12, .CW20, .CW30 and .CW60. You willget 12,6,4 and 2 characters per inch.

.CPn ("conditional Page Break") go to next page if the number of lines remaining in the current page is less than n.

.POn ("Page Offset") What you type in column 1 will start printing n columns from the left edge of the paper.

.MTn ("margin top") gives top margin n lines. The default is 3 lines.

.MBn ("margin bottom") gives bottom margin n lines. The default is 8 lines.

.HE ("header") prints a page heading in the top margin space. For example, .HE ELEMENTS OF WORDSTAR will print the heading 'ELEMENTS OF WORDSTAR' in the top margin. To cancel that command insert .HE.

.FO ("footer") prints a footer label in the bottom margin. For example, .FO continued will cause the footer 'continued' to be printed in the bottom margin. If a footer is specified page number is not printed. To cause the printing of page number one must give the command as .FO # continued

The default settings for the margins are shown in the Fig. 12.

	(line 1	heading <if any>	
top margin	(line 2		: two lino of
	(line 3		: header margin
first line of text			
last line of text			
	(line 1		: two lines of
	(line 2		: footer margin
	(line 3	footing <if any>	
bottom margin	(line 4		
	(line 5		
	(line 6		
	(line 7		
	(line 8		

Fig. 12.

The relationship between the header and the main body of the text, and the end of the main text and the start of the footer can be even more finely tuned using the commands .HMn and .FMn.

.HMn	("header margin") the number n gives the number of blank lines required between the header and the first lino of the text. From the Fig. 12 you see that the default value is 2.
.FMn	("footer margin") the number n gives the number of blank lines required between the last line of the text and the footer. From the Fig. 12 you see that the default value is 2.

Inserting Comments in the Text

If you want to give some documenting information for purpose of information to all the users of the file, you can do so after typing two consecutive dots in the first two columns. Any information typed afterwards will be treated as comments and will not be printed on paper. For example,

.. This is comment information, not to be printed on paper.

Actual Printing

So long we were telling how to create, edit and format texts. Now we will see how we can actually do the printing. The print command can be initiated either from the OPENING MENU by pressing P or from the EDIT MENU by pressing ^KP. As soon as you initiate the printing command the screen prompt asks for the name of the document to be printed. The user can now type the name and press the Esc key. WORDSTAR will now print the contents of the file with its own built-in or default format. If you press the CR key after typing the name of the file, several printing options appear on the screen one by one as shown in the Fig. 13.

```
Number of copies?
Pause between pages (Y/N)?
Use form feeds (Y/N)?
Starting page?
Ending page?
Non-document (Y/N)?
Name of printer?
```

Fig. 13.

The last question is very important, since the answer to this question enables you to get the document printed in a file for a review if required. You type the name 'preview' against the name of the printer and press the CR key. The document is now written in a file by name prview.ws. The file prview.ws can be reviewed on the screen and further corrections can be made to the document before you transfer it to the printer. For the question on starting page number you can give any desired number. If you want to start from 1, simply press the carriage return, otherwise type the number and press the CR key. For the question on ending page number, if you press the CR key the entire file will be printed. If you specify the final page, printing will stop after that specified page. For the question on form feeds, you answer Y, if you use continuous stationery. Then WORDSTAR will send the necessary line feeds to advance to the top of next page. If you use single sheets give the answer as N so that paper will not advance after the page is printed. For the question on pause between paper changes, you can answer Y, if you are using single sheet, otherwise N. Finally, see that the printer is ready. If so press the CR key. See that you get the fruits of your labour in black and white. The readers can try with the different options and see how the printing is done.

This is the most crucial lesson, since only in this lesson you are told how to get the output for all the efforts you put in. Readers can key this lesson and practice printing.

13

Lotus 1.2.3 Why, What?

What is LOTUS?

In recent years computers have become very powerful tools in solving a wide variety of human problems. Such problem areas include fields like financial accounting, payroll, inventory, budgeting, management information systems, decision support systems etc. Very powerful softwares have been developed to make the use of computers in these fields highly productive. LOTUS 1-2-3 is one such high productive software, which has been developed for use by the common man. By common man it is meant persons with no special knowledge about computers and programming languages, but with a thorough grasp of their specialised problems. For solving a problem with the conventional high level languages like FORTRAN, COBOL, BASIC, PASCAL etc., you have to tell two things to the computer, namely,

1. What is it to be solved and
2. The procedure for solving it

Will it not be wonderful if you have a software which will have built-in procedures for solving the different problems? This is precisely what you have in LOTUS. You simply tell or command what you want and need not tell how to get them. LOTUS has built-in procedures for working out most of the commands required in the data processing world. LOTUS is called a Command Language and you need only learn the commands to ask what you want without bothering as to how they are got. Hence Command Languages are a lot more easier to learn and use than the conventional high level languages. This is the reason why LOTUS is called a High Productive Software. LOTUS provides the user, what is called a menu driven approach. When the LOTUS software is loaded in the computer, it displays a menu on the screen asking the user to describe his problems more specifically. By a series of prompts LOTUS elicits the required parameters for solving the problem from the user himself and finally presents the solution in the desired format. LOTUS is called a three-in-one package, since it does three functions, that of a spreadsheet, a database management system and business graphics. It has also limited facilities for doing wordprocessing functions. The whole glamour about LOTUS 1-2-3 is because of its versatility to combine such sophisticated functions in one package. We will now see what these different functions mean.

What is a Spreadsheet?

Whenever we want to solve a problem, we invariably take a sheet of paper and a pencil and do some writing work. We can call the sheet of paper as a worksheet. What exactly we write and how do we write them? We know that any problem could be solved only if a formula is evolved. So we get hold of the appropriate formula for the problem and write it in some area or location. We call this area as formula cell and let us represent it schematically by highlighting it with bounding lines as shown in the Figure 1. Then we get the values of the variables involved in the formula (called the data values) and

Formula Cell

Fig. 1.

write them in different locations called dala locations or data cells. We can represent the data evils schematically by rectangles as we have done for the formula cell. Let us now consider the problem of finding the simple interest (SI and the compound interest (CI) for a set of values of principal (P), rate per cent (R) and number of years (N). We enter the values of P, R & N in the data cells and the formulae for SI & CI in the formula cells arranged in a row as shown in the figure 2. For getting the solution, we take the data from the data cells, substitute them in the formulae, compute manually and write the results in the formula cells. Suppose we want to find the simple interest and the compound interest for a sccond set of values of P, R & N, we prepare another row of 5 cells in the second line. For a third set of values we prepare another row of 5 cells in the third line and so on.

P =	R =	N =	P*N*R/100	P*(1+R/100) ^N-P

Fig. 2.

We find that there is some orderliness in the arrangement of the cells, i.e., the cells are arranged in rows and columns somewhat as shown in the Figure 3. The cells along a row need not have the same width, but the cells along a column have the same width. For the sake of simplicity we have shown only 5 rows and only 5 cells in each row.

Fig. 3.

In general the worksheet can be divided into a large number of cells arranged in several rows and columns, the number depending on the number of variables and formulae involved in the problem. This is a manual worksheet or a passive worksheet as it is called, where the results in each of the formula cells are computed manually. Such a worksheet is found to be useful for working a variety of problems like payroll, inventory, budgetting etc. Of course we have to enter all the data in the data cells and compute all the formulae in the formula cells completely manually. Will it not be wonderful if we have a worksheet in which the formula values in the formula cells are automatically computed as soon as we enter the data values in the data cells? It is this type of worksheet that is precisely given by LOTUS on the computer screen. Such a worksheet is called an active worksheet, also called the SPREADSHEET. In addition to automatic computation of formulae in the formula cells, LOTUS provides many other facilities like the re-usability of the same area for any number of problems, duplication of data and formula in any number of cells etc. So SPREADSHEET is nothing but an active worksheet provided by LOTUS on the computer screen. We can call a SPREADSHEET as a computer controlled worksheet. We know that computer power is exercised by means of wordy commands provided by LOTUS. So we call LOTUS as a command language for manipulating worksheets. Command languages are a lot more easy to learn and use as compared to programming languages like FORTRAN, COBOL, BASIC etc., and that is why LOTUS is very popular with computer enthusiasts.

We said that LOTUS gives a worksheet on the computer screen and it is made of a number of cells or locations arranged in rows and columns. It may be remembered that we have been asked to visualise the computer memory in the same fashion as made of cells arranged in rows and columns somewhat like a pigeon-hole cabinet box, which we see in post offices for .sorting letters. What LOTUS does is to project or bring out this visualisation of the computer memory on the computer screen. Each cell we see on the screen is an addressable memory location of the computer. This means, we can put dala in them and reference them by the addresses of the different cells. How does LOTUS gives the address to the different cells? LOTUS follows a convention of referencing the rows by the numbers 1, 2, 3 etc. and the columns by alphabetic letters A,B,C etc. The label or the address of each cell is coined by combining the column letter and the row number and putting it as a single entity. Using this notation the address of the first cell in the first column is Al, that of the first cell in the second column is B1 and so on. The Figure 4 shows a small portion of the

	A	B	C	D	E
1	Al	BI	Cl	Dl	El
2	A2	B2	C2	D2	E2
3	A3	B3	C3	D3	E3
4	A4	B4	C4	D4	E4

Fig. 4.

spreadsheet containing cells arranged in 4 rows and 5 columns, with the addresses of the different cells marked on them. LOTUS shows the column letters and the row numbers on the screen itself so as to enable the users to find the address of any cell in which the user wants to enter data or formula.

Computing Capability of LOTUS

LOTUS permits us to enter only one of two things in a cell, namely data or formula. Please remember that LOTUS is a special purpose software used for solving problems which can be expressed in formula form. Suppose you enter a dala 5 in the cell Al. This means that the variable A1 is assigned the values 5. Similarly if you enter 10 in the cell B, it means that the variable B1 is assigned the value 10. Suppose you enter the expression +A1 + BI in the cell C1 it means that you are entering the formula C1 = +A1 + B1 in the cell Cl. The beauty about LOTUS is, that when you enter a formula in a cell, the formula does not get itself entered in the cell, but it is only the computed value of the formula that is entered in the cell. This is what we call as the computing capability of LOTUS. Suppose we change the value in the cell Al from 5 to 10). Immediately the value in the cell C1 is recomputed and becomes 20, which is the value obtained by computing the formula using the current values of the the variables involved in the formula. We will see that this facility is of very great importance for studying what can be termed as "What IF" types of problems.

LOTUS Spreadsheet is an Electronic Blackboard

We say that the LOTUS Spreadsheet is something like an Electronic Blackboard, wherein the users can rub and write just like the ordinary blackboard. The main difference between the electronic blackboard and the ordinary blackboard is, that all the formulae entered in the electronic blackboard are computed automatically, whereas all the computations have to be done only manually in the ordinary blackboard. This means that whenever the values of the variables in the electronic blackboard are changed, the formulae are recomputed using the new values automatically. Remember that the computer is used only for their high speed, high degree of accuracy, high degree of reliability and complete automaticity. It is the job of the user to enter the right data and the right formulae in the different cells, otherwise the formula GIGO (Garbage In Garbage Out) will work. LOTUS is essentially an interactive type of language which gives quick response to our queries. So this language is preferred in certain applications where we have to monitor the results under rapidly changing environments. Numbers can be moved faster on the screen so as to reflect the changes that are taking place. LOTUS thus provides a sort of animation with numbers just like the animation we see in the cartoon films of Walt Disney's Mickey Mouse. The pictorial representation of the movement of inanimate objects is called animation. In the cartoon films, pictures move and in LOTUS numbers move. You are seeing the computer doing the calculations visibly and this has a powerful appeal.

A Typical "What IF" Type Problem

Consider a table as shown in the Figure 5 containing the register numbers, names and marks obtained in 5 different subjects by a large number of students taking an examination.

Reg. No.	Name	m1	rn2	m3	m4	m5	avg%	Result
...	...	...	...	...	...	...	...	...
...	...	...	...	...	...	...	...	...
...	...	...	...	...	...	...	...	...
...	...	...	...	...	...	...	...	...
...	...	...	...	...	...	...	...	...

Fig. 5.

The average percentage obtained by each candidate is shown in the 8th column and the result ('PASS' or 'FAIL') of each candidate is shown in the 9th column. Let us assume for the sake of simplicity that if the average percentage is >=50, the candidate is declared 'PASS', otherwise as `FAIL.' The appropriate formulae are replicated in the 8th and the 9th columns. Once the data values are entered in the other columns, LOTUS displays the values in all the fields in the 8th and the 9th columns. Suppose you feel that there are too many failures and you want to improve the result by applying some moderation.

Moderation can be applied by adding 2 or 3 or 4 marks etc., in each subject for all the students or marks can be added on a selective basis, i.e., only to those students who have got below a certain value and so on. In general there are several ways of applying moderation and you want to find out how the result will improve by applying the different moderation criteria. Of course one can write a Basic program for each case, get the outputs and compare them. This will be time consuming and laborious. LOTUS does this job almost instantaneously without any programming effort. Commands can be given for changing the marks suitably and the results under the different moderation criteria can be displayed in the different columns. After nuking a visual comparison, the moderation criteria appropriate for the situation can be chosen. This is a typical "What IF' type of problem.

There are several such "What IF" problem situations in real life. For example, a businessman would like to know, how his profits will be affected if he increases the selling price of a product by say, Rs. 2/- or decreases the selling price by Rs. 2/- or offers a free gift of some value along with each product sold and *so* on. In such cases LOTUS will help the user to quickly study the outcome of the different sales gimmicks. In fact, such manipulation of numbers and presentation of the results in meaningful tables are required in very many applications like budgetting, forecasting, inventory control etc. The conventional high level languages (HLL) like FORTRAN, COBOL, BASIC etc., are not very convenient in such cases. This is where LOTUS comes to the rescue of the users. We say that LOTUS is a specialised software or a very high level language (VHLL) admirably suited for solving what are called as "What IF' types of problems.

Database Management by LOTUS

We said that LOTUS displays the memory locations of the computer on the screen arranged in rows and columns. Once we enter the data and the formulae in the appropriate cells, the computations are done almost instantaneously in the formula cells and the results are displayed. This picture reflects the relationship between the data cells and the formula cells. The dala items are treated completely independently. The question may be asked whether structured data can be entered in the worksheet and whether LOTUS can provide commands to manipulate structured data. LOTUS does provide commands for structured data, organised as records and files. Suppose we enter the data items pertaining to one entity, say one employee, in the different cells along a row and enter similar data items for a number of other employees in different rows, we get what is called a record structured file. An arrangement of data items such that the fields in a row denote the diverse characteristics of a single entity and the fields in a column denote the same characteristic of different entities is called a database. LOTUS provides commands to manipulate such a database and produce a wide variety of meaningful reports. LOTUS can manage a fairly big database file containing as much as 2000 records, each record containing as much as 256 fields. The database management ability of LOTUS is adequate for many purposes.

Graphic Capability of LOTUS

We said that LOTUS displays the results in the worksheet in the form of a table, i.e., in a row column format. LOTUS provides commands to represent the values in the table by an X-Y plot or a graph. One has to choose the cells whose values are to be represented along the X-axis and the cells whose values are to be represented along the Y-axis. When the graph command is given LOTUS depicts the relationship between the X-fields and Y-fields by an X-Y plot. This is called the graphic capability of LOTUS. Such plots have been found to be very appealing in many business applications.

SUMMARY

In summary we say that LOTUS is a THREE-IN-ONE package or an Integrated Software, which gives the best of three different functions in the data processing world in one leading. When we use three different packages, we get into lot of interfacing problems. An integrated stuff has got its own advantages, in that it gives lot of saving in running time and learning time besides solving interfacing problems. Perhaps it may not cope up with bigger jobs, but we must say that LOTUS is not static and is ever growing and so it will always adjust itself to the growing needs of the modern man.

LOTUS COMPOSITION

The Composition of LOTUS

We said that LOTUS is a very high level language intended for communicating the procedural commands, for solving certain specialised problems in the computer. We know that computers can solve any problem only if it is given in formula form. A formula is made of constants, variables, operators and their combinations. So just like every other computer languages, LOTUS also is concerned with the rules for coding the above entities. LOTUS stuff (version 2) is made of the following finite number of entities:

1. 2 Constants
2. 2,097,715 Variables
3. 16 Operators
4. 81 Library Functions and
5. 10 Basic Commands

The point is, that the different entities are finite in number and this finiteness contributes to the ease of learning LOTUS. LOTUS uses a character set (all ASCII characters) and a set of grammar rules or syntax as it is called for coding the different entities like constants, variables, operators, expressions and commands.

Character Set

Every computer language has three different types of characters, namely, the alphabetic, the numeric and the special. The alphabetic characters consist of all English alphabets from A to Z, the numeric characters consist of the 10 digits from 0 to 9 and the special characters consist of the commonly used algebraic symbols like +, -.*,/,., „ =, (,), $, @, %, >, <, ?, etc. Learning the character set of LOTUS does not pose any special problem, since we are already familiar with these symbols.

Constants

Initially there are two types of constants, namely, the numeric and the label or the string. A numeric constant is coded by combining numeric digits to a maximum length of 15. A sign can be present in the leftmost position and there can be a decimal point placed anywhere. The numbers can be either in the floating notation or scientific notation. Examples: 2345, -12.34, 2.3E-4, -3.54E6, 7.678E+126, -.2345 etc.

A label constant is coded by combining any valid character including blanks to a maximum length of 240. LOTUS considers anything excepting numbers and formulae as labels. If labels are to be explicitly coded, they must be preceded by a single quote without any corresponding ending quote mark. Examples: KRISH, '1234, A1+B1, '+A1+B1 etc. If you simply write 1234, LOTUS will interpret it as a number. To treat this as a label, it must be preceded by the single quote mark. Similarly +A1+B1 is a formula, but A1+B1 is a label or a string. If the formula or a number is preceded by a single quote it will be treated as a label. Anything other than numbers and formulae will be treated as label by default and so no prefix symbol is necessary. That is why the item KRISH is not given any prefix symbol.

Variables

We know that variables are used for storing constants. As far as the machine is concerned, the variables represent the addresses of the memory locations. We have said that LOTUS displays the memory locations on the screen by means of cells arranged in 8192 rows and 256 columns. This means that there are 8192 x 256 cells or memory locations available in LOTUS. So there are only 8192 x 256 variables in LOTUS. Rows are referenced by numbers from 1 to 8192. Columns are referenced by letters A, B, C, ...Z, AA, AB, ...AZ, BA, BB, ...BZ, CA, CB, ...CZ, DA, DB, ...DZ, EA, EB, ...EZ, FA, FB, ...FZ, GA, GB, ...GZ, HA, HB, ...HZ, IA, IB, ...IV. The cell address is coined by combining the column letter and the row number. With this notation, the address of the first cell is Al and the address of the last cell is IV8192. Since the cell addresses will be seen on the screen itself, there will be no problem in identifying them. The main point is that the cell addresses or variable names are system defined and there are only finite number of variables in LOTUS. In conventional high level languages like BASIC, FORTRAN, COBOL, PASCAL etc., there is no limit to the number of variables that can be coined, since they are all user defined.

Operators

There are three types of operators in any computer language, namely, the arithmetic, the relational and the logical. The arithmetic operators are + for addition, - for subtraction, * for multiplication, / for division and ^ for exponentiation. The relational operators are = for equal to, > for greater than, < for less than, >= for greater than or equal to, <= for less than or equal to and <> for not equal to. The logical operators are #NOT#, # AND# and #OR#. All the operators have the same meaning as in thc conventional HLLs. These operators are performed as per the following hierarchy rules:

1. All operations within parantheses
2. Exponentiation
3. Multiplication and Division in the order in which they occur from left to right
4. Prefix + or -
5. Addition and Subtraction in the order in which they occur from left to right
6. All Relational Operators
7. NOT Operator
8. AND and OR Operators in the order in which they occur from left to right

Expressions

Expressions are coined by combining constants, variables and operators. Expressions are called the formulae in LOTUS and it is only the computed values of expressions that are given as solutions. When an expression is given in a particular cell location say Cl, then it is implied that the formula Cl=Expression is entered in that cell. The entity Cl= is implicitly present. We said that an expression is a formula and it leads to a value and any entity which leads to a value must conform to certain rules. A formula or an expression can start only with any one of the following characters: 0,1,2,3,4,5,6,7,8,9, +, -, @, (, # and $. It cannot contain space character. It can contain numbers and operators. It can contain cell addresses and numbers or cell addresses alone. Examples: 2+3/4, +A1-B1, +Al-3/4*6, +Al*Cl-4/Dl etc. If the first entity in an expression happens to be a cell address, then it must start with a sign, otherwise LOTUS will take it as a label or a string entity.

LOTUS Functions

LOTUS has a number of built-in Functions or Library Functions for computing the values of some frequently occurring expressions or formulae. These functions are given names for reference purposes. The names are usually followed by an argument enclosed within parentheses. The general form of a LOTUS Function is

@name-of-the-function(argument)

A LOTUS function invariably starts with the symbol @, which is pronounced as 'at.' So LOTUS Functions are also called 'at functions.' The argument can consist of a value or a range or a list or another function itself. Value is either a number or a formula or a cell address. Range is a group of cells specified by the top leftmost cell and the bottom rightmost cell separated by two periods. A Range can consist of a single cell, a row of cells or a column of cells or a block of cells. List is one or more values or ranges or formulae separated by commas. Every function returns a single value depending on the argument. Functions are divided into the following categories:

1. Mathematical Functions
2. Logical Functions
3. Date Functions
4. Financial Functions
5. Statistical Functions
6. Database Statistical Functions and
7. Special Functions

Mathematical Functions

1. @ABS(x) Returns the absolute value of the number in the argument. For example, @ABS(-23.4) returns 23.4.
2. @lNT(x) Returns the integer part of the number in the argument. For example, @LNT(23.4) returns 23.
3. @LN(x) Returns the logarithm of x to the Naperian base e. For example, @IN(2) returns .693147.
4. @LOG(x) Returns the logarithm of to the base 10. For example, @LOG(2) returns .301029.
5. @EXP(x) Returns the value of e raised to the power x.
6. @SQRT(X) Returns the square root of x. For example, @SQRT(100) returns 10.
7. @MOD(x,y) Returns the remainder of x divided by y. For example, @Mod(5,2) returns 1.
8. @ROUND(x,n) Returns the number x to n places right of the decimal point if n is

+ve, n places to the left of the decimal point if n is -ve and rounds to an integer if n is zero. For example, @ROUND(23.456,2) returns 23.46.

@ROUND (23. 456, -2) returns 0.

@ ROUND (23. 456,0) returns 23.

9 @PI — Returns the value 3.1415926. There is no argument for this function.

10. @RAND — Returns a random number between 0 and 1. There is no argument for this function.

11. @SIN(x) — Returns the sine of the angle x expressed in radian measure. For example, @SIN(@PI/4) returns .707106.

12. @COS(x) — Returns the cosine of the angle x expressed in radian measure. For example, @COSINE(@Pl/4) returns .707106.

13. @TAN(x) — Returns the tangent of the angle x expressed in radian measure. For example, @TAN(Pl/4) returns 1.

14. @ASIN(x) — Returns the angle in radian measure whose sine is x. For example, @AS1N(.707106) returns .785397.

15. @ACOS(x) — Returns the angle in radian measure whose cosine is x. For example, @ACOS(.707106) returns .785399.

16. ATAN(x) — Returns the angle in radian measure whose tangent is x. For example, @ATAN(l) returns .785398.

17. @ATAN2(x, y) — Returns the angle in radian measure whose tangent is y/x. The signs of x and y are considered separately, so that the angle can be in any quadrant. If both x & y are +ve, the angle is in the first quadrant. If both x & y are -ve, the angle is in the 3rd quadrant. If x is +ve and y is -ve, the angle is in the fourth quadrant. If x is -ve and y is +ve, the angle is in the 2nd quadrant. For example, @ATAN2(1,1)returns .785397.@ATAN2(-1,-1) returns-2.35619. @ATAN2(1, -1) returns -.785397. @ATAN2(-1,1) returns 2.35614.

Logical Functions

1. @TRUE — Returns the logical value 1.
2. @FALSE — Returns the logical value 0.
3. @ISERR(x) — Returns 1 if x has the value ERR, otherwise 0.
4. @ISNA(x) — Returns 1 if x has the value NA (not available), otherwise 0.
5. @IF(condition x, y) — Returns x if the condition is true; otherwise returns y. For example,

   @IF(9>8, A 1, B2) returns the value in A1.

   @IF(9<A1, B2) returns the value in B2.

DATE Functions

LOTUS stores every date by a number called the datenumber starting from January 1900.

1. @DATE(yy,mm,dd) Returns the date number of the given date.
   @DATE(00,01,01) returns 1.
   @DATE(99,12,31) returns 36525.
   @DATE(89,02,10) returns 32549.
2. @DAY(datenumber) Returns the day of the month of the datenumber. For example, @DAY(32549) returns 10.
3. @MONTH(datenumber) Returns the month of the year of the datenumber. For example, @MONTH(32549) returns 2.
4. @YEAR(datenumber) Returns the last two digits of the of the given datenumber. For example, @YEAR(32549) returns 89.
5. @TODAY Returns the datenumber of the date entered in the system.

Financial Functions

1. @FV(pmt,int,term) Returns the future value of an investment using the formula pmt((l +int) ^n-l)/ int, where pmt is periodic payment int is periodic interest rate and n is the number of periods. Suppose you enter 2000 in Al, .1 in BI, 20 in Cl and the function @FV(A 1,Bl,CI) in Dl, the value returned in Dl is 114549.9, which is the future value of a periodic investment of Rs.2000 for 20 years at 10% interest compounded annually.
2. @NPV(int, range) Returns the Net Present Value of a series of cash inflows given in the range, discounted at a fixed interest rate int. Suppose you enter .1 in Al, the cash inflows of 2000, 2000, 2000, 4000 and 4000 in B1, Cl, Dl, El & FI respectively and the function @NPV(A1,B1..F1) in G1, the value returned is 10189.
3. @PMT (prin, int, term) Returns the periodic payment on a loan prin, at interest rate int per period, and paid in term number of periods. Suppose you enter 5000 in Al, 1 /120 in B1, 10 in C1 and @PMT(A1,B1,C1) in Dl, then the value returned in Dl is 523.20. The formula used is pmt = prin*int/(l-(l+int) ^n-l).
4. @IRR(guess, range) Returns the maximum interest rate at which you can borrow money for given cash flows over a range of period so as to make the investment breakeven. The first value in the range is the cash outflow and is -ve and the other

values are cash inflows. Suppose you enter the initial guess as .05 in A1, the cash flows -1000, 120, 124, 128, 132, 136, 130, 120, 124, 128, 132, 120, 124 in BI, Cl, Dl, El, FI, Gl, HI, I1,J1,K1, LI, Ml & N1 respectively and @IRR(A1,B1..N1) in 01, the value returned is .0709. This means that for the given cash outflows und inflows, the breakeven interest rate is 7.09%.

5. @PV(pmt, int, term) Returns the present value of an annuity. Suppose your friend offers two plans for repayment of a loan taken from you. 20 annual instalments of 50,000 each or an immediate payment of Rs.400,000. If the interest rate is 12%, the present value of the instalment repayments as given by @PV(5000,.12,20) is 373472. We find that the lump sum payment is worth more today. The formula used is pmt(l-(1+int)^-n)/int.

Statistical Functions

1. @COUNT (list) Returns the count of the number of value cells in the given range excluding the label and the blank cell. Suppose you enter 24,78,90, 785,65 in B1, B2, B3, B4, B4 & B5 respy. Then enter @count(Bl..B5) in B6 and press the carriage return. The number 5 will be entered in B6.

2. @SUM(list) Returns the sum of the values in the list. This ignores the blank and the label cells. Using the same same values as in 1 enter the function @sum(Bl..B5) in B7 and press CR. The value 1042 gets entered.

3. @AVG(list) Returns the average of the values in the list. Enter the function @avg(Bl ..B5) in B8 and press CR. The value 208.4 gets entered in B8. This function is equivalent to @sum(list)/@count(list). Verify the same.

4. @MAX(list) Returns the largest number in the list. Enter the function @max(bl ..b5) in b9 and press CR. The value 785 gets entered in B8.

5. @MIN(list) Returns the smallest number in the list. Enter the the function @min(Bl..B5) in b10 and press CR. The value 24 gets entered in b10.

6. @STD(list) Returns the Standard Deviation of the values in the list Enter the function @STD(B1..B5) in B11 and press CR. The value 289.1564 gets entered in the cell b11.

7. @VAR(list) Returns the variance of the values in the list. Enter the function @var(bl ..b5 in b12 and press CR. The value 83611.44 gets

entered in b12. Check that this value is the square of standard deviation.

DATABASE Statistical Functions

The Database Statistical Functions perform the same calculations on a database as the ordinary statistical functions perform on a list. So a database must be set up in the worksheet and the criterion range must be established. Each database statistical function has three arguments, namely, the INPUT, OFFSET and CRITERION. Input is the range which includes all the database records and their field names. Offset is the column number containing the field, count being done from 0 from the first column of the input range. Criterion is the criterion range established by the user.

1. @DSUM(input,offset,criterion) Returns the sum of the values in the offset column of the input range that meets the criteria of the criterian range.
2. @DCOUNT (input, offset, criterion) Returns the number of non-blank cells in the offset column of the input range that meets the criteria in the criterion range.
3. @DAVG(input,offset,criterion) Returns the average of the values in the offset column of the input range that meets the criteria in the criterion range.
4. @DMAX(input,offset,criterion) Returns the maximum value in the offset column of the input range that meets the criteria in the criterion range.
5 @DMIN(input,offset,criterion) Returns the minimum value in the offset column of the input range that meets the criteria in the criterion range.
6. @DSTD(input,offset,criterion) Returns the standard deviation of the values in the offset column of the input range that meets the criteria in the criterion range.
7. @DVAR(input,offset,criterion) Returns the variance of the values in the offset column of the input range that meets the criteria in the criterion range.

The meaning of these functions will become clear after we study the database management function performed by LOTUS.

Special Functions

1. @CHOOSE(x,vl,v2,.....vn)

Returns any one of the values vl, v2, ...vn depending on the values of x. If x = 1, vl is returned, if x = 2, v2 is returned and so on.

2. @ERR Returns the value ERR when an error condition is present in the cell.

3. @NA Returns the value NA in a cell when data is not available.

4. @HLOOKUP(x,range,row-number)

It performs a horizontal lookup. The value of x is compared to each cell in the top row of the range moving horizontally from the beginning of the range. When it finds a match, it moves down by row-number of rows and returns the value in that cell. Suppose you enter the values in the worksheet as shown below.

	a	*b*	*c*	*d*	*e*	*b*
1	89					
2						
3	34	67	89	90		
4	45	56	33	9		
5	89	25	22	456		

Enter the function @hlookup(a1, a3..d5,2) in b1 and press the CR key. LOTUS searches for the value 89 in the first row of the range a3..d5. The value is in c3. Then it goes down by 2 rows down and gets the value 22 and returns it in the cell b1. This function will work only if the values are in the ascending order in the first row where the look up is made.

5. @VLOOKUP(x,range,column-number)

It performs a vertical lookup. The value of x is compared to each cell in the first column of the range moving down vertically from the beginning of the range. When it finds a match, it begins to move horizontally along that row by column-number of columns and returns the value in that cell. Suppose you enter the function @vlookup(al, a3..d5,2) in b2. Now LOTUS lotus looks up for the value 89 along the first column of the range a3..d5. The value 89 is in the cell a5. Then it moves 2 columns to the right and returns the value 22 in b2. While doing vertical look up the lookup values in the first column must be in the ascending order.

The above 51 functions only are available in the LOTUS version 1A. The additional functions available in LOTUS verion 2 are given below.

Three functions have been introduced to compute the depreciation on the cost of a capital equipment by the three methods, namely, the double-declining balance method, the straight-line method and the sum of the year's digits method.

1. @DDB(cost,salvage-valuc,life,period)

   Returns the depreciation by the DDB method. The formula used is (bv x 2)/n, where bv is the book-value in that period. This is obtained by subtracting the depreciation from the cost, n is the useful life of the asset. The period represents the 1st or the 2nd or the 3rd year und so on us the case may be. The depreciation is high in the first year, but decreases as years pass on.

2. @SLN(cost,salvage-value, life)

   Returns the depreciation by the straightline method. The formula used is (c-s)/n, where c is the cost, s is the salvage value and n is the useful life. The depreciation is uniform in all the years.

3 @SYD(cost, salvage-value, life, period)

   Returns the depreciation by the sum of the year's digits method. The formula used is 2(c-s)(n-p+l)/n(n+l), where c is the cost of the asset, s is the salvage value, n is the useful life and p is the current period. In this method also the depreciation value decreases as years pass on.

   Suppose you enter the cost 20000 in al, salvage value 1000 in bl and the useful life 5 in cl, the depreciation for the first five years are computed by the functions and entered as shown below.

	a	*b*	*c*	*d*
1	20000	1000	5	
2	years	ddb	sln	syd
3	1	8000	3800	6333
4	2	4800	3800	5067
5	3	2800	3800	3800
6	4	1728	3800	2533
7	5	1037	3800	1267

In b3 enter the function @ddb(al,bl,c3,a3). Copy this formula in the range b4..b7 using the command /cb3~b4..b7~. In c3 enter the function @sln(al,bl,cl) and copy this in the range c4..c7 using the command /cc3~c4..c7~. In d3 enter the function @syd(al,bl,cl,a3) and copy this in the range d4..d7 using the command / cd3~d4..d7~. Enter values 1, 2, 3, 4 and 5 in a3, a4, a5, a6 and a7 respy. You will get the depreciation table over a period of 5 years as shown above. Wherever you see the symbol - press CR.

There are two functions for making Investment Analysis.

1. @TERM(payment,Interest-rate,future-value)

   Returns the term in number of years required to earn the future-value by making equal annual payments at the given interest rate. Suppose you make an annual payment of Rs.1000 for certain number of years which gives a compound interest of 10%. If you want to find out when the value will become 20000 use the function @term(1000,.l ,20000). This will return 11.53. This means that in 11.53 years you will get Rs.20000.

2. @RATE(future-value,present vulue.term)

   Returns the interest-rate required to earn the future-value from the present given value. Suppose you want to find at what rate per cent the amount of 10000 will grow to 20000 in 5 years, use the function @rate(20000, 10000,5). This will return .15. The formula used is(fv/pv)^(l/n)-l.

The following Special Functions have been added in the LOTUS version 2:

1. @COLS(range)	Returns the number of columns in the given range. 2.
2. @ROWS(range)	Returns the number of rows in the given range.
3. @CELL(attribute, range)	Returns the attribute specified for the cell or the range of cells. The attributes that can be requested are address, row, column, contents, type, prefix, protect and format.
4. @CELLPOINTER(attribute)	Returns the attribute specified for the current cell.
5. @INDEX (range, column, row)	This is a lookup function which returns the value in the cell in the given range specified by the column and the row keys.

The following String Functions have been added in the LOTUS version 2:

1. @UPPER (lable or cell-address)	Transforms all the lower case letters in the label contained in the given cell and returns it.
2. @LOWER(Label or cell-address)	This is opposite of UPPER function. Transforms all the upper case letters in the label contained in the given cell and returns it.

3.	@PROPER(label or cell-address)	Transforms the first letter of the label contained in the given cell into upper case and returns it.
4.	@LENGTH(label or cell-address)	Returns the length of the label contained in the given cell in terms of the number of characters contained in the label including blanks if any.
5.	@TRIM(label or cell-address)	Removes the trailing and the leading blank spaces if any from the label contained in the given cell.
6.	@CLEAN (lavel or cell-address)	Removes any unprintable ASCII codes like Control Codes from the label contained in the given cell.
7.	@LEFT(label, n)	Returns n characters of the label counting being done from the left end of the label.
8.	@RIGHT((label, n)	Returns n characters of the label counting being done from the right end of the label.
9.	@MID(lable, m, n)	Returns n characters of the label counting being done from the mth position of the string from the left.
10.	@FIND(sub-string main-string, n)	Returns the position of the sub-string in the main-string, starting from the nth character of the main string, storting the count from 0.
11.	@REPLACE(string 1,n,x, string 2)	This deletes x characters from the string1 from the nth position and replaces the gap with the string2.
12.	@EXACT(stringl,string2)	This makes a comparison between the two strings and if they are identical, returns the logical value 1, otherwise 0.
13.	@STRING (value,number-of-decimal-places)	This converts a numeric value into a string after rounding the value to the number-of-dccimal-places specified.
14.	@VALUE(numeric-string)	Returns the numeric value of the string. If the string contains anything other than digits an ERR message is given.
15.	@N(RANGE)	Returns the numeric value of the first cell in the given range. If the first cell contians a label, this returns 0.
16.	@S(range)	Returns the label contained in the first cell in the given range. If the first cell contains a value, this returns 0.
17.	@ISSTRING(cell)	Returns the logical value 1, if the cell contains

a label, otherwise 0.

18. @ISNUMBER(cell) — Returns the logical value 1, if the cell ontains a value, otherwise 0.
19. @CODE(string) — Returns the ASCII value of the first character of the string.
20. @CHAR(value) — Returns the character whose ASCII value is given in the argument.

The DATE Function @TODAY in version 1A is replaced by @NOW in the LOTUS version 2.

1. @NOW Returns the datanumber for the current date and time as entered when DOS is booted.

The meaning of these functions will become clear when one uses them in problems.

From the next lesson onwards we will study about LOTUS Operations and Commands.

LOTUS OPERATIONS

Computer Terminal

All LOTUS operations are done through the computer keyboard. LOTUS operations mainly consist of keying two things, namely,

1. Keying the data and
2. Keying the Commands for manipulating the data.

So one must be familiar with the arrangement of the keys on the keyboard and also their functions. In a computer keyboard, we have the usual typewriter keys and in addition we have some extra keys such as ->, <- ,1, ^, PgUp, PgDn, Tab, BS, DEL, HOME, End, Esc, Ctrl, CR, NumLock, ScrollLock, F1 F2, F3, F4. F5, F6, F7, F8, F9, F10 etc., for performing certain special functions. These functions will become clear when we deal with the particular LOTUS operation. The arrangement of the different keys in a typical computer keyboard is shown in the Figure 6.

Entering the LOTUS Mode

LOTUS has been specially developed for IBM PC machines and their compatibles. PC machines usually come either with two Floppy Drives each with a capacity of 360 KB (called the simple PC) or with one drive of 360 KB capacity and one Hard Disk Drive or Winchester Drive of 20 MB capacity or slightly more (called as PC XT or PC AT depending on whether the machine is based on eXtended Technology or Advanced Technology). By referring to the manual, one can learn as to how to load the LOTUS software in the computer system. Initially, when the computer is booted, we are in the system mode and the computer displays the system prompt (A>) on the screen. To enter the LOTUS mode from the System

FI	F2	~ -	! 1	@ 2	# 3	$ 4	% 5	^ 6	& 7	* 8	(9	) 0	_ --	+ =	1 \	Esc	Num Lock	Scroll Lock	Sys Reg
F3	F4	→ ←	q	w	e	r	t	y	u	i	o	p	(	)	CR	7 Home	8 ↑	9 PgUp	prtSc *
F5	F6	Ctrl	a	s	d	f	g	h	j	k	i	: ;	″ ′			4 ←	5	6 →	-
F7	F8	Shift	z	x	c	v	b	n	m	< ,	> .	? /	Shift			1 End	2 ↓	3 PgDn	+
F9	P10	Alt	Space Bar										Caps Lock			0 Ins	Del		

Fig. 6.

Mode, type the word LOTUS and press the carriage return key (CR). You will get a one line menu called as LOTUS Access Menu. Now press the CR key again. LOTUS 1-2-3 displays a small part of the worksheet containing the first 20 rows and 8 columns on the screen as shown in the figure 2. The worksheet portion that is displayed on the screen is called the window. Since the entire worksheet is of very big size of the order of 30' by 70' or even more, the whole worksheet cannot be displayed on the screen at the same time because of the smaller size of the screen. But the entire worksheet can be scanned by moving the window using the LOTUS commands. All the columns arc of 9 characters width. This is called the default setting by LOTUS. But this width can be changed by over-riding LOTUS commands. One will find that the cell Al is highlighted by reverse video. This highlighted rectangle is called the cell pointer. The cell occupied by the cell pointer is called the current cell.

```
Al:                                                         READY
          A       B       C       D       E       F       G       H
  1
  2
  3
  4
  5
  6
  7
  8
  9
 10
 11
 12
 13
 14
 15
 16
 17
 18
 19
 20
1-Jan-1989-05:00 PM
```

Fig. 7.

Any entry or command one makes at this position affects the current cell. To make an entry or give command in any other cell, the cell pointer has to be moved to that particular cell and this is possible by using the appropriate LOTUS commands. The first three lines at the top of the worksheet constitute the control panel. The left edge of the first line contains information about the current cell address, the cell contents, column width, display format and protection status. In the opening worksheet shown in the figure 2, only the first line is seen and it contains the cell address Al at the left edge. Other details will be seen only when entries are made. At the right edge, there is a mode indicator which tells the current operating mode, whether READY, VALUE, LABEL, MENU, HELP etc. In the beginning, the mode indicator shows READY, indicating that at this time, entries can be made in the worksheet. The mode indicator will change depending on the nature of the entries. The second line will display any one of the following information:

1. the characters that one is typing
2. menu items
3. prompts or requests needed to complete a command.

The third line displays either a submenu or a one line description of the command currently highlighted in the menu. The left edge of the bottom most line contains the date and time as entered in the system in response to the DOS prompt. At the right edge of the bottom most line, there is the status indicator, which tells whether particular keys are on or off (CapsLock, ScrollLock, NumLock etc.). Error messages if any will also appear in the last line. This is the first LOTUS worksheet, or the opening worksheet. Now one must learn to scan the worksheet, make the necessary entries in the different cells and get the required output in the desired format.

Scanning or Viewing the Entire Worksheet

We said that LOTUS displays only a small portion of the worksheet on the screen because of its size limitation. To see the whole worksheet, one can move the cell pointer or the window over the worksheet using the appropriate commands as given below:

Moving the Cell Pointer One Cell at a Time

There are four arrow keys, namely the right arrow (→) the left arrow (←), the up arrow (↑) and the down arrow (↓). On pressing any arrow key, the cell pointer moves one cell in the direction of the arrow. As the cell pointer moves, notice that the address of the cell also changes as displayed at the left corner of the first line of the control panel.

Moving the Cell Pointer Directly to a Cell

Suppose the cell pointer is initially in the cell Al and one wants to go to the other three corners of the worksheet. Of course ore can do so by pressing the arrow keys several hundreds or thousands of times to reach those places. Instead one can use the function key F5. When one presses F5, prompt will appear in the control panel asking for the cell address. Suppose one keys A22 and presses CR. The cell pointer directly goes to that particular cell.

To go to another cell from this place press again F5, type the cell address, say 1V2048 and press CR. The cell pointer directly goes to the cell 1V2048. Press F5 and type A256 and press CR. The cell pointer goes to the cell A256. To come back to the first cell Al from aay position, press the HOME key. The function key F5 is called the GOTO key. In the direct interaction mode one cannot give a command GOTO A22. Later we will see that in the programming node we can write commands like (GOTO) A22.

Moving the Cell Pointer a Page at a Time

If one presses the PgUp key, the cell pointer moves up by one screenful of cells, i.e., 20 rows. If one presses the PgDn key the cell pointer moves down by one screenful of celts, i.e., ,2.0 rows. If one presses the CTRL left arrow, the cell pointer moves one screenful of columns to the left. If one presses CTRL right arrow, the cell pointer moves one screenful of columns to the right. In these cases both the CTRL key and the arrow keys must be pressed simultaneously. CTRL key is never used singly.

Moving the Window

Instead of moving the pointer, one can move the window by using the Scroll Lock key. If one presses the ScrollLock key, the status indicator at the bottom right end shows ScrollLock On. If one presses the arrow keys now, the window moves in the direction of the arrow and the cell pointer remains stationary. If one presses the ScrollLock key again, this feature is turned off.

Moving Round the Active Area Using the END Key

When one presses the END key, the status indicator shows END. Now the arrow keys function in the following manner:

1. If one presses the arrow key, when the cell pointer is in a blank cell, the cell pointer moves in the direction of the arrow to the next filled cell or the edge of the worksheet.
2. If one presses the arrow key when the cell pointer is in a filled cell, the cell pointer moves in the direction of the arrow to the last filled cell before a blank cell or to the end of the worksheet.
3. If one presses the HOME key, the cell pointer moves to the lower right corner of the active area.
4. The other keys function as usual. Entries and commands can be made by pressing the other keys.
5. By pressing the END key once again, this feature is turned off.

To Exit from LOTUS Mode & Return to System Mode

First of all bring your worksheet to the READY Mode using the Esc key freely. Now one must give the QUIT command as follows. Press the slash key (/) for invoking the command menu. Immediately you will get a menu in the control panel. The menu contains several options to the user. One selects the quit option by pressing Q. Prompt will appear in the control panel to confirm (Y/N). If one pressess N, one will revert to the LOTUS Access Menu. Now press E for EXIT & then Y for YES. Now one will be in the System Mode. It may be noted that it is also possible to enter the worksheet READY mode from the System mode directly by keying 123 and CR in succession. Such direct entrants can come out of LOTUS READY to System by keying /QY in succession. If one presses /QN, one will revert to the LOTUS READY mode.

So far we have seen how to enter the LOTUS mode, scan the big worksheet and exit from the LOTUS mode. The above mentioned operations excepting the END key operations must be practised, until one gets over what is called the stage fear.

Entering and Editing the Items in a LOTUS Cell

The LOTUS worksheet consists of a large number of cells arranged in rows and columns as we have said and seen before. Each cell has an address which is coined by combining the column letter with the row number. We have said that cell addressess can be treated as variables and used in the formulae as such. The value of a variable at any time is the value contained in the cell whose address is associated with that variable. In the beginning, when the worksheet is formed all the cells are empty and the worksheet is in the READY mode. LOTUS permits the user to enter any one of the following three entities in any cell, namely, a numeric data, a label data and a formula. Numeric data and formula can be entered only in the VALUE mode and label data can be entered only in the LABEL mode. LOTUS has provision for making corrections in a cell while keying and also to make corrections at any time after keying is over. These are called the editing features of LOTUS.

Entering Numeric Data in a Cell

Suppose you want to enter a number, say 1000 in the cell B10. When the worksheet is initially formed, the cell pointer is in the cell A1. Bring the cell pointer to the cell B10 making use of the arrow keys. See that the mode indicator shows READY. Start typing the digits. As soon as you type the first digit, the mode indicator shows VALUE, which indicates that you are entering a numeric value in that particular cell. The typed matter appears in the second line of the control panel. You will also find that a cursor, called the edit cursor moves along with the typed characters and is always positioned at the current typing position. For completing the entry you have two options. If you press the CR key, the typed number appears in the cell B10 and the cell pointer also is in the same cell. The number disappears from the second line but appears in the first line. In fact the contents of a cell always appear in the first line. The mode indicator returns to READY. The other method is to press any arrow key. Now the cell pointer moves one cell in the direction of the arrow. The typed number disappears from the second line. The mode indicator shows READY. The first line gives the contents of the current cell. The current cell is the cell in which the cell pointer is positioned at that time. Suppose you make a mistake while typing. Use the BS (back space key) key to erase any character preceding the current edit cursor position and retype the correct character. The old character disappears and the new character appears in that position. If you attempt to press the arrow keys to move the edit cursor, beep sound will come out indicating that you are using wrong keys. Suppose you type a non-numeric character. LOTUS will consider it as a syntax error and it will automatically revert to what is called the EDIT mode. The mode indicator shows EDIT. Now LOTUS allows you to edit the typed matter making use of the following keys:

1.	Left arrow	:	moves the edit cursor one character left.
2.	Right arrow	:	moves the edit cursor one character right.
3.	Tab	:	moves the edit cursor five characters right.
4.	^Right arrow	:	moves the edit cursor five characters right.
5.	^Left arrow	:	moves the edit cursor five characters left.
6.	Home	:	moves the edit cursor to the first character.
7.	End	:	moves the edit cursor to the last character.
8.	Del	:	erases the character just below the cursor.
9.	BS key	:	erases the character just below the cursor.
10.	CR key	:	Returns to the entry mode.
11.	F2 Key	:	Returns to the entry mode.

It is found that the key F2 acts as a toggle, i.e., if it is pressed when you are in the EDIT mode it returns you to the entry mode. If it is pressed when you are in the entry mode, it brings you to the EDIT mode. To complete any entry press either the CR key or any of the arrow keys. Suppose you want to cancel a partial entry which you have made in a cell and start typing afresh. Press the Esc key and you will be returned to the READY mode. Using the above information you can enter any numeric data in any cell.

Entering Label Data in a Cell

The Following Rules Govern the Entry of Label Data

1. A Label Data can start with any character other than 0,1,2,3,4,5,6,7,8,9 +, -, .) @, #, $. In case you want to start with the above symbols, you must use any one of the prefix symbols or the alignment indicating symbols as they are called.

   (single quote mark) for left alignment

   "(double quote mark) for right alignment

   ^ (caret) for center alignment

   \ (backslash) to repeat the entry across the cell.

2. In the absence of any alignment indicator symbol, LOTUS will enter any label data in the left justified position inside the cell. This is called the default setting of LOTUS.

When you type the first character of the label data, the mode indicator shows LABEL.

The methods for completing an entry and correcting or editing an entry are exactly the same as you used for numeric data. A label data can be as long as 240 characters. The cell width is only 9 characters. Suppose you have typed a label EMPLOYEE NUMBER containing 15 characters.Remember that for label data blanks also must be counted. After completing the entry you will see only the first 9 characters in the cell. Fortunately LOTUS will store the remaining characters in its memory and will display the entire label data when you increase the width of the cell by making use of column-width command which we will see later. You need not at all worry when you enter any data numeric or label longer than the width of the cell. The full dala can be made visible by doing Formatting operations.

Entering Formula in a Cell

The following rules govern the entry of formula in a cell:

1. A formula must start with any of the following characters, namely, 0,1,2,3,4,5,6,7,8,9,+,-,.,(,©,# and $. Otherwise LOTUS will take it as label data.
2. A formula must be typed without any spacing between the characters.
3. Editing rules are exactly the same as for entering data. When you start typing a formula in a cell, immediately the mode indicator shows VALUE. If you do not follow the syntax for a formula, the mode indicator shows LABEL. So by looking at the mode indicator you can find out whether you are entering the formula correctly. After completing the entry, press either the CR key or any of the arrow keys. In this case you will find that the formula does not get itself entered in the cell, but it is only the computed value of the formula that gets entered in the cell. We have already pointed out that this is what is called the computing capability of LOTUS.

Editing the Entries in a Cell

This is a very important aspect in LOTUS operations. Very often we make mistakes while entering data or formula in a cell and we must know how to correct them. Suppose you have made a wrong entry in a cell. This can be corrected in the following ways:

1. Bring the cell pointer to that particular cell making use of the four arrow keys and retype the correct entry completely and press the CR key. The old entry is erased and the now entry will get into that particular cell.
2. Bring the cell pointer to that particular cell making use of the arrows keys. Now press the F2 key which is called the Editing Function Key. The mode indicator shows EDIT. The contents of that cell is now brought to the second line or the editing line of the control panel. Now change the character or insert any character by bringing the edit cursor to that particular position, making use of the TAB, Right arrow, Left arrow, Home and End keys. After making the entry press the CR key. You will be returned to the READY mode. The corrected entry will be seen in that cell. After completing the entry if you press the F2 key you will be returned to the VALUE or LABEL mode as the case may be. The Edit Key (F2) operates as a toggle between Edit & Value Modes.

3. Suppose you want to erase completely the contents of a cell and leave it empty. There is only one way of doing this and this is by making use of the RANGE ERASE command. Bring the cell pointer to the cell whose contents are to be erased. Type /RE and press CR. You will find that the cell becomes blank.

Viewing the Cell Contents and the Cell Values

For viewing the contents of a cell, bring the cell pointer to that particular cell. You will see the cell contents on the first line of the control panel. If the contents is a formula, you will see the formula in the control panel. What you see inside the cell is the computed value of the formula or the cell value as it is called. Note clearly the distinction between the cell value and the cell contents.

Lotus Help

A very useful and an attractive feature in LOTUS is that it enables even the novice user to extricate himself from difficult situations by providing screenfuls of Help information appropriate to that situation. This Help facility can be accessed any time by simply pressing the FI key which is the Help function Key in LOTUS. The mode indicator shows HELP. LOTUS displays Help information about the operation currently in progress. Every Help Screen also includes a menu of additional Help topics. For selecting any topic, the pointer movement key is used to bring the cursor over that topic. Then the CR key is pressed. You will get Help information about the topic you have selected. If you press the BS key you can view the previous Help screen. To return to the worksheet, press the Esc key. LOTUS provides more than 200 screenfuls of HELP information and this is as good as the LOTUS manual. A typical Help Screen will look as shown in the figure 8.

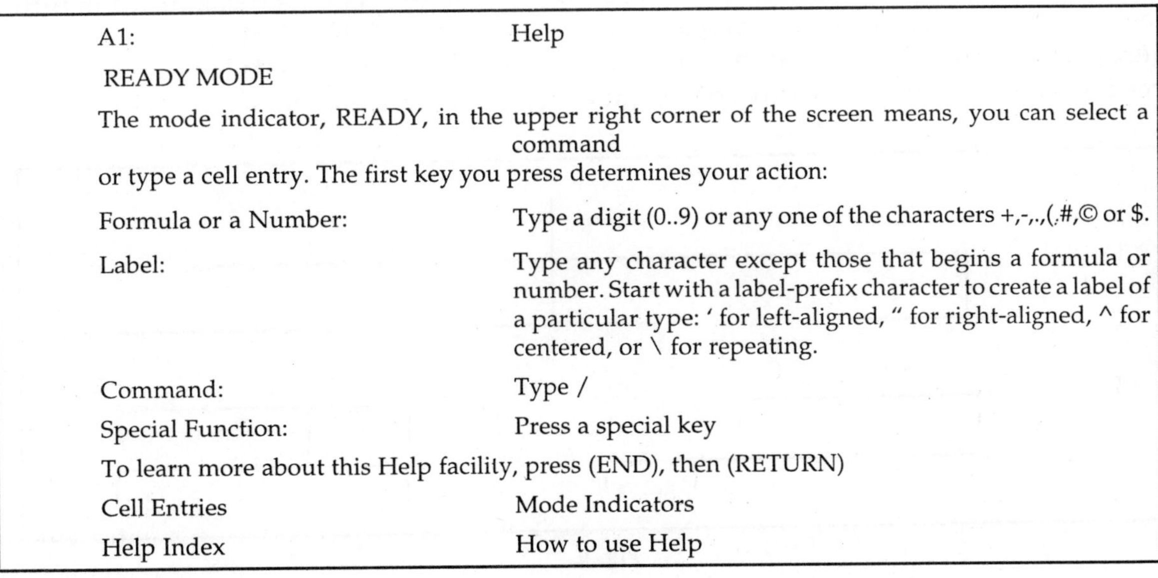

A1:	Help
READY MODE	
The mode indicator, READY, in the	upper right corner of the screen means, you can select a command
or type a cell entry. The first key you	press determines your action:
Formula or a Number:	Type a digit (0..9) or any one of the characters +,-,.,(.#,© or $.
Label:	Type any character except those that begins a formula or number. Start with a label-prefix character to create a label of a particular type: ' for left-aligned, " for right-aligned, ^ for centered, or \ for repeating.
Command:	Type /
Special Function:	Press a special key
To learn more about this Help facility,	press (END), then (RETURN)
Cell Entries	Mode Indicators
Help Index	How to use Help

Fig. 8.

The first line of the Help Screen tells at what situation, the Help has been invoked. In this case, the FI key has been pressed when the mode was READY. The last two lines give a menu of further Help topics from which, you can select any one by bringing the cursor over that topic and pressing the CR key. To return to the worksheet press the Esc key. We will see more LOTUS operations in the next lesson.

LOTUS COMMANDS (1)

What are the Things that One Must Learn about LOTUS Commands ?

This is the question which always looms large before everybody's eyes. Really LOTUS Commands are innumerable in number. Fortunately they are beautifully organised so that even a beginner can easily learn them. Of course there must be a sense of deep involvement in knowing about the beauty of LOTUS. The following are the essential things that one must learn in LOTUS:

1. Structure of the LOTUS Commands.
2. What are the available LOTUS commands, their meanings and functions.
3. How to code the different commands for
   (a) getting the desired output by direct interaction and
   (b) getting the desired output by executing LOTUS programs.

Structure of LOTUS Commands

LOTUS is a Command Language. LOTUS Commands have a generic structure. That is, every command may give rise to one or more sub-commands. Each sub-command in turn may give rise to further sub-commands. A command path will be terminated after doing some particular setting in the worksheet. We say that LOTUS commands have an inverted Tree Structure or a level structure somewhat as shown in the figure 9.

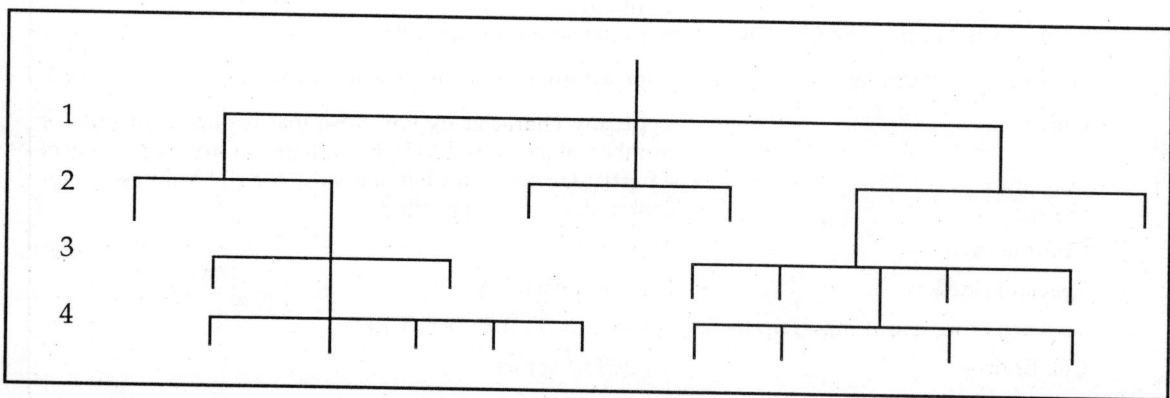

Fig. 9.

Basic Commands in LOTUS

There are 10 Basic Commands in LOTUS, also called the Basic Command Menu. They are as follows:

1. Worksheet Commands
2. Range Commands
3. Copy Commands
4. Move Commands
5. File Commands
6. Print Commands
7. Graph Commands
8. Data Commands
9. System Commands
10. Quit Commands

Invoking the Basic LOTUS Command Menu

Bring the worksheet to the READY mode. Press the slash (/) key. The screen displays the Basic Command Menu and it appears as shown in the figure 10. The mode indicator now shows MENU. The second line of the control panel gives the listing of the 10 Basic Commands. The first item of the Command Menu, namely, Worksheet is highlighted. This highlight is called the menu pointer. This menu pointer can be moved over other items in the menu by using the Left and the Right Arrow Keys. The 3rd line gives the sub-options for the Basic Menu Item which is highlighted at that time. In the beginning the item worksheet is highlighted. So the 3rd line gives the sub-options for the Worksheet Command.

Al:										MENU
Worksheet	Range	Copy	Move	File	Print	Graph	Data	System	Quit	
Global	Insert.	Delete.	Column		Erase	Titles.	Window		Status	Page
	A	B	C		D.	E	F		G	H
1										
2										
20										

Fig. 10.

Menu Levels

The opening menu which we got on pressing the slash key is called the first level menu. Some of the items in the main menu have further sub-menu levels, second, third and so on. For getting the second level menu for any item in the basic menu there are two ways:

1. Bring the menu pointer over that item using the appropriate arrow keys and press the CR key.
2. Simply key the first character of the Command Item whose next level menu is required.

At any stage, the main menu items appear in the second line and the sub-menu items corresponding to the highlighted main menu item appear in the third line of the control panel. When there are no more sub-menu levels, the user makes the final choice either by keying the first character of the final choice item or by entering the appropriate values for the LOTUS prompt as the case may be. In general LOTUS requires the final choice to be completed by pressing the CR key. Once the final choice is made along a menu path, the worksheet returns to the READY mode directly from any menu level. When you are traversing a the command menu path, you may sometimes require to go to the previous menu level. In that case press the Esc key. By repeatedly pressing the Esc key you can come back to the READY mode. If you want to come to the READY mode directly from any menu level, press the CTRL and the ScrollLock keys together. If you have completed the menu options along some menu path and if you want to cancel that particular sequence of commands, you have to start over again resetting the old sequence of commands. If you have not completed a menu path, corrections can be made at any level. Thus you see, that one can safely cruise through the different menu levels and make the appropriate choices.

Worksheet Command Tree

We have seen that there are 10 basic commands and each command has its own Tree Structure. The figure 11 shows the Tree Structure of the Worksheet command. Just below each command, the keystrokes required to invoke the next level command menu are also given. Later on we will see how these keystrokes sequence can be converted into instructions, when we write LOTUS programs. From the figure 11, you will find that some commands have further branches and some terminate without any branches. In general the last key which terminates a menu path will be the CR key.

Worksheet Command Functions

The worksheet commands are generally used to perform certain functions, which are global in nature, i.e., which affect all the cells in the worksheet. In addition to global functions, they do certain jobs in specified ranges also. Again global specifications can be overridden if necessary in specified cells by using the Range commands. Thus we are not completely pinned down by giving global commands.

Invoking the Worksheet Menu Options

When you press / W, you get the worksheet sub-menu containing the 9 items, Global, Insert, Delete, Column, Erase, Titles, Window, Status and further sub-menus. To get the submenu for the first item Global, press/WG. You get the submenu containing the 7 items Format, Label-prefix, Column-width, Recalculation, Protection, Default and Zero as shown

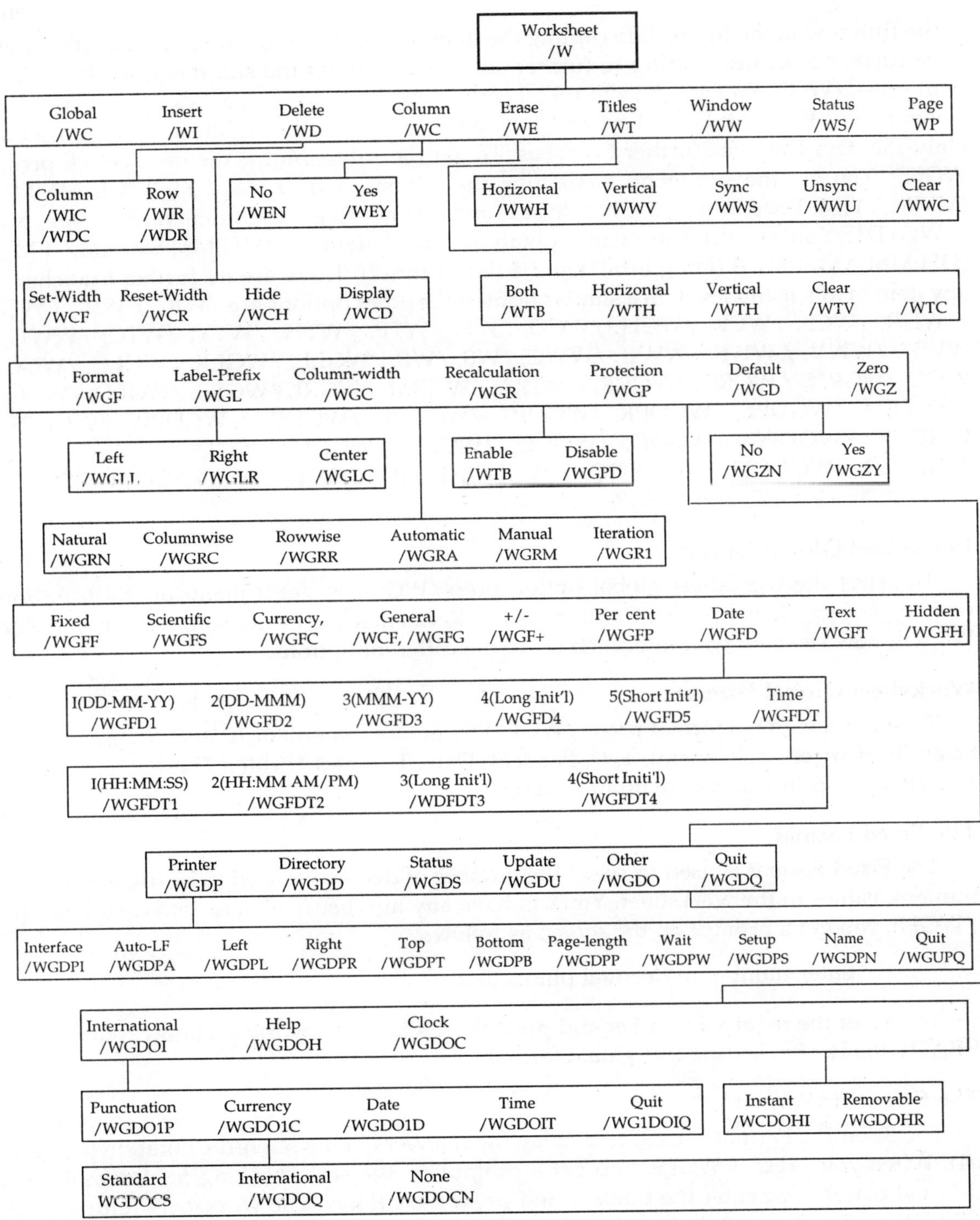

Worksheet /W
Global /WC
Insert /WI
Delete /WD
Column /WC
Erase /WE
Titles /WT
Window /WW
Status /WS/
Page WP
Column /WIC /WDC
Row /WIR /WDR
No /WEN
Yes /WEY
Horizontal /WWH
Vertical /WWV
Sync /WWS
Unsync /WWU
Clear /WWC
Set-Width /WCF
Reset-Width /WCR
Hide /WCH
Display /WCD
Both /WTB
Horizontal /WTH
Vertical /WTH
Clear /WTV
/WTC
Format /WGF
Label-Prefix /WGL
Column-width /WGC
Recalculation /WGR
Protection /WGP
Default /WGD
Zero /WGZ
Left /WGLL
Right /WGLR
Center /WGLC
Enable /WTB
Disable /WGPD
No /WGZN
Yes /WGZY
Natural /WGRN
Columnwise /WGRC
Rowwise /WGRR
Automatic /WGRA
Manual /WGRM
Iteration /WGR1
Fixed /WGFF
Scientific /WGFS
Currency, /WGFC
General /WCF, /WGFG
+/- /WGF+
Per cent /WGFP
Date /WGFD
Text /WGFT
Hidden /WGFH
I(DD-MM-YY) /WGFD1
2(DD-MMM) /WGFD2
3(MMM-YY) /WGFD3
4(Long Init'l) /WGFD4
5(Short Init'l) /WGFD5
Time /WGFDT
I(HH:MM:SS) /WGFDT1
2(HH:MM AM/PM) /WGFDT2
3(Long Init'l) /WDFDT3
4(Short Initi'l) /WGFDT4
Printer /WGDP
Directory /WGDD
Status /WGDS
Update /WGDU
Other /WGDO
Quit /WGDQ
Interface /WGDPI
Auto-LF /WGDPA
Left /WGDPL
Right /WGDPR
Top /WGDPT
Bottom /WGDPB
Page-length /WGDPP
Wait /WGDPW
Setup /WGDPS
Name /WGDPN
Quit /WGUPQ
International /WGDOI
Help /WGDOH
Clock /WGDOC
Punctuation /WGDO1P
Currency /WGDO1C
Date /WGDO1D
Time /WGDOIT
Quit /WG1DOIQ
Instant /WCDOHI
Removable /WGDOHR
Standard WGDOCS
International /WGDOQ
None /WGDOCN

Fig. 11.

in the fifth row in the figure 3. Excepting the items Column-width and Zero, the other items have further branches leading to further submenus. To get the sub-menu for the Format item press /WGF. You get the sub-menu containing 10 items, Fixed, Scientific, Currency,,, General, +/-, Per cent, Dale, Text and Hidden as shown in the eighth row in the figure 3. Only the item Date has further branches. To get the submenu for the item DATE press / WGFD. You get the sub-menu containing the 6 items, 1 (DD-MM-YY), 2 (DD-MMM), 3 (MMM-YY), 4(Long lntn'1), 5 (Short lntn'1) and 6 Time. To got the submenu for Time, press / WGFDT. You get the sub-menu containing the 4 items, 1 (HH:MM:SS: AM/ PM), 2 (HH:MM AM/PM), 3 (Long lntn'1) and 4 (Short Intn'l). There are no further branches for any item in this menu level. In a similar fashion the other options are /WIC, / WIR, / WDC, / WDR, /WCS, /WCR, /WCH, /WCD, /WE, /WTB, /WTH, /WTV, /WTC, /WWH, / WWH, /WWV, / WWS, /WWU, /WWC, /WS, /WP, /WGLL, /WGLR, /WGLC, /WGC, / WGC, /WGRN, / WGRC, /WGRR, /WGRA, /WGRM, /WGRI, /WGPE, /WGPD, /WCDPI, /WGDPA, /WGDPL, /WGDPR, /WGDPT, /WGDPB, /WGDPP, /WCDPW, /WGDPS, / WGDPN, /WGDPQ, /WGDD, /WGDD, /WGDS, /WGDU, /WGDOIP, /WGDOIC, / WGDOID, /WGDOIT, /WGDOIQ, / WGDOHI, /WGDOHR, /WGDOCS, /WGDOCI, / WGDOCN, /WGDQ and /WGZ.

Worksheet Global Option

To select the worksheet global option press/WG. You get a menu of seven options, namely, Format, Label-prefix, Column-width, Recalculation, Protection, Default and Zero. We will now see how we can branch off to the different options.

Worksheet Global Format

To select the global format press /WGF. You get a submenu of 10 items, namely, Fixed, Scientific, Currency,,, General, + /-, Per cent, Date, Text and Hidden.These items are used to format the cells containing numeric data.

The Fixed Format

The Fixed Format is used to select the number of decimal placed to be displayed in the numeric values in the worksheet. You can have any number from 0 to 15. When you press /WGFF, you get a prompt on the screen as follows:

Enter number of decimal places (0..15)

You enter the required number and press the CR key. The worksheet now returns to the READY mode after setting this global format.

The Scientific Format

The Scientific Format is used to display the numbers in the scientific notation (e.g. 2.3E-04). When you press / WGFS, you get a prompt on the screen asking for the number of decimal places. You enter the number and press the CR key. The worksheet returns to the READY mode after setting the scientific format.

The Currency Format

The Currency Format is used to insert the dollar sign($) before the numeric value. When you press / WGFC, you get a prompt on the screen asking for the number of decimal places. You enter the number and press the CR key. The worksheet returns to the READY mode after setting the currency format.

The Comma (,) Format

The Comma Format is used to insert commas between thousands in the integer part of the number. When you press /WGF, the comma format is set and the worksheet returns to the READY mode.

The General Format

The General Format is used to set up the default settings in LOTUS. In the default setting all numbers are rounded off to two decimal places on display. When you press /WGFG and the CR key, the General Format is set and the worksheet returns to the READY mode.

The+/-Format

The +/- format is used to denote all values into corresponding + or - symbols. A value 5 in the + format is denoted by +++++ and a value 5 in the - format is denoted by ——. When you type /WGF+ or /WGF-, the horizontal bar graph format is set.

The Per Cent Format

The Per cent Format is used to display all values as percentages by multiplying the value by 100 and adding a trailing % sign. For example, a value 0.1 will be displayed as 10%. Give the command /WGFP for setting this format.

The Date Format is used to denote the date in the desired form. When you press / WGFD, you get a submenu containing 5 options.

If you select the option 1, the date will be in the form 06-OCT-87.

If you select the option 2, the date will be in the form 06-OCT.

If you select the option 3, the date will be in the form OCT-87.

If you select the option 4, the date will be in the form 10/6/87.

If you select the option 5, the date will be in the form 10/87.

If you select the option T, you get a submenu containing 4 items for setting the format for time.

The above six formats are invoked by pressing /WGFDl,

/WGFD2, /WGFD3, /WGFD4, /WGFD5, /WGFDT respectively.

If you enter /WGFDT1, the time will be denoted in the form 08:56:50 AM

If you enter /WGFDT2, the time will be denoted in the form 08:56 AM

If you enter /WGFDT3, the time will be denoted in the form 20:56:50

If you enter /WGFDT4, the time will be denoted in the form 20:56

The Text Format

The Text Format is used to display formulae entered in the cells instead of their computed values. If you press /WGFT, the text format is set.

The Hidden Format

The Hidden format is used to hide the values in the cells. The cell contents will be seen in the control panel, but the cell itself will appear blank. If you press / WGFH, the Hidden Format is set.

The Global Label-prefix

The Label-prefix format is used to set the alignment of labels. If you press / WGL, you get a submenu with three items, Left, Right & Center. If you press / WGLL, the labels will be left-aligned, if you press /WGLR, the labels will be right-aligned and if you press / WGLC, the labels will be centered.

The Global Column-width

The Global Column-width command sets the column width of all the cells in the worksheet to any desired length. The default length is 9 characters. When you press /WGC, the screen prompt appears as

Enter Column Width (1 ..240)

You enter the desired value and press the CR key. Any column widths that were individually set with the worksheet Column set-width Command are not affected by Global Column-width command. For changing the widths of such columns one has to use the Reset option of that command.

The Global Recalculation

The Recalculation Command is used to control when, in what order and how many times a particular formula or a set of formulae must be recalculated. When you press the keys /WGR, you get a submenu containing six options for recalculation, namely, Natural, Columnwise, Rowwise, Automatic, Manual and Iteration. Let us consider these options one by one.

The Recalculation Natural

Suppose you have a formula in the cell C8, which involves the data or the formula in the cell B7, LOTUS calculates the formula in B7 before it calculates the formula in the cell C8. This also the default order for recalculation. The command keys /WGRN will do this setting.

The Recalculation Columnwise

When you give the command /WGRC, LOTUS does all recalculations columnwise starting from the leftmost column.

The Recalculation Rowwise

When you give the command /WGRR, LOTUS will do all recalculations rowwise starting from the topmost row.

The Recalculation Automatic

When you give the command /WGRA, LOTUS will do all the recalculations automatically each time you change the contents of the data cells. Automatic is also the default setting.

The Recalculation Manual

When you give the command /WGRM, LOTUS will recalculate all the formulae only if you press the CALC key. F9 is the CALC function key. When recalculation is manual, the CALC indicator appears in the lower right corner of the screen, whenever any cell entries have changed since last recalculation.

The Recalculation Iteration

The Iteration Command is used to repeat the calculations a specified number of times from 2 to 50. When you give the command /WGRI, the screen prompt appears asking for the number of iterations. You give any number from 1 to 50. Of course the number *1* is the default setting. The Iteration command will be obeyed only if circular references have been made. We will consider the concept of circular references later.

The Global Protection

The Protection Command is used to protect the entries in the cells being changed unauthorisedly or by some mistake. When you give a command / WGP, the screen prompt will appear asking for Enable or Disable. If you give the command /WGPE, the entries in the cells will be protected and you cannot change them by any Range Erase command. The only way you can unprotect the cell is to give the command / WGPD. The Worksheet Erase Command will erase also the protected cells.

The Global Default

When LOTUS is initially loaded, it comes with certain default settings as regards the printer, directory, certain display formats, clock display on the screen and the method of using HELP. This default can be permanently changed by the Global Default Command. The Global Default Command enables the user to set his own default settings regarding the above items, using the Global Default Update Command regarding the above items. Using the Global Default Update Command the new settings can be made the initial default setting whenever LOTUS is loaded. When you give the command /WGD, you get a submenu containing 5 items, namely, Printer, Directory, Status, Update, Other and Quit.

The Global Default Printer Option

When you press the keys /WGDP, you get a submenu containing 11 items, namely, Interface, Auto-LF, Left, Right, Top, Bottom, Pg-Lenglh; Wait, Setup and Name.

The Default Printer Interface

Printers are connected to the computers through special circuits called interfaces. There are again four choices for Interfaces, namely, Parallel, Serial, Second Parallel and Second Serial. The original default setting is Parallel. Now you can change the default to any of the four using the commands /WGDP11 or /WGDP12 or /WGDP14.

The Default Printer Auto-LF

Printer do not normally give a line feed after a carriage return. In the initial default setting, Auto-LF is No. When you give the command /WGDPA, the screen prompts asks for Yes or No. Type /WGDPAY or /WGDPAN as the case may be to set your own default.

The Default Printer Left

The initial default value for the left margin is 4 characters. The Default Printer Left option allows you to give other values for the left margin. When you give the command / WGDPL, the screen prompt asks for the left margin in terms of the number of characters. You type the required value in the range 1 to 240 and press the CR key. Your default value is now set up.

The Default Printer Right

The initial default value of the right margin is 76. This initial default value can be changed using the command /WGDPR. When you key this command, screen prompt appears asking for the value. Enter any value greater than the left margin you have specified earlier, but less than 240 and press the CR key. Your default value is now set up.

The Default Printer Top

The initial default value for the top margin is 2 lines. This initial value can be changed using the command / WGDPT. When you key this command, screen prompt appears asking for the new value. You can enter any value between 1 and 10 and press the CR key. Your default value is now set up.

The Default Printer Page-Length

The initial default value for the page length is 66 lines. This initial value can be changed/ WGDPP. When you key this command, screen prompt appears asking for the new page length. Enter any value between 20 and 100 and press the CR key. Your default value is now set up.

The Default Printer Wait

The printer does not normally pause or wait for further instructions after printing one page. The default option for Wait is No. When you use single sheets for printing you would like the printer to wait at the end of each page to enable you to insert the next sheet. You can set this default by giving the command /WGDPWY. The default is / WGDPWN.

The Default Printer Setup

Some printers need to be initialised before the printing is started. The initialisation consists of some control characters. Initial default setting is blank, i.e., no initialisation. If your printer requires initialisation codes, you can give them by using the command / WGDPS. The printer manual must be referred for any such codes.

The Default Printer Name

The default value for the printer name is the name of the printer selected when installing LOTUS. When you give the command / WGDPN, you will get a submenu containing the names of printers. You select the name you require and press the CR key. Your default printer name is now set up.

The Default Printer Quit

When you key the command /WGDPQ, you are returned to the default menu.

The Global Default Directory Option

When you type the command /WGDD, you will get the name of the current directory or the current disk prefix (A or B or C) in which LOTUS will write new files when you save them. This is the default value. You can also specify another name or another disk prefix as the case may be as new directory using the above command.

The Global Default Option

When your type gives the command /WGDS, the screen displays the current printer and directory default values. The settings are only displayed and you cannot change any of them here.

The Global Default Update Option

When you dive the command /WGDU, the new default settings given by you will be saved and used by LOTUS in all subsequent loadings. If you don't use this option, LOTUS will use your default only for your current work and will revert to its initial default for subsequent loadings.

The Global Default Other Option

When you enter the command/WGDO, you get a submenu containing 3 items, namely, International, Help and Clock.

The Default Other International

When you key the command /WGDO, you get a submenu containing 5 items, namely, Punctuation, Currency, Date, Time and Quit. When you key the command /WGDOIP, you get options for selecting the punctuations to be used for points and thousands separators in numbers, argument separators in @ Functions and separators for keywords in macros. You can select your option and press the CR key. The default values arc (.) and (,). When you key the command / WGDOIC, you get options for using any currency sign instead of the default symbol ($). You can select your option and press the CR key. When you give the command / WGDO1D, you get options for setting the Date format. When you key the command / WGDOIT, you get options for setting the Time format. When you key the command / WCDOIQ, you are returned to the Other menu.

The Default Other Help

When you key the command /WGDOH,you get two options, namely, Instant and Removable as regards the Help File. If you give the command WGDOHI, the Help file remains open throughout the session. If you give the command /WGDOHR, the Help file can be removed when not in use. This is possible if the Help file is in a removable Floppy Disk.

The Global Default Other Clock Option

When you give the command /WGDOIC, you get a submenu containing 3 items, namely, Standard, International and None. If you give the command / WGDOCS, the date will be displayed in the long format (DD-MM-YY) and Time will be displayed in the short format (HH:MM AM/ PM). This is the initial setting. If you give the command / WGDOCI, the date is displayed in the long international format (MM/DD/YY) and time in the short international format (HH:MM) using 24 hours day. If you give the command /WGDOCN, the date and time will not be displayed on the screen.

The Global Zero Option

When you give the command /WGZ, you get two options Yes or No. If you enter / WGZY, all zero values will be suppressed in printing. If you enter /WGZN, all zero values will be suppressed in printing and the zero value cells will appear blank. With this wo have completed all the worksheet global commands.

The Worksheet Insert Command

The worksheet insert command is used to insert one or more blank rows or blank columns. Suppose you want to insert a blank row in the third line, bring the cell point to any cell in row 3 say A3. Give the command / WIR and press CR key. The row 3 will become blank. The entries that were originally in row 3 will be shifted to row 4, the items in row 4 will be shifted to row 5 and so on. Suppose you want to insert three blank rows, say 3,4 & 5. Give the command /WIR A3..A5 and press the CR key. The rows 3,4 & 5 will become blank. The items in row 3 will be shifted to row 6, the items in row 4 will be shifted to row 7 and so on. Suppose you want to insert a blank column, say at column B. Bring the cell pointer to the cell BI. Give the command / W1C and press the CR key. The column B will become blank. The items in Column B will be shifted to column C, the items in column C will be shifted to column D and so on. Suppose you want to insert 3 columns blank, say B, C and D. Give the command /WICB1..D1 and press the CR key. The columns B,C & D will become blank. The items in the column B will be shifted to column E, the items in column C will be shifted to column F and so on.

The Worksheet Delete Command

The worksheet delete command is used to delete one or more rows or columns. Suppose you want to delete the row 2. Bring the cell pointer to any cell in row 2. Give the command / WDR and press the CR key. The entries in the row 2, the entries in row 4 will come to row 3 and so on. For deleting more than one row, give the command /WDRB2..C4 and press the CR key. The rows 2,3 and 4 will disappear. The entries in row 5 will now come to row 2, the entries in row 6 will come to row 3 and so on. To delete a column say B, bring the cell pointer to any cell in the column B and give the command /WDC and press the CR key. The column B will vanish. The entries in column C will come to column B, the entries in column D will come to column C and so on. For deleting say the columns B, C & D, give the command / WDCB1..D1 and press the CR key. The entries in the columns B, C & D will disappear. The entries in column E will come to column B, the entries in column F will come to column C and so on.

The Worksheet Column-width Command

The worksheet column-width command is used to change the width of the current column (the column in which the cell pointer is currently located). When you give the command / WC, you get a submenu containing the items, Set-width, Reset-width, Hide and Display. If you select the first item and give the command / WCS, the screen prompt asks for new column width. You enter any value between 1 and 240 and then press the CR key. The new column width is set overriding any other global settings done earlier. If you give the command / WCR, the column width returns to the default value of 9 characters overriding any other global setting done earlier. To hide the data in the current column without permanently destroying them, the command /WCH is used. To redisplay a hidden column, the command / WCD is given. Ranges can also be specified in the Hide and Display commands.

The Worksheet Erase Command

The Worksheet Erase command is used to erase the contents of the entire worksheet. When you give the command /WE, the screen prompt appears asking for Yes or No. If you give the command /WEY, the worksheet contents are erased and if you give the command /WEN, the worksheet contents are retained as they are.

The Worksheet Titles Command

The Worksheet Titles Command is used to freeze one or more rows or columns and make them appear on the screen, when you are scrolling through the entire worksheet. Usually the border rows and columns will contain some headers, which you want to be displayed even when you scroll through long rows and columns. Bring the cell pointer one row below the rows you want to freeze or one column to the right of the columns you want to freeze or blow and to the right of the rows and columns you want to freeze. When you give the command/WT, you get four options on the screen, namely, Both, Horizontal, Vertical and Clear. If you give the command/WTB, the rows above the current row and columns to the left of the current column are frozen. This means that the frozen columns and rows will always appear on the screen, wherever you are in the worksheet. If you give the command / WTH, the rows above the current row are frozen. If you give the command /WTV, the columns to the left of the current column are frozen. The command / WTC unfreezes all the existing titles or the existing frozen rows and columns.

The Worksheet Window Command

The Worksheet Window Command is used to split the screen display into two windows, so that two different parts of the worksheet can be observed together. The windows are independent, in that the cell pointer can be switched from one to the other and moved independently to display any cell in the respective windows. When you give the command /WW, the screen prompt gives five options, namely, Horizontal, Vertical, Sync, Unsync and Clear. When you select the first option and give the command /WWH, the screen splits into two horizontal windows with the top window containing all the rows above the current row. When you give the command /WWV, the screen splits into two vertical windows with the left window containing all the columns to the left of the current window. When you give the command /WWS, the two windows become synchronised. This means that for horizontal windows, if one window scrolls horizontally, the other also scrolls horizontally, keeping the same columns on the screen. For vertical windows, if one window scrolls horizontally, the other window also scrolls vertically, keeping the same rows on the screen in both the windows. If you select Unsync option by giving the command /WWU, the two windows can be scrolled independently. In order to clear either kind of windows and return to a single worksheet display, the Clear option is exercised by giving the command /WWC.

The Worksheet Status Command

The Worksheet Status Command is used to display the status of the settings for the worksheet global commands for Recalculation, Format, Label-prefix, Column-width Zero suppression and Protection. This also gives the amount of main memory available for the current worksheet. This command is invoked by typing /WS. The screen displays the different status information. You cannot make any changes row. Pressing the CR key will return you to the READY mode.

The Worksheet Page Command

The worksheet page command is used to insert a page break at the end of any row. To invoke this command, bring the cell pointer to the row below which you want the page to end. Type the command /WP. The rows below the cell pointer moves down to the next page.

End of Worksheet Commands

Out of the ten basic command trees, the worksheet command tree is the biggest in LOTUS and there are about 100 commands. Though we may not be using all the commands, it is worthwhile to know what is available, in the worksheet menu. We will discuss the other command trees in the forthcoming lessons.

14

The WordStar Environment

WordStar is a Very Powerful Word processing program. There are many features available to you as work, features that save you time and help produce the highest documents. Many people learn only few of the basic WordStar commands; they are able to generate the documents they need, but have to work harder than necessary to accomplish certain tasks.

This chapter focuses on the part of WordStar that you must deal with every time you work with the program: the WordStar working environment. Assuming that you have a basic knowledge of this environment, and that you have worked with the program before, we will share with you ways to save time and avoid problems as you work.

The chapter begins with ways of entering the WordStar program, and opening a document file quickly. We explain the basic menu structure of WordStar, and discuss working with these menus and the various commands that are available from each menu. WordStar has some useful help features, and we offer suggestions for using them effectively.

You can make changes in the various default settings that are in effect when you enter WordStar by using the installation program provided by MicroPro. You can also redefine the function keys on your computer, allowing you to enter your choice of commands with one keystroke. This chapter discuss each of these ways of modifying the WordStar program so you can change the working environment to suit your own needs.

Macro processors, such as ProKey, are programs you can use with WordStar to save time entering text and commands. They allow you to enter whole passages of text or entire sequences of WordStar commands with one keystroke. The chapter ends with tips for working with these useful auxiliary programs.

ENTERING WORDSTAR AND OPENING DOCUMENT FILES

To begin working with WordStar, you must get the program running on your computer. The tips and traps in this section explain a variety of ways to access WordStar from the operating system, including some tricks for getting into a document file quickly.

WordStar requires you to specify a logged disk drive where the files you will be working with can be found and where you want new files to be saved. Unless you include a drive designator with the file name, as in A:letter, WordStar assumes that any file you name is located on the currently logged drive. This section includes tips and traps concerning the logged drive, as well as some important considerations in handling your files.

Tip

If you press the space bar at the WordStar title screen, you will get to the opening menu more quickly.

When you enter the WordStar program with the command WS at the operating system prompt, you have to wait while a title screen is displayed. After a few seconds, the screen display changes to the opening menu. If you press the space bar as soon as the operating system prompt disappears from the screen, you can eliminate the pause at the title screen.

Tip

You can change the logged drive without waiting for the opening menu to be displayed.

As soon as you enter the command WS, your computer begins to access the WordStar program. You don't have to wait for the opening menu to be displayed before you begin entering commands; you can follow the WS command with any WordStar command that operates from the opening menu.

If you press L, then R and then the return key, you will change the logged disk drive to the B drive. The screen display will change quickly, and you will see the opening menu with the disk directory for the B drive.

You can put this together with the preceding tip to enter WordStar and change the logged drive quickly. Enter the command WS at the system prompt, press the space bar, and then type the commands to change the logged disk drive.

Tip

You can enter WordStar and open a document file with one command.

Let's say you are working with a double-floppy system, and the operating system is booted. On an IMB computer, you will see the DOS prompt.

A>

If the WordStar working disk is in drive A, and a document file (named report in this example) is on the disk in drive B, one way to edit this file is to enter WordStar, wait for the opening menu, select option D to open a document file, and enter report when you are asked for the file name. You can accomplish all this much faster, however, if you enter the command

ws b: report

at the DOS prompt. You will still have to wait while the title screen is displayed, but when you enter WordStar, the file report will be open and ready for editing.

Trap

If you go into a document file from the operating system, the logged disk drive will not be changed.

The preceding tip explains how you can enter a document file directly from the operating system. This can be a timesaver, but it must be used carefully. When you open a document file this way, the logged disk drive is not changed. For example, the command we discussed earlier,

ws b: report

was entered at the A> system prompt. The system was logged onto drive A, and that will remain the logged drive unless you tell WordStar to change it.

You can change the logged disk drive while you are editing a file with the command ^KL, or you can wait until you finish working with your file and change the logged drive at the opening menu. Until you make this change, WordStar will continue using drive A as the logged disk drive.

See the following tip for a quick way to change the logged drive before you enter WordStar.

Tip

You can change the logged disk drive with one command before you enter WordStar.

When you enter the WordStar program, the logged disk drive is established by the drive that was being used by your operating system. When you boot DOS (the IMB operating system) on a double-floppy system, the A rive is logged, and you see the prompt.

A>

you can change this to the B drive by entering b: at this prompt and you will see

B"

to reflect the change. Even if your WordStar working task is in drive A.

you can enter WordStar from the logged B drive by entering the command

a:ws

at the B> prompt.

Once you have the B> prompt on the screen, you can also go directly to the document file report, with the logged drive changed to the B drive by entering the command.

a: ws report

Notice that you don't need to specify b: before report because B is the logged drive.

Rap

You cannot enter a nondocument file directly from the operating system.

Several of the preceding tips explain how to enter WordStar and open a file directly from the operating system. If you do so, the file will be opened in document mode, as if you had entered the D command at the opening menu.

If you need to work with a nondocument file, you cannot open the file from the operating system. You must enter WordStar without opening a file, and select the N command at the opening menu.

Trap

If you change the disk that contains a document file when the file is open, you risk losing data.

When you are working with a document, only part of the file is in the computer's memory at any time. WordStar moves portions of the file between memory and disk storage, using temporary files on the disk, until you are not limited by the size of your computer's memory, but it means that the disk that contains a document file must remain in the logged drive whenever the file is open.

If you change the disk in the logged drive while you are working with a file, you may be removing the temporary files that WordStar needs to save your document in its complete form. When you write text from one file into another as explained in the section on working with blocks), both files must be available to WordStar without changing the disk that contains the document you are currently editing. If you get a DISK FULL error message, changing disks will not help.

Never change the disk that contains your document file until you close the file and the opening is on the screen.

Tip

If you change the disk in the logged drive, you can get a directory of the new disk by logging the same drive again.

The preceding trap explains why you should never change the disk in the logged drive until you close your files. Once you have done that, and WordStar is displaying the opening menu, you can safely change your data disk.

However, WordStar does not automatically access the new disk, so the file directory on the screen will still show the files on the old disk. To get the new directors just log the same disk drive again, by entering L and the name of that drive at the opening menu.

Trap

When you enter text onto the screen display, it is not automatically saved in a disk file.

WordStar never saves the current version of a file to your disk unless you enter a command to do so. This is a very helpful feature, since it gives you the option not to save the results of an editing session. If you accidentally delete part of a file, or make changes and decide you don't like them, you can abandon the current version of your file by entering ^KQ. WordStar will ask you if you want to abandon your work, and if you respond Y, the current version will not be saved.

In order to give you this flexibility, WordStar never saves your work until you enter a save command. When you finish working with a file, the command ^KD saves the file and returns you to the opening menu. You can also use ^KX which saves the file and exits WordStar at the same time.

Because of the vulnerability of open files, it is a very wise policy to save your work frequently. See the following tip.

Tip

Protect your datal: Use the save and resume command (^KS) often while you are working with your files.

Any time a file is open, it is vulnerable to a power failure, to malfunctioning equipment, or to human error. Protect your data and the time you have invested in the file by saving your file frequently as you work.

The save and resume command, ^KS, saves the current version of your file to disk without closing the file. You should develop the habit of using this command, to keep the disk version of your file as up-to-date as possible while you are working.

Backup copies of your data disks are also an important part of protecting your files.

THE WORDSTAR MENUS

When you enter WordStar, you are presented with the opening menu. This menu is displayed whenever you do not have a data file open, and it lists the commands that WordStar can execute in this no-file mode. Once you open a document file with the D command you will see the main menu. You can access several other menus from the main menu; each lists a related group of the commands that are available to you while you are working with a file.

The tips and traps in this section explain the structure of these nested menus, and offer some tricks for working with them efficiently.

Tip

If you enter a control command at the opening menu, you will not get the results you expect.

WordStar has two basic modes of operation: the no-file mode and the open-file mode. The commands that can be executed depend on which mode you are currently operating in.

The opening menu shown, displayed whenever WordStar is running and a file is not open. The only commands that can be executed in the no-file mode are the ones listed on this menu, commands that manipulate or print files, run other programs, and so on. There are all one-letter commands, in this mode, you must hold down the control key for all commands.

Once you open a file, WordStar changes its mode of operation and you can use the control commands, as listed for you in the various WordStar menus. There are no one-letter commands in this mode; you must hold down the control key for all commands.

If you try to enter a control command at the opening menu, it will not have the same result as entering that command when a file is open. If the command letter is the same as one of the one-letter commands on the opening menu, WordStar ignores the control key and executes that command. For instance, if you are in no-file mode and you enter ^O, which displays the onscreen menu when a file is open, WordStar executes the O command, which copies a file. If you enter a control command with a letter that is not listed in the opening menu. WordStar just ignores the command . you must open a before you can use the control commands.

Tip

You can short any of the one-letter commands by pressing the Esc key before you type anything else.

The one-letter commands are available to you at the opening menu. Let's say you enter O, the command to copy a file. What you will see on the screen, a request for the name of the file to copy from, and a list of control codes for responding to this prompt. According to this list, you need to enter ^U to cancel the command; if you do this, you will get the message

INTERRUPTED*Press ESCAPE Key

and you will have to press the Esc key to resume working with WordStar.

If you realise you don't want to execute this command, you can get the same result much more quickly by skipping the first step. Just pressing the Esc key before you respond to the command question will abort any of the one-letter commands. If you begin to answer the question, and then decide to cancel the command, you must use the ^U command

Tip

When WordStar asks you for the name of a file to print or to edit, you can repeat you last response to the same question by pressing ^R.

If you enter the command P, to print a file, or D, to open a document file, WordStar will ask you for the name of the file to be printed or edited. You can repeat the last response you gave to that question by simply pressing ^R.

Suppose you have finished editing a document file named report. you save the file with ^KD, and enter P at the opening menu to print out this file. As you read through the printed document, you decide to make a few more changes in the text, so you enter the command D to open the report file once again.

When WordStar asks you for the name of the file, you do not have to type out the word report again. Just press ^R, and the file name will appear on the screen; press the return key to enter this file name. Once you make the changes in the text, you can use the same ^R response to save time when you print the file.

If you use ^R the first time you print a document after entering WordStar, you will get the name of the first file you edited in this work session. Otherwise, pressing ^R enters the last response you gave to that particular prompt, of you print one file and then edit another, ^R will name the file that was printed if you use it after the P command, or the last file that was edited if you use it after the D command. Always double-check the file name that appears on the screen before you press the return key to use that file.

Tip

Access the correct editing menu if you need to find a particular WordStar command.

Once you open a document file, WordStar will display the main menu, unless you are working at help level 2 or lower. This menu lists the most basic commands for entering and editing text, commands to move the cursor, scroll the screen, delete text, and so on. More editing commands are available to you, and these are listed on the other five editing menus. you will save time if you refer to the correct menu when you are looking for a particular command.

The help menu, accessed with ^J shows you how to set the help level, and offers onscreen documentation for many WordStar features. See the section on help later in this chapter.

Each of the other four menus contains commands that are grouped together because their functions are related. See the tips following this one for a discussion of each of these menus.

Tip

Use the quick menu when you want commands that move you through your file quickly.

The quick menu, accessed with ^Q is shown. The commands in the quick allow you to accomplish the following tasks quickly:

- Move the cursor all the way across the screen or to a block or place marker in your file
- Delete an entire line of text
- Find particular text in your file
- Replace selected text in your file
- Repeat a particular command without reentering it

Tip

Use the onscreen menu when you want to control the formatting of text on the screen.

The onscreen menu is shown, and is accessed with ^O when a document file is open. These commands and toggles help you

- Set the margins, tabs, and line spacing
- Center text on a line
- Turn word wrap and right justification ON or OFF
- Control display of the ruler line, page breaks, and print control characters.
- Turn hyphen-help and soft hyphens On or Off

A toggle works like a switch-in other words, each of these parameters is either ON or OFF whenever you are working with a document. You are change the setting from ON to OFF, or vice versa; by entering ^O followed by the letter for that particular toggle.

Tip

If you want to check the current settings of the various format toggles, call up the onscreen menu.

As explained in the preceding tip, many of the WordStar format settings are controlled by toggles, which are set to either ON or OFF whenever you are working with a document file. The current status of each toggle is displayed on the onscreen menu. If you need to check one of the settings, just press ^O when you have a file open. The menu will be displayed, and if you choose to change one of the settings, you can do so by entering the letter for that toggle.

Tip

You don't have to leave your document file to copy, print, rename, or delete a file, or to change the logged disk drive.

Although all of these operations on entire files are available at the WordStar opening menu, you can also perform them while you are editing a document file by accessing the ^K block menu.

Tip

Use the block menu when you need commands for handling entire files or blocks of text within a file.

You can call up the block menu, shown by pressing ^K from within a document file. These commands allow you to

- Save a file, and close the file or resume work with it after the save
- Abandon a file after an unsuccessful edit
- Insert temporary place markers into you text
- Work with a block of text, marking it and then moving it, deleting it, or copying it
- Change the logged disk drive
- Copy, print, rename, or delete an entire file

The logged disk drive is discussed earlier in this chapter, and file operations are explained in the chapter on working with files, Place markers and block operations.

Tip

Use the print menu to insert commands for special effects in your printed document.

You get to this menu by pressing ^P when you are editing a file. These commands allow you to use special effects when you print your document such as boldface and overprinted lines.

Tip

You don't have to wait for the menu to be displayed before you enter the second letter of a control command.

The control commands are available to you when you are working in a document file, and each one is accessed through one of the menus described in the preceding tips. If you are not sure which command you need, you can press the control key and the first letter of the command, and then wait for the menu to be displayed. WordStar will wait for you to either enter the second letter of the command, or press the space bar if you decide not to execute a command from that menu.

If you already know the command you want to enter, you can just press the appropriate keys, without waiting for the menu to be displayed. The command will be executed immediately.

Tip

When you enter the second letter of a control command, it makes no difference if you hold down the control key or not.

Suppose you want to change the setting of the justification toggle. The command you need is ^OJ: WordStar will accept the command as ^OJ or as ^O^J. You must press the control key for the first letter of the command, but after that it makes no difference to WordStar.

There is one exception to this; when you are entering a number as the second part of a place marker command, you cannot press the control key. But WordStar accepts all of the two-letter control commands in either form.

Tip

You can interrupt the execution of any WordStar command by pressing ^U.

The ^U command interrupts the execution of virtually any WordStar command. When you press ^U, WordStar stops whatever it is doing and displays the message

INTERRUPTEDPress ESCAPE Key

If you press ^U and you do not see this message, WordStar was not executing a command, so there was no process to be interrupted.

To abort one-letter commands at opening menu see the top about using the Esc key earlier in this chapter.

WORDSTAR HELP FEATURES

The WordStar help features offer you several levels of onscreen assistance:

- Reference screens explains many WordStar commands and functions. You can view this onscreen manual while you are working with a document, without having to close the file.
- Commands messages explain the various options you have for the particular command you have entered. (Some WordStar commands require you to enter text or make choices before they are executed.)
- Menu displays list the various commands you may choose to execute, and show the current settings of the toggles.

When you first begin working with WordStar, or when you attempt to master a new set of commands it is helpful to have all of the menus and explanations on the screen as you work. Once you become more proficient, you can remove these help features from the screen, giving yourself more space for viewing your document.

Tip

You can access the WordStar onscreen manual from the help menu.

You can access this menu by pressing ^J when you are working in a document file. The H option, for setting the help level, is explained in the top that follows the next trap. All of the other options on this menu are the topics in the onscreen manual. You can refer to this manual without closing your document file. For instance, if you select F (flags in right-most column), you will see the help screen. Each of the symbols that can appear in the flag column is explained for you. When you have finished referring to this screen, press the space bar to clear it from your monitor.

Some of the help screens have more than one part; you can view them in sequence by pressing the space bar to move from one to the next. You can also press ^U at any time, to interrupt the help display and return to your document.

Trap

Your workspace is very small when you leave the main menu display on the screen.

The main menu, discussed earlier in this chapter, lists some of the most basic WordStar commands. It takes up large portion of the screen, as you can see, so that only a small part of your document file is displayed. Since most people master these commands rather quickly as they work with WordStar, it is helpful to remove the menu from the screen, and open up a much larger area for your text. How much more work space is available when you suppress the main menu, and the following tip explains how to suppress this menu display.

Tip

You'll have a larger workspace on the screen if you choose help level 2 or lower.

The default setting for help is level 3, the maximum help setting. Unless you change this default with the WordStar installation program (as explained later in this chapter), help will be set at level 3 whenever you enter WordStar. At this level, the screen display includes all of the menus and command explanations. In particular, the main menu remains on the screen while you work with a document file, as discussed in the preceding trap.

Help level 2 is essentially the same as level 3; all of the command messages are displayed, and the various editing menus are displayed when you enter the first letter of a control command. The only difference at level 2 is that the main menu is not displayed while you work in a document file. As you can see, this gives you much more room to view the text in your file.

If you choose to work at help level 1, none of the menus will be displayed, but you can still use all of the WordStar commands. The various options for a particular command will not be displayed at this level, but you can access the onscreen manual with ^J followed by the letter for the help screen you would like to view.

The lowest help setting is level 0, which provides no assistance at all; all command messages are unavailable, although you can still use the onscreen manual, just like level 1.

Many people find help level 2 the most efficient setting. The main menu is removed from the screen, so you have a large workspace. The other editing menus are available to you as you need them. If you pause after you enter the first letter of a control command, the menu is displayed; if you enter the second letter immediately, it is not. This feature makes level 2 the most flexible of the help settings.

Tip

You can always get more help if you need it.

Suppose you are editing a document with help set at level 2, so you have the maximum screen area for your text. The main menu is not visible when you are working at this help level.

If you want to consult the main menu, you can enter ^JH3 any time you have a document file open to quickly reset help to the maximum level. You can enter the whole command at once, without waiting for the screen display to change. Once you are finished with the main menu, just enter ^JH2 to return to help level 2.

REINSTALLING WORDSTAR

Many of the features of the WordStar working environment are established automatically when you load the program. The initial help level is set at 3, justification is ON, and so on. These settings are called the default values; the settings that WordStar uses unless you issue a command to change them.

Some of the default settings may not suit your word-processing needs. If you prefer to work at help level 2, you must issue the commands to change the help setting each time you enter WordStar. If you rarely right-justify a document, you have to reset this toggle every time. You can, however, change the default settings for these WordStar features by reinstalling the program, so that whenever you enter WordStar, the environment will be already customised for your needs.

If you are using, WordStar on an IBM computer, each of the built-in function keys has a particular command assigned to it and can be used to enter the command quickly. If you have WordStar version 3.3 or higher, these commands are displayed across the bottom of the screen as you work. Some of these short-cuts are more helpful than others; you might like to assign different commands to the function keys to save time entering commands you use very often. You can redefine these function keys and change the message that is displayed across the bottom of the screen by reinstalling WordStar.

The following tips and traps explain how to use the installation program that comes with WordStar version 3.31. If you have another release, check the installation manual provided with your software, and use the commands required by your version of the program.

Tip

Before you can begin reinstalling WordStar, you must have the installation files available on a disk.

You will need the following files to reinstall WordStar:

WSU.Com

WS.Ins

WINSTALL.EXE

You can copy these files from the original WordStar disk.

To begin the reinstallation procedure, get the operating system running on your computer and place the disk with these three files in the logged drive. Enter WINSTALL at the operating system prompt.

Tip

If the WS.INS file is not on the disk in the logged drive, the installation program will not run.

As explained in the preceding tip, you must have certain files available to run the installation program. In particular, the file WS.INS must be on the disk in the drive indicated by your operating prompt. If it is not, you will get an error message, the installation program will stop running, and you will be returned to the operating system.

If the DOS prompt A> is on the screen, WS.INS must be in the A drive; there is no way to tell the installation program to look for this file on another drive.

Tip

If you don't have room for new files on your disk, the installation program will not run.

The WordStar installation program begins by making a copy of WSU.COM on your working disk. If there isn't enough space for this copy you'll get a message that an error occurred while copying the file, the installation program will stop running and you will be returned to the operating system.

This is why are recommend using a temporary disk for the reinstallation procedure. The disk with your WordStar program files can get very full, particularly if you have auxiliary programs like MailMerge and CorrectStar on it also. It may be impossible to reinstall WordStar directly in that disk. When you finish reinstalling on a temporary disk, a new file will have been created, named WS.COM, which you can then copy to the disk with your WordStar program files.

Tip

Follow the instructions on the screen until you see the installation menu.

The installation program displays several screens of information for you to read, and will offer you a chance to exit the program. As you work with this program, you will often be asked to confirm the choices you have made; just press return if the information on the screen is correct.

The installation menu is shown in Figure 1. To change WordStar default settings or to redefine the function keys choose option C, Menu of WordStar Features.

Tip

To change one of the WordStar default settings, select the appropriate letter from the features menu.

***** Installation Menu *****

If you are installing a new copy of WordStar, you must select latter a to install your printer. If your printer is not listed on the Menu of Printers, return to this menu and select latter B. If you want to change a particular WordStar Feature choose latter C.

A Menu of Printers

B Custom Installation of Printers

C Menu of WordStar Features

X Exit from INSTALL

Enter the latter of your choice (A/B/C/X).

Fig. 1. The installation menu

Figure 2 shows the features menu from the installation program. Let's say you want to change the initial help setting (see the section on help earlier in this chapter). Press A, and you will see the screen display in Figure 3, which tells you that the current setting is level 3 and explains each of the possible help settings.

Enter the letter for the help level you want, for example, to set help at level 2, press B. The screen will clear, and you will see the following message:

Help level is now 2.
If this is correct, enter Y or <RET>,
If not, enter N.

If you press return, the default setting will be changed and you will be returned to the features menu.

You can also change the initial setting of many of the WordStar toggles. Suppose you would prefer to have the justification toggle set to

***** Menu of WordStar Features *****

To modify a WordStar Features, select the appropriate letter, choose the modification, then return to this menu is continue or exit to the Installation Menu ("X")

A	Initial help level	K	Left margin
B	Decimal Point character	L	Right margin
C	Non-document mode	M	Number lines/page
D	Initial directory display	N	Page offset
E	Initial Insertion toggle	O	Form Foods
F	Justification toggle	P	Data Field separator
G	Hyphen help toggle	Q	Variable name symbol
H	Omit-page-numbering toggle	R	Default disk drive
I	Top page margin	S	Function keys
J	Bottom page margin	T	Color Installation

X Exit in Installation menu

Enter the letter of choice (A-T/X).

Fig. 2. Features menu

Initial help level

You can set the level of onscreen help to provide more or less information as you need it. The help level is currently 3.

A Help level 3
All menus and explanations displayed

B Help level 2
Main editing menu (I-key commands) suppressed

C Help level 1
Prefix menus (2-key commands) also suppressed

D Help level 0
Command explanation also suppressed
Enter the latter of your choice (A/B/C/D),
or press <RETURN> to leave exchanged.

Fig. 3. Resetting the initial help level

Off when you begin working with WordStar. Select option F at the features menu, and you will see the screen display in Figure 4. Enter C to change the default setting, and then press return when you are asked to confirm the choice.

Justfications taggle

This sets WordStar to start with justification on. Year text
will be right justified as you type.

Justificaiton features is correctly ON

Enter "C " t change to OF
or press (Return) to leave unchanged.

Fig. 4. Resetting the justification toggle

Tip

To change the definitions of the function keys, select option S at the features menu.

When you press S at the features menu, you will see the screen display shown in Figure 5. Across the top, you see the function description line, which will appear long the bottom of the screen as you work in WordStar. Below the description line, each of the current function key assignments is listed for you. Select the letter corresponding to the function key you would like to redefine.

Let's say you want to redefine key F1, now defined as the command ^JH, which sets the help level. Press A to choose this key and WordStar will ask you to confirm your entry. After you do so.

Changing the function key is easier than the instructions indicate in Figure 5. Let's redefine this key to the command sequence ^KS^QP, the save and resume work command followed by the command to return the cursor to its position before the save. This is a very useful function key assignment because you should be using this command sequence frequently as you work.

Enter the same command letters that you see to issue the command when you are working in WordStar. Each letter is preceded by a colon (:) as you can see in Figure 8, so the installation program will interpret it as a command letter. You enter each letter of the command sequence separately, to enter the ^K and ^ Q you hold down the control key as you press the letter, just like you do when you give that command in WordStar. When you finish the command, enter a period (.) to indicate the end of the sequence.

Figure 6 shows the screen display, which lists each entry you have made. Once you finish the command sequence and enter the period, it will show you the complete command, with the message

Function key #1 sequence is now: ^KS^QP

Check the sequence carefully, then press return to confirm the entry or N to change it.

```
You can enter a value is ASCII, decimal, or hexadecimal codes.
Precedes each entry with these prefixes.
ASCII              :   (^A enters ASSCII ^A, a single value)
Hexadecimal        :   (, 41 enters hexadecimal 41)
Decimal            :   (261 enters decimal 61)
To enter a sequences of characters, enter each one separately, followed by <RETURN>
Press <RETURN> to leave the value exchanged.
Enter a period (.) and press <RETURN> to terminate a sequence and to eliminate all subsequent values.
These special characters require beneficial Input:
<RETURN>                , 89
Period                  , 28
^H (backspace: ^H       , 89
Maximum entries for function key **** is 6.
Current          New
Value            Value
^J               —
```

Fig. 5. Changing a function key definition

A command sequence for a function key can be up to six values long. Each value may be a letter, like P in ^KS^QP or a letter entered with the control key pressed, such as ^K in the same command. If your command sequence includes pressing the Esc key like the commands to set a margin at the current cursor location, you just press Esc to enter that value, and the "[" symbol will appear in that position on the screen display.

```
Press <RETURN> To leave the value exchanged.
Enter a period (,) and press <RETURN> in terminate a sequence and in eliminate all subsequent values.
These special characters require hexadecimal input:
<RETURN> (^M)           ,83
Period (.)              ,22
^H (backspace:  ^N)     ,88
Maximum entries for function key 81 is 6.
Current             New
Value               Value
^J                  : ^K
N                   : S
Function key 8 sequence is now : ^KS^QP
If this is correct, enter V or <RETURN>. If not, enter N. -
```

Fig. 6. A completed function key definition

Tip

You cannot enter a period, ^H, or the return key in a function key definition.

The WordStar installation program requires you to enter a period to indicate the end of the command sequence. If you try to enter a period for one of the values within the command, the installation program will think you have finished the whole command sequence. Therefore, you cannot enter a WordStar dot command, like .CP5 for a conditional page break, in the same form you would use within WordStar. Similarly, the installation program does not allow you to enter ^H or the return key directly into the command sequence. See the following tip for a way to get around this problem.

Tip

Use the hexadecimal codes to enter a period or the return key as a value in a function key definition; use ^S instead of ^H if you need a backspace command.

As explained in the preceding trap, the installation program does not allow you to enter a period, ^H, or a carriage return directly into the command sequence for a function key definition, if you need the return key or a period, you must use a coded entry:

For the return key, enter ,OD

For a period within the command sequence, enter ,2E

The ^H command has the same effect a ^S, moving the cursor left one space. Use ^S if you need a backspace in a function key definition.

Most WordStar commands do not use these characters, but they are available if you need them. Suppose you have a file named RUL, which contains all of the ruler lines you use for formatting your documents. You could redefine one of the function keys with the command sequence ^KRRUL<return>, to read this file into a document with one keystroke. You would enter the values ^K, R, R, U, and L, and then ,OD for the return key.

Tip

If you use shift-6 for the control symbol in a function key definition, the installation program will beep and refuse to accept the letter for that value.

Pressing shift-6 places the control symbol (^) on the screen, but the symbol, will not be interpreted correctly by the installation program. To enter ^K as a value in a function key definition, you must hold down the control key and press K; this will be accepted, and the screen display will show ^K for that value.

Tip

When you redefine a function key, change the description line text that will be displayed on the screen while you are working with WordStar.

Once you confirm the new definition for a function key you will see the screen display shown in Figure 7. Press C to change the text, and enter a brief (up to six letters) description for the key's new function. This new text will be displayed at the bottom of the screen when you work kin WordStar, along with all other function key definitions.

> **Tip**
> *Be sure to save the changes you have made when you exit the installation program.*

After you finish changes to customise WordStar, select X to return to the installation menu, and X again to leave the program. You will see the exit options menu, shown in Figure 8.

Press A to save these changes. The installation program will produce a version of WordStar with the default settings and function key definitions you have chosen.

```
Formation key 81 description line ext is currently : HELP
        Enter "C" to change,
        we press <RETURN>  to leave exchanged. C

        You may now enter the text which you wish to appear on the function key description line, a
        maximum of 6 characters will be stored. Press <RETURN>, if you require nothing printed on the
        description line for this function key.

        Enter now description line text:  S & E-
```

Fig. 7. Changing the function key description

```
The changes made during this  session of INSTALL are stored
is a temporary file. You may now save those changes is your
installed file  A:WS. COM.

These are your current value:

Terminal                :   IBM PC, KT and 3270 Computers
Printer                 :   IMB Parallel Printer

              ***** Exit Options Menu *****

A    Save the changes made during this INSTALL session.
B    Omit this session of INSTALL without saving changes
C    Change any of your choices is INSTALL

Enter the letter of your choice (A/B/C).
```

Fig. 8. The exit options menu

USING A MACRO PROCESSOR WITH WORDSTAR

A macro processor is a program that allows you to enter a sequence of commands or a portion of text with a single keystroke. With a macro processor, like Prokey by RoseSoft or SuperKey by Borland, you can redefine the value of certain keystrokes. For example, if you assign specific text to the ^F10 key, such as the text you enter when you begin typing a letter (dot commands for page formatting and printing, a ruler line to set the margins and tabs, and your name and address) ProKey will enter all of this text into your document when you press ^F10.

Any sequence of keystrokes can be included in a macro. Some ways to use Prokey with the above example of writing a letter include the following.

- Entering text. You can include text such as your name, your company name, and your address in a macro definition.
- Placing text on separate lines. You can include the return key in a macro, so you can enter multiline text like the heading for a letter or a sequence of dot commands.
- Centering text. You can have ProKey center your name and address on the page b including the keystrokes ^OC after the text for each line.
- Setting margins and tabs. You can enter and activate a ruler line by having ProKey type it on the screen, activate it with ^OF, and then erase it with ^Y, so it will not be printed in your document.
- Boldfacing. You can have ProKey boldface your company name by surrounding it with the keystrokes ^PB.
- Positioning text. You can have ProKey move the cursor into position for the date, will for you to enter the date, and then move the cursor to the location where you want to begin entering text.

You can also use a macro processor to reduce a sequence of commands to a single keystroke. Suppose you frequently enter and edit text with single spacing and then reform the document to double spacing before printing. You could assign the following sequence of commands and keystrokes to a particular key, and one command will set the entire sequence in motion:

^KS	Save the document and positions the cursor at the beginning of the file.
^OS 2	Changes line spacing to double spaced.
^QQ ^B 1	Reforms the entire file at the fastest setting.

There are several different macro processors available, each with its own features. All of them allow you to redefine the meaning of certain keystrokes, but the particular commands you use will vary with each program. The tips and traps in this section focus on some of the ways you can use a macro processor with WordStar; see the manual that comes with your macro processor for the specifics of creating the macros to accomplish these tasks.

Tip

Write macros to replace sequences of commands that you use very often.

The most helpful macros are the ones that save time entering keystrokes and handling routine tasks. Each WordStar user needs a personalised set of macros, depending on the tasks the particular user performs most often. Some possibilities include:

- Addressing an envelope
- Changing between two formats within a document
- Moving a block of marked text, reforming the paragraph, and hiding the block markers
- Entering a heading that is centered, boldfaced, and underlined
- Entering a series of dot commands at the top of a document

The rest of the tips in this section include sample macros, use these examples to help you think of the particular time-savers you can use as you work with WordStar.

Tip

Use a macro to make it easy to enter a word, phrase, or passage that appears repeatedly in a document.

A macro can be simply a word, phrase, or passage of text, without any executable commands. You can use a macro like this to save time when you are typing a document, and you can make the text as long as your macro processor allows.

For example, if you are typing a legal document that uses the word plaintiff repeatedly, you can assign that word to Alt-p. Then you can enter plaintiff with one keystroke. If you writing a script where the names of the characters must be entered before each of their lines, you can assign each of the these character names to a macro and save a lot of typing time.

Tip

You can use a macro for the special printing toggles, and both parts of the print command will be inserted for you.

To tell WordStar to print a certain passage in boldface, you must insert ^PB commands at the beginning and the end of the passage. A macro can do this for you with one command. Using ProKey, you could define the Alt-b macro like this;

```
<begdef> <altb> <ctrlp> <vfld>...<vfld><ctrlp>b<enddef>
```

Now, when you press Alt b, a ^B symbol is inserted into you text, and the cursor changes to the ProKey block-shaped cursor. Type in the text you want boldfaced. Then press the return key and a second ^B is inserted to end the boldfacing. The usual WordStar cursor will be positioned immediately after the second ^B symbol. Pressing the return key here does not insert a carriage return into your text, but, rather, it tells ProKey to end the boldfacing.

Tip

If you use ^R in a macro definition to insert a file name after the print command, you may not get the file name you want when the macro is executed.

After the enter a print command, either P at the opening menu or ^KP from within a document file, WordStar asks for the name of the file you want printed. Pressing ^R tells WordStar to enter a previous file name for you. If you printed any documents so far in your work session, the name of the last document you printed will be inserted after the file name prompt. If you have not done any printing in this work session, the name of the first file you edited when you entered WordStar will be inserted. If you have not edited or printed a file-in other words, if you begin your work session by entering P and then pressing ^R-the ^R command will have no result.

Because the result of pressing ^R varies depending on when you use it in a work session, you should not use this command in a macro definition. If you do, the macro will be of limited value, and you will have to remember that it can only be used when the ^R command would insert the name of the file you want printed.

The next tip explains a much more reliable way to handle the file name question within a macro.

Tip

If you assign the name of the file you are working with to a macro when you open the file, you can use that file name in other macros later on.

Whenever you print a document with WordStar or with MailMerge, you have to enter the name of the file you want printed. Therefore, if you want to write a macro that prints a document, you must insert the file name within the macro definition. For example, if you use the current file name in a macro definition, you can write a macro to save the current version of a file, print it with the default settings, and resume work at the current cursor position.

The first step is to store the file name in a macro when you open the file. The usual way to open a file is to press D at the WordStar opening menu and then type in the name of the file. You can write a macro to do this, and at the same time, to store the name of the file you open in a second macro. To create this macro with ProKey, you must type the following command line; the keystroke Alt-f is redefined to open a file and store its name in the Alt-n macro:

<begdef> <altf> <begdef> <altn> <vfld>...<vfld> <endef> <enter> <enddef>

Let's look at each part of the macro:

<begdef>	Marks the beginning of a ProKey macro definition.
<altf>	Defines the Keystroke, which, in this case, is holding down the Alt key and pressing F.
d	Indicates the first keystroke the macro will enter: the command to open a document file.
<begdef>	Appears again because another macro is being defined within the Alt-f macro.
<altn>	Defines the keystroke for the nested macro, holding down the Alt key and pressing N.
<vfld>....<vfld>	Tells ProKey to pause and wait for the file name to be entered from the keyboard. ProKey changes the cursor to a block and waits for you to type in the file name.
<enddef>	Marks the end of the Alt-n macro definition.
<enter>	Indicates pressing the return key after the name of the file has been typed in, to tell WordStar to open this file.
<enddef>	Marks the end of the Alt-f macro definition.

With this macro in memory, when you press Alt-f and enter the file name at the ProKey cursor block, the file will be opened and the name of the file will be assigned to the Alt-n keystroke. If you press Alt-n, the file name will be entered on the screen and if you include Alt-n in another macro, it will be replaced by the name of the file when that macro is executed.

Now you can write the macro, mentioned at the beginning of this tip, to save, print, and resume working. The following command line is the ProKey definition for this macro, assigned to the Alt-p keystroke.

<begdef> <altp> <ctrlk> <ctrlq> p <ctrlk> p <altn> <esc> <enddef>

The Alt-p macro executes ^KS to save the file and resume working with it. ^QP to return the cursor to the position where the save command was entered, and ^KP to print while editing. Then the name of the file is typed in by the Alt-n macro to tell WordStar which file to print, and the Esc key is pressed to bypass the printing options.

15

Using MailMerge

Mailmerge is a Program That Runs in conjunction with WordStar and is by far the most useful of the auxiliary programs available. MailMerge enables you to build a document as it is printed, using data from different files as well as data entered at the keyboard. This can be a tremendous time - saver in many word - processing tasks.

With MailMerge you can do the following:

- Merge data and form documents to produce customised versions of a standard document, such as a form letter or a contract.
- Combine more than one file into a document, either in sequence or nested within one another.
- Insert boilerplate passages into a document as it is printed without having to read one file into another.
- Produce a customised version of a standard document with minimal editing time.
- Include certain passages in some documents and not in others without editing each document separately.
- Produce a customised copy of a document for each of the people on list, or for certain selected people only.

If you purchased the WordStar Professional package, MailMerge is included on the Options disk; otherwise, it is available as a separate program. It greatly enhances the power and flexibility of WordStar and is worth taking the time to learn. Many people find that they end up using MailMerge for virtually all of their WordStar printing tasks.

This chapter includes tips and traps on working with each of the options that are included in the MailMerge program. It begins with the basic tools; *the master document,* which serves as a template for customised documents, and the *variables,* the information that changes for each specific document.

You will learn how to use MailMerge to combine data in different files in a variety of ways, depending on the word - processing task you need to accomplish. You will also learn how to print a series of documents with specific data for each one entered at the keyboard as it is printed, and how to customise the format and content of each document as it is printed.

Working with MailMerge

> **Trap**
>
> *You cannot run MailMerge without the WordStar programs available on the same disk.*

MailMerge operates only in conjunction with WordStar; it cannot be used on its own. Copy the file MAILMRGE.OVR from the distribution disk to the disk with your WordStar program files; if you are working with a hard - disk system, add this file to the same directory as the WordStar program files.

When you want to work with MailMerge, enter WordStar, change the logged disk drive to the drive that contain your data and document files, and then select option M from the opening menu.

> **Tip**
>
> *All of the WordStar commands can be used in documents that will be printed with MailMerge.*

MailMerge operates within the WordStar environment, giving you more options without eliminating any of the WordStar functions. A MailMerge document can contain any of the WordStar dot commands, and they will give the same results as when they are used in a WordStar document.

> **Tip**
>
> *The screen line displays a flag (M) when a MailMerge dot command is entered into a document.*

MailMerge for commands are entered exactly the same way as the WordStar dot commands: each begins with a period in the first column of a screen line, and the particular dot command is entered immediately after the period, with no intervening space.

You write a MailMerge document using WordStar; you use the MailMerge program itself only when you are printing the document. Whenever a screen line begins with a MailMerge dot command, WordStar displays the M flag on the far right of the screen.

If you begin a screen line with a period in the first column, WordStar checks the characters after the period. If these characters are not one of the WordStar or MailMerge dot commands, you will see a question mark in the flag column. Keep you eye on the flag column as you enter your documents, and correct your entry whenever this question mark is displayed; it is telling you that the command you have entered cannot be interpreted by WordStar or MailMerge.

Tip

If you use the WordStar print function to print a document that contains MailMerge dot commands, the MailMerge dot commands will not work.

Once you include MailMerge commands in a document, you must use MailMerge to print the document correctly. WordStar without MailMerge interprets those commands as comment lines and just ignores them when the document is printed.

Tip

Proofread a MailMerge document by printing it out with the WordStar print function.

When you prepare a document for MailMerge to print, it will include MailMerge dot commands and keywords for variable values. These must be entered correctly, with the proper format and spelling, and the variable names must be entered consistently throughout the document.

You should always proofread a MailMerge document so you can make corrections as needed before you begin a printing task. An efficient way to do this, especially with a long document, is to print the file with WordStar. If you suppress the page format (which is one of the printing options explained in Chapter 4), all of the dot commands in your document will be printed out and the keywords for your variables will be printed as you entered the, Figure 1 (in the following section) shows a MailMerge file printed this way; the file appears on paper exactly as it appears on the screen.

Tip

You cannot print a file using MailMerge while you are editing in WordStar.

One of the useful features of WordStar is that you can edit one file while you are printing another (as explained in Chapter 4), but this option is not available to you if you are printing with MailMerge. You must exit edit mode and select MailMerge at the opening menu is order to print a MailMerge document.

Creating the Master Document

Each MailMerge printing task is controlled by a master document: a file that tells MailMerge what text to print, which other files to access, and so on. This document serves as a template for printing, and can include the following:

- Text to be included in every copy of the document.
- Variable names, which will be replaced with specific data as each copy of the document is printed.
- Commands that tell MailMerge where to find the data to replace the variables in each copy of the document.
- Commands to insert the contents of another file.

- Commands that tell MailMerge to insert certain text in some of the documents and not in others.
- Commands to establish the format of the documents.

Figure 1 shows the master document for a form letter that will be customised with MailMerge. The tips and traps in this section explain the various components of this document.

```
. OP
. DF ref.dta
. RV last, title, first coname, street, city, state, zip, pline
. SV date, July 3, 1986
. CS
. DM This person is interested in &pline&.
. AV "Catalog page:", page
                                                          &data&

&title& &first& &last&
&coname/O&
&street&
&city&, &state&, &zip&

Dear &title& &last&,
We are delighted that you are interested in learning about our &pline&, one of several product lines
available from Ace Equipment, Enclosed is a copy of our catalog. You will find &pline& on page
&page&.
We have a customer service agent in your area, who can answer any questions you might have about
our products, and can assist you in placing your order:
. FI &state&
. IF &state& <> "CA" GOTO endsale
Unit II the end of this month, we are offering a special discount to our customers in California. Be sure
to see the yellow sale pages at the front of the catalog for this exciting offer.
. EP endsale
Thank you for your inquiry: we at Ace Equipment would like to work with you to meet your
equipment needs.
                                   Sincerely,

                                   Caron Brown
                                   Ace Customer Service
. PA
```

Fig. 1. A MailMerge master document

Tip

Use the WordStar formatting commands to control the format of your MailMerge documents.

Figure 1 includes the dot commands .OP and .PA at the beginning and end of the document. These WordStar commands are used to control the format of the page for each letter. Whenever you use MailMerge to generate repetitive documents, you will need to use dot commands to control page numbering and to begin each document on a new page, as explained later in this section.

You can use any of the WordStar formatting commands in a MailMerge master document, so you can produce exactly the format you need when you print your documents. There are also special formatting commands you can use when you insert files with MailMerge which are discussed in detail in the formatting section of this chapter.

Tip

Use variable names to indicate the places in your master document where variable data will be inserted.

You can see many variable names in the master document in Figure 1; each one is surrounded by ampersands when it appears in the body of the letter. A variable name serves as a place marker in the document and tells MailMerge where to place a particular data item.

When MailMerge prints this letter, it will generate one copy for *each* of the people listed in a separate file, called the data *file.* Each of the variable names in ampersands will be replaced by the data for that person, which is called the *current value* of the variable. For example, the letter in the figure is headed.

Dear &title &last&,

When MailMerge prints the letter for Mr. Names Warren, the current value of the title variable is "Mr.", and the current value of last is "Warren". MailMerge prints these current values wherever the variable names are placed in your document; therefore, this copy of the letter will be headed.

Dear Mr. Warren,

When MailMerge moves on to printing the next copy of the letter, the current values of the variables will change, and the data about the next person in the data file will be inserted into the letter.

A variable name can be up to 40 characters long, and must begin with a letter. Subsequent characters can be letters, numbers, or hyphens, but no spaces or other punctuation are allowed. Place each variable name in your master document in the exact location where the variable data should be printed, and surround each one with ampersands. MailMerge replaces each variable with its current value.

In the letter in Figure 1 the variables include the date, which is printed at the top of the letter, the name and address data for each person who will receive the letter; and the variable pline, which will be replaced with the name of the product line the person is interested in. The person's name and address data is printed above the text of the letter:

&title &first& &last&

&coname/O&

&street&

&city&, &state& &zip&

The comma between city and state and the spaces between the variable values will be printed exactly as they are positioned on these lines.

The particular product line will be printed in the first paragraph where the variable name &pline& appears. The other variable, &page&, must be types in by the user for each letter, and changes depending on the product line. It will be printed in its designated position within the letter.

Tips

Use dot commands to tell MailMerge where to find the values for the variables in your master document.

As explained in the preceding tip, you use variable names, surrounded by ampersands, to indicate the places in your master document where the data that customises each document should be placed. MailMerge can find the values for these variables in three different places:

1. In a data file. When you are printing out many customised versions of the same document, you can place the variable data in a separate file, called a data file, which MailMerge accesses.
   See the next section of this chapter, which contains tips and traps on working with data files.
2. Entered at the keyboard. You can instruct MailMerge to ask for the current values of the variables before each document is printed. See the section on data entry from the keyboard later in this chapter.
3. In the matter document itself. If a data item has the same value for all of the documents printed in one session, you can specify the value in the document itself. See the top on using the .SV command later in this section.

You must tell MailMerge where to find the variable data for your master document before you use any variable names in the text. In Figure 1 each type of data is used. The .DF and .RV commands tell MailMerge to find certain variables in a data file. The .AV commands tells MailMerge to ask for the value of the page variable and accept a keyboard entry for the data. The date variable will have the same value for all of the letters printed on a certain day, so it is assigned a value in the master itself, using the .SV command.

Trap

MailMerge leaves a blank line in the heading of your letters if there is no entry for one of the address lines.

Let's say you need to print out a form letter for several people on a mailing list. Some of the addresses include a line with the company name, and some do not.

If you head your letter like this,

&title &first& &last&

&coname&

&street&

&city&, &state& &zip&

an address without a company name will be printed with a blank line between the name and the street address. See the following tip for a way to get around this problem.

Tip

Use the omit if blank symbol, /O, with a variable that might not have an entry.

The letter in Figure 1 shows how the omit if blank symbol is used. The address includes a line for the company name, which will not be needed for some of the letters. When the variable is positioned in the master document, /O is included within the ampersands:

&coname/O&

This tells MailMerge to omit the entire lien from the document if there is no current value for the company name.

The omit if blank symbol can only be used for a variable that appears on a line by itself in document, like the company name in an address. It does not work with a variable name within a sentence, because it tells MailMerge to omit an entire screen line.

Tip

Use the file insert command, .FI, to tell MailMerge to insert the entire contents of another file into a master document.

In the letter in Figure 1, the name and address of the customer service agent for each state is stored in a separate file, which has the name of the state for its name. The command

. F1 and State&

tells MailMerge to insert the file for the person's state at this position in the letter. See the section on inserting files later in this chapter.

Tip

Use conditional printing commands to include certain text in some documents and not in others.

The letter in Figure 1 includes a conditional printing command structure, which begins with the command

.IF &state& < > "CA" GOTO endsale

and ends with

The text that appears between these commands will be included in letters to people who live in California, and will be omitted otherwise. See the last section of this chapter for tips and traps on using these conditional printing commands.

Trap

If you're not careful when you print repetitive documents with MailMerge, the page numbers and top and bottom margins will not come out correctly.

When MailMerge prints the same master document over and over, customising each copy with the current values of the variables, it considers the entire printing job as one document. Unless you give the proper commands, the pages will be numbered consecutively, and the top and bottom margins on each page will vary. The following tip explains how to handle this problem.

Tip

Whenever you print repetitive documents, include commands to control page numbering and page breaks.

As explained in the preceding trap, MailMerge numbers the copies of an entire printing task consecutively unless you include the necessary dot commands. If you are printing from a master document that has only one page, like the form letter in Figure 1, you do not want your documents to have page numbers at all. Place the command

.OP

at the top of the master document to turn off the page numbering.

If your master document has more than one page, you want each copy to begin with page one. Use the command

.PN 1

at the top of the first page, to have page numbering start over again each time the document is printed.

.PN 1

at the end of the first page, to have page numbering start over again each time the document is printed.

At the end of your master document, you need to include a page break command, .PA to tell MailMerge to begin the next copy of the document at the top of a new pate. The placement of this command is critical; the needs to be the last line of your master document, and should not be followed by any blank lines. When MailMerge reaches the .PA command, it immediately moves to the top of the next page. If the command is followed by blank lines, MailMerge will skip down that many ones before beginning the next copy of your document. These skipped lines will add up as a document is printed many times, and your form letters will gradually creep down the page.

Be sure to end a repetitive document with .PA on the very last line. Check the flag column for the carriage return symbol (<) and delete any ones after the .PA command.

Tip

If a variable will have the same value for all of the documents printed at one time; establish the value in the master document with the .SV command.

The form letter in Figure 1 includes a variable for the date the letter was printed. This date remains the same for all of the letters printed at one time, but needs to be changed when letters are printed on another day. It is inefficient to use the .AV command for this variable, since you would have to enter the same data at the keyboard for each letter that you print. You can't use the .RV command because the date is not a record in a data file. Instead, the date variable is given a value in the master document itself, with the command

.SV date July 3, 1988

When letters are printed on another day you must change this line of the master document before the printing begins. That way, you only have to enter the date once.

The set variable command is structured like this:

.SV variable name, current value

Note that there are no quotes around the current value; all of the characters after the command will be considered part of the data for the variable.

In Figure 1, the date variable appears only once in the text of the master document. The .SV command does not actually save you any time here because you could simply change the date in the letter before you print it. Instead, this .SV command serves as a reminder that the date needs to be changed.

Sometimes, however, the .SV command can save you a lot of work. Suppose you are printing a form letter to all of the employees in a large company. The letter mentions the department where the person works in several different places in the letter. You can enter one department name in .SV command, and then print all of the letters for that department. MailMerge will insert the department name everywhere the variable appears in the letter. After those letters are done, just change the department name in the .SV command, and you are ready to print the letters for the next department. MailMerge changes the value of the variable throughout the document.

Place the .SV command near the top of your master document so it is easy to edit this line when necessary.

Working with Data Files

Once you have written a MailMerge document, as explained in the previous section, you can use it to generate a series of repetitive documents, with each copy customised for its recipient. When you need to print a large number of documents, you can place the variable values for each letter in a separate file, called a data file, and instruct MailMerge to print a letter for each entry in that file. Once you have entered your mailing list into a data file, you can see the file over and over, with different master documents, to produce many customised mailings.

The tips and traps in this section explain how a data file is structured and how to write one that MailMerge can use. This section also covers the commands you need to include in your master document so that the information in the data file will be correctly placed into the document.

Tip

Structure your data file so that MailMerge can use it.

Figure 2 shows part of a data file: a list of names and addresses for a mailing list. Each line of the file is called a *record* and contains, information about one person on the list. Within a record, each discrete piece of data - the last name, first name, street, and so on - is called a *field.*

```
Martin, Mr..James, Ace Electric, 110 East St.., Oakland, CA, 94569
Wilson, Ms., Pat, "C &P, Inc," 2020 Main St., San Jose , CA, 94678
Brown Mr., Tom, EI Capitan, P.O. Box 2122 San Francisco, CA, 94632
West, Mr., Edward., 1238 East Second St., Alaneda, CA, 94722
```

Fig. 2. Records in a data file

There are three important rules for setting up a data file that MailMerge can work with:

1. The fields which each record must be separated by commas.
2. Each record must end with a carriage return.
3. The order of the fields within each record must be consistent throughout the file.

See the tips and traps in the rest of this section for a more detailed explanation of the data file structure.

Tip

If the fields in your data file are not placed in the same order in every record, MailMerge will not insert the data into your documents correctly.

Suppose you have these two records in a data file:

Smith, Mr., John,East Co., 1100 Main St., Oakland, CA, 94867

Wilson, Susan, Ms., Ace Electric, 95 Elm St., Alameda, CA, 93654

Because the first names and the titles are placed in a different order in each record, you could end up with letters addressed to Mr. John Smith and Susan Ms. Wilson.

When MailMerge takes the data from a record, it assigns the fields to the variables in the same order every time. You use the RV command, explained later in this section, to specify the order of the fields in your file, and the data are assigned to the variables in that order. If you tell MailMerge to find the last name first, followed by the title and then the first name, each record in the data file must have the fields listed in precisely that order. MailMerge considers whatever appears in the first field to be the last name, whatever is in the second field to be the title, and so on, and inserts the data into your master document accordingly.

Whenever you use a data file, be sure all of the records have their fields listed in the same order.

Tip

If you write a data file in WordStar's document mode, MailMerge will not be able to use the data in the file.

When WordStar is in document mode, the word - wrap function inserts spaces and/or soft carriage returns within the lines of text. A data file cannot have extra spaces or returns in its records.

Tip

You can write a data file with WordStar if you use the nondocument mode.

As explained in the preceding trap, a data file for MailMerge must be written without the word - wrap function. When WordStar is in nondocument mode, which you enter by typing N at the opening menu, word wrap is turned off. You can enter the records for your data file; the only spaces and carriage returns in the file will be those you have inserted. You can also edit your data file in nondocument mode; the WordStar editing functions operate in this mode as well as.

Tip

MailMerge can use a data file written with another software product, as long as the records are in the correct format.

If you have a data file that generated with a database program, you can use it with MailMerge, as long as the fields are separated by commas and each record ends with a carriage return.

Trap

If there is a comma within one of your data items, the data will not be inserted correctly into the master document.

Suppose this record was part of the data file in Figure 2:

Brown, Mr., Thomas,AAPCO; Inc., P.O. Box 2455, Boston,MA, 02374

MailMerge considers a comma to be the marker for the end of a field, so the comma in AAPCO, Inc. will cause AAPCO to be assigned to the variable for the company name, Inc, to the street address, P.O. Box 2455 to the city and so on.

Whenever a comma is part of the contents of a field, you need to let MailMerge know that this comma does not mark the end of a field. The following tip explains how to do so.

Tip

If there is a comma within a data item, surround the contents of that field with quotes.

As explained in the preceding trap, a comma within a data item will be interpreted as the end of the field when MailMerge reads the data in the record. If your data item contains a comma, you need to delimit that field with quotes, so that MailMerge will read the entire contents of the field.

To enter the record in the preceding trap correctly you should type the following:

Brown, Mr., Thomas, "AAPCO, Inc.", P.O. 2455, Boston, MA, 02374

When MailMerge finds a field surrounded by quotes, it considers every character within the quotes to be part of the data item.

Tip

If you skip a field in a data record, the variable information will not be inserted correctly into your master document.

Let's say you need to enter a record that does not have a company name in the data file in Figure 2. You can't just omit that field altogether (as in the following example) or you will throw off the printing for this record, and for all subsequent records in your data file:

Evans, Ms.,Ann, North Main St., Atlanta, G.A,34521

MailMerge cannot evaluate the contents of field to decide if it is a company name or a street address; whatever data you place in a particular position in a record is assigned to the variable that corresponds to that position. If MailMerge runs out of fields in one record, it will move to the next record, to give a data value to each variable. In this case, 1122 North Main St. will be considered the company name, and each field from on in the data file will be assigned to the wrong variable. The following tip explains how to handle this situation.

Tip

If a field has no contents, use a comma with no intervening space in the data record.

The preceding trap explains the problem that arises if you skip a field in a data record. You must include every field in every record in your data file.

If a field has no contents, indicate this to MailMerge by using a comma, with no characters at all in that field position, not even a space.

To enter the record in the preceding trap correctly you must type

Evans, Ms., Ann., 1122 North Main 9t., Atlanta, GA, 34521

The second comma immediately following the first name tells MailMerge that there is no data for the company name.

Trap

You can use MailMerge to create a data file with the records structured correctly.

If you have a lot of data records to enter into a file, or if you would like an inexperienced WordStar user to enter the data for you, can use MailMerge to enter the data into a disk file. You can establish the structure of each record, and be certain that all of the data will be entered correctly.

Figure 3 shows a master document that would create a data file structured like the file in Figure 2. Since the data will be written to a disk file rather than printed, each "document" that is generated will be a data record on the disk, to a printed page.

Let's go through the purpose of each part of this master document, First, use dot commands to suppress all page formatting.

.MT O gives you no blank lines at the top of a "page"

.MB O gives you no blank lines at the bottom of a "page."

.PO O gives you no left margin.

.PL 1 gives you a "page" that is one line long.

```
. MT  0
. MB  0
. PO  0
. PL  1
. AV "Titler", title
. AV "Last name:", last
. AV "First name: ", first
. AV "Company name:", coname
. AV "Street address:", street
. AV "City:" city
. AV "State:", state
. AV "zip code:", zip
&last&, &title&, &first&, &coname&, &street&, &city&, &state&m &zip&
```

Fig. 3. Using MailMerge to enter data records

Next, tell MailMerge to ask for keyboard entry of each data item by using the .AV command, which is explained in the next section of this chapter:

.AV "Title:", title

.AV "Last name:", last

.AV "First name:", first

.AV "Company name:", coname

.AV "Street address:", street

.AV "City:", city

.AV 'State:", state

.AV "Zip code:" zip

Now you need the command to print the data record to the disk file (use quotes to delimit any field that might have an embedded comma, as explained in an earlier trap and tip):

&last&, &title&, &first&, "coname&", &street&, &city&, &state&, &zip&

These are all the commands you need. Now you can use this master document with MailMerge to create a data file on your disk.

When you enter MailMerge, you are asked for the name of the master file and then presented with a list of questions about the printing format. The first question is:

DISK FILE OUTPUT (Y/N)

Answer Y and you will be asked for the name of the disk file. Enter the file name for your data file. When you get the question

NUMBER OF COPIES (RETURN FOR 1)?

answer with a number large enough to allow you to enter all of your data records.

MailMerge presents you with each of the .AV command prompts. Enter the data for a record and it will be printed as a data record on your disk. MailMerge includes the commas between fields and the quotes around the company name exactly as they are specified in the master document. Once you have finished entering records, cancel the printing, as explained in the section on working with the .AV command.

Tip

Use the .DF and .RV commands is your master document to tell MailMerge where to find the data items for the document.

When MailMerge takes data from a data file and inserts the values into a master document, it needs to be told two things:

1. Which file the data records are in
2. The order of the fields in each record

Before the text of your master document, include the two dot commands with this information:

.DF data file name

.RV variable 1, variable 2, variable 3,......

You must place the data file command, .DF, before the read variables command, .RV, since data cannot be read until the correct file has been accessed. Include both commands or MailMerge will not be able to read the data records.

In the master document in Figure 1, these commands appear at the top of the document:

.DF ref. dta

.RV last, title first, coname, street, city, state, zip, pline

The .DF command tells MailMerge to use the file named ref.dta, and the .RV command lists the nine fields that will be found in each data record in exactly the order they are listed in the data file.

Trap

If the order of the variable names in the .RV command does not match the order of the data items in each record, MailMerge will not insert the data correctly into your master document.

The .RV command tells MailMerge to read the information in a data record and to assign each field, in order, to the variables named in the .RV command. The order of these assignments is critical; MailMerge assigns the contents of the first field to the first variable, the second field to the second variable, and so on. If the variables are listed incorrectly in your .RV command, data will be inserted in the wrong places in your documents. Be sure you write each .RV command so the variables are in exactly the same order as the fields in your data records.

Tip

You can use more than one .RV command, if you need more than one line to list all of the variable names.

Each .RV command is limited to one line. Sometimes, this will not give you enough room to list all of the variables in your master document. However, MailMerge accepts more than one *RV command, as long as each one begins with .RV in the first column. The following example shows an acceptable way to access data:

.DF maillst.dta

.RV last, title, first, coname, street, city, state, zip

.RV areacode, phone, reference

Trap

If your .RV command does not list a variable to correspond to each of the fields in a data record, the data will not be inserted correctly into your master document.

Consider a data file containing records with these fields.

last name, title, first name, position, company name,
street, city, state, zip code

Suppose you are sending out a letter that does not mention the person's position, so that the data in this field will not be inserted into your master document. You can't leave this item out of your *RV command altogether, as in the following example:

.RV last, title, first, coname, street, city, state, zip

If you do so. MailMerge will assign the data in the position field to the variable coname, and all of the subsequent fields will be assigned incorrectly as well. You must assign the position field to a variable, even if it will not be used in the master document.

The information in a data record is assigned in order to the variables in your .RV command; you cannot skip a field. Whenever you write the .RV command, be certain each field in the data records is assigned to a variable.

Tip

When you use the .DF and .RV commands in a master document, MailMerge automatically prints one document for each record in the data file.

The .DF and .RV commands allow you to generate one document for each record in your data file. When a master document contains these commands, MailMerge will print one copy of the document for each data record.

When you print a file with MailMerge, you are asked for the number of copies to be printed. If your master document contains the .DF and .RV commands, this question refers to the number of copies of the document for each data record. One is the default setting and it produces one document per data record; change this number only if you need more than one copy of the document for each record in your data file.

Entering Data from the Keyboard

Some of the data that can change in your documents will not come fro a data file. Perhaps you are printing out the bills for certain month; a new billing date needs to be entered each month, but this will not be in a record in your data file. Or perhaps you are sending out letters to people who are not on your permanent mailing list, or printing a contract with information that will only be used once.

When you are printing a document or series of documents with MailMerge, you can instruct MailMerge to ask for certain data to be entered at the keyboard. MailMerge displays a prompt on the screen asking for data, and the data that is entered will be assigned to the variable you designate when you write the command.

The tips and traps in this section explain how to write the commands that tell MailMerge to ask for data from the keyboard, and how to print documents containing them.

Tip

Use the .AV command when you want to supply variable data from the keyboard as documents are printing.

The ask for variables command, .AV, tells MailMerge to display a message on the screen and then accept a keyboard entry for a certain variable. There are two forms for this command:

.AV variable name

.AV "message to display", variable name

When the dot command is followed by the variable name, the screen display will show that variable name, followed by a question mark.

For example,

.AV last

will produce this line on the screen:

last?

The cursor will be in the space following the question mark, ready to accept a keyboard entry, and whatever you type will be assigned to the variable last.

You can choose to display another prompt for the data by using the second form of the .AV command. For instance,

.AV "Enter last name:" last

result in this screen display:

Enter last name:

The cursor will be in the space after the colon. Again, the data you enter will be assigned to the variable last, the variable named in the .AV command.

```
. OF
. DF postings.dta
. PV last, title, first, coname, street, city, state, zip
. CB
. DN Now printing letter for &last&, &first&.
.AV "Appointment date", data
. AV "Time:" time
&title& &first& &last&
&coname/O&
&street&
&city&, &state& &zip&
Dear &title& &last&,
We have received your application for a position on our advisory staff,
and would like to meet with you in person to discuss several important
issues about this committee and the contributions you might make.

We have scheduled you for a meeting on &date& at &time&. If this is not
convenient, places call Margarat Janison at (800)746-1200 to arrange
another appointment.

We are looking forward to meeting you.
                                        Sincerely,

                                        John Adamson
                                        Vice President
. PA
```

Fig. 4. Using the .DM command with variable data

Tip

You can display a long message when you request data from the keyboard and you can include the current value of variables in the message.

Figure 4 shows the master document for a letter that will be sent to each person in a data file. The name and address information is supplied in the data file; the .DF and .RV commands at the top of the document instruct MailMerge to find this data in the file. Each person's letter will also include an appointment date and time; this data will be supplied from the keyboard as each letter is printed.

Notice how the screen display is defined:

.DM Now printing letter for &last&, &first&

.AV "Appointment date:" date

.AV "Time:", time

The person entering appointment dates and times needs to know which person's letter is currently being printed so the correct date and time can be entered. This means that the current values of the variables last and first should be displayed as each letter is printed. The display message command, .DM instructs MailMerge to do this.

There are no quotes around the text that .DM displays; everything that appears in the command line after the .DM will be displayed. The variable names surrounded by ampersands, &last& and &first&, will be replaced by the current values of those variables. This means that when MailMerge is preparing to print a letter to James Healy, the screen display will show

Now printing letter for Healy, James

Appointment date:

Once the date is entered, the person entering data will be asked for the appointment time.

You can use the .DM command any time you would like a message displayed on the screen while a document is printed. You can display the current value of any variable by including its name, enclosed in ampersand, in the text of the .DM command.

Tip

You can limit the number of characters that MailMerge will accept in response to the .AV command.

If you follow the variable name in the .AV command with a comma and a number, MailMerge will accept only that many characters in the keyboard entry. For example

.AV "Enter the 2 - letter code." code 2

causes the cursor to stop after the second character has been entered and wait for a carriage return.

You can use this command to guard against mistakes; for example, you can prevent the user from entering more than three digits for an area code.

Tip

Clear the screen between documents that have .AV commands, so the screen display will not be cluttered.

MailMerge displays the prompts for .AV commands one under another and scrolls the screen display upward as more lines, are needed. This can result in a cluttered screen, especially if a document has several .AV commands.

You can instruct MailMerge to clear the screen between documents by placing the clear screen commands, .CS at the to of the master document.

Trap

If a master document contains only .AV commands for accessing data, only one copy of the document will be printed.

Unless you instruct MailMerge otherwise, a master document that does not read data from a data file will be printed once, and then you will be returned to the WordStar opening menu. The next tip explains how to get around this limitation.

Tip

You can print many documents from a master document that contains only .AV commands without going through the WordStar opening menu each time.

As explained in the preceding trap, unless you tell MailMerge otherwise a master document that contains only .AV commands to access data prints only one copy. When you enter M at the WordStar opening menu and then name the master file for MailMerge to use, you are presented with a list of questions about the printing. If you would like to print many documents using master document that contains only .AV commands, answer the fourth question.

NUMBER OF COPIES (RETURN for 1)?

with the number of documents you want to print.

If you're not sure how many documents you will need, you can enter a very large number. Once you have finished generating documents, just cancel the printing with the P command.

Trap

You cannot cancel a print command when MailMerge is waiting for a response to the .AV command.

When the cursor is positioned after a prompt for the .AV command, MailMerge considers any keys that are pressed as text, not as commands. To interrupt a print command, you need to enter the command P, but if you type P when MailMerge is waiting for a response to the .AV command, the letter P will be entered as the value of a variable, not interpreted as a command. The next tip explains how to get past this problem.

Tip

You can cancel a printing command when MailMerge is asking for keyboard entries with a two - key sequence.

As explained in the preceding trap, you cannot enter the cancel print command, P, when MailMerge is waiting for data entry from the keyboard. You need to enter the command when MailMerge is between .AV commands, so it will be interpreted as a command rather than data. You can do this by pressing return at the .AV prompt, and then pressing P very quickly.

Inserting Files

You can use MailMerge to insert an entire file within another when a document is printed. This is a very efficient way to handle boilerplate files (standard passages of text that need to appear in many documents) it saves time and disk storage space. If you keep a master list of the contents of your boilerplate files, you can quickly insert the text you need into any document, without having to copy the boilerplate file into the document file.

MailMerge's insert feature also allows you to print multiple files, one after another, with consecutive page numbers and no page breaks. This cannot be done using WordStar alone. It's much easier to edit smaller files than large ones, and you can avoid DISK FULL errors as well. If you will have a very ling document, you can enter and edit the document in pieces, keeping each in a separate file, and then use MailMerge to combine them into a disk file or a printed document.

The tips and traps in this section show you how to combine more than one file in a document.

Tip

You can insert the entire contents of a file into a document with the .FI command even if the file is on a different disk than the master document file.

The file insert command, .FI, tells MailMerge to print the entire contents of a certain file. Figure 1 has an .FI command on it that is used to insert a particular name, address, and phone number into a document.

The .FI command is written as follows:

.FI file name

The file to be inserted can be on a different disk from the master document. In that case, follows the file name with the command CHANGE. For example, to insert a file named outst.dis, which is on a different disk than your master document, use the command.

.FI outst.dis CHANGE

When MailMerge reaches this command, it will pause and display the following message:

Insert diskette with file outst.dis, then press RETURN.

Once the file has been read from the disk, you will be asked to reinsert the disk with the master document file.

The name of the file to be inserted can be a variable value as in the example in Figure 1. MailMerge will replace the variable name with its current value, and then insert the file with that name.

Tip

You can nest files within one another, up to seven files deep.

You can nest files with MailMerge. This means that a file named in the .FI command can contain the .FI command itself; MailMerge will begin inserting the first file into the document, stop and insert the second file at the .FI command, and then return to finish inserting the first file.

Up to seven files may be inserted, one within another; if you try to nest more files than this you will get an error message and the eighth .FI command will be ignored.

Tip

You can chain - print any number of files, one after another.

Suppose you have three files that you would like to combine into one document, with consecutive page numbers and no page breaks. At the bottom of the first file insert the .FI command naming the second file, and at the bottom of the second file insert the .FI command naming the third file. The files will be printed in a chain, one after the other.

Before you print these files, you should remove any dot commands that would create page breaks or would reset the page numbers so the files will print as one document.

Formatting

When you are working with WordStar alone, the screen display shows you what your document will look when it is printed. As you edit the text, you reform paragraphs with ^B to integrate the changes into the format you have chosen for your document. If you decide to change this format, you specify the parameters and then reform each paragraph on the screen before printing.

MailMerge works quite differently; the program itself combines text with variable, data, or integrates entire files within one another, without displaying the result on the screen. Each document is formatted as it is printed, using a process called *print time line forming*. You can allow this to happen automatically or you can instruct MailMerge to vary the format of a document to your specifications.

The following tips and traps explain how print time line forming operates, and show you how to make changes to generate documents in exactly the format you need.

Tip

MailMerge reforms paragraphs automatically when variable data is inserted into a master document.

The default setting for print time line formatting is DIS, which stands for discretionary. When you use MailMerge in this mode to generate documents with variable data such as form letters, the paragraphs are reformed as the variables are replaced with their current values. Print time line forming adjusts each paragraph where text is inserted, so that the margins, line spacing, justification, and other attributes of master document are preserved.

Trap

Page breaks can occur differently than shown on the screen when variable data is inserted into a master document.

If you are using MailMerge to print a multipage document that will have variable text inserted, the page breaks indicated on the screen are based on the lengths of the variable names you have used. When these variables are replaced with data, print time line forming reforms each paragraph, as explained in the preceding tip. Depending on the length of the inserted text, the page breaks can occur either before or after those you see on the screen. The next tip explains how to control the position of a page break.

Tip

When you use MailMerge to print a multipage document including variable text, use the .CP command to prevent awkward page breaks.

As explained in the trap above, when variable data is inserted into a master document, the position of the page breaks can change. You can prevent pages from breaking in inappropriate places by using a conditional page break, the .CP command, which starts to new page when the number of lines you specify in the command are not available on the current page.

The .CP command is actually a WordStar command, not a MailMerge command.

Trap

MailMerge may split parts of inserted data that should not be separated.

There are many common expressions that include spaces or hyphens and which should not be split at the end of a line of text. For example, "Mr. Evans" should be printed together on one line, not separated at the space, and "(803)254 - 8216" should not be split at the hyphen. When print time line forming is in the default mode, these expressions may not be handled correctly if they fall at the end of a line of text. The two different ways to prevent these expressions from being separated are discussed in the following two tips.

> **Tip**
>
> *If you want a paragraph to be reformed when it is printed, but do not want a particular space to be placed at the end of a line of text, use a non - break space (^PO) when the data is entered.*

Because MailMerge formats paragraphs while a document is printed without displaying the results on the screen, you don't have a chance to make changes in the format of an individual document before it is printed. As explained in the preceding trap, you could end up with "Mr" at the end of one line and "Evans" on the line below.

You can tell MailMerge not to separate the parts of a particular data item, even when it occurs in a paragraph that should be reformed. Just use non - break space when you enter the variable data, either as an item in a data file record or as the response to an .AV prompt on the screen. To keep "Mr. Evans" from being split type ^PO in the space.

The screen display will show ^O between the words, and MailMerge will not separate them when the document is printed.

> **Tip**
>
> *If you do not want MailMerge to reform paragraphs when your document is printed, turn print time line forming off with the .PF OFF command.*

Figure 5 shows a form letter that includes a small table of names and telephone numbers. The phone numbers outside of the local area include area codes, while the local numbers do not. It is important to keep each telephone number on one line, and those numbers with area codes included will extend into the right margin of the letter.

If print time line forming is operating, the letter will print as shown in Figure 6, with the longer phone numbers split at the hyphen. You can prevent this by turning print time line forming off for this part of the letter. Figure 7 shows how this is done.

As you can see, print time line forming is controlled with .PF commands. To turn it off, insert

```
.PF OFF
```

on the line above the text that should not be reformatted. After the table, insert the command

```
.PF DIS
```

to return print time line forming to the default mode, so the closing paragraph will be reformed by MailMerge when the letter is printed.

```
. OP
. DF   netwk.dta
. RV   last, title, first, coname, street, city, state, zip
. CS
. DM   This letter is addressed to &last&, &first&.
. AV   "Contact 1 :    Name:" name1
. AV   "                  Street Address:" add1
. AV   "                  City, State Zip:", add2
. AV   "                  Phone:" phone1
. AV   "Contact 2: Name: ", name2
. AV   "                  Street Address:" add3
. AV   "                  City, State Zip:" add4
. AV   "                  Phone:", phone2
&title& &first& &last&
&coname/O&
&street&
&city&, &state& &zip&
Dear &title& &zip&
We are pleased that you will be working with us  as part of our
information-sharing network. Here are two of the people who will also be
involved in your potion of the project:
&name&                  &add1&                &phone1&
                        &add2&
&name2&                 &add3&                &phone2&
                        &add4&
Please call me at (415) 942-1100 if you have any questions.
                                            Sincerely,

                                            Jim Brown
                                            Network coordinator
. PA
```

Fig. 5. Document with variable names close to right margin

Trap

If you use the .PI command to include an entire file in a document, you can end up with parts of your document justified differently on the right - hand side.

Mr. William Bennett
1257 lincoln Place
Conford, Massachusetts 02773

Dear Mr. Sonnett,

We are pleased that you will be working with us as part of our information-sharing network. Here are two of the people who will also be involved in your portion of the project:

Anne Hobson	P.O. Box 2714 Loncoln, MA 02566	627-2943
John Gravett 6754	267 Broadway Antloch, CA 94972	(415)921-

Please call as at (415)942-1100 if you have any questions.

Sincerely,

Jim Brown
Network Coordinator

Fig. 6. Inserted text split between two lines

When you use the .FI command to tell Mail/Merge to include an entire file, either inserted within another file or chain - printed after it, you need to be careful about the justification of your document. When print time line forming is in the default DIS mode, MailMerge right justifies the inserted text according to the format of its own file, whether or not this matches your master document. You could end up with a right - justified insert within a document with a ragged edge, or vice versa. The next tip explains the commands you can use to prevent this problem.

Tip

You can control the justification of inserted files.

As explained in the preceding trap, text that is included in a document with the .FI command will given a justified or ragged right edge depending on the format of its own file. This may or may not match the other file(s) included in the document.

You can use commands to determine the justification of an inserted file without having to reformat the file. You can tell MailMerge to make the inserted text match the rest of the document, or , for effect, print the inserted text with a different justification.

To do so, you must place two dot commands, each on its own line, above the .FI command that names the file being inserted. First, to turn print time line forming on, use

.PF ON

Then you must use the OJ command, which stands for output justification. To give the inserted text a justified right edge, use

.OJ ON

```
. OP
. DF  netwk, dta
. RW last, title, first conam,e street, city, state, zip
. CS
. DM This letter is addressed to &last&, &first&.
. AV    "Contact 1:    Name:", name1
. AV    "                 Street Address:", add1
. AV    "                 City, State Zip:", add2
. AV    "                 Phone:",  phone1
. AV    "Contact 2:    Name:", name2
. AV    "                 Street Address:" add3
. AV    "                 City, State zip:" add4
. AV    "                 Phone:", phone2
&title& &first& &last&
&coname/O&
&street&
&city&, &state& &zip&
Dear &title& &last&
We are pleased that you will be working with us as part of our information-sharing
network. Here are two of the people who will also be involved in your portion of
the project:
. PF OFF
&name 1&                    &add1&              &phone1&
                            &add2&
&name2&                     &add3&              &phone2&
                            &add4&
. PF DIS
Please call us at (415)942-1100 if you have any questions,
                                                Sincerely,

                                                Jim Brown
                                                Network Coordinator
. PA
```

Fig. 7. Preventing inserted text from being split between two - lines

To produce a ragged right edge, use

.OJ OFF

Once the inserted file has been printed with the justification you have chosen, you need to return MailMerge to the default settings, so the rest of your document will be formatted correctly. Follow the .FI command with

.OJ DIS

.PF DIS

to reestablish the default settings.

Trap

Documents printed by MailMerge may have awkward line spacing.

When you are working with WordStar alone, you have the option of inserting hyphens when you reform paragraphs. Unless you have turned hyphen - help off, WordStar pauses and asks if you want a word hyphenated. You can then choose to insert a soft hyphen, which will be printed only if breaking up the word will create more even line spacing.

Since MailMerge reforms paragraphs while it prints each document and doesn't display the text on the screen you cannot insert soft hyphens as each paragraph is reformed. This can result in a less finished look for your final document. See the following tip for a way to insert soft hyphens.

Tip

To create the most even the line spacing possible in a MailMerge document, insert soft hyphens manually in your file.

As the preceding trap explains, MailMerge does not pause to give you the option of hyphenating words that occur at the end of a line of text. If you want your document to have the most line spacing possible, you can insert soft hyphens manually. A soft hyphen will be printed only if dividing the word in that position would result in more even line spacing.

Figure 8 shows two paragraphs printed by MailMerge. The first paragraph has no soft hyphens, and you can see that it has a very ragged right - had edge. The second paragraph has soft hyphens inserted in several of the words; the right margin appears much smoother.

> This paragraph was printed using MailMerge. Several variables of different lengths were inserted into the text no soft hyphens were inserted, and print time line forming was allowed to form this paragraph as it was printed. The right-hand margin that results is rather uneven.
>
> This paragraph was also printed using MailMerge, with variables of different lengths inserted into the text. This time soft hyphens were included in several words, so print time line forming was able to hyphenate these words if they occurred last on a line. You can see the results.

Fig. 8. Using soft hyphens in a MailMerge document

To produce a soft hyphen when the hyphen key is pressed, enter ^OE to turn on the soft hyphen toggle. Once this is done, all you have to do to type a soft hyphen is press the hyphen key, if you need to type a hard hyphen (which will always print, regardless of the position of the word), you must press ^P and then the hyphen key. When you have finished inserting soft hyphens, enter ^OE again to reset the hyphen key to a hard hyphen.

How can you know when inserting soft hyphens would be helpful? Try printing a sample copy of your document, with values inserted for the variables. If the right edge is very ragged, you can go back and insert soft hyphens into the appropriate words in your master document.

Conditional Printing

If you have version 3.31 or higher of MailMerge, you can use the conditional printing commands to produce customised documents. These commands allow you to print selectively: to vary the contents of a document, depending on the values of variable data, or to print a document only for selected records in your data file.

The conditional printing commands tell MailMerge to take variable data, either from a data file (accessed by the .DF and .RV commands), from a keyboard entry (in response to the .AV command) or from the document itself (given in the .SV command), and test them against data specified in the conditional printing command. Portions of a document, or even the entire document, will only be printed if the variable data passes the test.

The following tips and traps show you how to write conditional printing commands, how to structure the testing conditions, and how to use this feature to generate documents customised to your needs.

> **Tip**
>
> *You can instruct MailMerge to include a particular paragraph (or set of consecutive paragraphs) in certain documents and not in others.*

Figure 9 shows a form letter that will be printed for each record in a data file. The third paragraph will only be included in those letters addressed to people who do not live in California. Note the command preceding that paragraph.

.IF &state& = "CA" GOTO

This is a conditional printing command. The .IF command tells MailMerge to compare the current value of the variable state with given data, "CA". The variable name must be enclosed in ampersands, as shows, and the given data is enclosed in quotes. If there is a perfect match, MailMerge will skip over the next between this command and the end market, .EF, and continue printing with the line following this market. If the data does not match, all of the text will be printed.

The general form for the .IF command is:

.IF &variable name& = "data to be matched" GOTO

(text)

.EF

```
. OP
. DF members, dta
. RV title, first, last, coname, street, city, state, zip

&titles& &first& &last&
&coname/O&
&street&
&city&, &state& &zip&

Dear &title& &last&,

One of our most important goals for the upcoming year is to improve the quality
of the support services offered to our members. Our first step has to be to find out
what services would be most useful to you.

Please take a few minutes to fill out the enclosed questionnaire, and return it is us
in the envelope provided.

. IF &state& "CA" GOTO
We are particularly interested in learning how we can best serve the needs of our
members who, like you, do not live in California. Please be sure to fill out the last
section of the questionnaire, headed "for Out-of-State Members Only.

Thank you very such for your assistance.

                                        Sincerely,


                                        Fred Williams
                                        President
. PA
```

Fig. 9. Using conditional printing commands

This command structure tells MailMerge to omit the included text if the current value of the variable matches the given data. Each .IF command must be used with a corresponding .EF to indicate the end of the text that may be omitted.

There is a second conditional printing command, .EX which is used in a structure similar to .IF. For example;

.EX &state& = "CA" GOTO

(text)

.EF

This command has the opposite effect of .IF; the .EX command tells MailMerge to print the included text if the current value of the variable matches the given data and to omit it if there is not a match. In this example, the text would be included in letters addressed to California, and skipped for any other state.

If you think of GOTO as meaning "skip this text" you can think of the .IF command as saying "If the condition is met, skip this text." Similarly the .EX command can be thought of an "Except if the condition is met, skip this text."

Trap

MailMerge does not consider the upper and lowercase forms of the same letter to be a match.

Consider the conditional printing command used in Figure 9;

.IF &state& = "CA" GOTO

This is intended to instruct MailMerge not to print the paragraph about out - of - state members in letters to members who live in California. If a data record contains CA in the state field, the value will match the given dta, and the paragraph will be skipped. However, if the state field contains Ca instead, MailMerge will not accept it as a match, and the out - of - state paragraph will be included in the letter.

There are two ways to avoid this trap. You can check each record in your data file to be sure all California entries have both letters capitalised and then use the conditional printing command as shows above. Alternatively you can reward the command, using a complex condition that covers possible abbreviations for California:

.IF &state& = "CA" .OR. &state& = "Ca" GOTO

Complex conditions are covered in detail later in this section.

Tip

You can print conditionally for a range of values of the variable data, as well as for a perfect match.

Mailmerge can compare the current value of a variable to given data in several different ways. All conditional printing commands have the same general form:

.IF (or .EX) expression GOTO

The expression contains three parts:

&variable name& comparision character (s) "given data"

The comparison character tells MailMerge what kind of relationship you want between the value of the variable and the given data. For example,

.IF &city& < > "San Francisco" GOTO

tells MailMerge to skip the following text (down to the .EF marker) if the current value of the variable city is not Sen Francisco. Similarly

.IF &zip& <"90000" GOTO

tells MailMerge to skip down to the .EF marker if the current value of zip is less than 90000.

These are the comparision characters you can use in conditional printing commands:

=	equal to
<>	not equal to
<	less than
>	greater than
< = or = <	less than or equal to
> = or = >	greater than or equal to

You can use all of these comparisons with words as well as with numbers: MailMerge considers one letter less than another if it is earlier in alphabetical order. Words are compared based on their first letter, so the command

.IF &lastname& < = "F" GOTO

tells MailMerge to skip the following text for last names that begin with the letters from A to F.

Trap

If some of your data values begin with uppercase letters and others with lowercase letters, your conditional printing commands will not work correctly.

The command

.IF &category&> "D" GOTO

will skip the following text (down to the .EF marker) for categories that begin with uppercase letters E through Z, as expected, but it will also skip the text for any category that begins with a lowercase letter. This happens because MailMerge makes comparisons using the ASCII sequence, which is standard in the computer industry. Each letter is assigned as ASCII code number that is used to make comparisons. The uppercase letters are assigned smaller ASCII code numbers than the lowercase letters, so any lowercase letter is considered greater than an uppercase letter.

Whenever you have a nonnumeric variable that will be used in a conditional printing command, be sure the data values are entered consistently, with the first letters wither all lowercase or all capitalised, so you can avoid this trap.

Tip

You can insert files conditionally into your documents.

The file insert command, .FI, discussed in detail earlier in this chapter, is a very useful tool for handling boilerplate text. You can keep each piece of bolierplate in its own file, and use this command to insert the text as needed in any document you are writing. MailMerge also allows you to insert these files conditionally, depending on the current value of the variable data.

Let's say you have a file, outst.txt, which must be inserted in any contract with a party from another state. Assuming your company is located in California, and that the state where the contract party resides is spelled out in the state variable, you could include this command structure in each contract that you write:

```
.IF &state& = "California" GOTO
.FI outst.txt
.EF
```

The text in the file outst.txt will be included in contracts with parties residing outside California, and omitted otherwise.

Tip

You can print a document for selected records in a data file.

Ordinarily, the .DF and .RV commands tell MailMerge to print a copy of a document for each record in your data file. With the conditional printing commands, you can produce documents for specifically selected records by including the entire text within the conditional command structure.

Suppose you have a mailing list data file, mlist.dta, that includes people from several cities, and you would like tc send a letter to the people who live in Los Angeles. At the top of the letter, place the .DF and .RV commands as usual:

```
.DF mlist. dta
.RV title, first,last, coname, street, city, state, zip
```

Below these commands, and before the text of the letter, place the conditional printing command:

```
.IF &city& <> "Los Angeles" GOTO
```

Now enter the entire text of the letter. Follow the text with the .PA command as usual for a repetitive document (see the first section of this chapter). Place the .EF marker at the very end of the file, after the .PA command.

This way, your entire letter has become the text to be included or omitted, depending on whether or not the city in the current data record is Los Angeles. Nothing at all will be printed if a data record contains any other entry in the city field.

Tip

You can use more than one comparison in a conditional printing command.

Sometimes one comparison is not enough to precisely specify in particular range of data values. Suppose you would like to include a certain paragraph in letters to people who live in zip code areas from 02368 through 02760, inclusive. You can use a complex condition such as the following.

.EX &zip& >= "02368" AND &zip& < = "02760" GOTO

The text that follows this command (down to the .EF marker) will be skipped if the zip code does not fall within the specified range.

The logical connector .AND. between the two conditions tells MailMerge that both conditions must be met by the current value of the variable. If the data meets one condition but not the other, it will not pass this text.

MailMerge also has another logical connector, .OR, that accepts data if it meets wither of the two conditions. This time, suppose you want a particular paragraph included in letters to people who live in Los Angeles or in San Francisco, and omitted from letters addressed to any other city. You can use the .OR. connector as follows:

.EX &city& = "Los Angeles" .OR &city& = "San Francisco" GOTO

Now only one of the conditions must be true of MailMerge to include the text.

Note the form of these complex conditional commands:

.EX expression .AND. expression GOTO

.IF expression .OR expression GOTO

Both the .AND and .OR connectors must be surrounded by periods, as shows here, and must be in uppercase letters. Each expression is a comparision between the current value of a variable and given data, and each expression must be complete, as explained in the following trap.

Trap

If a complex conditional command is not complete, you will get an error message and the command will be ignored.

A complex conditional command, explained in the preceding tip, is written in this form:

.IF (or .EX) expression .AND. (or .OR.) expression GOTO

Each of the expression must have three parts:

&variable name& comparision character "given data"

MailMerge cannot interpret a conditional command unless each expression includes all of these components. For example, the command

.IF &state& = "CA" .OR. "Ca" GOTO

would produce an error message because the expression that follows the .OR. connector is incomplete. It needs to be written as

.IF &state& = "CA" .OR. &state& = "Ca" GOTO

with a complete expression on each side of the logical connector.

Trap

If you have one conditional printing command nested within the structure of another, MailMerge might skip to the wrong .EF marker.

Consider this portion of a letter, which includes two nested conditional printing commands:

.IF &state& <> "California" GOTO
(first part of text for California letters)

.IF &city& <> "San Francisco" GOTO
(text for San Francisco letters)

.EF
(second part of text for California letters)
.EF

If a letter is being printed for a person who does not live in California, the first .IF command tells MailMerge to skip text down to an .EF end marker. However, the first .EF in the document marks the end of the San Francisco text, not the end of the California text. MailMerge will include the second part of the text intended for California letters in letters to other states. See the following tip for a way to get around this problem.

Tip

If you have one conditional printing command nested within the structure of another, use labels to tell MailMerge which end marker corresponds to each conditional command.

The preceding trap shows an example of nested conditional printing commands and explains the problem that can result. You can place one conditional printing command within another and have it work correctly if you use labels to indicate which .EF marker corresponds to each of the conditional commands.

Let's add labels to the example above, so it will print letters as intended:

.IF &state& <> "California" GOTO end CA
(first part of text for California letters)

.IF &city& <> "San Francisco" GOTO end SF
(text for San Francisco letters)

.EF endSF
(second part of text for California letters)

.EF and CA

A different label follows each GOTO, and the identical label is placed after the .EF marker that corresponds, to each conditional printing command. When MailMerge sees a label, it skips all text until it finds the .EF marker with the same label. Now letters to states other than California will not include any part of the California text.

A label can be from 1 to 20 characters long. It must begin with a letter; after the first character you can use letters, numbers, or a hyphen, but no other punctuation and no spaces. Leave one space between GOTO (or .EF) and the label. The .EF marker must have exactly the same label as its corresponding conditional command.

16

Flowchart Language I

When we solve a problem with the definition of an algorithm, we must communicate that algorithm using a language. So far we have seen the use of three different languages for the expression of algorithms.

Computer language is used to communicate; we may be communicating an algorithm to other people or we may be communicating it to a computer. The type of language used for this process depends on the purpose of the communication. In the final instance we wish that a computer should execute the algorithm. Since the only language understood by a computer is its machine language, an algorithm must ultimately to expressed in that language. However, we have seen that a translator can convert an algorithm written in other languages into one written in machine language. These languages are more comprehensible to a person than machine language so that it is easier to understand a program when it is being written and when it is being corrected or changed.

If a programmer encodes algorithms in a machine-level language he has to be very cognizant of the organisation of the computer. Instead of writing "A ← + C X D," he has to be concerned with the computer's accumulator, and whether the arithmetic has to be performed on integers or floating-point numbers. These computer details tend to obscure the procedure used in the algorithm; therefore, we often prefer to use languages that omit these details and concentrate mainly on the solution procedure. Such languages are called *high-level languages.* They are also called *procedure oriented languages* (POLs for short). If a system program is available to translate an algorithm written in a POL into the same algorithm written in machine language, we an use that POL to communicate the algorithm to the computer.

If we are going to communicate an algorithm to the computer, it must be input via a machine-readable medium. The usual input is via punched cards or typewritten lines, so most POLs are designed around these. This means that the language may use only a restricted number of characters-usually the decimal digits 0-9, the upper-case letters A-Z, and about twelve to twenty-seven other special characters. Furthermore, the algorithm in a POL must be a sequence of cards or lines. We can view the cards as a sequence of lines-or a long string of characters. Either way, the input appears as one long block of characters.

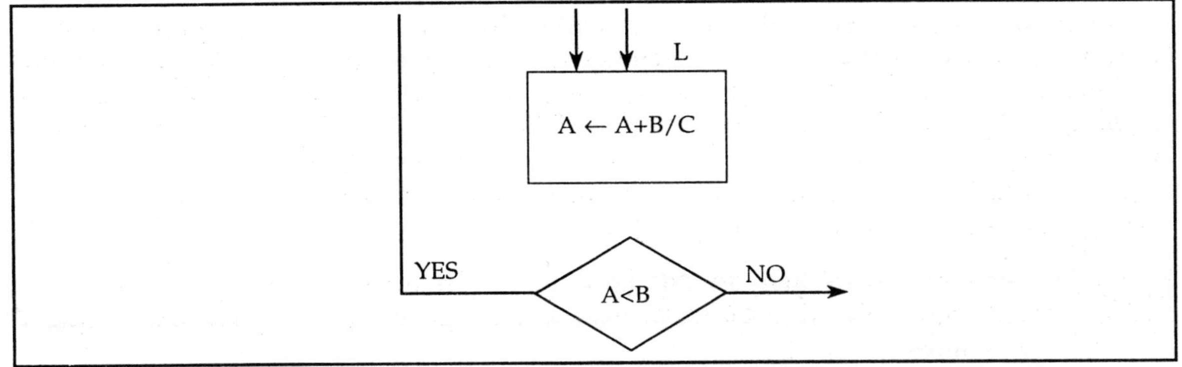

Fig. 1. A loop

Even though we may break up the string of characters by judicious use of cards with blanks or comments on them (much as we use paragraphs in this book to break up the text into self-contained sub-blocks) a long string of characters does not display the flow structure of the algorithm very clearly. For example, the loop in Figure 1 is fairly obvious because it is written in a flowchart language. However, in a language that is written as one sequence of characters or lines (a *linear* language), a loop will have to be encoded by the use of a *transfer* instruction equivalent to the machine language BRNCH. "GO TO" is the PL/I equivalent of a branch instruction. In PL/I the loop would be written as either L:A=A+B/C;IF A<B THEN GO TO L;

or L: A = A + B/C;

IF A<B THEN GO TO L;

The latter form has been made a little clearer by the use of spaces and indentation, but it is still necessary for a person to search for the label L to determine that this is a program loop.

We will use flowcharts for stating algorithms in this book. It is relatively easy for a person to follow and to change a procedure expressed as a flowchart. The conversion of flowchart programs to programs written in linear languages is straightforward and is covered in the supplementary texts on specific languages.

Common POL linear languages include FORTRAN, ALGOL, PL/I and BASIC. Each has slightly different rules for expressing common operations such as assignments and branches. (You will have to refer to a manual for a particular language to find the specific rules for that language.) In this chapter we are going to introduce some precise rules for writing programs in a flowchart language. Since there is no flowchart language that is universally accepted, our rules may differ from rules found in other books. What is important is that you be consistent in whatever rules you adopt. Then your programs will be unambiguous and it will be easy for you to convert your flowchart programs into programs in the POL that you are using.

Flowcharts consist of symbols connected by flowlines. We will call the symbols "boxes" because we will be using the word "symbol" in other contexts. The shape of each box indicates the type of statement that appears inside. In this chapter we will discuss the boxes for assignment, input, output, connection, and decision. These have already been used informally; here we will give rules for their use. The purpose of these rules is to allow us to write algorithms unambiguously. We will introduce additional types of statements (i.e., shapes of boxes) that make programming easier.

Two elementary boxes that do not need to be discussed further are (START) and (STOP). START must appear just once in any complete program, while STOP may appear any number of times.

Assignment Statements

Assignment is the operation of calculating the value of an expression and storing that value in a designated cell in memory. An assignment statement should be written in the form

"lefthand side" ← "righthand side"

where "lefthand side" is the name of a variable - that is, the identification of a cell in memory - and "righthand side" is an expression that can be evaluated. Valid assignment statements include, for example,

A ← 17.5
B ← A X 5.3 - 21.43
Z ← (X + Y) X Z

The following are *not* valid assignment statements:

5.1 ← A (5.1 is a constant, not a cell in memory)
B + C ← X(B + C is not a cell in memory)
X ← (Righthand side is missing)
X ← Y X Z (Arrow assignment operator is missing)

An assignment box is a rectangular box that an contain one or more assignment statements, as shown in Figure 2. This box contains statements that exchange the values of A and B. The statements inside the box are executed sequentially in the order given. Note that only one box is executed at a time. This leads to an important restriction on assignment boxes; namely, only one flowline may *leave* the box. This path indicates the unique path to be followed after each assignment statement inside the box has been executed. Several flowlines may enter an assignment box, as shown in Figure 3. Box 4 is executed immediately after either Box 2 or Box 3 has been executed.

TEMP A
A ← B
B ← TEMP

Fig. 2. Assignment box

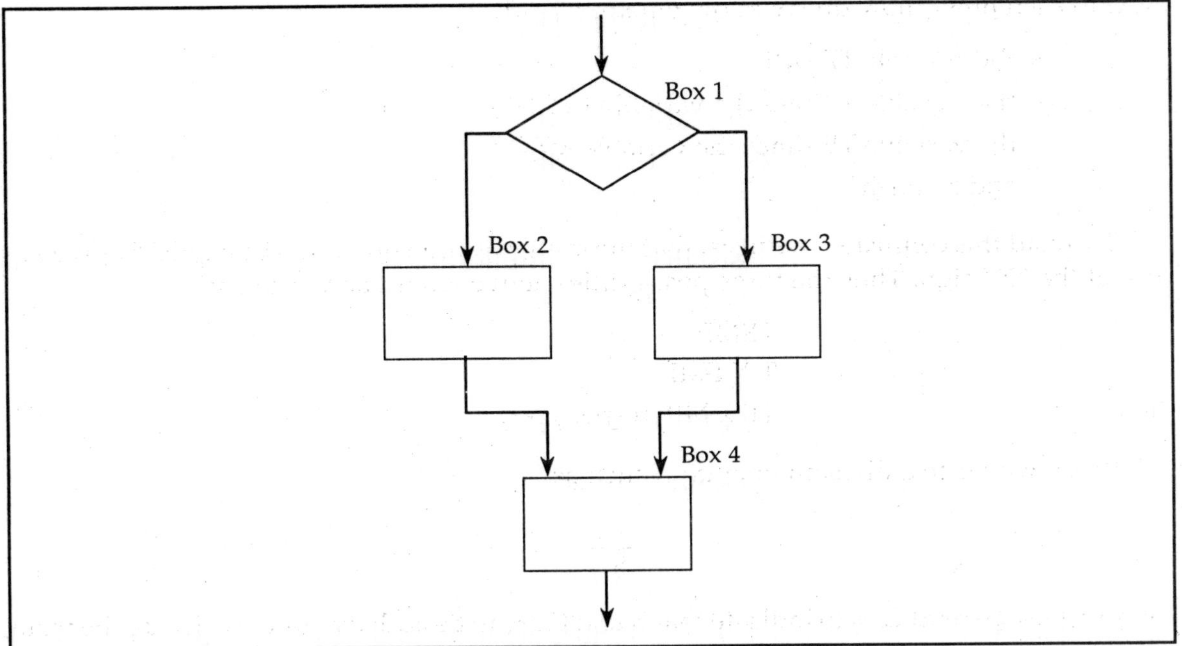

Fig. 3. Two flowlines to an assignment box

Each assignment statement has an expression on the right-hand side. In science we are accustomed to writing expressions in a variety of ways, for example

(i) $\dfrac{A + 5B}{16.4 + C}$

(ii) $(x^2 + y^2)^{1/2}$

(iii) $\dfrac{-B + \sqrt{B^2 - 4AC}}{2A}$

Typical computer input devices do not provide for superscripts such as B^2 or built-up fractions such as $\frac{B}{A}$. Therefore POLs do not include them. To make our flowchart language reasonably close to POLs, we will similarly restrict our expressions. For this reason, we must introduce special symbols for superscripting and division. These symbols are ↑ and /, respectively. Thus we write B^2 as B ↑ 2 and $\frac{A}{B}$.as A/B.*

In the expression given in example (i) above, we also used one other common mathematical abbreviation: we write "5B" for "5 times B." In mathematics we can also write "AB" for "A times B." Unfortunately, we will be using variable names with more than one character. For example, we have already used "TEMP" as a name for a temporary location in many earlier examples. If we allow a person to indicate multiplication by writing two variable names next to each other, how do we know whether TEMP is

the variable TEMP?

the variable T times the variable EMP?

the variable TE times the variable MP?

and so forth.

To avoid this confusion, we insist that the multiplication operation be explicitly given by use of the "X" sign. Thus the three possibilities above would be written as

TEMP

T X EMP

and TE x MP, respectively.

When we write a division operation such as

$$\frac{A}{B + C}$$

we must use parentheses to indicate that B and C are to be added before we divide the result into A. Thus we write A/(B + C). If we wanted to say

$$\frac{A}{B}+C$$

we could write (A/B) + C.

When we first learn arithmetic, we learn that 4 - 3 + 2 means (4 - 3) + 2, which is 3. That is, we learn that we do the left-hand operation first. If we had done the right-hand operation first, we would have 4 - (3 + 2) = 4 - 5 = -1. If we want to override the left-hand-first rule, we use parentheses. Thus, A - (B - C) means "take C from B, and then take the result from A."

For multiplication, we rules of arithmetic differ slightly. A X B + C is the same as (A X B) + C, but A + B X C is the same as A + (B X C). That is, multiplication is "more important" than addition and subtraction, so multiplications are done before additions and subtractions. The rule "multiplication is more important than addition and subtraction" saves us having

* We introduced ÷ for the division operation. We will delay further discussion of the differences between ÷ and / until Section 16.2.

to use parentheses in many cases. Although (A X B) - (C X D) is correct, it is faster and simpler to write A X B - C X D. Formally we say that "multiplication takes *precedence over addition* and subtraction. "We will think of division as being related to multiplication much as subtraction is related to addition. Subtraction and addition have the same *precedence level;* that is, neither takes precedence over the other, so if no parentheses are present, the operations are done from left to right. The same is true for consecutive multiplications and divisions.

Examples

The following pairs are equivalent :

A + B - C + D = ((A + B) - C) + D

A - (B + X) - Y = (A - (B + X) - Y

A X B / C X D = ((A X B)/C) X D

(= $\frac{A+B}{C} \times D$ in conventional form)

A X B / (C X D) = (A X B) / (C X D)

(= $\frac{A \times B}{C \times D}$ in conventional form)

Both multiplication and division have a higher precedence than addition and subtraction, so multiplications and divisions are done before additions and subtractions.

Examples

The following pairs are equivalent:

A X B - C / D = (A X B) - (C / D)

X - Y / (U - V) = X - (Y / (U - V))

(= $X - \frac{Y}{U-V}$ in conventional form)

A X B - C X D + F = ((A X B) - (C X D) + F

A X (B + C) / D - (E - F) / G

A X T1 / D - (E - F) / G

Fig. 4. First reduction

Note that after the multiplications have been done in the last example, the additions and subtractions are done from left to right.

We can visualise the evaluation of an arithmetic expression as a series of reductions, each consisting of the execution of one of the arithmetic operations to form an intermediate result. If we start with the expression A X (B + C)/D - (E - F)/G, the first reduction is to evaluate B + C to get an intermediate result, say T1. This is shown in Figure 4. Thus the single assignment statement

T ← A X (B + C)/D - (E - F)/G

is equivalent to the pair

T1 ← B + C

T ← A X T1/D (E - F)/G

The next reduction consists of the evaluation of E - F to get another intermediate result, say T2. This is shown in Figure 5. Thus the assignment statement above is equivalent to

T1 ← B + C

T2 ← E - F

T ← A X T1/D - T2/G

These reductions continue until there is only one operation left to perform. At this time the original assignment statement has been replaced by a sequence of single-operator assignment statements. For the above example, we get

T1 ← B + C

T2 ← E - F

T3 ← A X T1

T4 ← T3/D

T5 ← T2/G

T ← T4 - T5

A X T1 / D - (E - F) / G

A X T1 / D - T2 / G

Fig. 5. Next reduction

Fig. 6. Representation of a single reduction

The process can be represented by pictorially as follows. A single reduction is diagrammed as a triplet with three lines joining it to its reduced form. This is shown for the reduction T1 ← A + B in Figure 6. In this Figure , A and B are the operands for the operation +T1 is the operand that results from this operation. A similar Figure can be drawn for T2 ← E - F. The next operation is T3 ← A X T1. The first operand for the multiplication operation is A; the second is T1, which is represented by the diagram in Figure 6. Consequently we represent the steps T1 ← B + C and T3 ← A X T1 by the diagram in Figure 7.

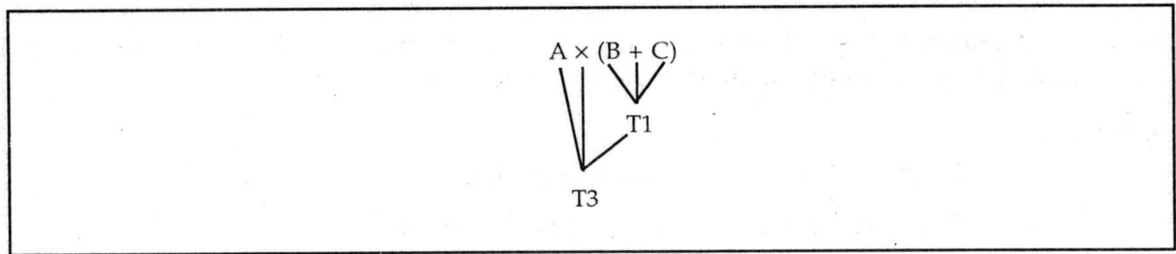

Fig. 7. Representation of two reductions

Continuing in this way, we finally represent the evaluation of the expression by Figure 8. This diagram displays the sequence of execution of the operations. In fact, it shows that there are several possible sequences. T1 must be evaluated before T3 and T4 can be formed; T2 must be evaluated before T5 can be formed. However, we could evaluate T1, T3 and T4 before or after T2 and T5 are formed. Thus we could do the evaluation in the order T1, T3, T4, T2, T5, T, or in the order T2, T5, T1, T3, T4, T. Other sequences are also possible in this example. The choice of sequence does not affect the value of the expression as long as restrictions implied by Figure 8 (and hence by the original expression) are obeyed. The compiler will usually choose an order that has a short machine-language equivalent.*

We introduced the "up-arrow" symbol, ↑, for exponentiation.

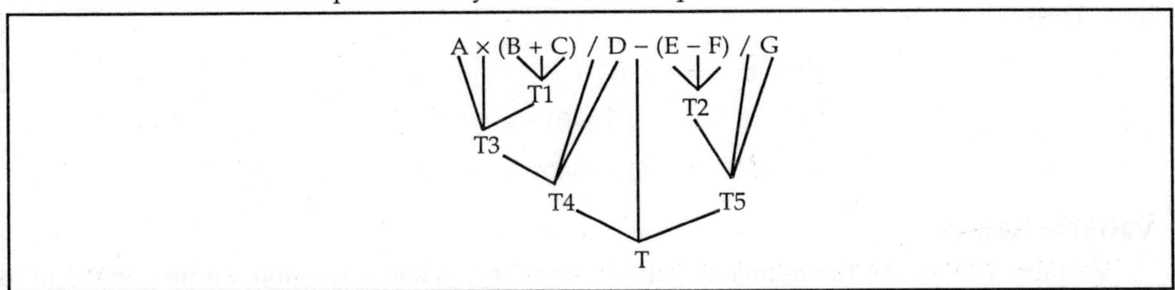

Fig. 8. Representation of the evaluation of the expression

---

* Note that the complier could choose whether to evaluate A + B + C as (A + B) + C or as A + (B + C). In Chapter 6 it wil be seen that these may give ifferent results because of numerical errors. Therefore compilers should use the left-to-right rule and evaluate (A + B) + C. Most do.

Thus B ↑ 2 is our way of writing B^2. X ↑ 0.5 is our way of writing $X^{½}$. This is mathematically the same as $\sqrt{X}$. The exponentiation operation must be assigned rules so that it fits in with the scheme for the other arithmetic operations. What does ↑ 2 X C mean? If we write this in the conventional mathematical way as A^2 X C, we know that it is (A^2) X C; that is we square A and multiply it by C. Similarly P + Q ↑ 2 is our way of writing P + Q^2, in which we square Q and add the result to P. We use the rule that ↑ has a higher precedence than multiplication and addition. Similarly, it has a higher precedence than division and subtraction. Thus we amend our rules to require than in the absence of parentheses, exponentiations are done first, then multiplications and divisions, and finally additions and subtractions. Operations at the same level of precedence are done from left to right.

Examples

A ↑ B + C X D = (A ↑ B) + (C X D)

X - Y / Z ↑ P X Q = X - ((Y / (Z ↑ P) X Q)

A ↑ B ↑ C = (A ↑ B) ↑ C

(Some POLs obey exponentiation operations from right to left; that is, A ↑ B ↑ C is the same as A ↑ (B ↑ C), which is equivalent to the mathematical expression A^{B^C}. We have adopted the left-to-right rule for consistency with the other operations.)

Binary and Unary Operators

Usually the operators +, -, x, / and ↑ are used with two operands - that is, two variables or constants that provide the data for the operation. Therefore, they are called *binary operators.* The two operators + and - can be used in a special way with only one operand. For example, we might write Z ← -X or A ← +B. We call the operators + and - *unary operators* when they are used in this way. (Binary is also called *diadic* and unary is also called *monadic.*) The unary arithmetic operators take precedence over all of the binary operators and must be performed first. Thus,

-A + B = (-A) + B = B - A

A ↑ - B = A ↑ (-B) = A^{-8}

C / +D = C / (+D) = C/D

Variable Names

Variable names are the names of cells in memory. When a variable name is used in an expression, the contents of the cell with that name is used. Many POLs restrict the length of variable names. Some FORTRAN compilers, for example, allow six or less characters starting with a letter and containing only letters or digits. Because space inside boxes is usually an important consideration in flow-charts, we will follow the same restrictions in the rest of this book.

Constants

We have been writing expressions using variable names and numbers but have never given any definite rules for valid ways to write numbers. We will allow ourselves to write numbers in the natural way. For example,

523	-1.25
10.74	$-3_{10}11$
-27.1	$0.2517_{10} - 12$
+3	-4

They can be signed (that is, have a plus or minus sign). They may or may not have a decimal point and can have a decimal exponent written after a subscript "10." (We assume that this character is available, as it is in ALGOL. Many languages - for example, PL/I are FORTRAN - use the character "E" instead.)

Exercises

1. Which of the following names are valid?
   (a) GOOD
   (b) BAD
   (c) A + B
   (d) 6J6
   (e) A123

2. Write the following expressions in the form allowed in our flowcharts:
   a. $\frac{A+B}{C+D}$
   *b. X^{2y}
   *c. (A + B)C
   d. $\frac{P^3+G}{4.5-\frac{A}{B}}$

3. Rewrite the following assignment statements using sequences of single arithmatic operation assignment statements such as A ← B X C. You can use as many storage cells T1, T2,... as you need.
   a. P ← Q + R X S
   b. D ← (G + H) ↑ (l/J)
   c. U ← V ↑ W X (X - Y)/(Z-U)

4. What are the possible sequences of execution of the operations in these assignment

statements?

*a. $A \leftarrow B \times C + D/E$

b. $P \leftarrow Q \uparrow (R - S) - T/U$

Questions

1. Which pairs of operators have the same precedence level?
2. Is there an operator that has a higher precedence than at lest one other operator and a lower precedence than a third?
3. Give an expression that uses both unary and binary minus operators.
4. Mathematically it does not matter if we evaluate A + B + C as (A + B) + C or as A - (B - C). Is this true for every operator?

DATA TYPES

In the statement of an algorithm we use names to refer to data. When the algorithm is encoded as a machine-language program, these names refer to memory cells. Data referred to in the algorithm usually has an implied type. For example, if we talk bout "names in the phone book," we are talking about character strings; if we talk about " a telephone number in New York City," we are talking about a seven-digit decimal number, if we talk about "the population of France," we are talking about an integer; or if we talk about "the distance between the spacecraft and earth in miles," we are talking about a real number, one we would want to represent as a floating-point number in the computer.

When we define an algorithm, we specify operations that must be performed on the data. In most cases, the type of the result will also be implied, For example, if we indicate the stop. "Find the population of North America by adding together the populations of the USA and Canada" we also know that the result is an integer. If we used the names PNA, PUSA and PCAN for populations of North America, the USA and Canada we could formally write this step as

$$PNA \leftarrow PUSA + PCAN$$

A person reading this step would know that the addition operations are to be performed with integers if he knows that the names PNA, PCAN, and so forth, refer to integer variables. There is an important difference in the use of the names in machine-language programs; they refer to cells in the memory, not to variables. The computer does not know that they represent populations. As the names of cells in memory, they do not have an associated data type. The cell PUSA can be used to store an integer, a real number in floating-point representation, a logical variable or some other data type. The type of data is "known" to the machine only by the instructions that use it.

If the variable PCAN is used in an integer addition operation, the computer knows that PCAN contains an integer. The same is true of PUSA and PNA. Let us look again at the problem and the three ways we have stated the solution.

Solution in English language	Add the populations of the USA and Canada. The result is the population of North America.	Integer data type is implied by name "population."
Solution in flowchart language	PNA ← PUSA + PCAN	Data type?
Solution in machine language	LOAD PUSA ADD PCAN	Data type implied by instructions.

To complete a statement of the solution in flowchart language we must also indicate the type of data involved. This information is needed so that a translator knows which operations to use in the machine-language version of the flowchart language. Therefore, we must declare the type of variables being used in a flowchart. This is done in *declaration statements.* We place them inside rectangular boxes with no connecting flowlines. They will be put at the top right-hand corner of our flowcharts. An example is given in Figure 9.

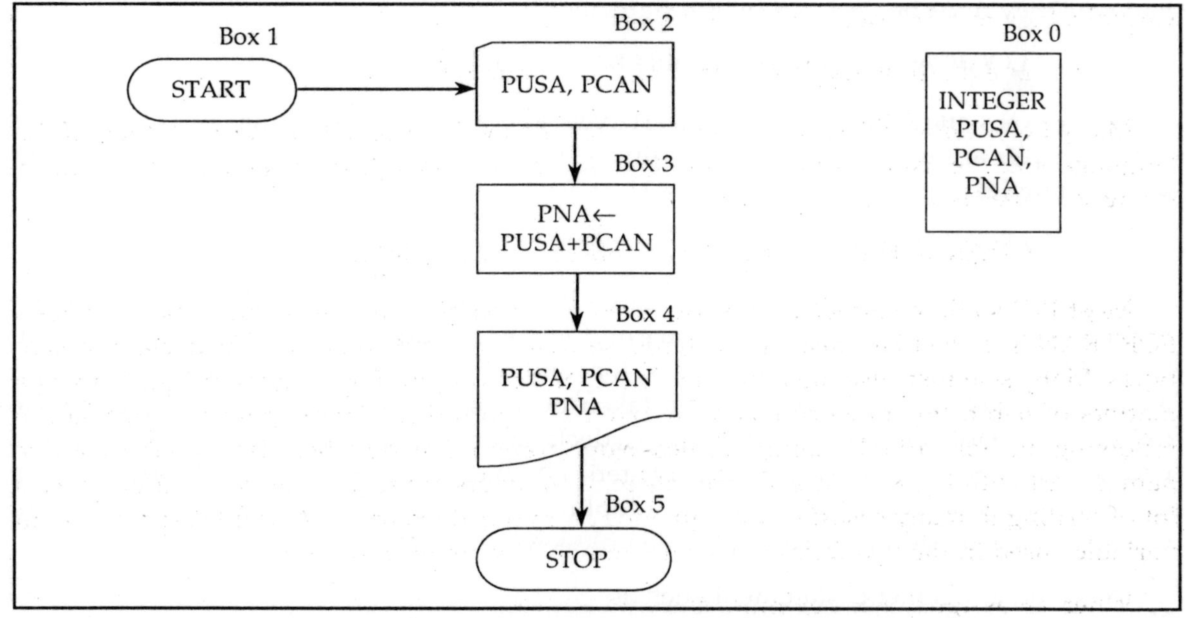

Fig 9. Flowchart showing declaration statements

Here we declare the three variables PUSA, PCAN, and PNA to be integers. With this information we can interpret the statements in the flowchart. Thus Box 2, the READ statement, tells us that the first step is to input the next two numbers from the card reader and to store them as integers in the cells PUSA and PCAN. The assignment statement in Box

3 is to be carried out with integer arithmetic, while Box 4 is to print integers.

A declaration box is never executed, since no flowlines enter it. Declaration statements are called *non-executable* statements. They tell the reader facts that apply to the whole flowchart.

Formally, our declaration box is a rectangle "on its side" - that is, taller than it is wide. It can contain statements such as

INTEGER variable 1, variable 2,.... variable n

where variable 1, variable 2, etc., are the names of variables that are to be integers. Similarly we will allow real numbers (which will be represented in floating point) to be declared by a statement such as

REAL variable rl, variable r2,.... variable rn

This ways that the variables named are to be stored in floating-point representation.

They can take on values "True" or "False". If a set of names is to be used for a logical variable, they must be declared by the statement

LOGICAL variable l1, variable l2,.... variable ln

Many POLs allow character string variables. You will become familiar with them if the language you are using has this capability. A typical declaration statement for character string variables is

CHARACTER variable *c1*, variable *c2*, ... variable *cn*

Most POLs allow variables to be declared in statements similar to these. Some POLs - FORTRAN in particular - also allow the programmer to omit some specific declarations of types. Many scientists use the letters i,j, k, l, m and n to stand for integers in equations as a matters of habit. this practice has been taken over into these languages by adopting the following rule for variable names: "Unless a declaration is made otherwise, variables whose names start with I, J, K, L, M or N are integers; all others are real." This convention saves a lot of writing in many cases, so we will adopt it in our flowcharts. We will assume that all variables used in the text follow this rule unless we state otherwise.

When an assignments statement such as

$$N \leftarrow I + J X K$$

is used, it is fairly obvious that we expect the arithmetic to be done with integers, since all of the variables are integers, but what does

$$A \leftarrow I + J X K$$

mean? Since the expression involves integers only, it can be evaluated to get an integer result. However, the left-hand side is a floating-point variable, so the value of the expression must be converted into the equivalent floating-point representation before it can be stored. We did not give any instructions in the descriptions of our computer's machine language for converting from fixed to floating point, but we assume that such exist. Hence, the machine-language version of the assignment above will use integer arithmetic to evaluate the expression and then convert the result into floating-point representation.

Example

If l = 3, J = 2, and K = 5, the value of the expression l + J X K is 13.

This must be converted into .13 X 10^2 to be stored as a floating-point number in cell A. This is a case of

Rule 1

If in the assignment statement

"variable" ← "expression"

"expression" is an integer quantity and "variable" is a real number, the integer is converted into floating-point representation before the assignment. This rule can result in loss of accuracy. For example if l = 3, j = 1000, and K = 1123, l + J X K is 1123003. Since our floating-point numbers have only five digits of precision, this integer would be converted into

. 11230 x 10^7

If, in the example, I had been 573, the expression l + J X K would have been 1123573. This time we would convert it to the floating-point number .11236 X 10^7 because, **whenever a number has to be shortened to store it in floating point, we want the closest approximation, so we round it.**

Now let us consider the following: We are given the average annual water consumption per person in the U.S. in gallons (a real number), say AGAL. We wish to estimate the number of people (say NPEOP) served by a given water company by taking the number of gallons that the company delivers in a year (say GAL) and dividing it by the average consumption per person, that is

$$\text{Number of people} = \frac{\text{annual water used}}{\text{average annual water used per person}}$$

or

NPEOP ← GAL/AGAL

The right-hand side is the quotient of two floating-point numbers; the left-hand side is naturally an integer (number of people). What rule shall we use?

Rule 2

If in

"variable" ← "expression"

"expression" is a real number and "variable" is an integer, the floating-point value of "expression' is truncated to an integer.

Example

NPEOP ← GAL/AGAL

if GAL = .10752 x 10^{11} and AGAL = .10000 X 10^6, then GAL/AGAL = .10752 X 10^6 so NPEOP would become 107520.

The rule above tells us what to do with an expression on the right-hand side after it has been evaluated. We still need rules for evaluating it. If all variables in a given expression are of the same type (integer or floating), the arithmetic must be performed using that type. For example, the number of tires an automobile manufacturer must order is five times the number of cars (NCAR) - assuming five tires per car. We naturally expect 5 x NCAR to be evaluated as an integer.

We wanted to divide two integers. In this case it is not apparent which answer is natural. For example, if we divide the number of cars in the U.S. (NCARS) by the number of people (NPEOP) in the U.S., we get the average number of cars per person. The latter is not an integer, so we want this division to be done in floating point. We will write this as

NCARS/NPEOP

and say that the division operation represented by "/" always uses floating-point arithmetic.

Example

If NCARS = 632657 and NPEOP = 2000000 NCARS/NPEOP is .3163285, which will be represented as .31633 X 10^0.

If we specifically want an integer result, we will use the "÷" sign for the division. The rule for l ÷ J is to form the correct fixed-point value and truncate by discarding all digits after the decimal point.

For example, we can find the remainder after dividing l by J from the expression

l - (l ÷ J) X J

We are thus led to

Rule 3

If the operands for the arithmetic operators +, -, X and ↑ are both integers, the result is an integer. If the operands for the arithmetic operators + , -, X, and ↑ are both real numbers, the result is a real number. The operator ÷ always gives an integer result; the operator / always gives a real result.

When an operator is to be applied to operands of different types, one operand must be converted to be the same type as the other before the arithmetic is performed. Since it is possible to convert integers (if they are small enough) into floating-point representation without loss of accuracy, whereas most numbers in floating-point representation will either be rounded or overflow if they are converted to integers, we chose to convert integers into floating-point numbers before the arithmetic operation. This leads us to

Rule 4

If one operand for the arithmetic operators +, -, X, and ↑ is an Integer and the other is a real number, the result is a real number.

Example

$$L \leftarrow I \times J \times (K + B)$$

The order of operation execution is:

1. Multiplication of I and J. Result is an integer.
2. Addition of K and B. K is converted to a real number since B is a real number. Result K + B is a real number.
3. Multiplication of (I X J) and (K + B). Since (K + B) is a real number, (I X J) is converted to a real number. The result is a real number.
4 Assignment. The value computed in step 3 is truncated to an integer and stored in cell L.

The above example illustrates the importance of the order of evaluation of an expression. The left-to-right rule for multiplication indicates that I X J is formed and then multiplied by (K + B). If, instead, the expression were to be evaluated as I X (J X (K + B)), the result might be different because of rounding or overflow. For example, if I and J are both 10^6 and K and B were both 1, the evaluation of I X J X (K + B) would give an overflow when I X J (= 10^{12}) is formed, whereas I X (J (K + B)) gives 2 X 10^{13} correctly. Alternatively, if we started with I = 123453 J = 2, K = 1, B = .1 X 10^1, then

I X J X (K + B)	= 123453 X 2 X (1 + .1 X 101)
	= 246906 X (.2 X 10^1)
(Convert I X J to floating point)	– (.24691 X 106) X (.2 X 10^1)

$= .49382 \times 10^6$

whereas

I X (J X (K + B))	$= 123453 \times (2 \times (1 + .1 \times 10^1))$
	$= 123453 \times (2 \times .2 \times 10^1)$
(Convert J to floating point and multiply)	$= 123453 \times (.4 \times 10^1)$
(Convert I to floating point)	$= (.12345 \times 10^6) \times (.4 \times 10^1)$
	$= .49380 \times 10^6$

Usually we do not have to be concerned with these small details, but we should be aware of potential hazards in unusual situations.

Constants

An expression uses operands that can be variable names or constants. Constants are stored in the computer memory by the compiler so that they can be used in the evaluation of an expression. Therefore the compiler must know in what form to store them - as integers, floating-point numbers, logical values, or character strings.

Numerical constants will be stored wither an integers or floating-point numbers. A numerical constant will be stored as an integer if it contains fo decimal point and no exponent. Otherwise it will be stored as a floating-point number.

Examples

Integers	**Floating-point numbers**
15	1.5
-173	$-25_{10}3$
1	$2.7_{10}-4$

Character string constants are written by surrounding the string by quotes. For example, 'THIS IS A CHARACTER STRING'. We sidestep the problem of how these constants are stored in memory (we have seen that characters can be stored). We will see one use for character strings in the next section on output.

The logical constants are written "TRUE" and "FALSE". Here we use the double quotes sign to indicate that the four characters TRUE and five characters FALSE are neither a name nor a character string.

The evaluation of an arithmetic expression is affected by the type of a constant in exactly the same way as it is affected by a variable.

Examples

The result of	is the type
2 + 1	Integer
2.0 ↑ 1	Real
2 - A	Real
2.0 X A	Real

Exercises

1. Give the type of the following constants, if valid;
   *a. -1.7
   *b. 25
   c. $-2.5_{10}3$
   d. 'TRUE'
   e. "FALSE"
   *f. "STRING"
   *g. '$1.7_{10}3$'
   h. $2.5-_{10}3$
   i. -17
   j. $25_{10}0$
2. Which of the following expressions are type integer and which are type real, assuming that no specific declarations have been made?
   a. A + Z X 1
   b. 1 ↑ J - 2
   c. X ↑ 2 - 3
   d. 1/ J + K
3. What value is assigned to the variable on the left of the assignment in the following statements if the variables A, B, C, l, and J contains the values 3.5, 1.7, -10.5, 10 and -3 respectively?
   *a. D ← 1 X 3 - J
   *b K ← C / A + 3.4
   *c. E ← 1 / J + 4
   d. K ← J ← 2 + A / B
   e. D ← (l + J) X B
   f. E ← A ÷ B + 1 - 7
   g. L ← C ÷ (-B) X 1

INPUT/OUTPUT STATEMENTS

We introduced boxes shaped like cards and torn printer paper for input and output. These boxes may have one or more paths leading to them, indicating different reasons for which they may be executed. However, they must have exactly one path *from* them to the unique box whose execution must immediately follow.

The input box is drawn as in Figure 10. It contains a list of variable names. When the box is executed, values are read from the cards in the card reader and assigned to the variables in the list. Execution of this box will cause four numbers to be read and stored in A, l, X and T23. Only variable names may appear in the list, as its purpose is to provide a set of cells in memory where input data can be stored. It would not make sense, for example, to write a constant in an input box as shown in Figure 11. '2.75' is not the name of a cell in memory, so no data can be read from a card and stored in '2.75'. A READ statement functions like an assignment statement in that values are assigned to the variables. Thus any memory cell specification valid for the left-hand side of an assignment is valid in a READ statement.

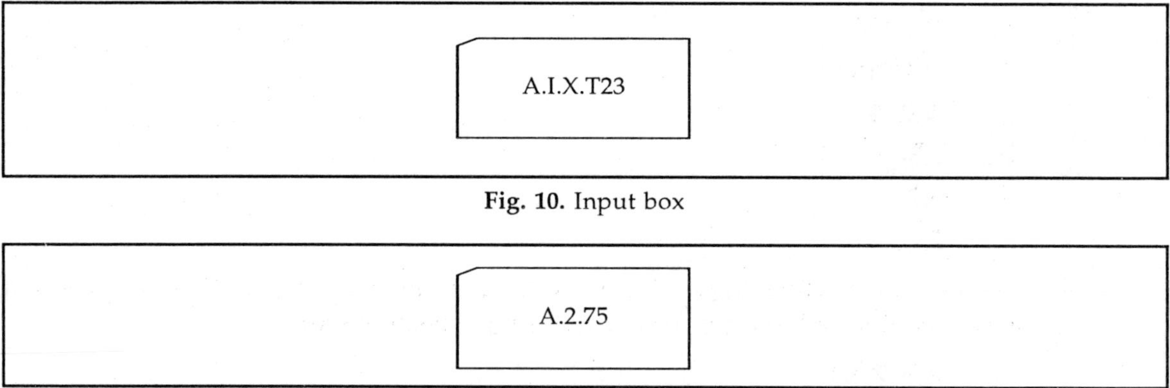

Fig. 10. Input box

Fig. 11. Invalid input box with constant

The statement in Figure 10 reads four numbers from a card. How are these numbers punched? We will use what is called *list-directed input/output*. The numbers are assumed to be punched in a form such that there is a clear demarcation between consecutive data items-either a group of spaces, a comma, or both. Thus if the data on the next two cards in the card reader is

17.52,375   82
921.25_{10} +7   29.5,19,3,1

execution of Figure 10 would be equivalent to

A ← 17.52
l ← 375
X ← 82
T23 ← 921.25_{10} +7

As many cards as necessary are red to get the required data. Reading can stop in the middle of a card (we read cards from left to right). In the example in Figure 10, the remaining four numbers on the second cards would not be read because reading would stop on the space between 921.25_{10} +7 and 29.5. If the program looped back and executed Figure 10 again, it would start reading from there, and assign the values 29.5, 19.3 and 1 to the variables A, I, X and T23, respectively.

The names of the variables in the READ statement determine the representation used when the data is stored in memory. If the data on the input cards has a different form, conversion is necessary. This follows the rules for assignment statements given in the last section. In the example in Figure 10, X is a floating-point variable. If 82 is read for the value of X, it will be stored as $.82 \times 10.^2$

A simple form of output is shown in Figure 12. A list of variable names appears in an output box. This causes values of the variables to be printed on the output printer when the box is executed. They are printed in a list-directed fashion; that is, each is printed in a suitable form and spaces are left between it and the next. The actual page layout depends on the language used and the type of output equipment. (You can find this information in local manuals, or by observing your output and experimenting.)

In addition to variable names, we can put constants in output lists. These constants are printed directly. For an example, see Figure 13. The output list contains four values: the character string FOR I =,the variable name I, the character string A =, and the variable name A. If Box I in Figure 13 is executed with I = 3, A is set to $.27000 \times 10^1$. Box 2 causes the output

FOR I = 3 A = $.27000_{10}$ +01

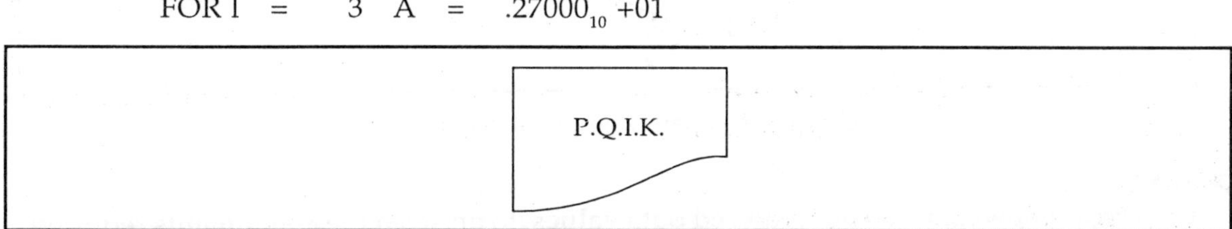

Fig. 12. Output box

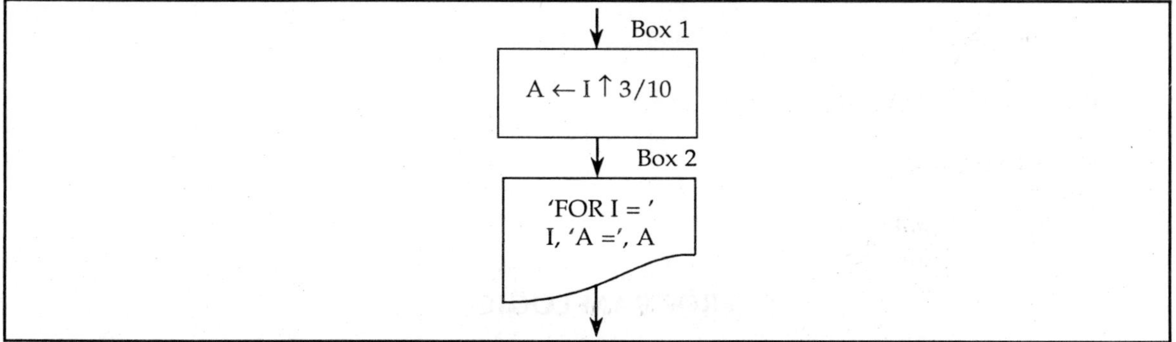

Fig. 13. Output list

The character string has been printed directly. The quotes have been removed because the constant is the string inside the quotes. The quotes are used to distinguish string constants from names and other parts of the language.

The members of an output list are just like the right-hand sides of assignment statements; they provide values to be printed just as the right-hand sides provide values to be assigned. Therefore, anything that is valid for the right-hand side of an assignment statement is valid in an output list. Hence expressions can be used in output lists. The example shown in Figure 14 is a valid output statement. Alternatively, it can be replaced by Figure 15.

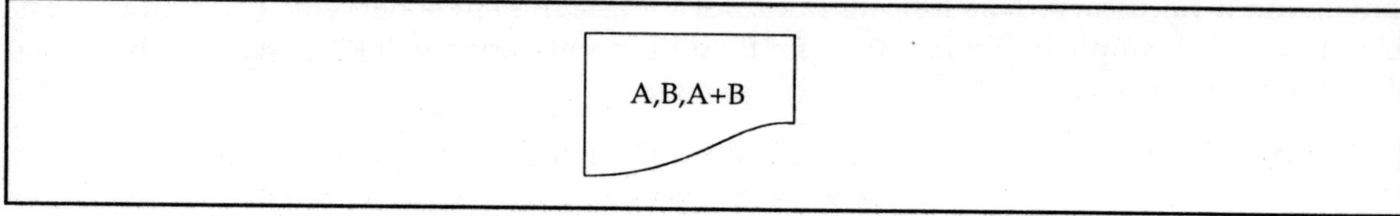

Fig. 14. Output statement including expression

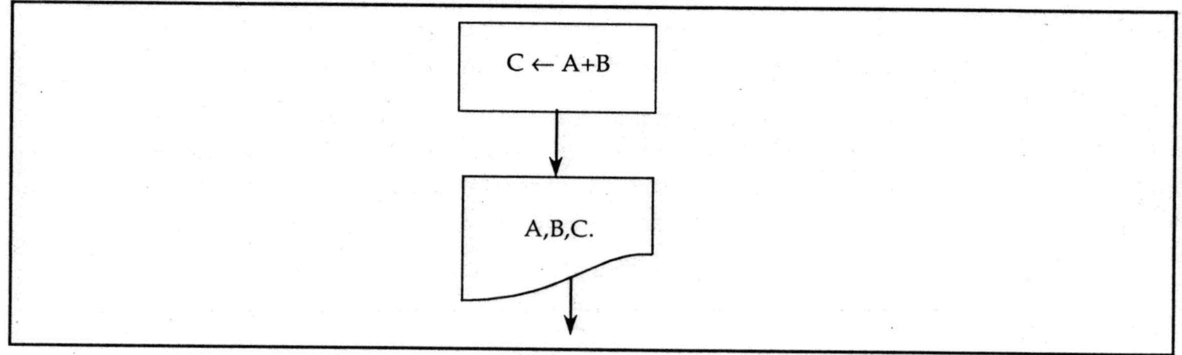

Fig. 15. Alternative output statement

Exercises

1. Draw a flowchart to read required data values, to perform the assignments required, and to print both the input and the result for:

*a. $P \leftarrow \frac{X^2 - Y}{Z}$

b. $Z5AB \leftarrow [A \times B]^{C/D}$

c. $TEMP \leftarrow \frac{P}{Q+R}$

$OUT \leftarrow \frac{TEMP + 3.5}{TEMP - 3.5}$

PROGRAM LOGIC

The power of a computer derives from two sources; its ability to process information rapidly and accurately, and its ability to test data and take action dependent on the outcome of the test. In a flowchart representation of a procedure, the diamond-shaped decision box is used to select between alternative flowpaths. The stop, "if A is less than B, take action X; otherwise take action Y," translates into the flowchart shown in Figure 16.

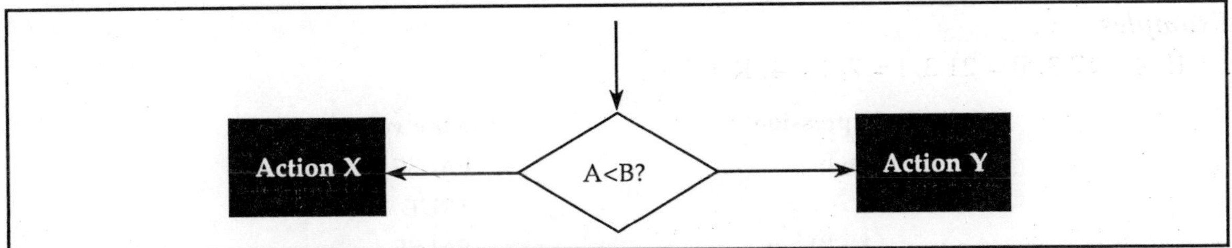

Fig. 16. Program decision

So far we have used questions that cn be answered YES or NO inside decision boxes. These are frequently phrases as true/false statements. In the future we will use these statements. Thus "A<B" is a statement that is either TRUE and FALSE. The flowlines leaving the box will be labeled TRUE and FALSE. When a decision box is executed, the expression inside is examined. If it is TRUE, the flow-line labeled TRUE is followed to find the next box that must be executed. Otherwise, the flowline labeled FALSE is followed

TABLE 1
Relational Operators

Operator	*Meaning*
$<$	Less than
$>$	Greater than
$\leq$	Less than or equal to
$\geq$	Greater than or equal to
$=$	Equal to
$\neq$	Not equal to

The expression in a decision box frequently uses one of the *relational operators* shown in Table 16.1. Relational operators are similar to binary arithmetic operators in that they use two numerical or character operands.* They differ in that the value of such an expression is logical; that is, it has the value "TRUE" or "FALSE". Any expression that has a logical value can appear in a decision box, in particular, a logical variable, say L, could appear by itself. The TRUE branch from the box is followed if the value of L is "TRUE" ; otherwise, the FALSE branch is followed. A logical variable can be assigned a value by assignment statements such as

$$L \leftarrow \text{"TRUE"}$$

and

$$L1 \leftarrow P \geq Q$$

* The relational operators = and ≠ can be used to compare any two operands of the same type for example, both logical. Some languages allow all relational operators to be used on all types of data.

In the first example the right-hand side is a logical constant; in the second it is a logical expression. Later in the section we will introduce other logical expressions. Any of these can appear in a decision box or on the right-hand side of an assignment statement if the left-hand side is a logical variable.

Examples

If A = 17.3, B = 21.3, l = 7, J = 4, K = 3

the expression	**has the value**
A > B	FALSE
l≠ A	TRUE
(A - B) ≥ 0	FALSE
(J + K)	TRUE

In the last example we compare the value of a variable with the value of an expression. In fact we can write this as J + K = l by using additional precedence information. The precedence of each of the arithmetic operators (+, –, ×, /, ÷ and ↑) is higher than the precedence of each of the relational operators. Thus the order of execution of the operations is to do the arithmetic operators first, then the relational operators. The precedence of each of the relational operators is the same, so they are done from left to right.

Examples

1. The precedence of the operators in A X B≠ l + J is shown in Figure 17.

   The value of the expression is value of the logical variable T3 where T3 is constructed by

$$T1 \leftarrow A \times B$$

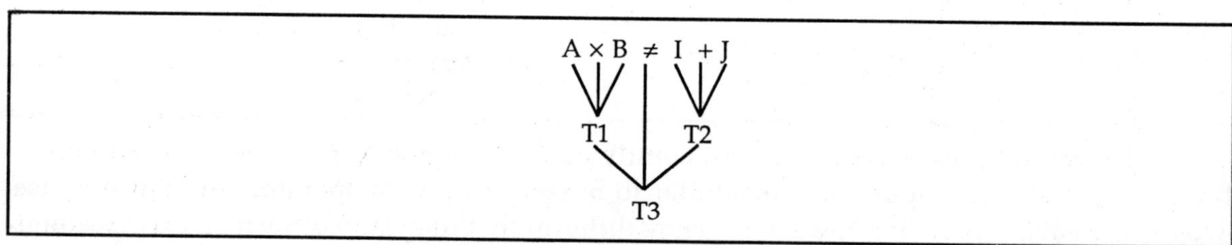

Fig. 17. Precedence in A X B≠ l + J

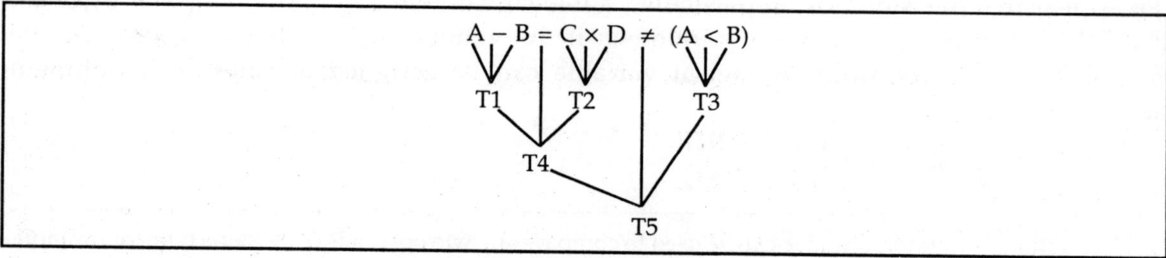

Fig. 18. Precedence in A – B = C × D≠ (A<B)

2. The precedence of operators in A – B = C × D≠ (A<B) is shown in Figure 18.

The precedence levels of = and≠ are the same, so the leftmost operator, the =, is performed first.

We use decision boxes to implement control actions required in the problem statement as in Figure 18; we also use them to test for conditions that are introduced in the algorithm.

Example 16.1 - Average

Problem: Read in a deck of cards, each of which contains two numbers. The first is a seven-digit student ID number, the other that student's score on an exam. Compute the average exam score of all the students and print it.

Since the average score is the total of all the scores divided by the number of students, we must find the number of students. This can be done by setting an integer variable N to zero and then, as each card is read, adding one to N. Thus after the last student card has been read, N will contain the number of students. We must also find the total score. This can be formed by *accumulating* the sum of all student scores read in another variable, say SUM. This part of the algorithm is shown in Figure 19.

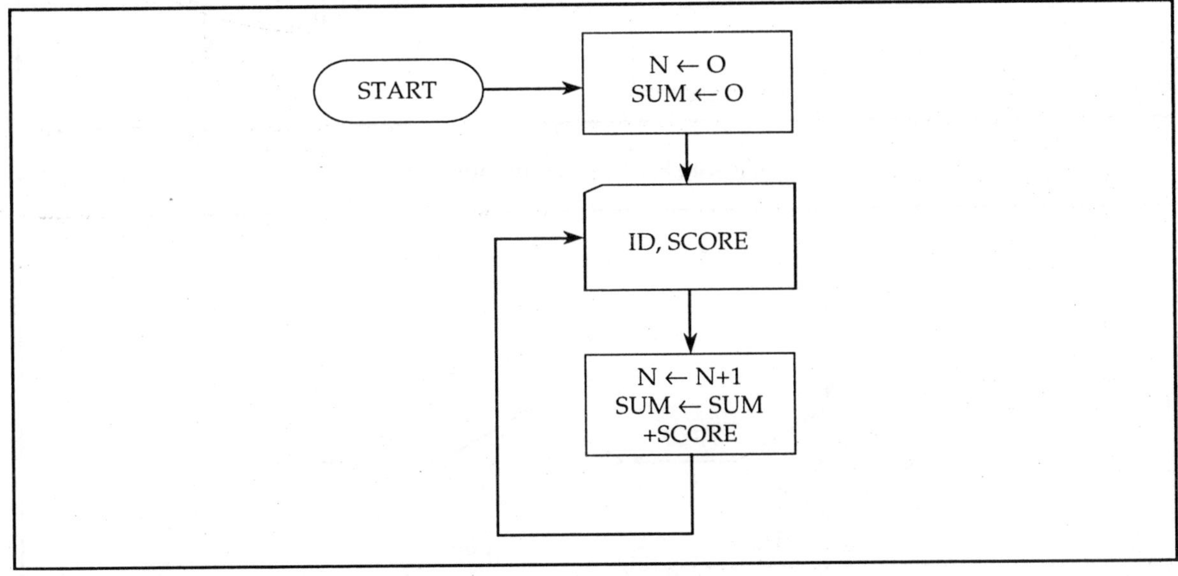

Fig 19. Accumulating SUM

The process must be stopped after the last student card has been read, so we need a way of testing to determine whether we have come to the last card. To do this we use the common technique of adding another card after the deck of student cards. This card is distinguished from the others because it contains "impossible" information. In this example, all student ID's are positive numbers, so we put a negative number on the card as a fake ID; the exam score can be anything since it is not processed. After reading a card, we test to see

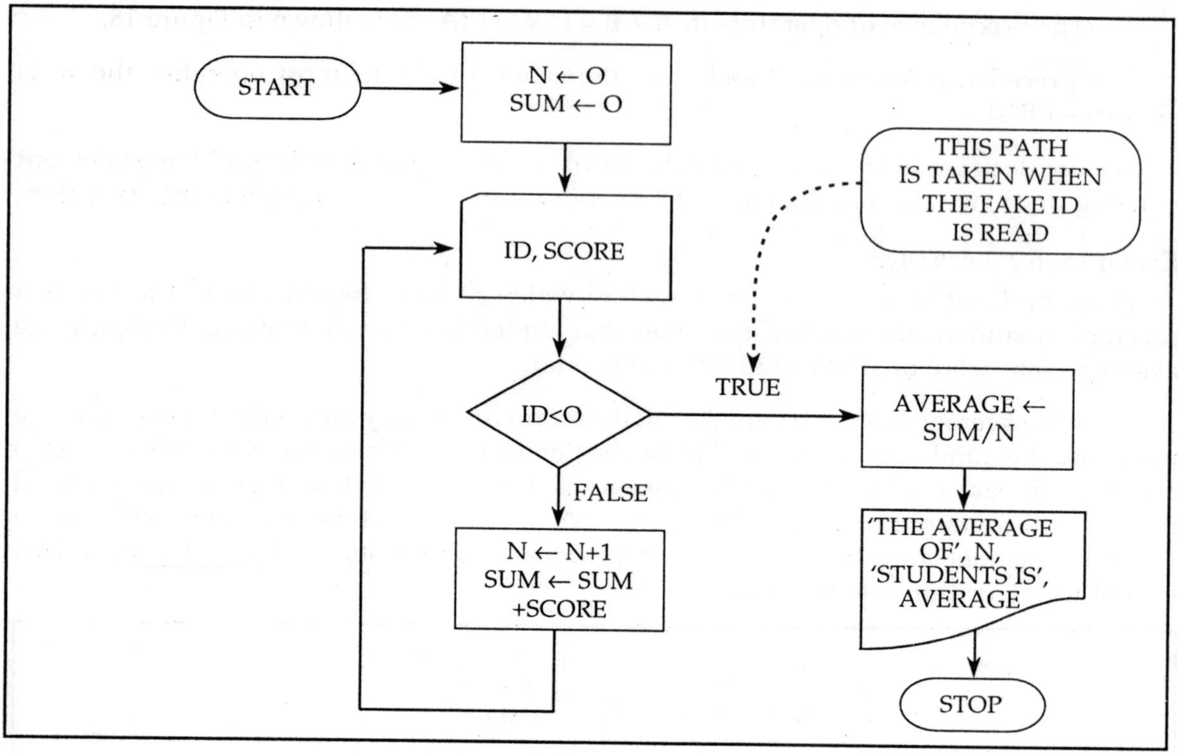

START
N ← O
SUM ← O
THIS PATH
IS TAKEN WHEN
THE FAKE ID
IS READ
ID, SCORE
ID<O
TRUE
AVERAGE ←
SUM/N
FALSE
N ← N+1
SUM ← SUM
+SCORE
'THE AVERAGE
OF', N,
'STUDENTS IS',
AVERAGE
STOP

Fig. 20. Average computation

A>B
TRUE
C=D
TRUE
BOX P
FALSE
FALSE
BOX Q

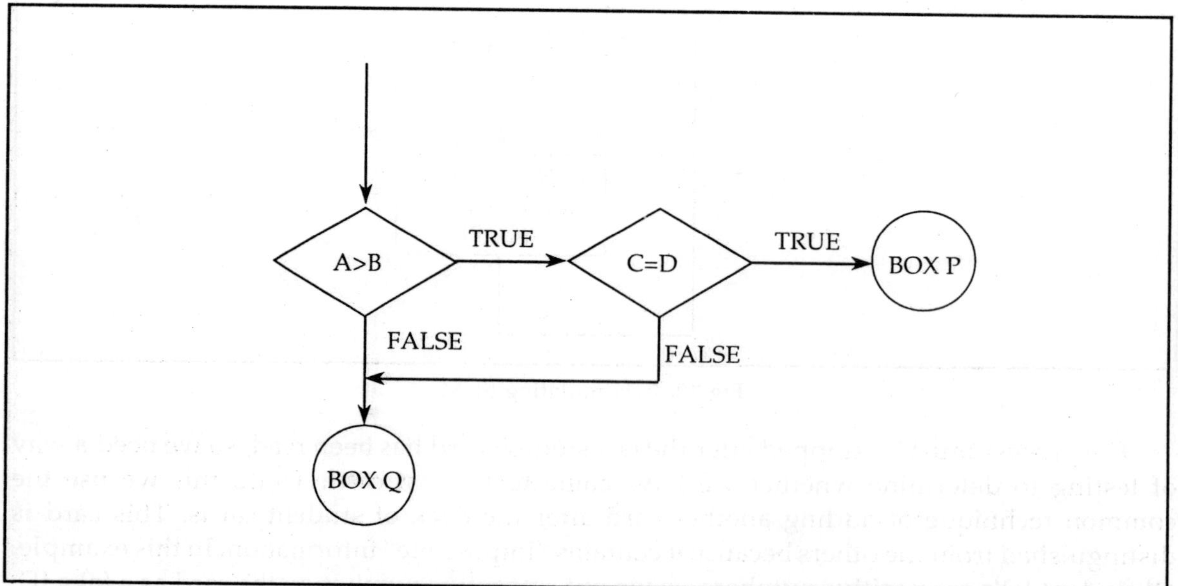

Fig. 21. Flowchart of a compound decision

whether the ID is negative. If it is, then we have already read and processed the last student card. The flowchart of the complete algorithm is given in Figure 20.

Logical Expression

In some problems a compound decision must be made. An example of a compound decision is "Go to Box P if both A>B and C = D, otherwise go to Box Q." One way of writing this is shown in Figure 21. Compound decisions of this form are common, so languages provide shorthand ways of writing single, logical expressions that are true in the desired cases. In the above example, we wished to know if the expressions "A>B" and "C = D" both had "TRUE" values. For this we use the logical operator "AND". This is a binary operator, both of whose operands must have logical values. The result of the "AND' operator is "TRUE' only if the value of both operands is "TRUE". Otherwise, the result if "FALSE". Thus, if A = 3.1, B = 2.4, C = 17.5, D = 17.5, then (A>B) "AND" (C = D) has the value "TRUE".

If P and Q are logical variables or expressions, P "AND" Q is a valid logical expression. Its value is shown in Table 2.

The logical operators "OR" and "NOT" can also be used, "OR' is a binary operator, and P "OR" Q is "TRUE" if either P or Q or both have the value "TRUE". If either P or Q is "FALSE," the expression is "FALSE. If either P or Q is not a logical variable, then P "OR" Q is meaningless."NOT" Q is "TRUE" if Q is "FALSE" and vice versa. "NOT" is a unary operator. The values of "OR" and "NOT" are shown Tables 3 and 4. Thus, we can shorten Figure 21 to Figure 22.

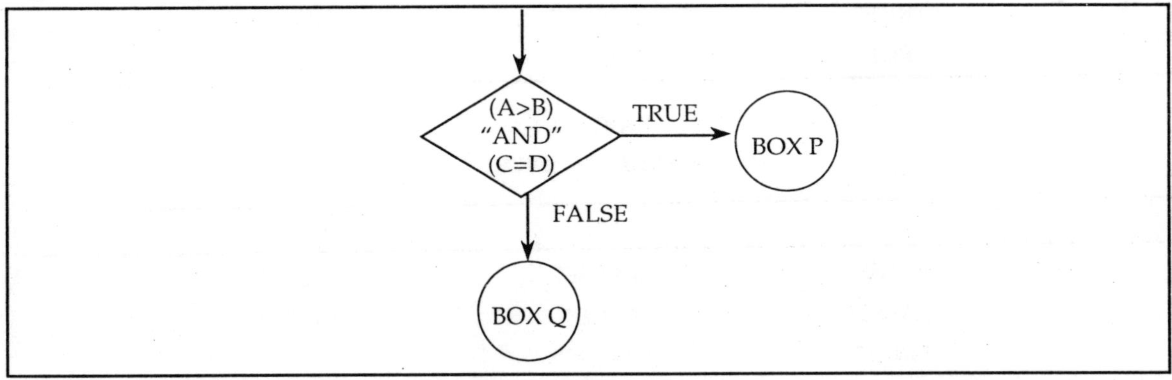

Fig. 22. Short form of Figure 21

When a logical expression involves more than one operator, we must know the precedence rules that determine the other of execution of the operators. The logical operators have lower precedence than arithmetic and relational operators. Within the logical operators, "NOT" has the highest precedence and "OR' the lowest. A complete list of precedence levels is shown in Table 5. Thus A "AND" B "OR" "NOT" C is equivalent to (A "AND" B) "OR" ("NOT" C). Other examples are

A "OR" B "AND" C is A "OR" (B "AND" C)
A "AND" "NOT" B is A "AND" ("NOT" B)
X>P + Q "AND" l = J is (X > (P + Q) "AND" (l = J)

The decision boxes we have introduced have exactly two paths leaving them. (They can have one or more paths entering.) The exit paths are labeled TRUE and FALSE. From now on we will abbreviate these to T and F although you should be careful not to confuse handwritten forms of the two. Sometimes we wish to test for several cases; for example, we may wish to go to Box P if A < 0, Box Q if A = 0, or Box R if A > 0. This is shown in Figure 23.

Figure 24 shows a shorter way of writing this using more than two exits labeled with the conditions under which they are to be taken. If many exits are possible, we will draw a decision box as in Figure 25. This would go to Box U if B < 1, Box V if B = 1, Box W if B = 2, and Box X if B > 2.

TABLE 2

VALUE OF "AND"

P	Q	P "AND" Q
"FALSE"	"FALSE"	"FALSE"
"FALSE"	"TRUE"	"FALSE"
"TRUE"	"FALSE"	"FALSE"
"TRUE"	"TRUE"	"TRUE"

TABLE 3

VALUE OF "OR"

P	Q	P "OR" Q
"FALSE	"FALSE"	"FALSE"
"FALSE"	"TRUE"	"TRUE"
"TRUE"	"FALSE"	"TRUE"
"TRUE"	"TRUE"	"TRUE"

TABLE 4

VALUE OF "NOT"

Q	"NOT" Q
"FALSE"	"TRUE"
"TRUE"	"FALSE"

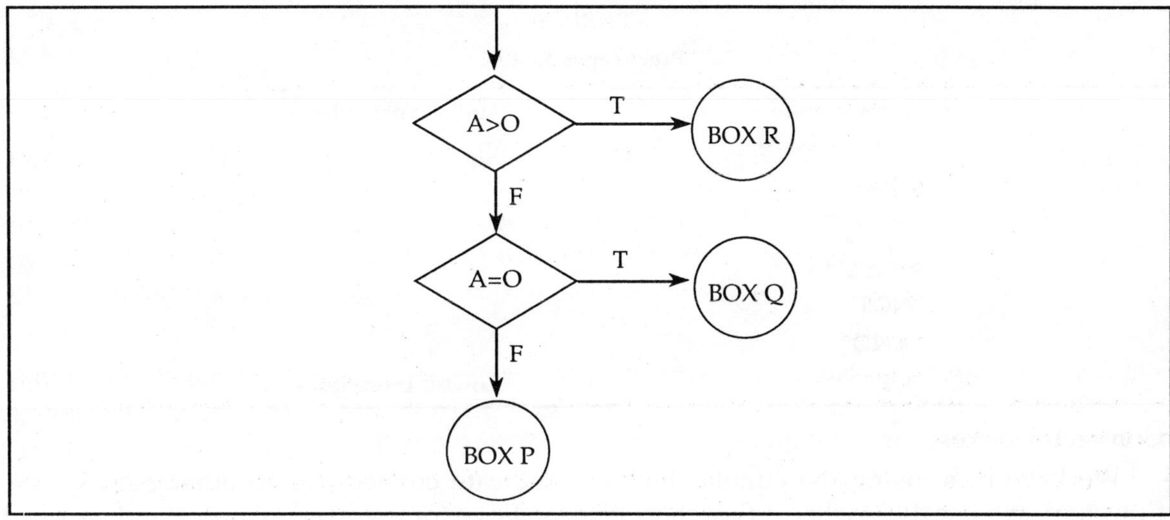

Fig. 23. Testing for several cases

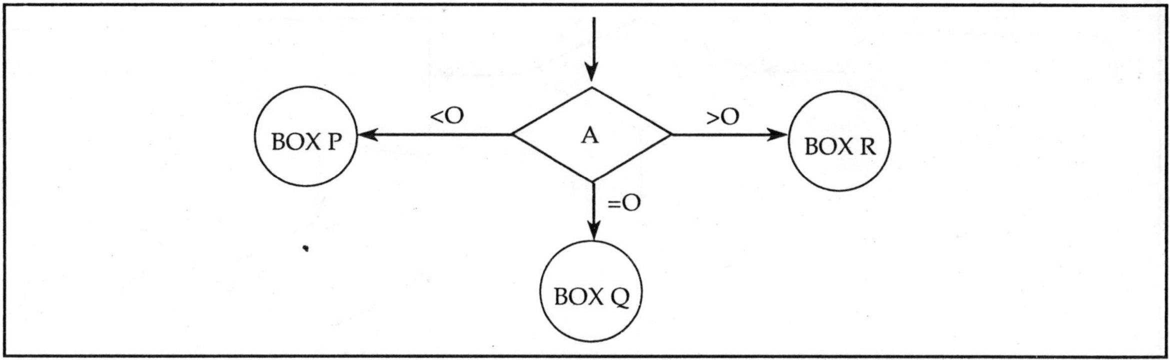

Fig. 24. Short form of Figure 16.23

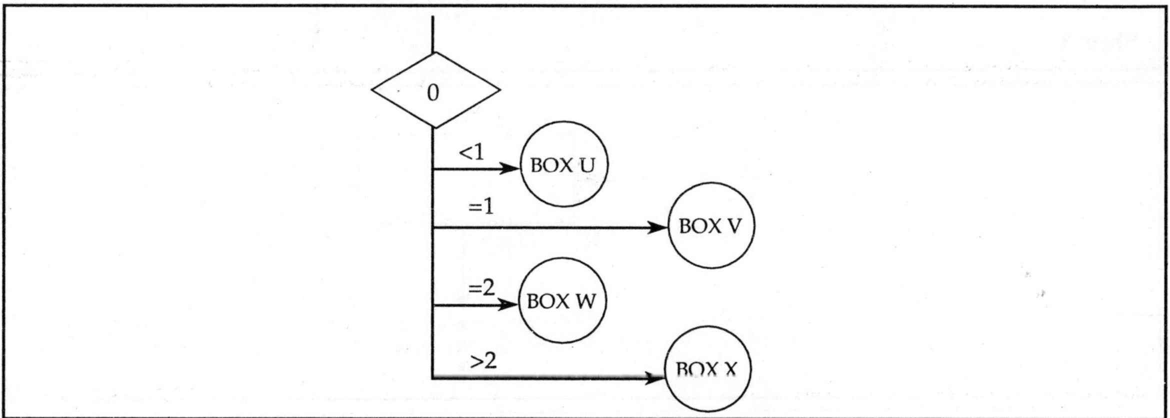

Fig. 25. Decision box with many exits

TABLE 5

Precedence Levels

Unary + and -	Highest precedence
↑	
X / ÷	
+ −	
> < ≥ ≤ = ≠	
"NOT"	
"AND"	
"OR"	Lowest precedence

Connector Boxes

We have been using the circular boxes to indicate connections to other parts of the flowchart. We use these when a flowchart gets too large for one sheet of paper and we need a path going from one sheet to another.

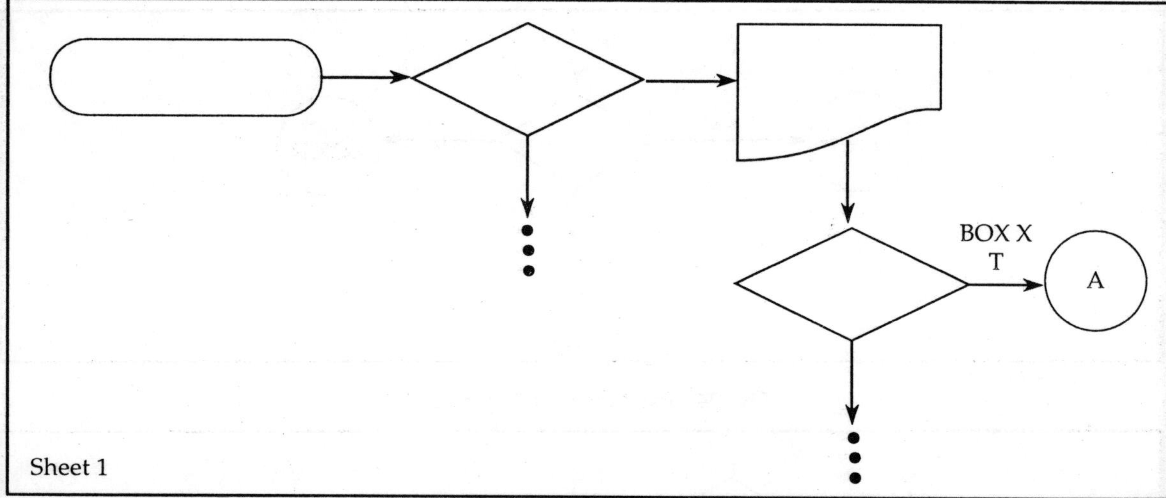

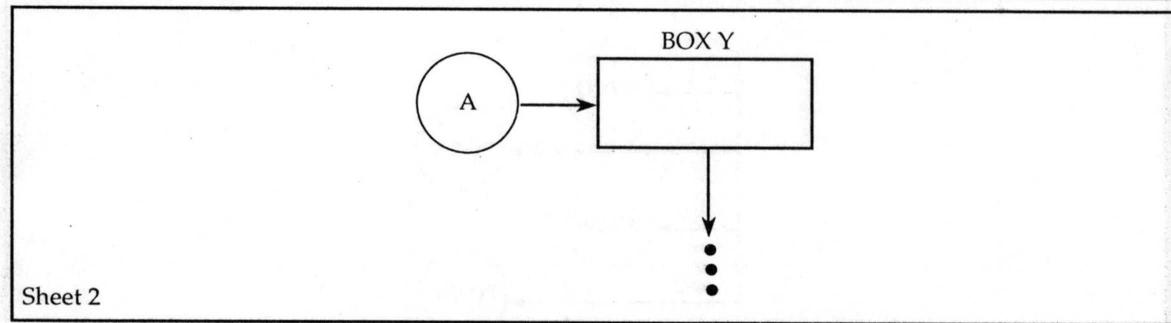

Fig. 26. Connector boxes

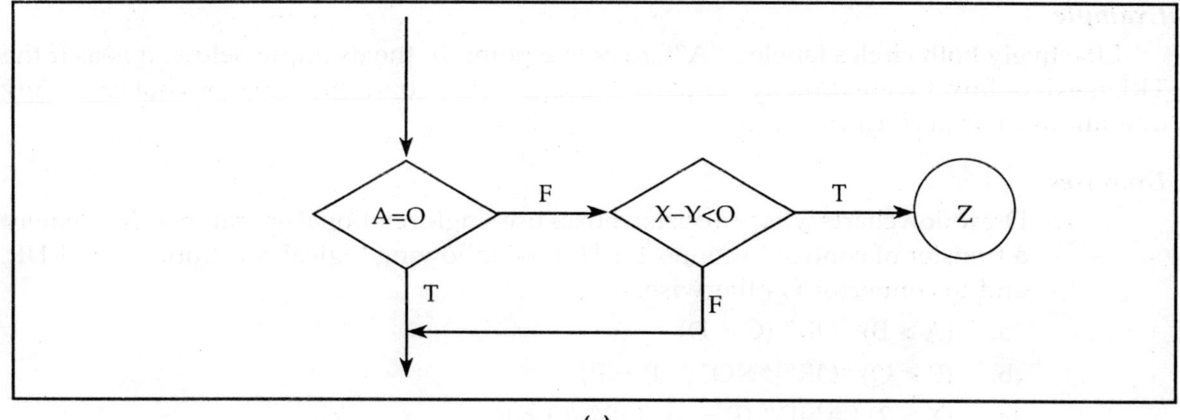

(a)

(b)

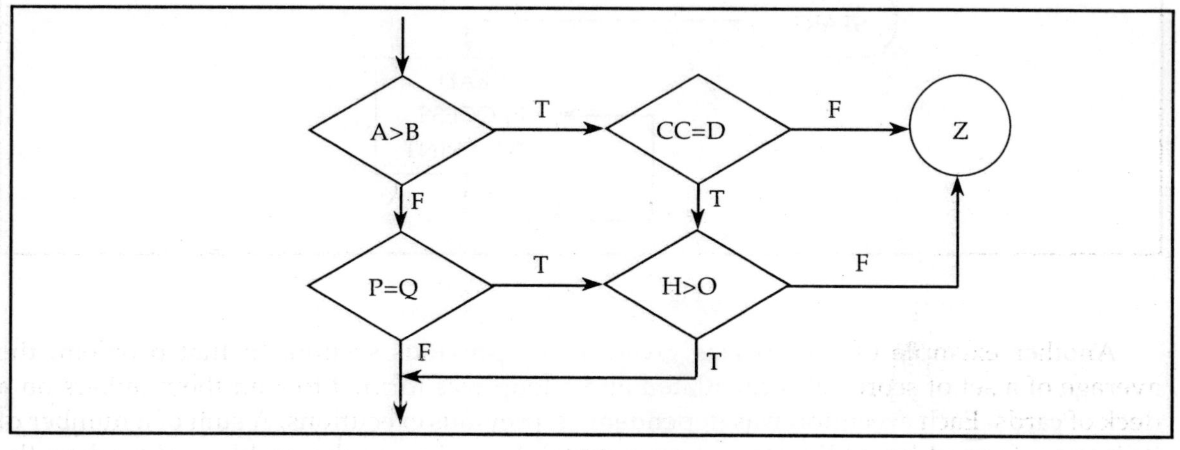

(c)

Example

Effectively both circles labeled "A" are at one point. In the example below, it is as if the TRUE exit of Box X were directly connected to Box Y. The connector box does not cause any operations to be performed.

Exercises

1. Draw flowcharts whose decision boxes use single relational operators to implement a transfer of control to connector H if the following logical conditions are TRUE, and to connector G otherwise.

   *a. (A > B) "OR" (C = D)

   b. (P < Q) "OR" "NOT" (R = P)

   *c. (X > 2) "AND" (P = 3) "OR" (Q < R)

   d. (X < 0) "AND" (Y = 3) "OR" (X > 0) "AND" (Z < 0)

2. Give a logical expression that is true if the following flowcharts transfer control to connector Z.

PROGRAM LOOPS

One of the ways in which computers are able to out-perform people is in the repetitive execution of identical tasks on different data. A procedure was written to compute the tax for an individual. It functioned by reading in data, processing it, and printing the answers. By transferring back to the start of the procedure, data for a second individual can be read and processed similarly. Thus the one program can be used to perform any number of tax calculations. This program loop was formed as shown in Figure 27.

The loop terminates when the data is exhausted. Each execution is independent of all previous executions and provides the numerical answer of another specific case.

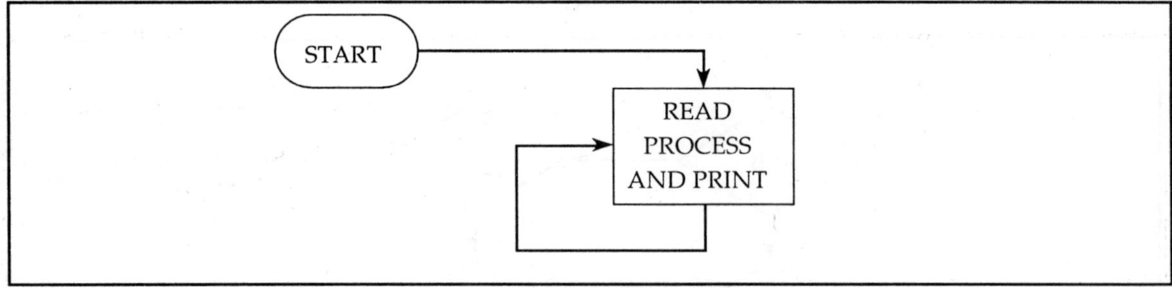

Fig. 27. Program loop

Another example of a loop was given in the previous section. In that problem, the average of a set of scores was calculated and a loop was formed to sum the numbers on a deck of cards. Each execution was dependent on previous executions. A sum of a number of items was formed by adding to a running total. If we ignore the problem of reading the input, the basic form of the loop is as shown in Figure 28

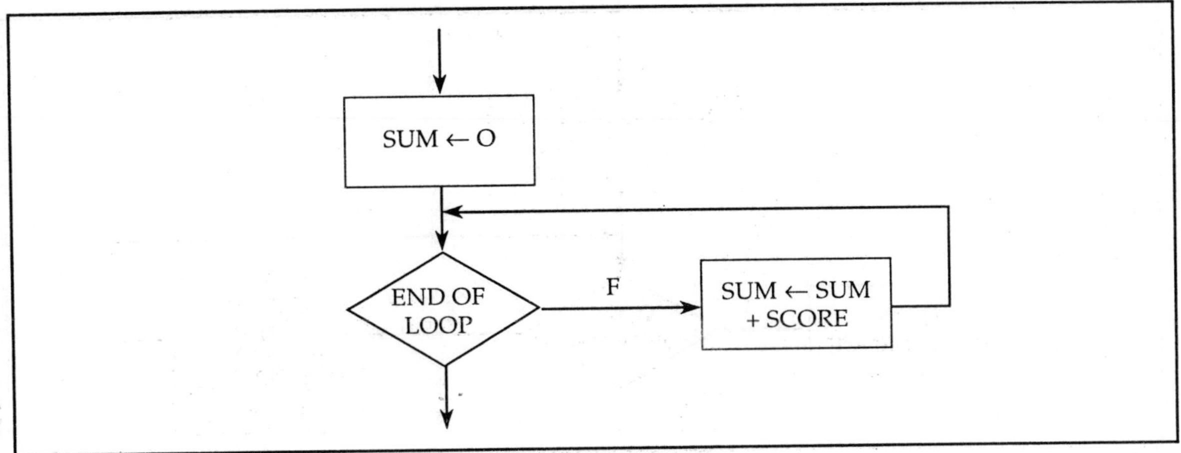

Fig. 28. Basic loop

The three boxes in Figure 28 display the three important procedures associated with this kind of program loop - the initialisation (setting SUM to zero), the end test (checking for the last card), and the processing inside the loop (forming the running sum).

This kind of loop, which we will call a *cumulative loop*, processes data left from a previous execution (in this case the value in SUM). Before the first execution, the variables that are to be processed must be initialised. In this case, SUM must initially be zero.

Example 16.2 —

Finding the Difference Between Largest and Smallest

Write a procedure that will read a set of cards, each containing one positive integer, and find the difference between the largest and smallest of these integers.

Again we do not know how many cards have to be read, so we will add one more card with a negative integer on it an as *end-of-file* indicator.

The largest and smallest numbers of a set of numbers is best found using the method we would use by hand. We would look at the first number and say, "If I do not find anything larger or smaller, then this is the largest and smallest." If we did find something larger or smaller as we read through the numbers, we would choose that one as the largest or smallest. The basic form of the loop is shown in Figure 29. (In terms of our flowchart language, this can be written as in Figure 30) If there are no cards containing positive integers, the program in Figure 29 will set LARGE and SMALL to a negative number and DIFF to be zero.

The problem statement did not day what was to happen if there were no integers in the set, so we have, in effect, corrected the problem statement by setting LARGE and SMALL to be negative as an indicator for this special case.

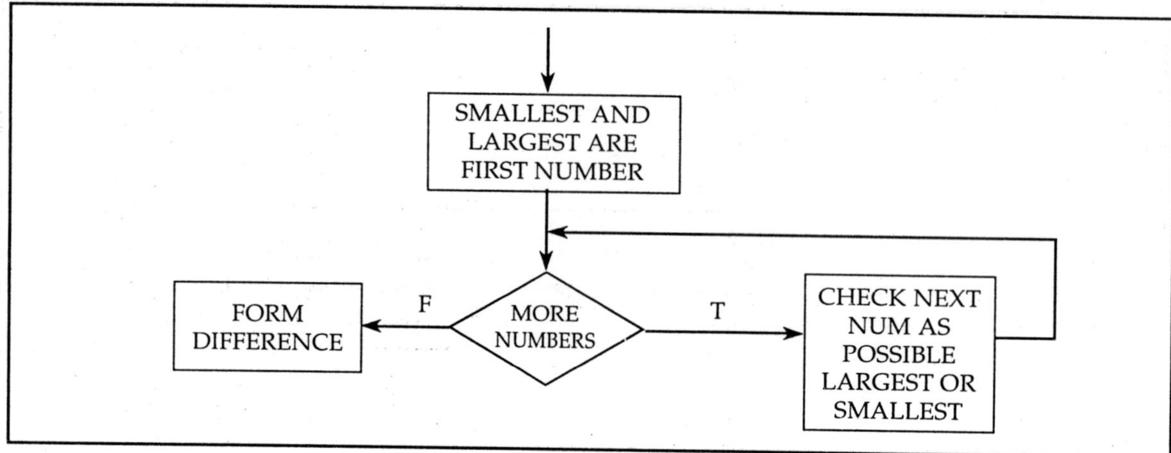

Fig. 29. Form of program to find largest difference

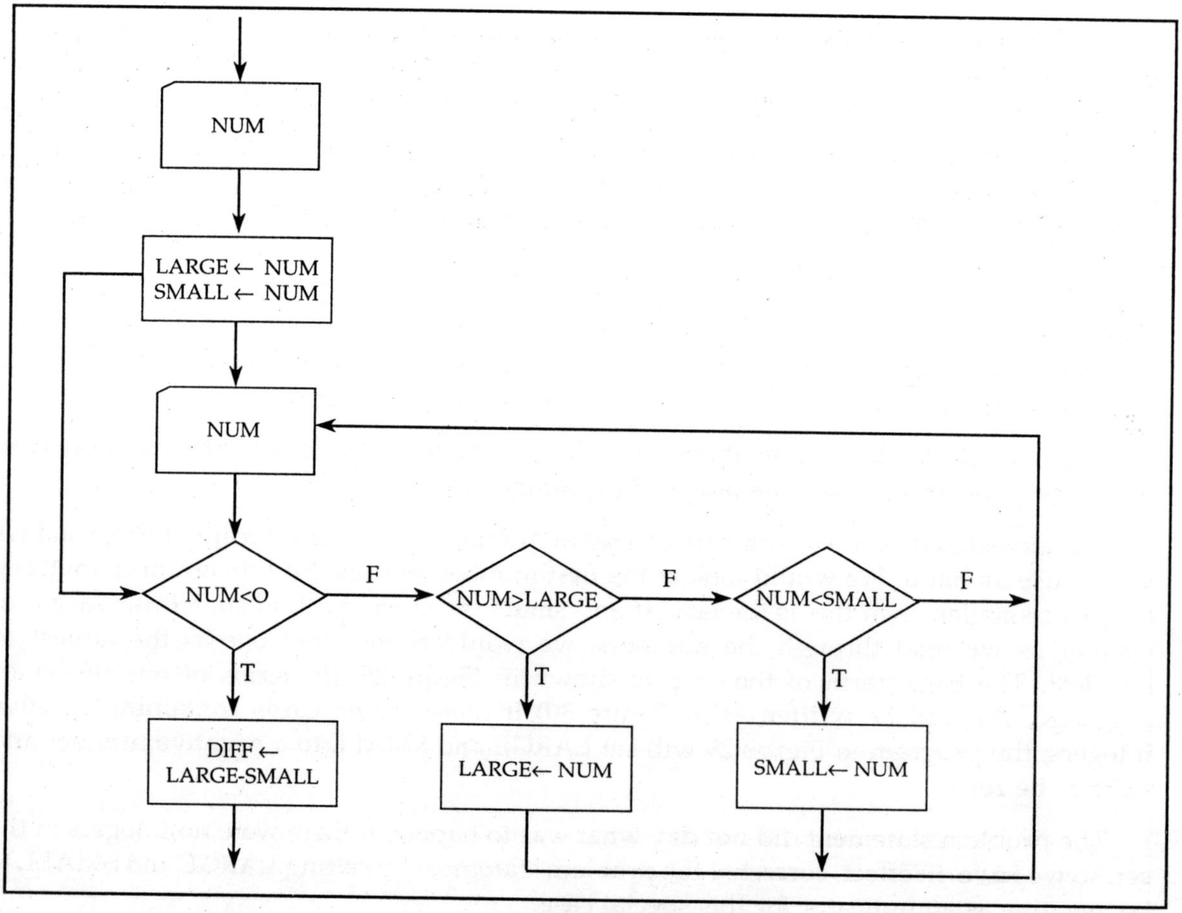

Fig. 30. Flowchart of the procedure

Example 16.3 — The Method of Bisection

A common problem in numerical processing is to find a value of x that satisfies an equation such as

$$x^3 + 3x - 5 = 0$$

The graph in Figure 31 shows the function $x^3 + 3x - 5$. As can be seen the function is below the x-axis at x = 0 and above it at x = 2. Since the function is a continuous line, it must cross the x-axis somewhere between x = 0 and x = 2. Hence for some value of x between zero and two, $x^3 + 3x - 5 = 0$.

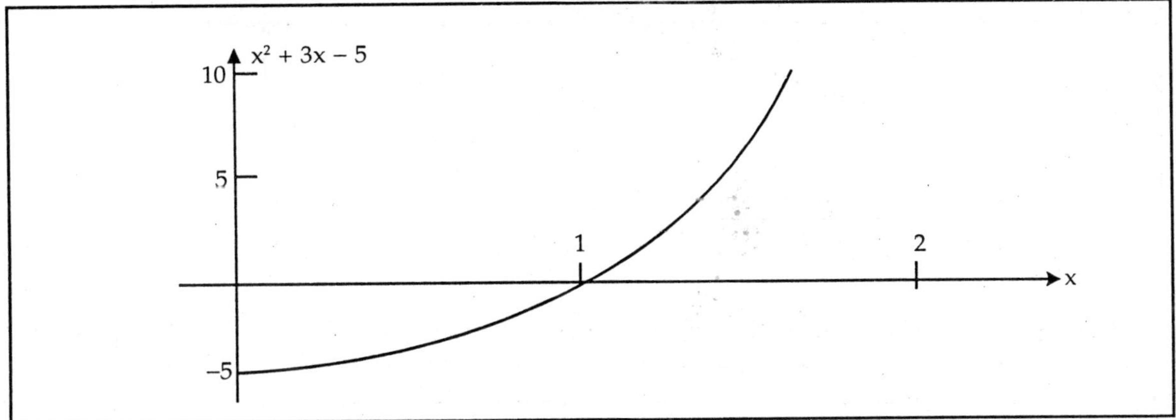

Fig. 31. $x^2 + 3x - 5$

If we set the value of LOW to be zero and HIGH to be two, then there is a solution of the problem between LOW and HIGH, as shown in Figure 32. The important characteristic of the two points LOW and HIGH is that the value of the function is negative at LOW and positive at HIGH. Now let us find the point MID midway between LOW and HIGH as shown in Figure 32. If we look at the sign of the function at MID we have two cases:

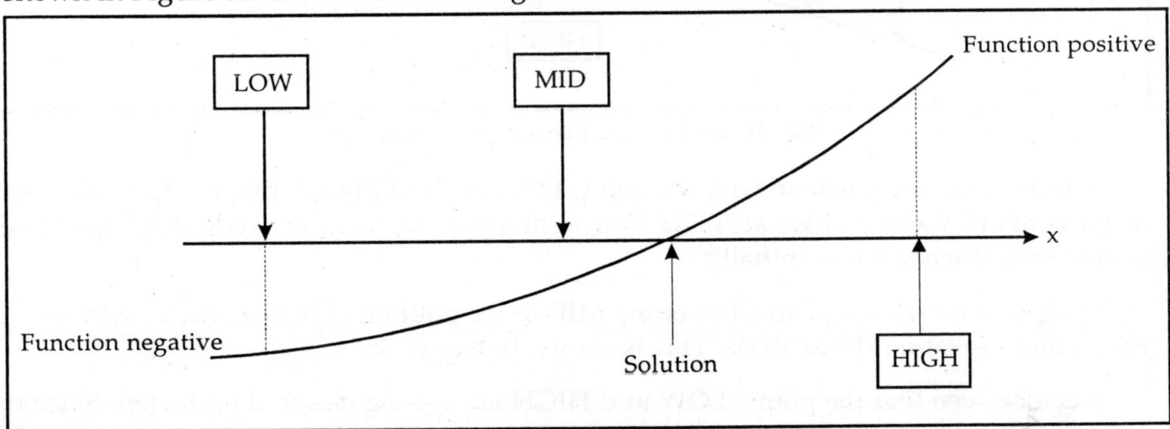

Fig. 32. Relation of computed points to solution

Case 1

Function is negative at MID (as shown). Since the function is positive at HIGH, a solution lies between MID and HIGH. Consequently, we can move LOW over to the point MID to get Figure 33. (Note that the solution still lies between LOW and HIGH.)

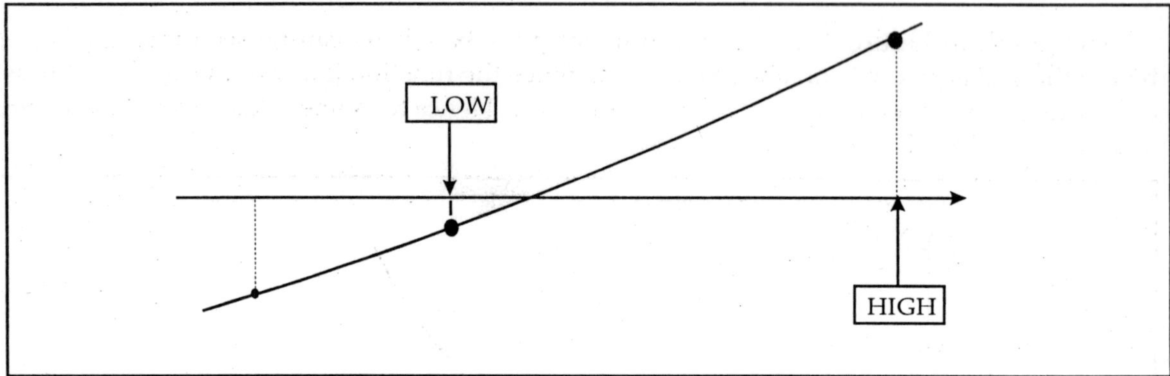

Fig. 33. Halving the interval negative at MID

Case 2

Function is positive at MID. In this case a solution lies between LOW and MID. Consequently, we can move HIGH over to the point MID as shown in Figure 34.

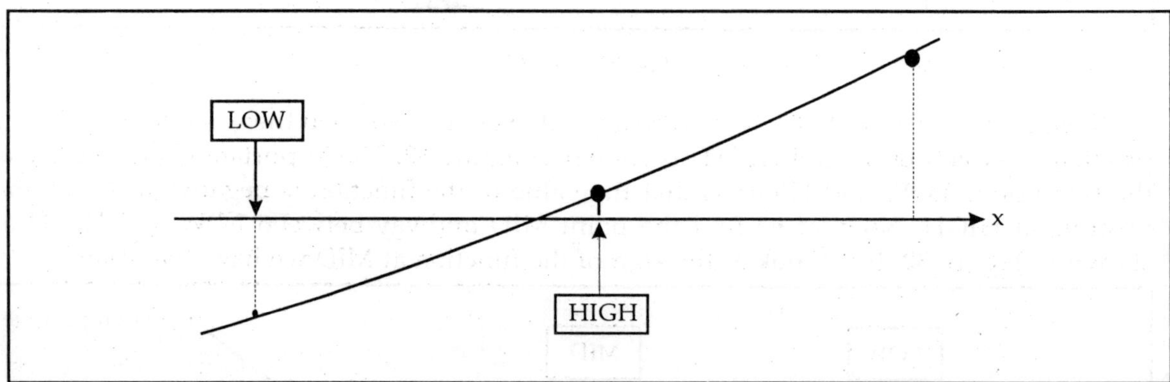

Fig. 34. Halving the interval positive at MID

In either case, we finish up with the points LOW and HIGH such that the function is still negative at LOW and positive at HIGH. Furthermore, the distance between LOW and HIGH is now half of what if was initially.

This process can be repeated by setting MID to the midpoint between the new LOW and HIGH and repeating the analysis. This is shown in Figure 35.

It can be seen that the points LOW and HIGH are getting closer at each step. Since the solution of the original problem lies between LOW and HIGH after each step, we are getting

10
5
1
2
x
–5
LOW
MID
LOW
LOW
LOW
MID
HIGH
MID
HIGH
HIGH
HIGH
Initially
After first step
After second step
After third step
etc.

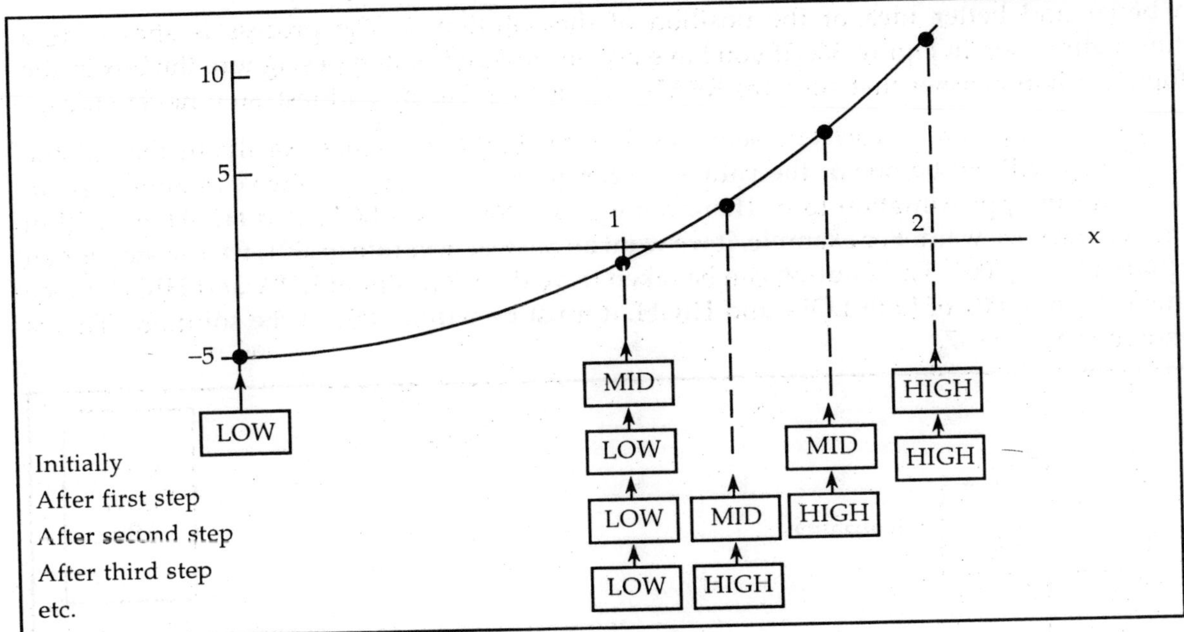

Fig. 35. Successive approximations

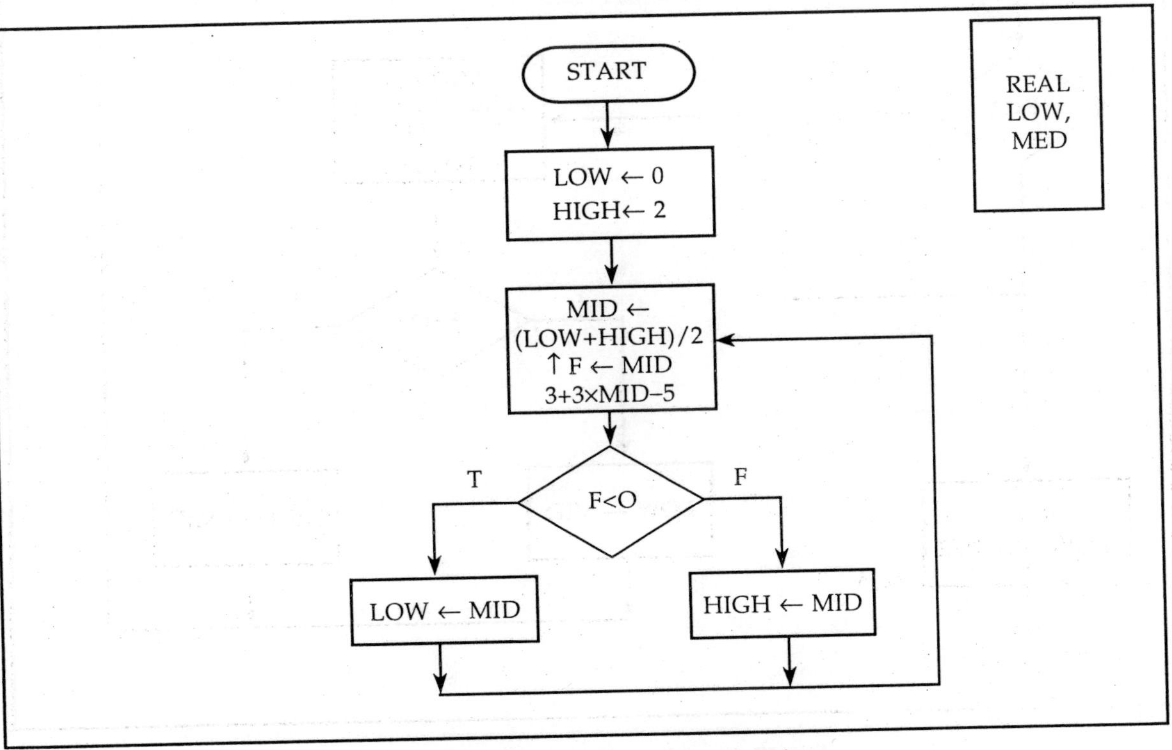

START
LOW ← 0
HIGH← 2
MID ←
(LOW+HIGH)/2
↑ F ← MID
3+3×MID–5
F<O
T
F
LOW ← MID
HIGH ← MID
REAL
LOW,
MED

Fig. 36. Basic flow for bisection procedure

a better and better idea of the position of the solution x. The process is shown as a cumulative loop in Figure 36. (If you have not yet covered data types, ignore the box in the top right-hand corner that contains REAL...). This loop has no end test, so it never stops.

In the computer, we can represent only a finite number of values exactly. In general, the solution x will not be one of the values we can represent exactly, so we can only hope to compute an approximation to it. Therefore we can stop when LOW and HIGH are within the accuracy we want. For example, if we want an answer accurate to .001, we can stop when HIGH-LOW ≤ .002. The solution can be taken to be the midpoint of LOW and HIGH. Since this is within .001 of both LOW and HIGH, it must be within .001 of the solution.* This is shown in Figure 37.

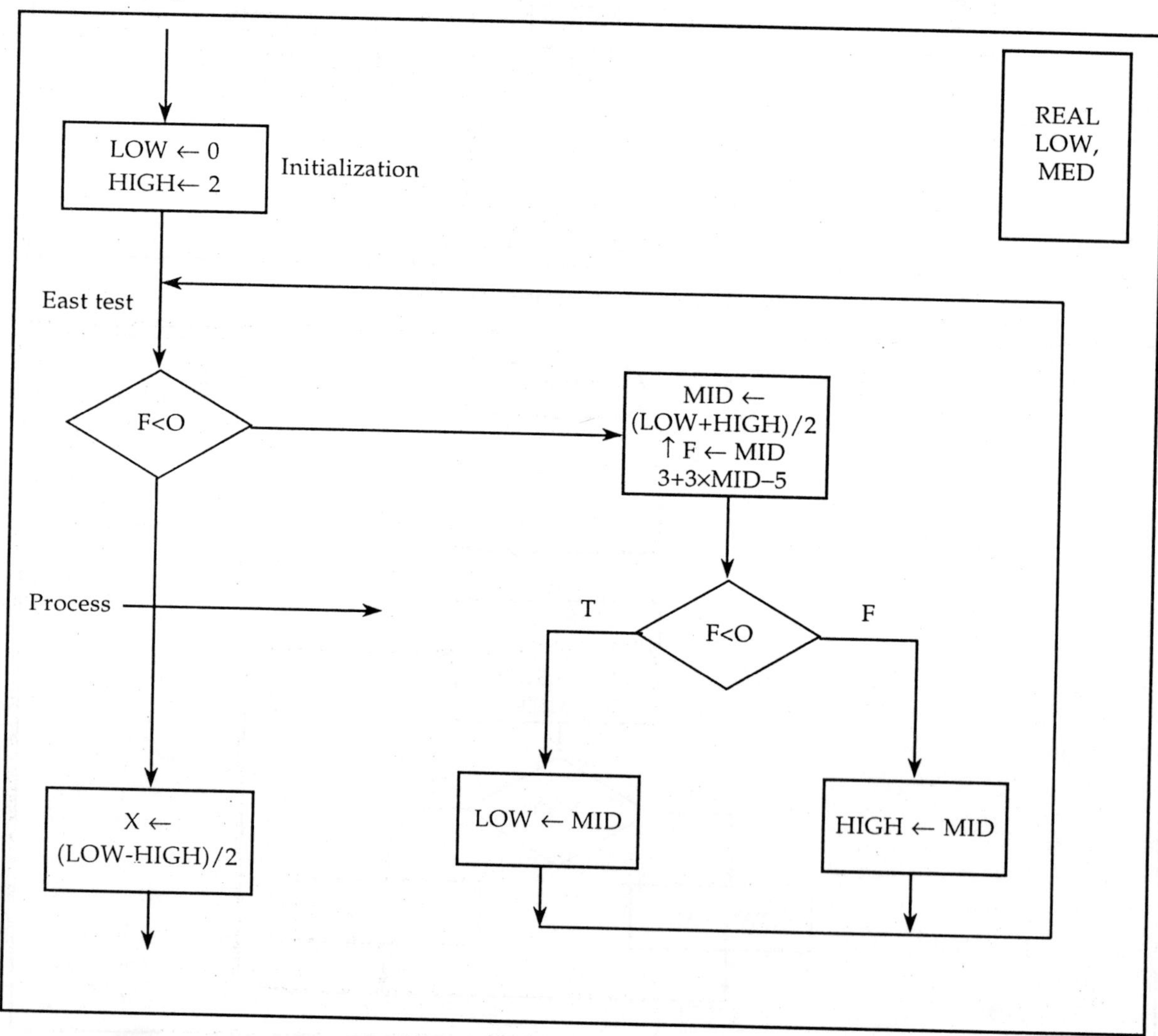

Fig. 37. Flowchart of bisection procedure

Example 16.4 - Population Growth

The following is an example of what is called simulation. We want to estimate the population of the world at future times. To do this we set up a mathematical model of the processes we believe control the population and compute its behaviour. We assume that the model has a constant population throughout the year, that on January 1 of each year a number of people are born, and that this number is a fixed given fraction of the population on December 31 of the previous year. This fraction is the annual birthrate. Further, we assume that on January 1 of each year a number of people die. This number is a fraction of the number of people alive on the day before, but this fraction (called the deathrate) is assumed to be proportional to the number of people alive on that December 31.

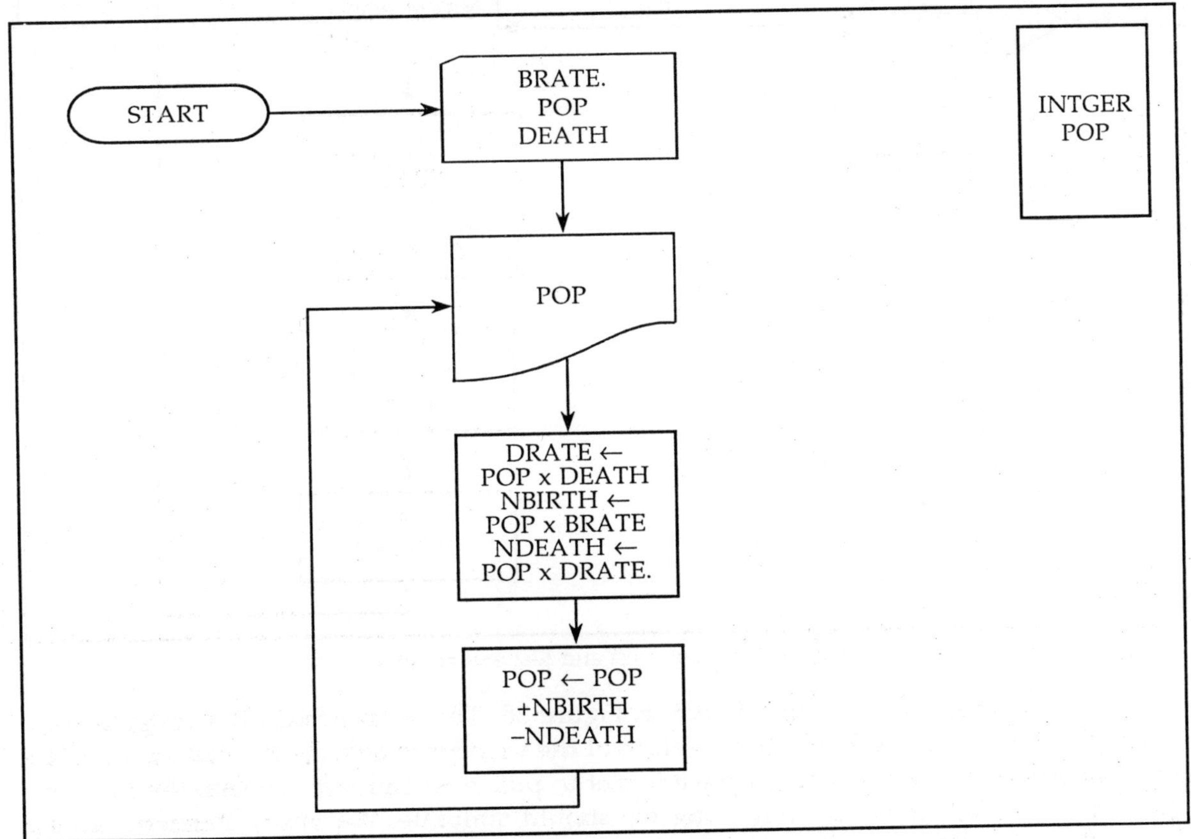

Fig. 38. First solution for population problem

We compute the behavior of this model by keeping back of the population and by calculating the change in the population from one year to another. Let us suppose that the birthrate is a real number to be input into BRATE, and the initial integer population is to be input into POP. Suppose also that the deathrate (DRATE) is a given fraction (DEATH) of the population, and that DEATH is to be input.

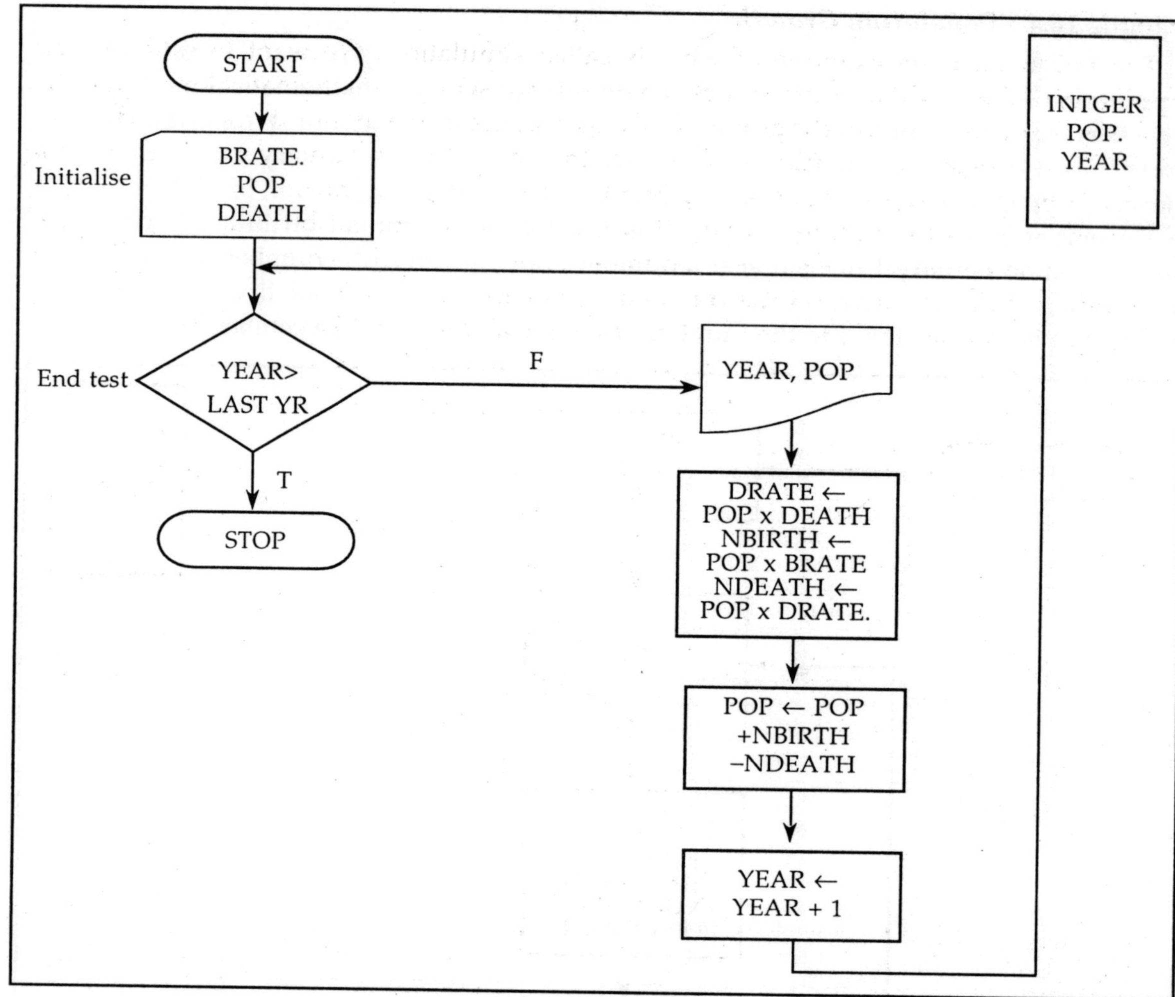

Fig. 39. Solution with end test and counter

We first propose the solution shown in Figure 38. The output from this program is a series of population sizes with no indication of the year for which the population has that size. The loop does not stop because we forgot to put in an end test - in fact, the problem specification failed to say for how long we should simulate. We must, therefore, add a *counter* that says how many years have elapsed and an end test that stops the loop. To do this we also require as input the integer date (YEAR) on which the first population is specified and the year up to which we must simulate (LASTYR). The solution is shown in Figure 39. The loop is stopped when the value of YEAR exceeds the last year to be simulated.

We have seen three examples of loops, each with a different stopping criterion. They were

- End of input in Examples 16.1 and 16.2.

- Accuracy. Each pass through the loop, called an *iteration*, improved the answer in Example 16.3. When the answer reached the desired accuracy, the iteration was stopped.
- A count. A counter (YEAR) was used to record passes through the loop. When it reached a terminal value, the simulation was stopped in Example 16.4.

Many loops are controlled by counters. The important steps in the counting process are:

- Initialisation: Setting the counter to its first value.
- Incrementation: Incrementing the counter, in this case by one, at the end of the processing in the loop.
- Testing: Seeing if the counter has exceeded its final value.

The use of one as an increment is not fundamental. If our model had specified that the population changed only on February 29, the counter could have been increased by 4. Or we could have two days a year when births and deaths are permitted, in which case the counter would have to be increased by 0.5.

QUESTIONS

1. What are the three important procedures associated with a program loop?
2. When a counter is used to control the termination of a loop, what are the three numbers that determine its action?

PROBLEMS

*1. A deck of cards, each containing a pair of numbers A and B, is to be read. Write a program to do this and to find the sum S1 of those numbers B for which A < B, the sum S2 of those numbers B for which A = B, and the sum S3 of those numbers b for which A > B. Print S1, S2 and S3. You may assume that the numbers A and B are both positive.

2. Suppose that in Example 16.3 we knew only that the sins of the values of $x^3 + 3x -5$ initially differed at x = LOW and x = HIGH, but did not know which was negative and which was positive when the program was to be written. The solution in Figure 36 works only for the case that the sign at x = LOW is negative. Modify it so that it checks the sign at x = LOW for the initial value of LOW, setting the logical variable ZNEG to be "TRUE" if that sign is negative. "FALSE" otherwise. Then modify the rest of the flowchart so that it works in either case.

ARRAYS

In one of the earlier examples we input a set of student exam scores and calculated their average. Let us amend that problem and ask also that the computer print out the difference between each student's score and the average score. All the scores must be processed and the average score must be calculated before we can compute the difference between each student's score and the average. Consequently we must pass over the list of student scores twice, the first time computing the average, the second time computing the difference. There are two methods of doing this. the first method is require that the deck of student scores be returned to the input hopper of the card reader after the first reading- a slow and inconvenient process. The second method is to store the scores in memory after the first reading. In this section we will look at technique that are helpful to the second method.

Each student card contains a score that will require one cell for storage. A different cell will have to be used for each score. We could try to allocate a set of cells by using the names SCOREA, SCORED.... etc., for cells for the first student, the second student, ... etc. Then the input section of the flowchart would look something like:

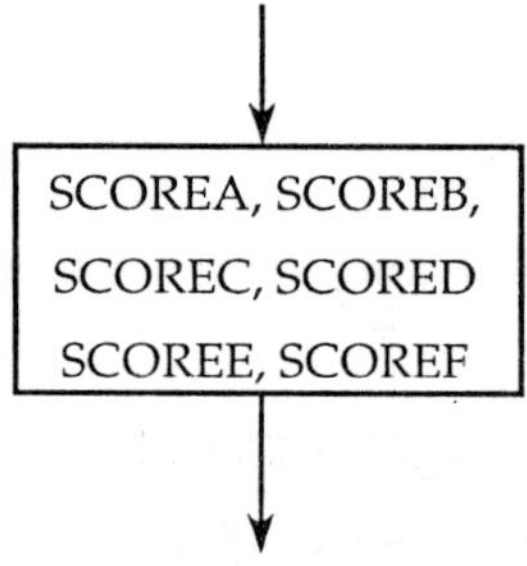

This approach would work fine if there were exactly six students. What if there were more or less? Since we do not know how many students there are, we cannot give individual names to the unknown number of different cells. What we need is a set of cells for the scores. This set should be arranged so that we can read into any one of them and get the results back from any one of them. In other words, we want to arrange the set of scores in a data *structure* such that we can access each.

There are various types of data structures. An array is a set of cells in memory such that we can access any one of them directly. By "accessing an element directly" we mean that we can refer to a particular one, such as the tenth. The mathematical notation for vectors is a useful one for arrays. In mathematics, a vector B is a set of N numbers, called B_1, B_2, B_3.....B_N. We refer to the 1th as B_1. Because our input devices cannot handle subscripting, we will write B_1 as B[l]. The set of N elements B[1], B[2], ...B[N] is an array of elements that we can access directly. We will allow arrays in our flowchart language. The student scores can then be stored in SCORE[1], SCORE[2]....etc. The score of the lth will be stored in SCORE[l]. The input section of the solution now takes the form of a loop that reads first to SCORE[1], then to SCORE[2], etc. A counter l is initialised to one and incremented by one. This is shown in Figure 40. Note that we can use SCORE[l] wherever we can use a simple name like SCORE, because it represents a cell in memory. The second part of the problem uses a similar loop to form the difference between each score and the average; however, this loop is controlled by a counter.

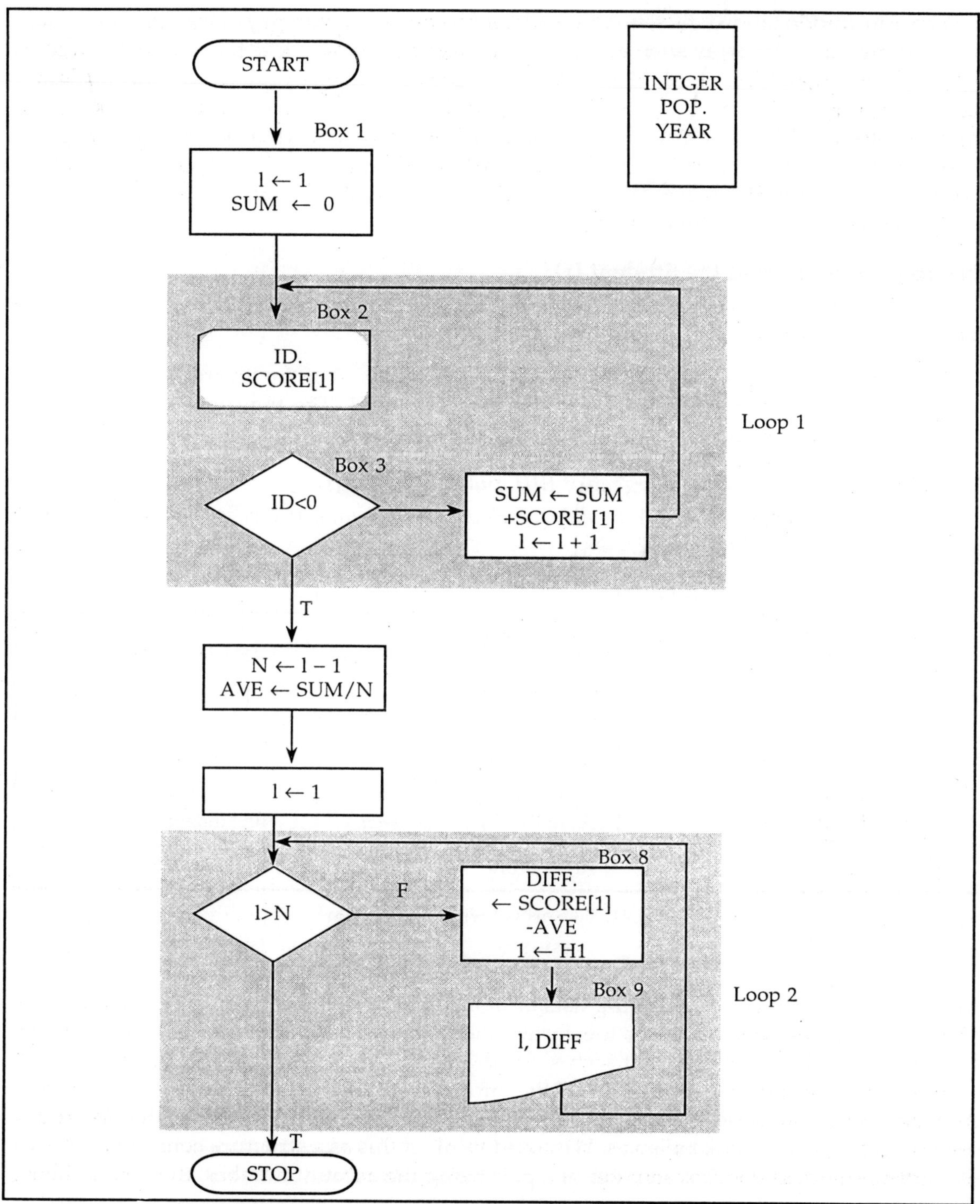

Fig. 40. Using two loops

You can understand data structures better if you know the way they are stored and accessed memory. An array such as we used is stored in a *contiguous* block of cells, that is, as set of cells with addresses M, M + 1, M + 2..... and so on. The first cell of the block contains the first element of the array. Thus SCORE[1] is stored in the first cell of the block used for the array SCORE. If we think of the address of the first cell of the array SCORE as having the name SCORE, then SCORE[1] is in location SCORE, SCORE[2] is in location SCORE+1,.......SCORE[l] is in location SCORE +l-1, and so on. Section 16.6.2 discusses how arrays are handled in machine language.

Example 16.5 - Printing the Student ID

In the student problem above, we wish to print the student ID along with the difference between his score and the average.

This can be handled by using an array ID such that the ID of the lth student is stored in ID[l], while his score is in SCORE[l] as shown in Figure 41. The flowchart in Figure 40 is modified by changing Boxes 2, 3 and 9 to that shown in Figure 42.

Example 16.6 — Putting the Largest of B[l] and C[l] into A[l]

Suppose we have three arrays, A, B, and C, each with N elements, and we wish to put the largest of B[l] and C[l] into A[l] for l =1, 2,....N.

The solution is shown in Figure 43.

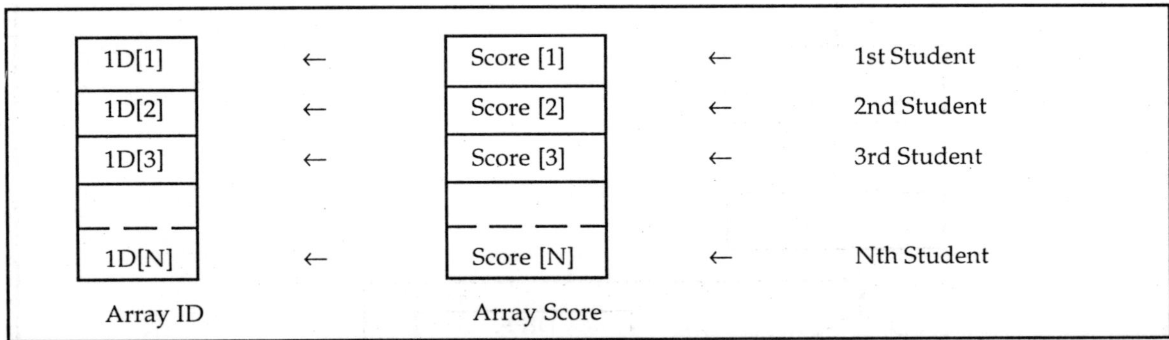

Fig. 41. Two arrays with related data

HIGHER DIMENSIONAL ARRAYS

Arrays were introduced as a storing lists of items that were to be directly read or written. The data was assumed to be of the form where it was naturally a *linear array* or *one-dimensional array*- a list of student scores, for example. Often we encounter data that has a more complex structure. In example 16.5 the information consisted of list of ID numbers and student scores. Suppose we have a list of bank account identification numbers and a corresponding list of bank balances. We could think of this as a structure consisting of a list of pairs of numbers-the first member of a pair being the account number, the second being the account balance. A natural way to store this information is in a *two-dimensional array* is shown in Figure 44.

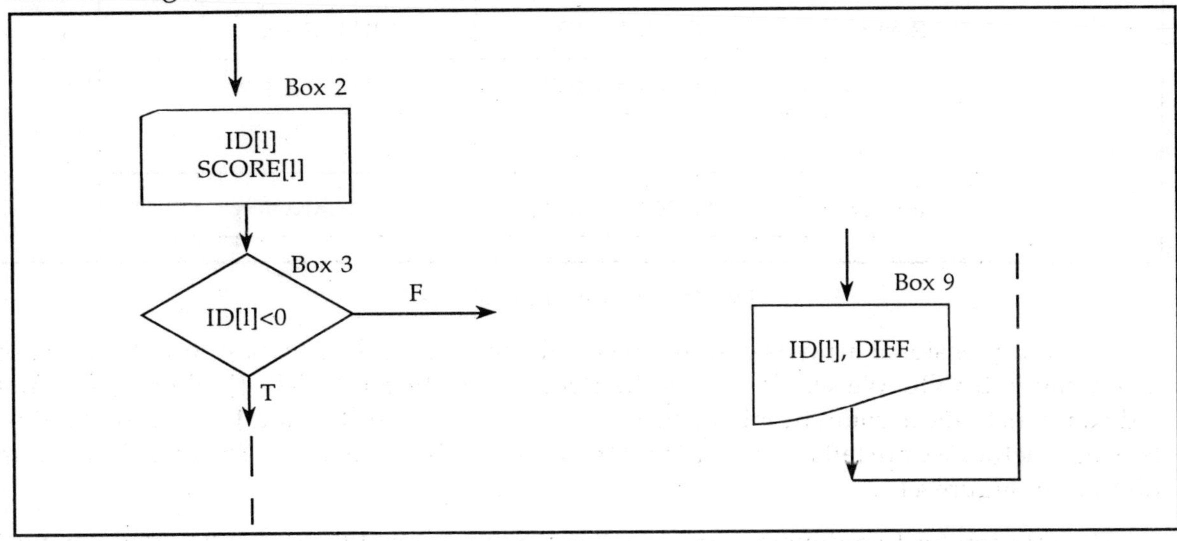

Fig. 42. Modification to Fig. 16.40

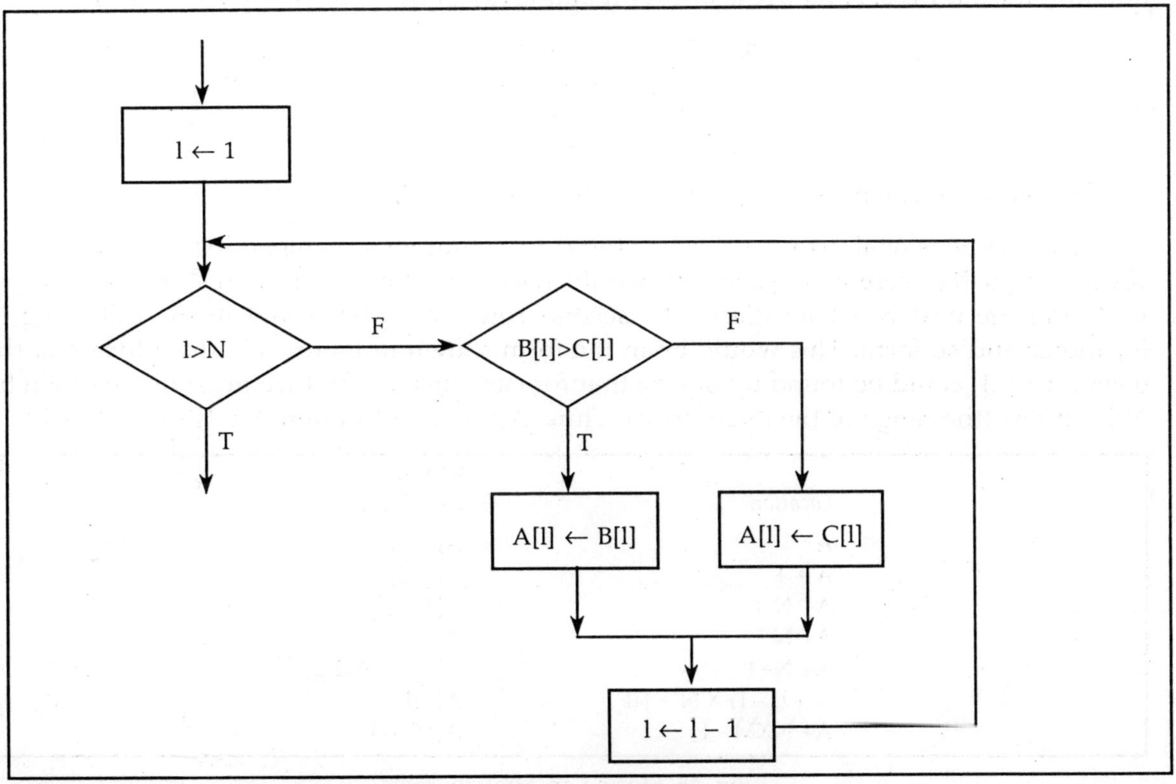

Fig. 43. Solution for Example 16.6

	Column 1	Column 2
Row 1	ACCOUNT ID1	BALANCE 1
	ACCOUNT ID 2	BALANCE 2
Row N	ACCOUNT ID N	BALANCE N

Fig. 44. Two-dimensional array

A two-dimensional array is one that has both rows and columns. Suppose the name of this array is BANK. We would access the items by writing BANK[l, J] where l, the first index, refers to the account number [the row number in Figure 44], and J, the second index, tells us whether we are talking about the ID (J = 1) or the balance (J = 2). Thus J is the column number in Figure 44.

The rotation for two-dimensional arrays is a natural translitertion of the mathematical notation for matrices. A matric is a rectangular array of numbers written in the form

$$A_{11}\ A_{12}\ A_{13}\ \ldots\ldots A_{1N}$$
$$A_{21}\ A_{22}\ A_{23}\ldots\ldots A_{2N}$$
$$A_{M1}\ A_{M2}\ A_{M3}\ldots\ldots A_{MN}$$

The general element is A_{ij}, which we must write as A[l, J].

A two-dimensional array could be stored in contiguous memory locations in any of several ways. If it were *stored by row* we would start at location A, say, and store the first row in A and the next N - 1 locations; the second row would be stored in the following N locations; and so forth. This would be in the form shown in Figure 45. The address of the element A[l,J] could be found by noting that for each increase in l we must move down by N locations (the range of the J subscript). Thus, A[l, J] is in location A + [l - 1] X N + J - 1.

Location	*Element stored*
A	A[1, 1]
A + 1	A[1, 2]
A+ N-1	A[1,N]
A+ N	A[2,1]
A+ N+1	A[2,2]
A + (l - 1) X N + J-1	A[l,J]
A+ NXM - 1	A[M, N]

Fig. 45. Storing an array by rows

If the two-dimensional array were stored by *columns, the* first column would be stored in the first M cells starting at A, the second column in the next M, and so on. This time the address of A[I,J] would be A + (J - 1) X M + I-1. Some POLs store matrices by column (FORTRAN, for example) and some by row (PL/I, for example). We will avoid the issue by never making major use of the way in which arrays are stored.

Example 16.7 — Weighted Sum of Array

An example of the use of a two-dimensional array is the set of student scores in a course. Each student takes several exams and does homework assignments. He receives a score for each of these. Therefore there is a one-dimensional array of scores for each student. This could be called SCORE[J], J = 1,.....N, assuming that there are N different exams or homework assignments. However, there are many students, say M, in the class, so we will need many arrays. The best way to handle these is to group them into a two-dimensional array. Thus A[I,J] can contain the score of the Ith student on the Jth exam. It contains N X M scores.

Location	*Element stored*
A	A[1,1]
A + 1	A[2, 1]
A+ M - 1	A[M, 1]
A + M	A[1,2]
A+ M + 1	A[2,2]
A+ (J - I) X M + I - 1	A[I,J]
A + NXM - 1	A[M, N]

Fig. 46. Storing an array by columns

Suppose that the instructor wishes to compute a total score for the Ith student. He does this by forming the expression.*

A[I,1] + A[I, 2] +......+A[I,N]

A more common way of arriving at the score for the whole course is to form a *weighted* sum. The instructor may have announced that each of six homework assignments counts 10% towards the grade, the mid-term counts 15%, and that the final counts 25%. In that case he would want to form

A[I,1] X 0.1 +......+ A[I, 6] X 0.1 + A[I, 7] X 0.15 + A[I, 8] X 0.25

This is a weighted sum. In general we want to form

$$C(1) = \sum_{J=1}^{N} A[1,J] \times B[J]$$

where B[J] are the weights. (This calculation occurs frequently in scientific work and is called the product of a matrix and a vector.) It can be dome using a double loop. The inner one computes the sum of the N products. The outer one changes I over the range 1 to M. A solution is shown in Figure 47.

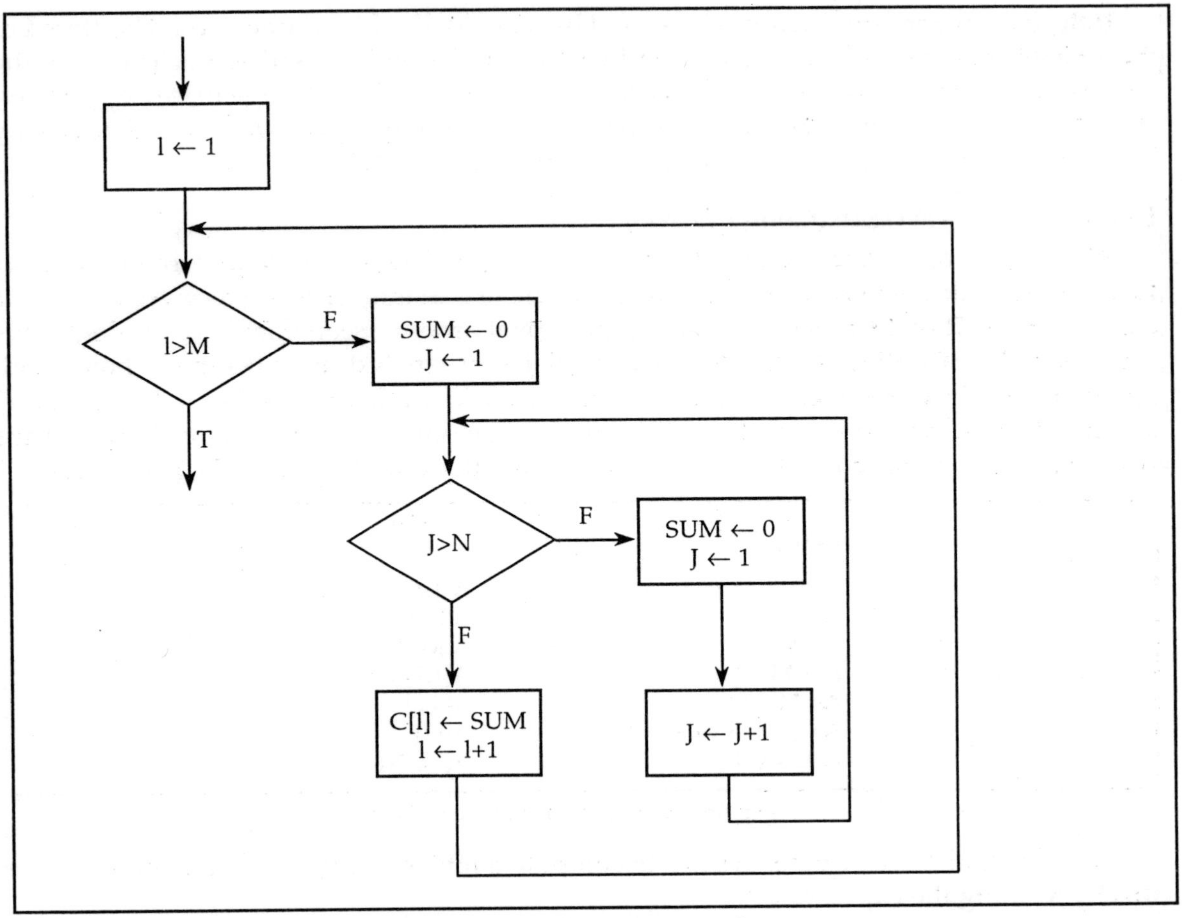

Fig. 47. Solution for Example 16.7.

In some problems we encounter even higher dimensional arrays. *A three- dimensional array.* for example, is an array of two-dimensional arrays. It is accessed by specifying three subscripts. Thus, if the array is B, we can refer to B[I,J,K]. A "picture" of a three dimensional array is given in Figure 48. One frequent use of three-dimensional arrays is to store approximations to a physical variable-for example, temperature or the flow of air around an airplane wing. Assume that approximations to temperature are stored as a set of points on a *rectangular grid* in ordinary three-dimensional space. Looking at Figure 48 we can see that we can fill up a region of space with these points so that there is always a point within a small distance. If the temperature does not change too rapidly as one moves from one place to another, the temperature at an arbitrary point is reasonably approximated by the temperature at the nearest point in the matrix.

---

* This is written more concisely with the mathematical operator Σ meaning sum. Thus $\sum_{J=1}^{N}$ A[I,J] means sum A[I,J] for all values of J form 1 to N.

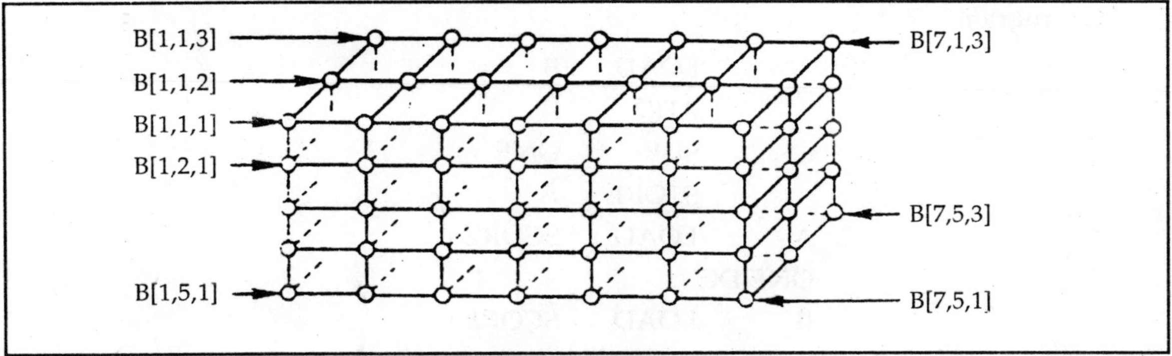

Fig. 48. Three dimensional array.

QUESTIONS

1. If array element A[13] is in location 1451, in what location is element A[29]?

*2. If A[2,3] is in location 1756 and A[3, 3] is in location 1760, where is A[4, 4]?

3. If A[1,1] is in location 245, A[3,4] is in location 262, and A[2,2] is in location 253, where is A[5,3]?

4. If A[2, 2] is in location 127 and A[7,5] is in location 144, where is A[6, 6]?

PROBLEMS

*1. The array A[l] contains N elements, l = 1......N. Write a program of find the largest difference between two consecutive elements; that is, the largest value of A[l] - A[l +1] for l =1, 2.....N -1.

2. Modify the program you write for problem 1 to also find the *index* of the largest difference; that is, to find a J such that A[J] - A[J + 1] is maximum.

3. The array VALUE[l] contains M elements. Write a program to find the number of elements less than the average value of all element and the number of elements greater than that average.

4. Assume that [l,J] l =1,....M, J = 1,....N contains the Jth score of the lth student. Assume that W[J] contains the weight of the Jth problem.

Write a program to rank *the students by storing into K[l] the position of the lth student in the class.*

Handling Arrays in Machine Language

The machine language form of the program has to be able to access the elements of SCORE. How does it do this? Recall from preceding that instructions are stored in memory cells just like data. Therefore we can do arithmetic on them. Suppose we wish to LOAD the lth element of SCORE, where l is stored in a cell with that name.

The program

```
            LOAD    B
            ADD     l
            SUB     ONE
            STORE   A
A           LOAD    SCORE
ONE DC              1
B           LOAD    SCORE
```

will do this. Location B contains a constant that is equivalent to "LOAD SCORE" as an instruction. If the address SCORE is 3127, this constant is 000 03127. If l contains the number 11, then LOAD B. ADD l puts 000 03138 into the accumulator. The SUB ONE reduces this to 000 03137, which is then stored in location A. Consequently, when the contents of cell A are executed as an instruction, they represent "LOAD SCORE + 10". Modern computers provide other faster techniques, called *indexing*, for doing this type of operation, we will not discuss them here.

BUILT-IN FUNCTIONS

We pointed out that although the computer has only a few basic capabilities such as addition and testing, many other common operations can be formed from or approximated by combinations of these. Because such other operations are common we adopt a special notation for them and allow them to be used directly. An example we have met already is the square root process. If we have a number stored in cell X, we know that it is possible to get an approximation to $\sqrt{X}$ by use of the basic arithmetic operators. We will denote this by SQRT(X) SQRT is called a function. Because it is one provided by our language, it is called a *built-in function*. (It is built-in to the language, not to the hardware of the machine.)

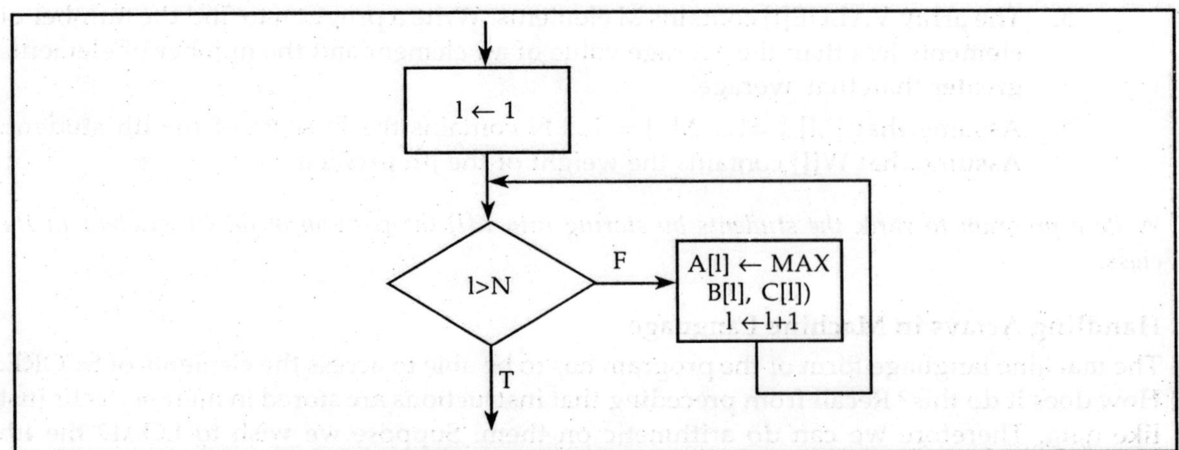

Fig. 49. Use of built-in functions for Example 16.6

We can use the expression SQRT(X) whenever the value of an expression approximately equal to $\sqrt{X}$ is needed. Thus

$$B \leftarrow A + SQRT(X)$$

is valid, as is

$$Q \leftarrow B + SQRT\ (X + Y)$$

The latter example first forms the value of X + Y, then finds its square root, and finally adds B to it before storing it in Q.

Other built-in functions that we will use include.

ABS)X	Value is the magnitude (absolute value) of X
TRUNC(X)	Gives the integer part of X by truncation
ROUND(X)	Gives the integer part of X by rounding
SIN(X)	Gives an approximation to sin X
COS(X)	Gives an approximation to cos X

The above functions have a single *argument*; that is, the variable X whose value determines the value of the function. The following have two or more arguments:

MAX (A, B)	Gives a number that is the maximum of A and B. MAX (A, B, C) gives the maximum of A, B, and C, and so forth
MIN(A, B)	Gives the minimum of A and B

These functions do not add to the power of the language; they do abbreviate the writing. Thus, Example 6 in the previous section can be written as in Figure 49.

17

Flowchart Language II

The symbols introduced here are adequate to solve any problems we may meet. In this chapter we are going to introduce additional symbols that make a problem solution and its flow-chart easier to prepare and follow. These symbols correspond to some concepts to program organisation and problem solution that will be introduced in this chapter.

PROGRAM LOOPS

We examined program loops and saw that they arose in several ways. Among these were:

- Loops that read data and terminate on some special condition—for example, a dummy final card with recognisable data such as a negative number.
- Iterative loops that solve a problem—perhaps by a trial and error process. These loops stop when the completed solution is sufficiently accurate.
- Counting loops in which a number of items are to be processed. This number is known at the start of the loop, so a counter can be used to count passages through the processing in the loop. The loop is stopped when the counter reaches a final value.

The counting type of loop occurs so frequently that we introduce special symbols for such loops. The important characteristics of this type of loop are:

- A variable is used as a counter.
- An initial value is required for the counter (often 1).
- An increment amount is required for the counter (often 1).
- An end value is required for the counter.
- The section of code that is processed inside the loop must be specified.

If a counting type of loop were to be executed for values of I between J and N, that is, for I = J, J +1, J +2.......N, we could write the flowchart shown in Figure 1.

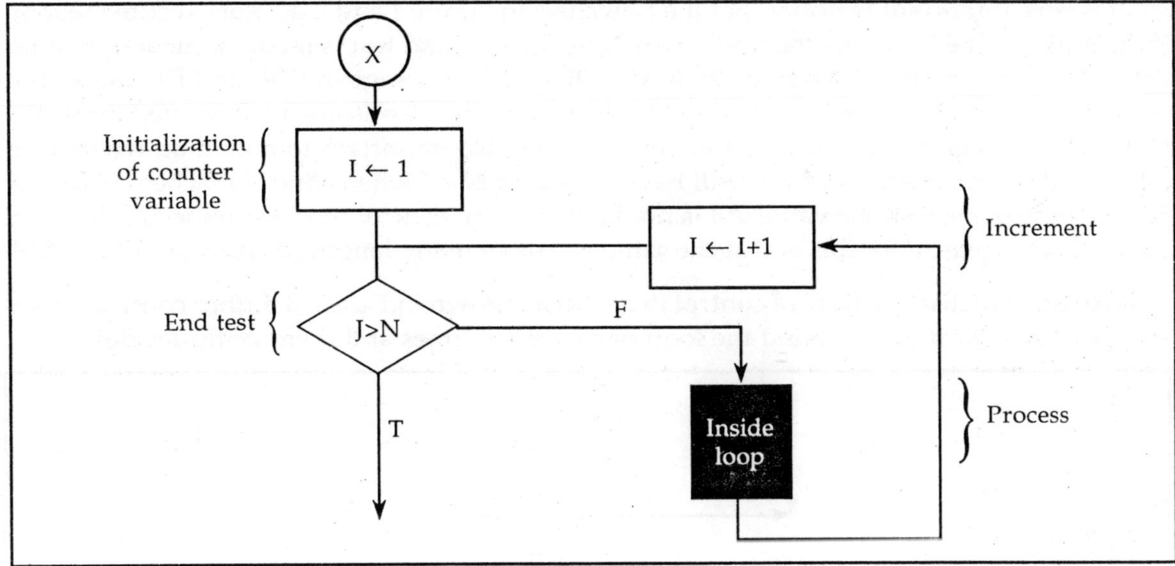

Fig. 1. Counting loop

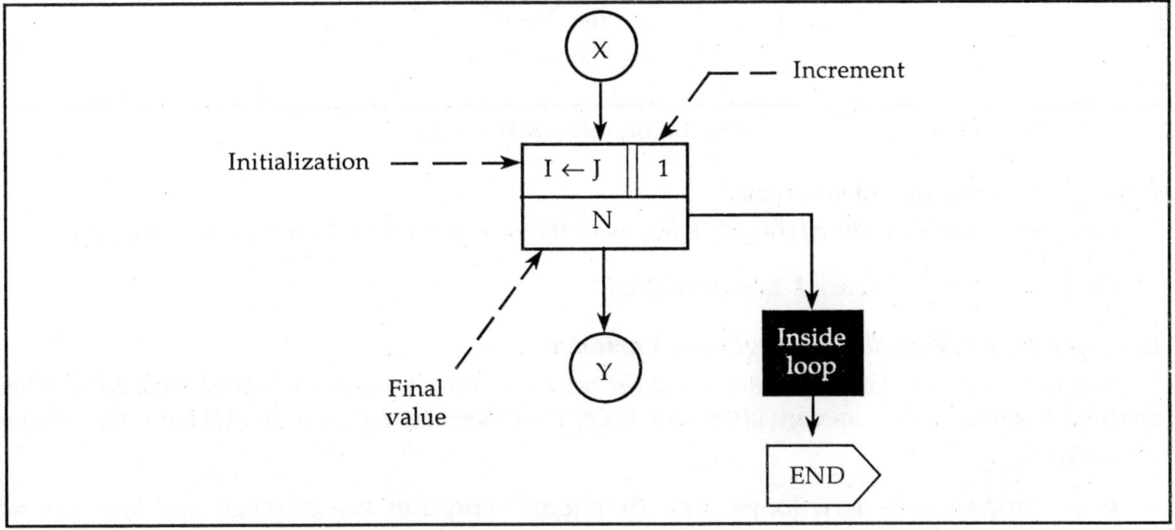

Fig. 2. Loop control box

This flow can be written in the more concise form shown figure 2. in which two new boxes have been introduced. The rectangle contains an assignment statement that specifies the variable used as a counter (called the *controlled variable*), the increment to be added after each execution of the loop, and the final value to be used. For now we assume that execution stops when the value of the controlled variable exceeds the final value. The End box, although not strictly necessary, emphasises that we have reached the end of the loop processing and are about to branch back to the incrementing stage.

It is very important to notice that the flowchart in Figure 1 and 2 do not execute the loop if the initial value J exceeds the final value N as the first and test is made immediately after the initial assignment. This agrees with ALGOL and PL/I usage in FOR and DO loops, but no with FORTRAN usage in DO loops. In the latter, the loop is always executed once; the first and test is made after the first increment. It is also important to note that, whereas in Figure 1 the controlled variable I will have the value N + I when control reaches connector Box Y, we assume that the value of I is not known when control reaches connector Box Y in Figure 2. Our reason for this is that the same is true in many languages such as FORTRAN.

We can visualise the flow of control in a loop as shown in Figure 3. Either control passes straight down or it goes around the loop one or more times and then continues down.

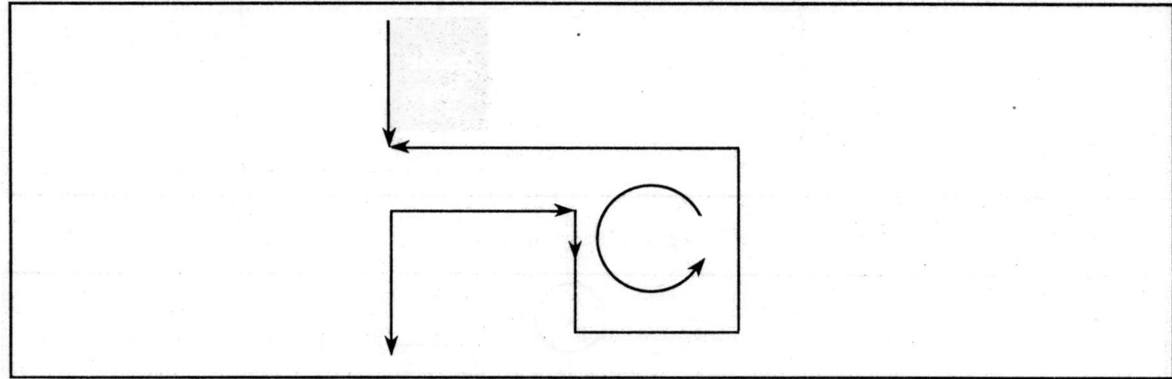

Fig. 3. Control flow in a loop

Example 1— Adding Two Arrays

Suppose we wish to add A[I] to B[I] and store the result in C[I] for each I between 1 and 20.

The flowchart in Figure 4 achieves this.

Example 2—Finding the Average and Variance

Suppose we wish to find the average and the variance of the N numbers A[I] through A[N]. (The variance is defined as the average of the squares of the differences between the A[1] and the average of the A[1].)

One solution uses two loops. The first loop computes the average and the second computes the variance. These loops occur sequentially because the result of the first (the average) is needed in the second. The solution is given in Figure 5. Note that the loops are exclusive; that is, no part of one is inside the other.

Example 3— Searching

Suppose we have an array of numbers A[1], A[2], ...A[N] and wish to find out if a given number B is equal to any one of the A[I], I = 1 to N.

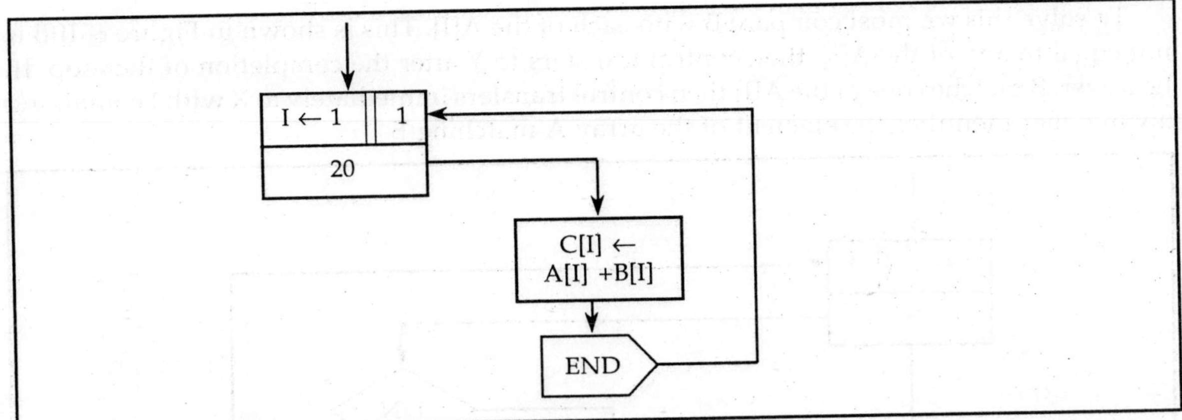

Fig. 4. Solution for Example 1

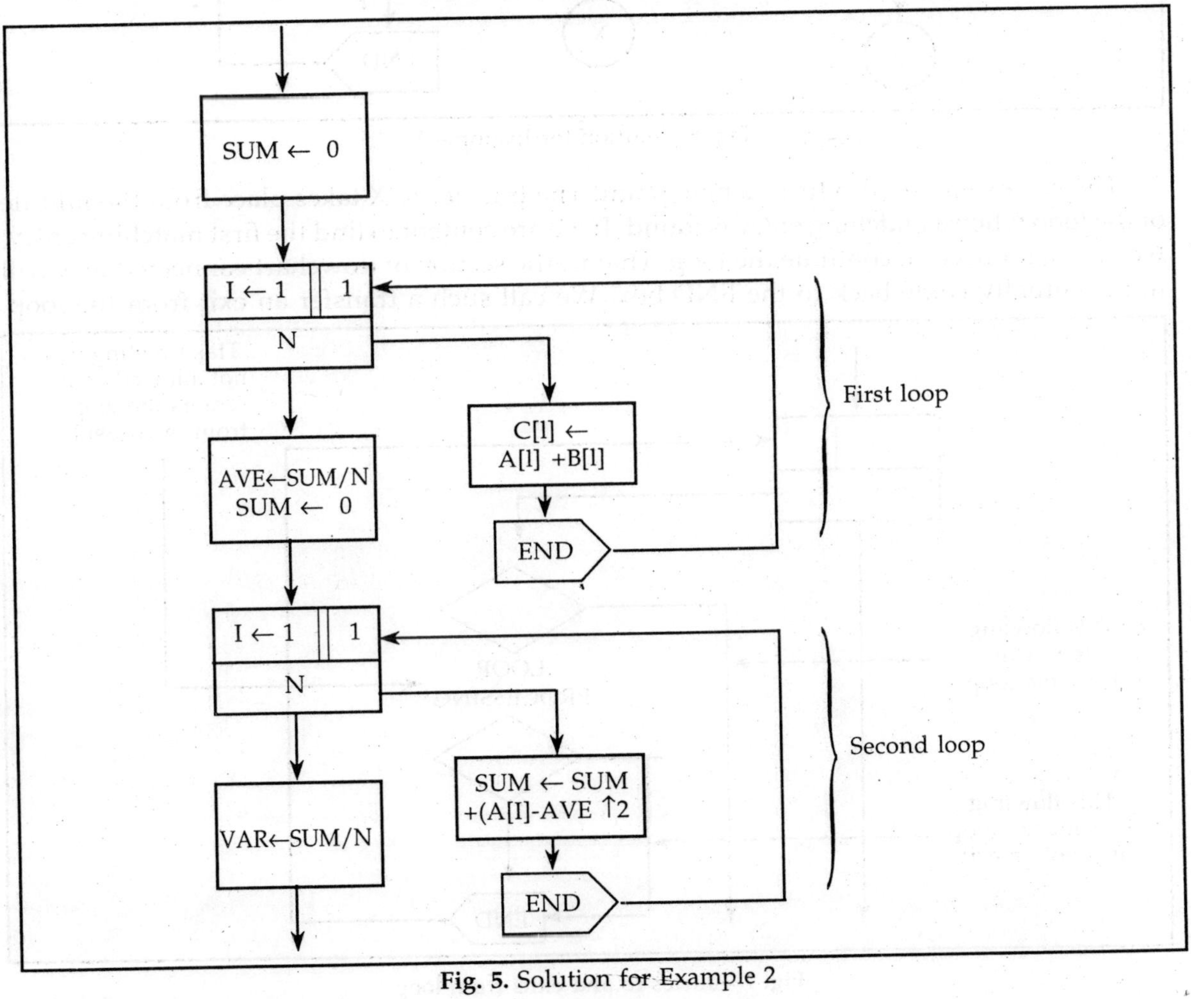

SUM ← 0

I ← 1 | 1

N

C[I] ←
A[I] +B[I]

END

First loop

AVE←SUM/N
SUM ← 0

I ← 1 | 1

N

SUM ← SUM
+(A[I]-AVE ↑2

END

Second loop

VAR←SUM/N

Fig. 5. Solution for Example 2

To solve this we must compare B with each of the A[I]. This is shown in Figure 6. If B is not equal to any of the A[I], then control transfers to Y after the completion of the loop. If, however, B matches one of the A[I] then control transfers immediately to X with I containing a value that identifies the element of the array A matching B.

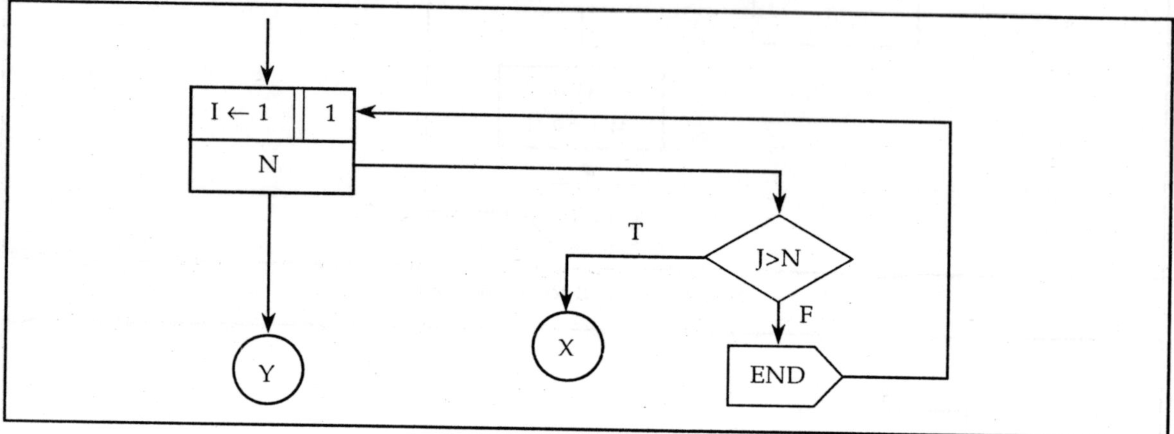

Fig. 6. Solution for Example 3

The last example introduces a new point. The transfer to X takes placc from the middle of the loop when a matching entry is found. If we are content to find the first matching entry, we no longer need to continue the loop. That is, the section of flowchart connected to X will not eventually come back to the END box. We call such a transfer an exit from the loop.

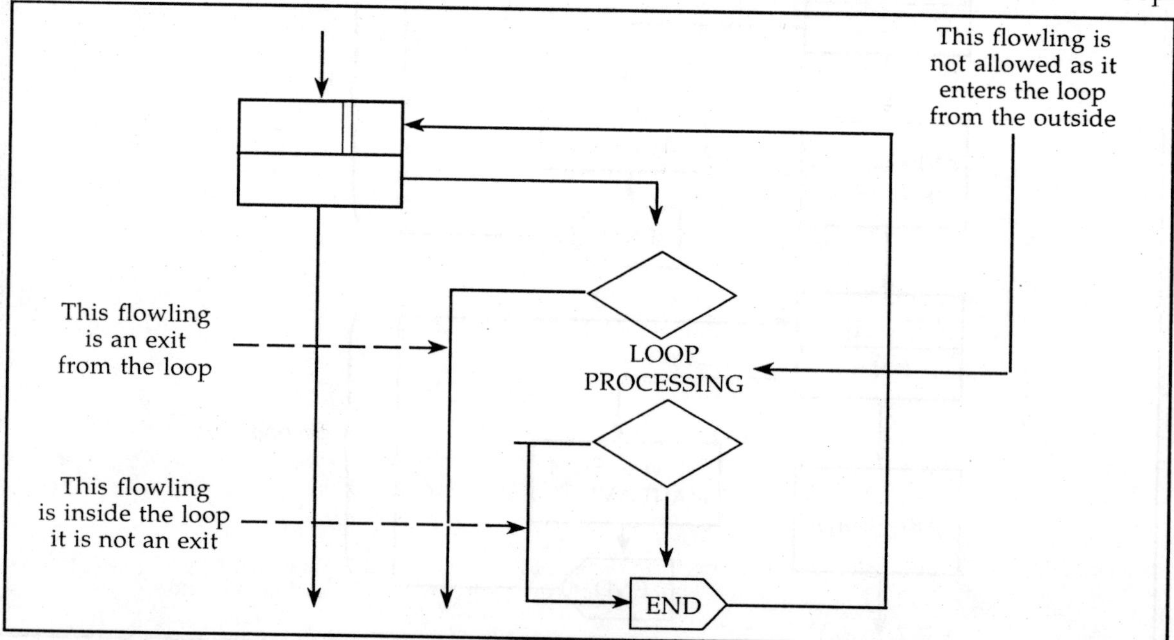

Fig. 7. Entries to and exits from loop

There can be any number of exits from the processing in a loop. However, there may not be any paths entering the processing of a loop from outside of the loop. A loop is defined by a loop control box and a matching END box as shown in Figure 7. The reason that paths may not enter the loop processing is that the initial conditions and incrementing must be started by passing through the loop control box.

Example 4—Different Increments

So far we have used increments of one. In this example we use a different increment. Suppose the odd-numbered locations in the array I(J), J = 1, 2, ... contain bank account identification numbers and the next higher even-numbered locations contain the account balances in cents for those accounts. Thus if I(7) contains 1275317, the balances of the customer with that account number is stored in cell I(8). The problem is to print the balance of the account whose number is stored in IAC. Assume that there are 100 accounts, so the array I uses 200 cells.

The solution is to search through the odd-numbered cells to find the account number. A flowchart solution is shown in Figure 8.

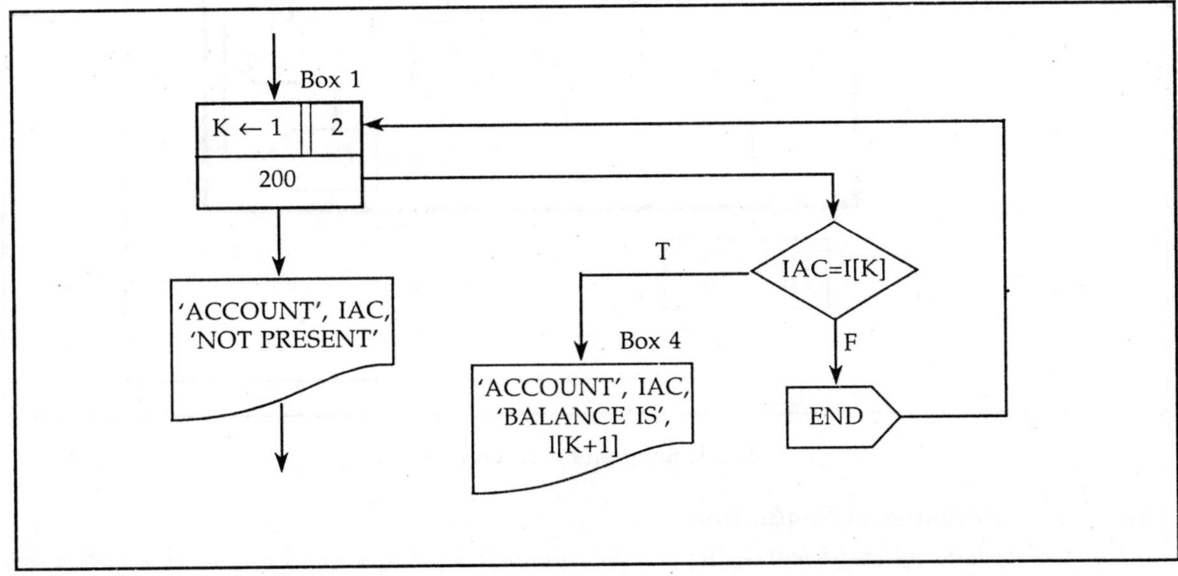

Fig. 8. Solution for Example 4

Two things should be noticed about this flowchart. In Box 1 we specified an increment of 2 starting at 1, but the end test is 200. The variable K will never take on the value 200, since it assumes only the odd integers. However, the end test stops the loop when the controlled variable K passes the end test. Thus the loop is executed with values of K = 1, 3, 5,.... 199. When K is incremented to 201. the end of test stops the loop. The second thing to be noted is in Box 4. There are array variable I uses an index that is an expression, namely K + 1. We will allow expressions to be used to index into arrays, although some programming languages are more restrictive.

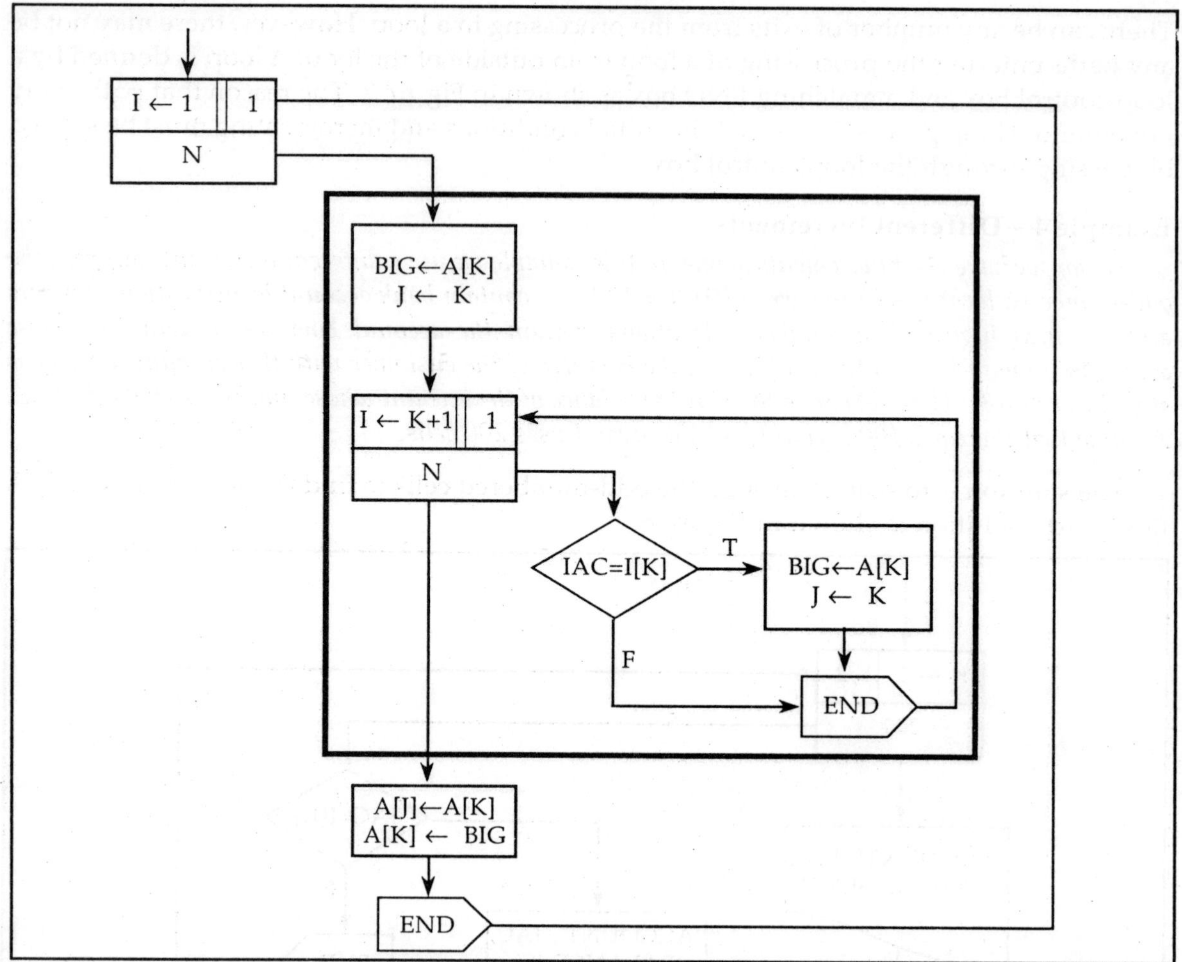

Fig. 9. Solution for Example 6

Example 5—Polynomial Evaluation

Suppose we have the coefficients $a_1, a_2, \ldots$ *of the polynomial* $p = a_n + a_{n-1}t + a_{n-2}t^2 + \ldots + a_t t^{n-1}$ *stored in array A[1], A[2],... and that we wish to compute p when t and n are given in locations with those names.*

Problems of this sort arise when we want to estimate the value of common mathematical functions. For example, the logarithm of 1 + x is given by

$$0 + x - \frac{x^2}{2} + \frac{x^3}{3} + \frac{x^4}{4} + \ldots$$

if x is less than one. We can approximate log (1 + x) by evaluating the first n terms of this sum for moderate size n.

If we evaluate p as it is written, we will use 2n – 3 multiplications; n – 2 to evaluate each power of t up to t^{n-1} and n – 1 to multiply each of the a; by t^{n-1} for i = 1.... n-1. Therefore we factor the expression into the following form:

$$p = a_n + t \times (a_{n-1} + t \times (a_{n-2} + t \times .... + t \times (a_2 + t \times a_1) ....))$$

N × (N – 1)/2 times* so, for example, if N is 100, it is executed 4950 times. This is independent of the original order of the items. Even if they were already in order and needed no sorting. 4950 passes through the inner would be required.

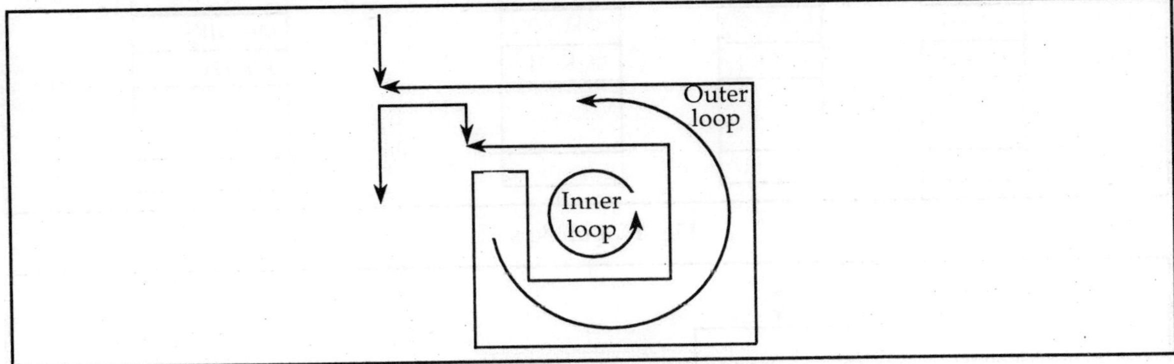

Fig. 10. Nested loops

Example 7—Bubble Sort

This method requires fewer steps if the data is partially in order. We search down the array A[I], starting from I = 1 and continuing until we find an element out of order. Thus if A [1]≥ A[2] ≥ . . . ≥ A[K], but A[K] < A[K + 1], the (K + 1)th element is the first element out of order. We then search back from A[K], moving elements down on slot until we find the right place to put A[K + 1]. This is diagrammed in Figure 11.

The name of the method arises from the fact that the element A[K +1] is allowed to rise up to its place in order, like a bubble in a bottle of fluid. The inner loop for this process is shown in Figure 12.

Notice that we are using a negative increment in the loop. Because of this, we do not expect the loop to stop until the counter K is reduced *below* the end test value of one. Second, notice that the loop has an exit to Box. 9. If this is taken, the right place for the old value of A[K +1] is cell A[I + 1]. If the loop terminates normally, the right place for the old value of A[K + 1] is at the top of the array. In this case we must ensure that I contains zero before going to Box 9 since we do not know the value of the controlled variable I after a normal termination.

---

*This can be seen by writing down the series once in the order given and once in reverse to get:

(N - 1) + (N - 2) + (N - 3) + ...+ 3 + 2 + 1
1 + 2 + 3 +......+ (N-3) + (N-2) + (N - 1)

if we add, we find that twice the value of the series is

N + N + N + ... + N + N + N

There are N - 1 terms present, so the sum of twice the series is N X (N - 1). Hence the value of the series is N X (N - 1)/2.

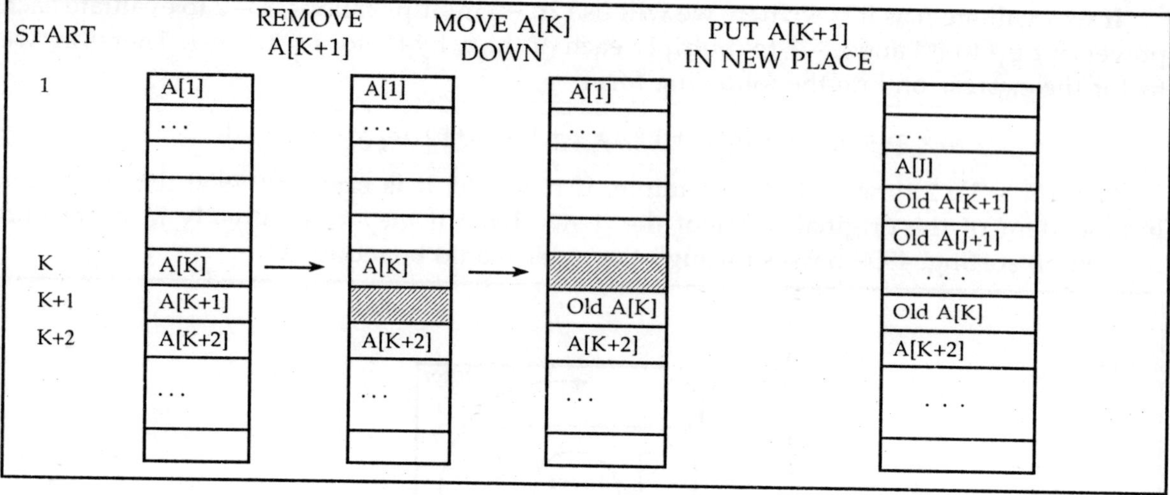

Fig. 11. Bubble sort

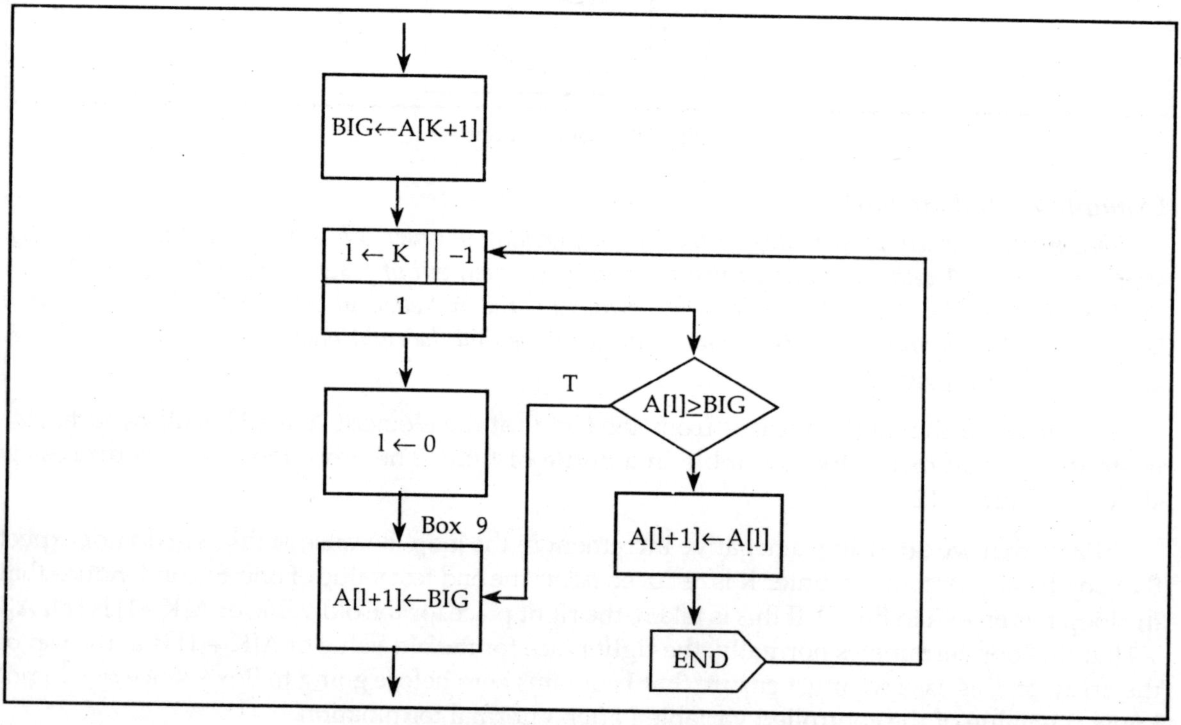

BIG←A[K+1]

l ← K | −1 | 1

A[l]≥BIG

T

l ← 0

Box 9

A[l+1]←A[l]

A[l+1]←BIG

END

Fig. 12. Inner loop

After the process in Figure 12 has been executed, the first K + 1 elements of A are in order. The search can then continue down the table to see if other elements are out of order. The full program is given in Figure 13. If the array is already in order, the TRUE exit will never be taken from Box 2, so one pass through the data will be sufficient to "sort" it.

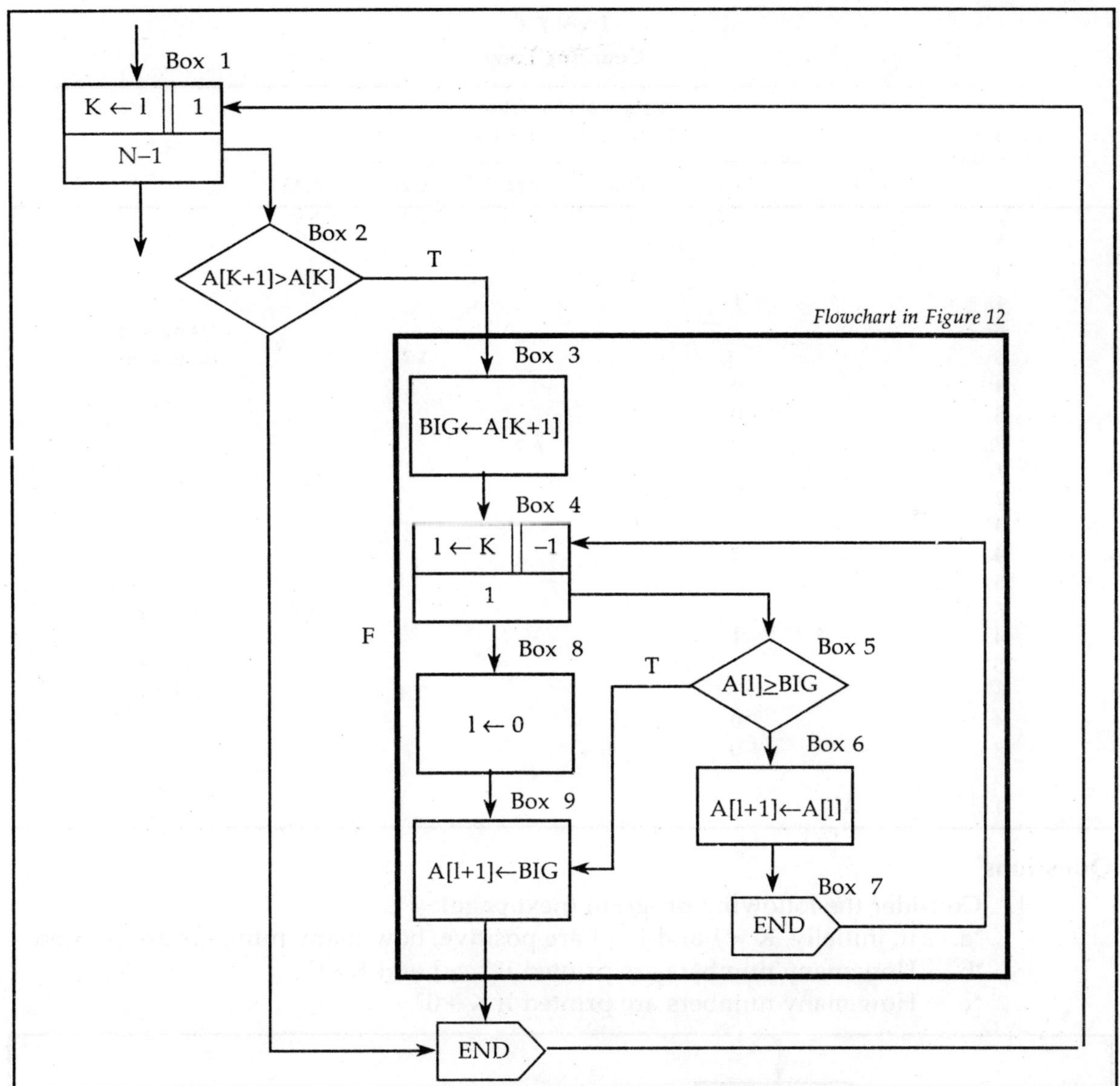

Fig. 13. Solution for Example 7

Of course, the worst case will still take N × (N – 1)/2 passes through the inner loop. This case occurs when the original data is in reverse order, as the following example shows.

Suppose the array A contains the three elements 1, 7, 2, 3, and 8, 7. The values of the important variables and the flow through Figure 13 are shown in Table 1.

TABLE 1
Counting Loop

Box to be Executed	Values of Variables (Only Changes Shown)						
	K	I	BIG	A[1]	A[2]	A[3]	
1	1			1.7	2.3	8.7	
2							
3			2.3				
4		1					
5							1st pass of
6					1.7		inner loop
4		0					
8		0					
9				2.3			
1	2						
2							
3			8.7				
4		2					
5							2nd pass of
6						1.7	inner loop
4		1					
5							3rd pass of
6					2.3		inner loop
4		0					
8		0					
9				8.7			
1	3						

Questions

1. Consider the following program (next page):
   - *a. If, initially, K = 1 and L ≥ J are positive, how many numbers are printed?
   - *b. How many numbers are printed if L ≥ J and K>0?
   - *c. How many numbers are printed if K # 0?

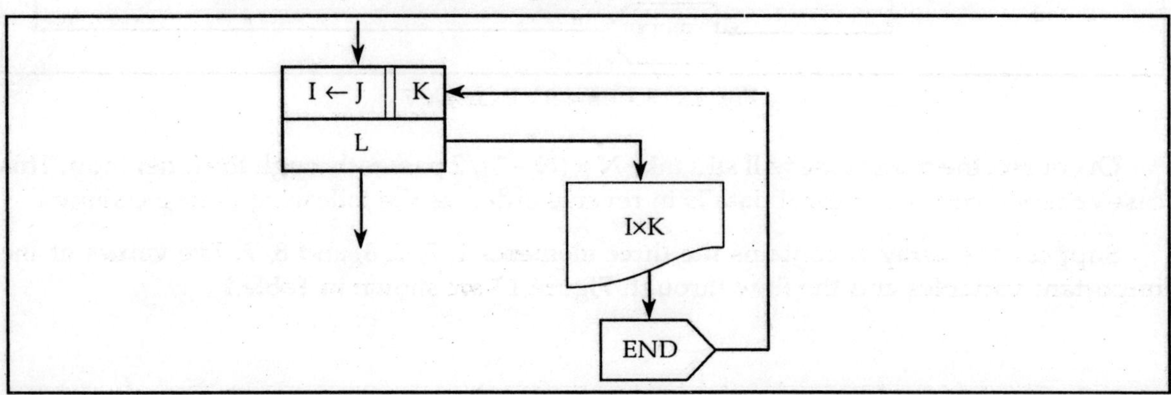

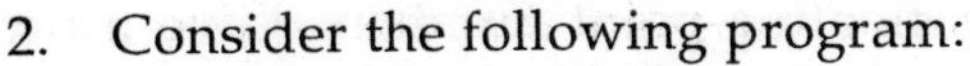

2. Consider the following program:

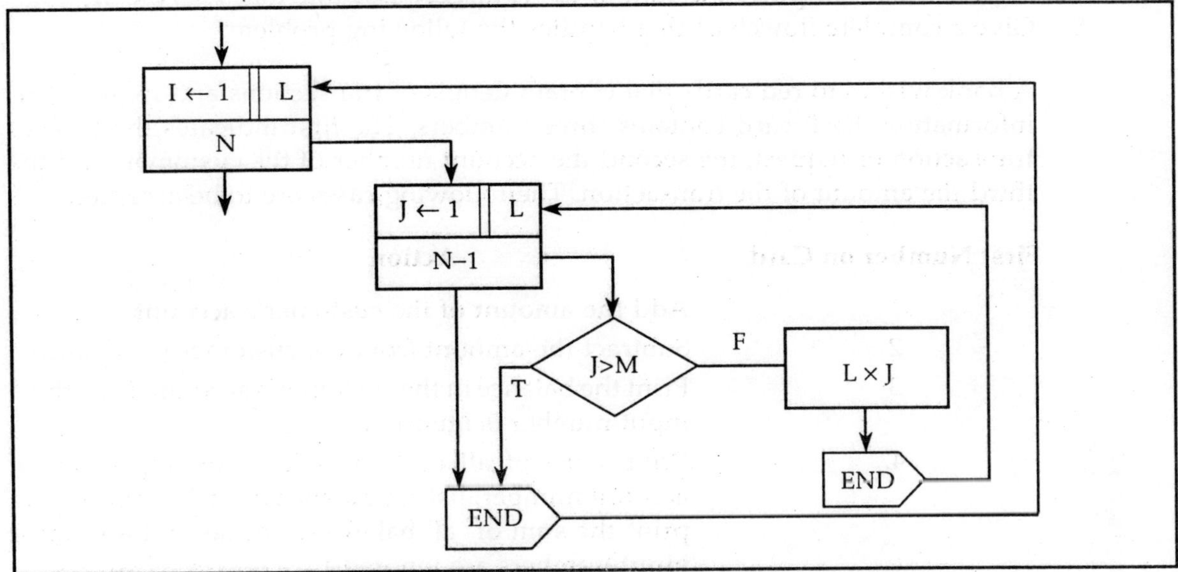

   a. If L = 1 and M ≥ N – 1, how many numbers are printed?
   b. If L > 0 and M ≥ N-1, how many numbers are printed?
   c. If L > 0, how many numbers are printed?

Problems

*1. The array A[I], I = 1,....N contains N numbers. Give a flowchart segment that computes the difference between the smallest and the largest.

2. Using only one loop, give a flowchart segment that finds the second largest number in the array A[I], I = 1,....N. Assume that N ≥ 2.

*3. Give a complete flowchart that reads N cards, each containing two numbers A[I] and B[I], I = 1,......N, in that order. Then compute the means

$$AX = \frac{1}{N}\sum_{I-1}^{N} A[I] \text{ \{This means } \frac{1}{N}\text{ (A[1] + A[2] + ... + A[N]).\}}$$

and

$$BX = \frac{1}{N}\sum_{I-1}^{N} B[I]$$

Finally compute and print the correlation

$$C = \frac{1}{N}\sum_{I=1}^{N}(A[1] - AX) \times (B[I] - BX)$$

4. An array X[I], I = 1,.....M., contains floating-point numbers. Give a flowchart segment that computes the sum of the N largest. Assume that $1 \leq N \leq M$.
5. Give a complete flowchart that handles the following problem:

   A bank wishes to red cards that contain details of transactions and requests for information. Each card contains three numbers. The first indicates the type of transaction or request, the second the account number of the customer, and the third the amount of the transaction. The following cases are to be accepted.

First Number on Card	Action
1	Add the amount of the customer's account.
2	Subtract the amount from the customer's account.
3	Print the balance in the customer's account. (The third input number is ignored.)
4.	Print a list of all customers in ascending order of account number, list the balance in each account, and print the sum of all balances.(The second and third input numbers are ignored.)
5	Open a new account with the third number as the initial balance.

If an addition or subtraction is attempted on a nonexistent account, an appropriate message should be printed. If a subtraction is made that would make the balance negative, the transaction should not be performed, but an appropriate message should be printed.

Initialise your data so that the bank has no customers.

INPUT/OUTPUT

In this section we examine some additional features of input and output boxes, and see how they might be applied in various problems. So far we have assumed that an input box contains a list of cell names. These names were either simple variable names such as A or X, or elements of arrays such as B[1], where I is the name of a cell that had already been assigned a value. It is possible that the read statement that includes B[I], in its list could also assign the value to I, as long as it does that first. Thus, the flowchart in Figure 14 reads an integer and assigns that value to I; it then reads a floating-point number into B[I]. If the input card contained "5, 15.71," the result of the read operation above would be to set 1 to 5 and B[5] to 15.71.

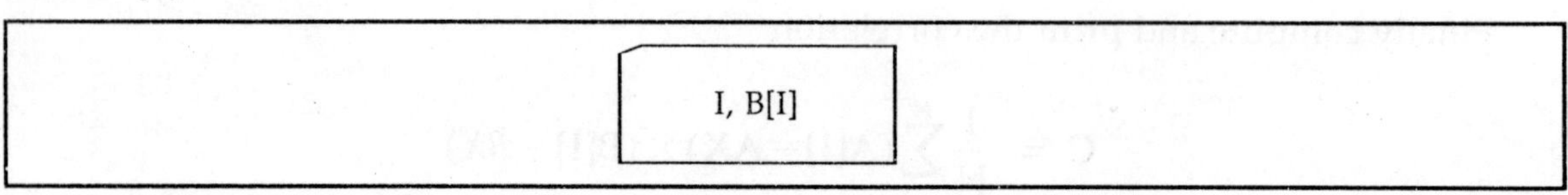

Fig. 14. Reading an integer and using it as an index

Example 8—Inserting into an Array

Suppose we have taken a series of temperature readings at some of the points and we have recorded the I, J and K of the points, and the temperatures T[I,J,K]. We wish to read these temperatures into the proper places in the array T.

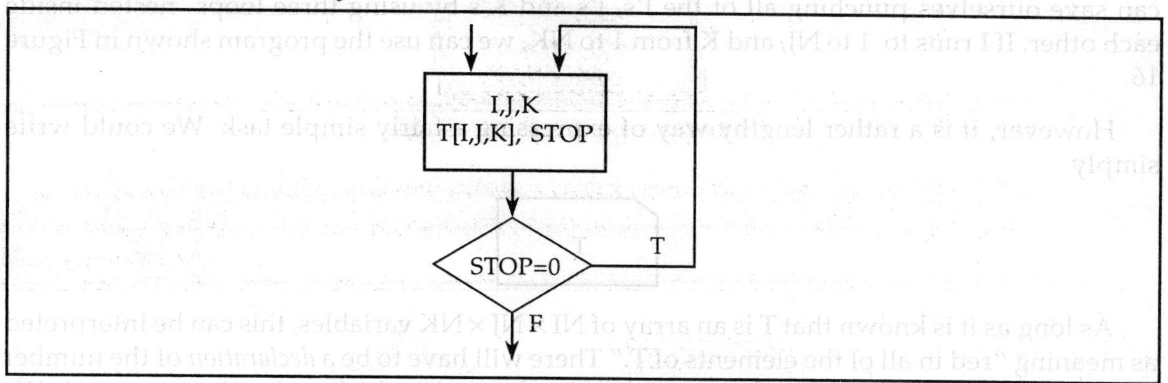

Fig. 15. Example 8.

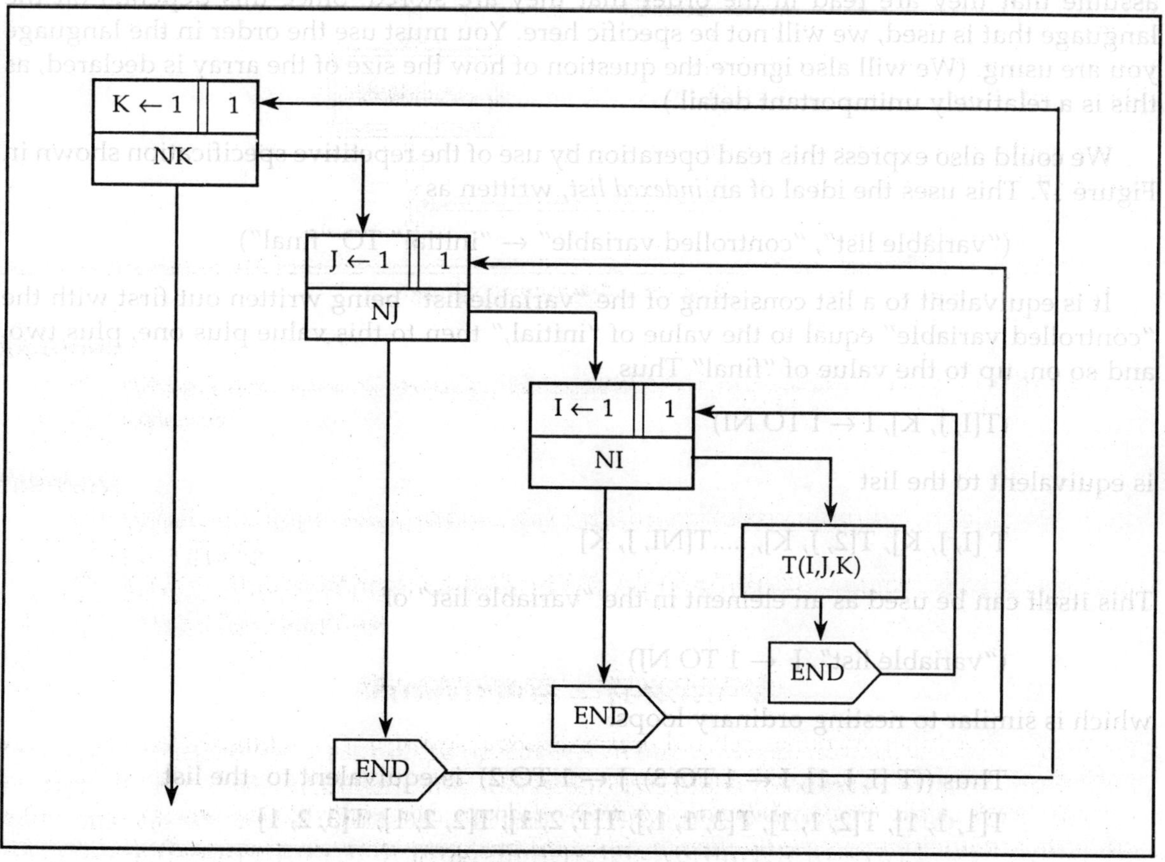

Fig. 16. Example 8 (2)

Since we do not know how many cards to expect when we write the program, we assume that each card has the numbers, I, J, K, T[I, J, K], and zero punched on it in that order, except for the last card which has I, J, K, T[I, J, K], and a one punched on it. A program to read in this data is shown in Figure 15. If temperature readings are taken at all points, we can save ourselves punching all of the I's, J's and K's by using three loops nested inside each other. If I runs to 1 to NJ, and K from 1 to NK, we can use the program shown in Figure 16.

However, it is a rather lengthy way of expressing a fairly simple task. We could write simply

T

As long as it is known that T is an array of NI × NJ × NK variables, this can be interpreted as meaning "red in all of the elements of T." There will have to be a *declaration* of the number of elements in the array T and we will have to know in which order they are read. We assume that they are read in the order that they are stored. Since this depends on the language that is used, we will not be specific here. You must use the order in the language you are using. (We will also ignore the question of how the size of the array is declared, as this is a relatively unimportant detail.)

We could also express this read operation by use of the repetitive specification shown in Figure 17. This uses the ideal of an *indexed list*, written as

("variable list", "controlled variable" ← "initial" TO "final")

It is equivalent to a list consisting of the "variable list" being written out first with the "controlled variable" equal to the value of "initial," then to this value plus one, plus two, and so on, up to the value of "final" Thus

(T[I, J, K], I ← I TO NI)

is equivalent to the list

T [I, J, K], T[2, J, K], ...T[NI, J, K]

This itself can be used as an element in the "variable list" of

("variable list", J ← 1 TO NJ)

which is similar to nesting ordinary loops.

Thus ((T [I, J, 1], I ← 1 TO 3), J ← 1 TO 2) is equivalent to the list
T[1, 1, 1], T[2, 1, 1], T[3, 1, 1,], T[1, 2, 1], T[2, 2, 1], T[3, 2, 1]

Finally this doubly indexed list can be used as a "variable list" in another loop, as in Figure 18. (Programming language also allows for increments of other than one. You should find details in your language manuals.)

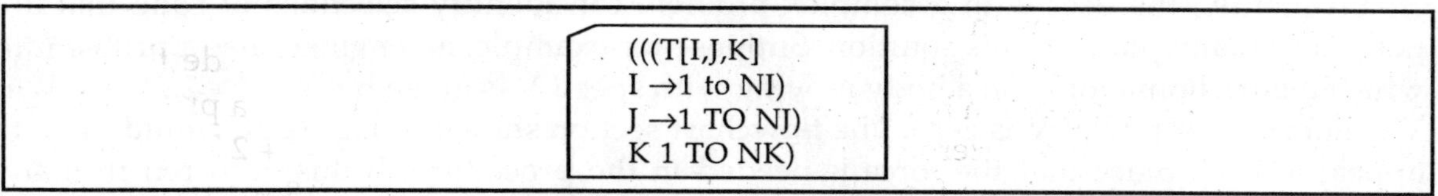

Fig. 17. Repetitive specification

An indexed list can be a part of another variable list. Thus, the sequence A[1, 1], A[1, 2], A[2, 1], A[2, 2], B[2].....etc., can be specified in an input or output list by ((A[I,J], J ← 1 TO 2), B[1], I ← 1 TO N).

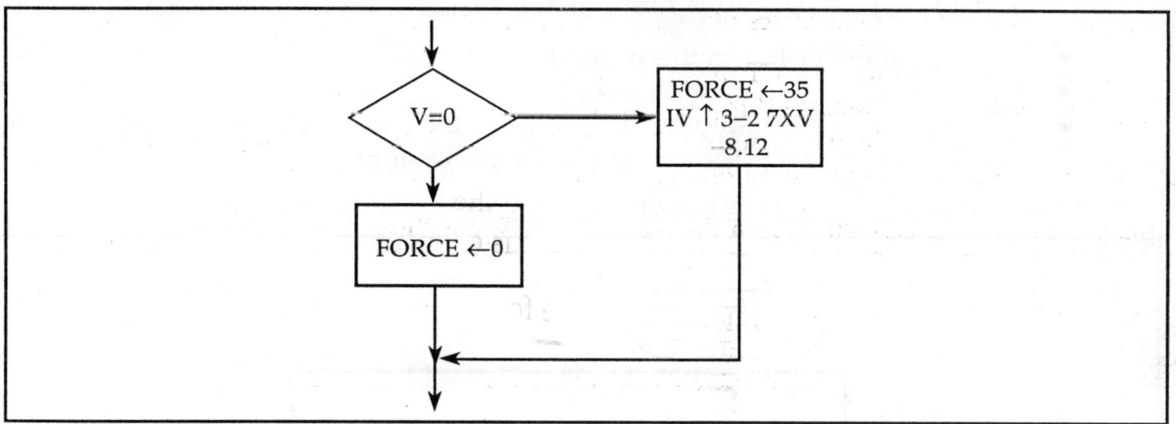

Fig. 18. Computation of force

Questions

1. What is the order of reading the elements of T in Figure 17 if NI = 3, NJ = 2 and NK = 2?

Problems

*1. Write one input statement to read the numbers N, I, and the variables A[I, J] for J = 1 TO N.

2. Draw a flowchart that reads the list (I, A[I,J] = I TO N) without using an indexed list in your read box.

PROCEDURES — FUNCTIONS

We introduced a number of additional operations which, although not basic, can be expressed in terms of the basic arithmetic and decision operations. Examples of these additional operations, called *built-in functions,* include COS(X) and MAX(A,B). Since, these built-in functions are frequently used by programmers, it is worthwhile to provide them within the system. The user does not have to reprogram such an operation each time he needs it in a procedure.

Frequently, the user with a complex problem can identify selections of code that are needed in many places in his solution. Suppose for example, an engineer has a problem in which the frictional force on a body moving with speed V is given by $3.5V^3 + 2.7V + 8.12$ if V is not zero, or by 0 if V is zero. The flowchart section shown in Figure 18 would have to appear at each place that the force is needed in the procedure. If this occurred in many different places, the engineer would soon wish that he had a built-in function named FRICT that computed the frictional force directly, so that he could write FORCE ← FRICT (V). Consequently, we allow the user to define his own functions by means of flowchart procedures.

The important characteristics of a function are:

- It has a name - FRICT in this example.
- It has parameters - V in this example.
- It has a rule for computing the value of the function from the value of the parameters - given by flowchart 5.20 in this example.

We will define a function by a flowchart of the form shown in Figure 19.

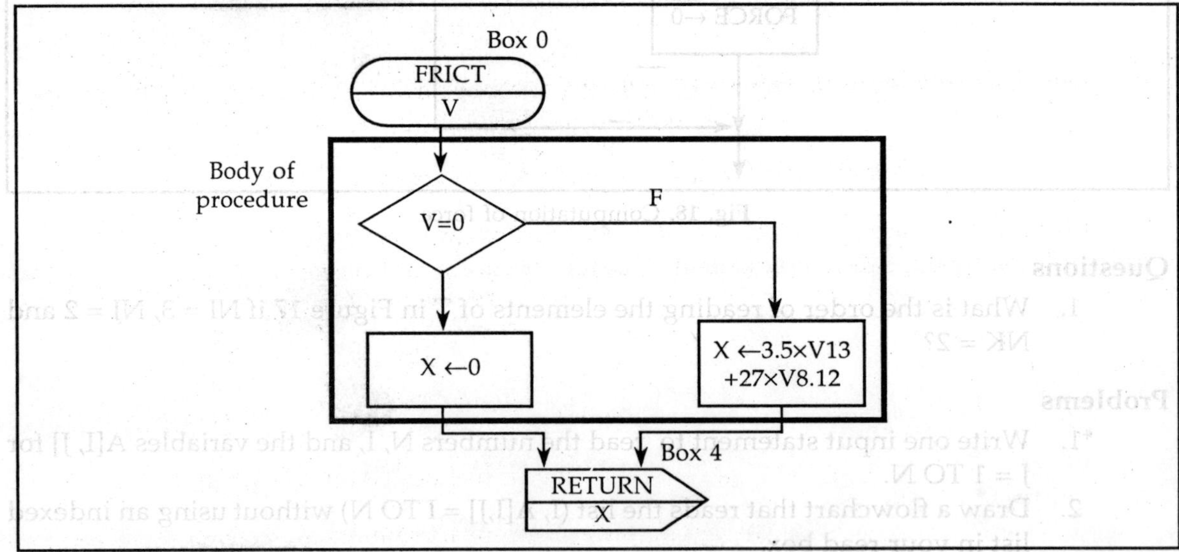

Fig. 19. Defining a function

This flowchart introduces two new boxes. Box 0 contains the name of the function being defined in its upper half and a list of parameters in its lower half. (Parameters are also called *arguments*.) Box 4 is a RETURN box that tells the computer the computation of the function FRICT is complete. Its value is given in the lower half of the RETURN box. (In this case it is X.) The function is defined by the actions given in the body of the procedure.

When a flowchart such as this forms part of the solution to a problem, we interpret it to mean that the user may now use the name FRICT as a function of one parameter, just as the built-in function COS is a function of one parameter. A function can be used in any place that a "right-hand side value" can be used because it can be processed to yield a value. Thus we can use a function as part of an expression in an assignment statement such as "A ← P × FRICT(Q)", or in a logical expression such as "17.5 < FRICT (R × 2.5)," Notice that the *actual parameter value* specified when we use the function need to be the name used for the parameter when we define the function. Thus, when the engineer writes FRICT(Q), it is equivalent to writing (3.5 × Q ↑ 3 + 2.7 × Q + 2.7 × Q + 8.12) if Q is not zero, or to writing 0 if Q is zero. That is, the actual value of the parameter (Q) is substituted for the parameter (V) used in the definition. We say that V is a *dummy variable* because it is a place holder for a value to be fed in when the function is used.

When the engineer uses the function FRICT, he does not want to be concerned with the way it works or with the names of variables he happened to use when he defined it. If he should happen to be using a variable named X in a section of program where he also uses the function FRICT, he does not want that variable changes by the use of FRICT. (Such a change is called a *side-effect.*) Therefore, variables used inside a function definition are normally assigned to memory locations local to that definition. The variable X in Figure 19 is part of the code for FRICT and cannot be referenced in any other flowchart. (In a later section we will see how to override this by use of global variables. The usage here is similar to FORTRAN; in PL/I and ALGOL, it is necessary to declare specifically that variables are local to a function.)

A function is a complete piece of program known as a *procedure*. When it is used we say that it has been *called* or *invoked*. The program that uses it is said to *call* it. The computer transfers control from the calling program to the called program when the value of the function is to be calculated. The called program is executed until a RETURN box is encountered. One and only one expression must appear in the bottom half of this box since the result of a function must be a single value that can be returned as the value of the function.

Example 9—Greatest Common Divisor

The greatest common divisor of two integers J and K is the largest integer I that divides both J and K exactly. There is a unique such integer since 1 divides both J and K, while any number larger than either number certainly does not divide both. There are a finite number of integers between 1 and the minimum M of J and K. The largest positive integer less than or equal to M that divides both J and K is the required answer.

This argument shows both that the problem has a solution and gives one method of solution by an enumerative method. Although it is a good method, we will use it as an example of a function. We will give a better solution in a second example.

The task is to define a function IGCD (J.K.) whose value is the greatest common divisor of I and J. A solution is shown in Figure 20. Note that two parameters, J and K, are used. A function may use any number of parameters. This solution checks each value of I starting from MIN (J, K) working down until it finds a value that exactly divides both J and K).

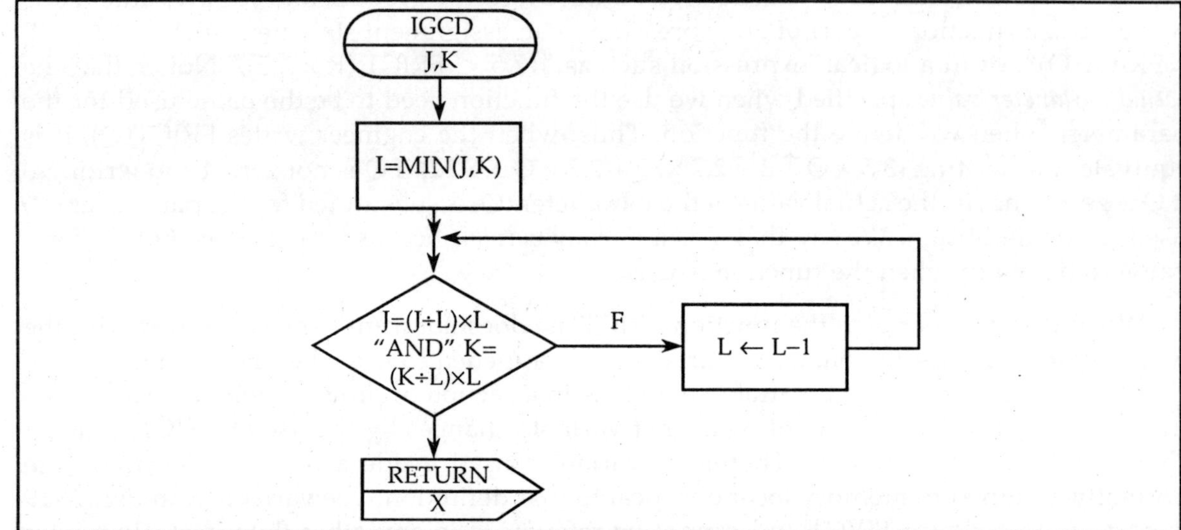

Fig. 20. Solution for GCD

Example 10—Euclidean Algorithm

The Euclidean algorithm is a faster method for finding the greatest common divisor of two numbers J and K. It works as follows:

1. Suppose J ≥ K, (If not, exchange them.)
2. Divide J by K to get a remainder L and quotient M.

   If L is zero, K divides J. Since K is the largest integer that divides itself, K is the greatest common divisor of J and K.

   If L is not zero, we have from the definition of the quotient M and the remainder L that

   $$J = K \times M + L \text{ and } L < K$$

   Therefore any integer that divides J and K also divides L, while any integer that divides K and L also divides J. Hence the greatest common divisor of J and K is also the greatest common divisor of K and L. If we replace J by K and K by L we now have the same problem to solve, but with smaller numbers. Thus we can repeat the process. Eventually the number K will be reduced to the greatest common divisor, at which time K will divide J exactly.

The solution is shown in Figure 21.

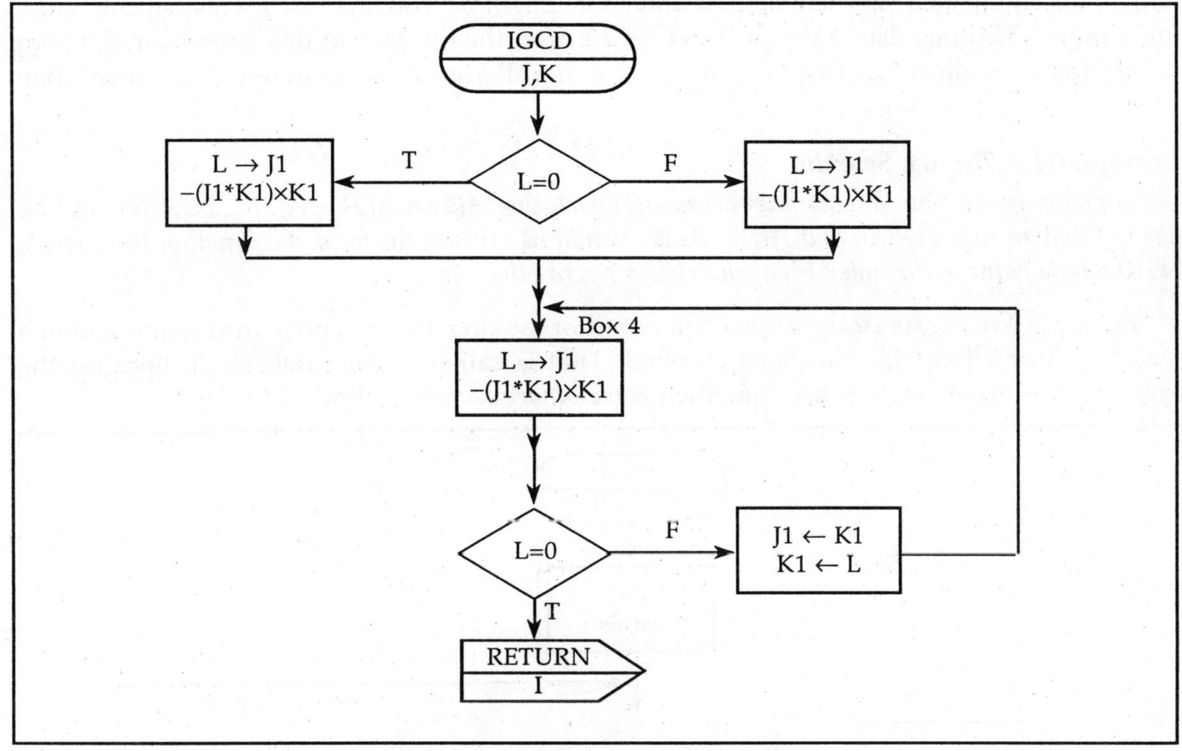

Fig. 21. Solution for Example 10.

The solution given in Figure 21 uses three local variables. L, J1 and J1, K1 and K1 were used to hold the larger and smaller of J and K. It appears that we could have used J and K themselves by simply switching them if J is not larger than K. There is a very important reason for not doing this, J and K stand for variables in the calling program; if we change them in the function procedure, the corresponding variables would be changed in the calling program. We do not like to have variables changed by procedures unnecessarily.

TABLE 2

States of J1 K1, and L After Loop Execution

Loop Pass	J1	K1	L
1	95	55	40
2	55	40	15
3	40	15	10
4	15	10	5
5	10	5	0

The difference in speed between the two solutions is illustrated by the case IGCD(55.95), which has an answer of 5. The loop is flowchart 2 will be executed for I = 55, 54.....6, and 5 for a total of 51 times. The states of J1, K1, and L after the five executions of Box 4 in the loop of Figure 21 are shown in Table 2. Thus the method Figure 21 is about ten times faster than that in Figure 20 in this case.

Example 11— Binary Search

Suppose we have an ordered liner array A[I] such that A[1] < A[2] < A[3] .....< A[N], and we wish to find an index I such that A[I] = B. We would like this in the form of a function ISRCH (A, N, B) whose value is the index I if such exists, or zero otherwise.

Example 3 used the straightfoward method of looking at each entry until either a match was found or all entries had been checked. That is called a *sequential search.* Because the array A is in order, we can use the much aster *binary search* method.

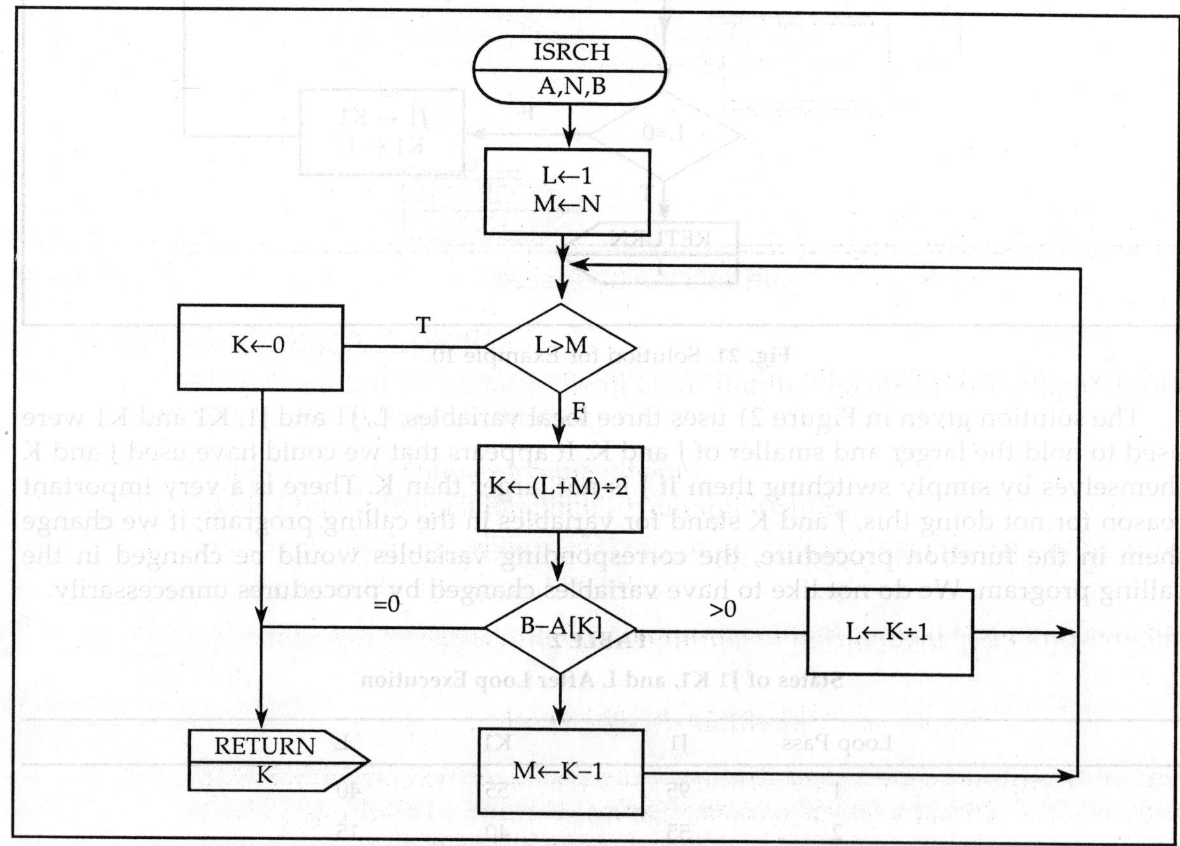

Fig. 22. Solution for Example 11

This method is very similar to the method of bisection discussed in Example 16.3. We start with two indices, L = 1 and M = N. If there is an I such that A[I] = B, then L ≤ I ≤ M. We choose an integer K about midway between L and M, say K = (L + M) ÷ 2. We compare A[K] with B. If they are equal, we have found a suitable value of I. If B > A[K], then we know that if there is an I it satisfies K + I ≤ I ≤ M. Hence we set L to K + 1 and continue the process. Similarly, if B < A[K], we know that if there is a suitable I it satisfies L ≤ I ≤ K – 1, so we set M to K – 1 and continue. The process must stop when a match is found, or when we reach the state L > M. There is no I satisfying L ≤ I ≤ M any longer, so the entry is not in the table.

Effectively, this method divides the table into two pieces at each step and determines which piece could contain the value B. Its flowchart is shown in Figure 22.

Questions

1. How many values can be returned by a function procedure?
2. Consider the function on page 566:
   a. What is the value of the expression F(3)?
   b. What is the value of F(6)?
   c. What does the smaller flowchart assign to A?

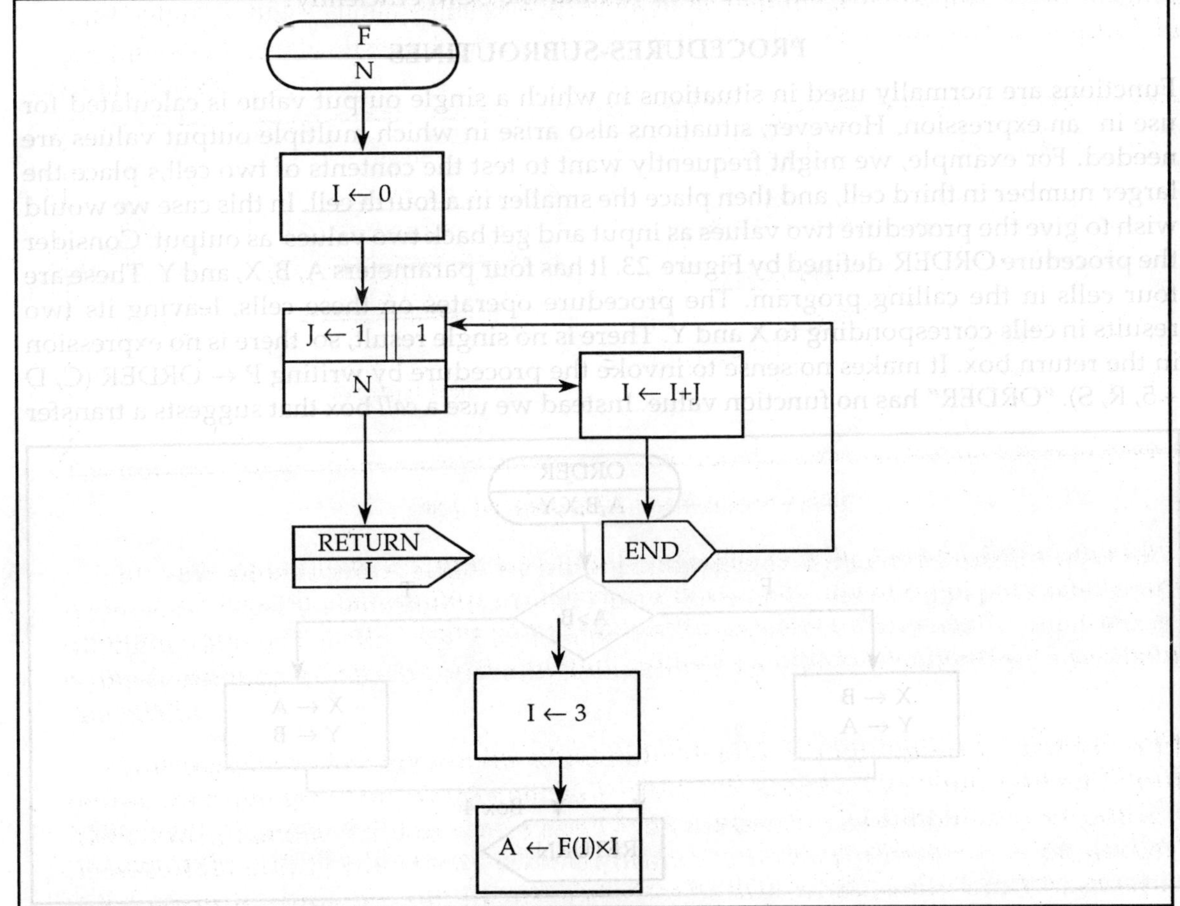

Fig. 22A.

Problems

*1. Write a function flowchart for MAX(A, B), assuming that it is not available as a built-in function.

2. Write a function flowchart that has the same effect as that in question 2 and that does not use a loop.

*3. Write a function flowchart SEARCH whose value is an integer I such that B = X[I], B is an input parameter, X is an array of N elements. If there is no I such that B = X[I]; the value of SEARCH should be 0.

4. The smallest common multiple (SCM) of two integers I and J is defined to be the smallest integer such that both I and J divide the SCM exactly. Devise an algorithm to find the SCM and express it by means of a function procedure flowchart that defines ISCM(I, J) to be the SCM of I and J. Do not worry about efficiency.

5. If you already have a function IGCD(I,J) that finds the greatest common divisor efficiently, now can it be used to fund the SCM efficiently?

PROCEDURES-SUBROUTINES

Functions are normally used in situations in which a single output value is calculated for use in an expression. However, situations also arise in which multiple output values are needed. For example, we might frequently want to test the contents of two cell,s place the larger number in third cell, and then place the smaller in a fourth cell. In this case we would wish to give the procedure two values as input and get back two values as output. Consider the procedure ORDER defined by Figure 23. It has four parameters A, B, X, and Y. These are four cells in the calling program. The procedure operates on these cells, leaving its two results in cells corresponding to X and Y. There is no single result, so there is no expression in the return box. It makes no sense to invoke the procedure by writing P ← ORDER (C, D + 5, R, S). "ORDER" has no function value. Instead we use a *call* box that suggests a transfer

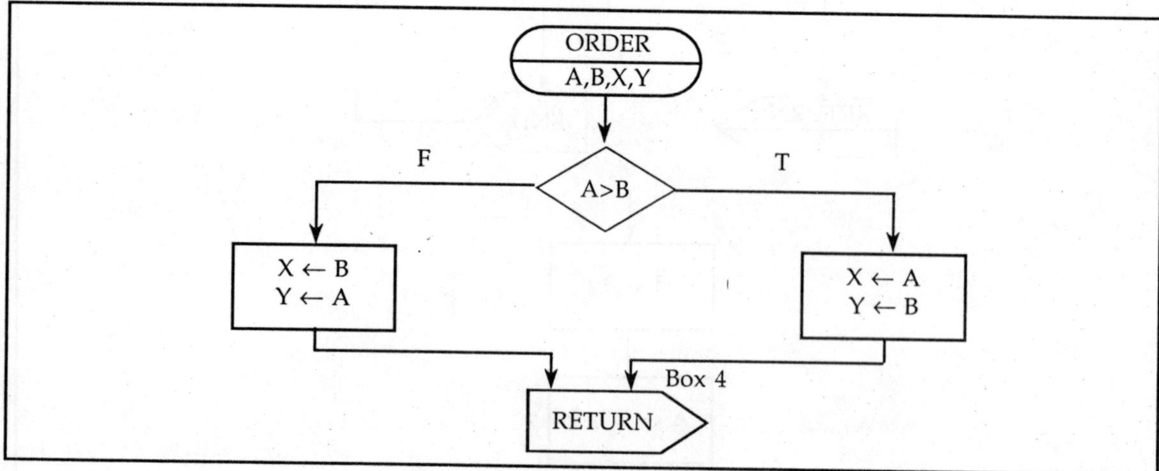

Fig. 23. The procedure ORDER

to the subroutine. It is shown in Figure 24. The name of the procedure is given in the top half of the box, the list of parameters is given in the lower half.

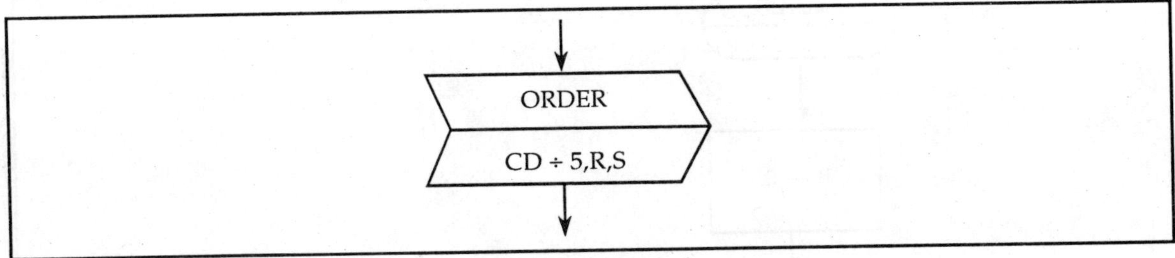

Fig. 24. Call box

This type of procedure is called a *subroutine*. Its output is provided by some of the parameters (in this case by X and Y) in the definition. If we invoke ORDER by the flowchart in Figure 24. the output is placed in cells R and S of the calling program. We call the parameters X and y *output parameters*. It is obvious that the actual values used for output parameters when a subroutine is invoked must be the names of cells so the output values can be stored.

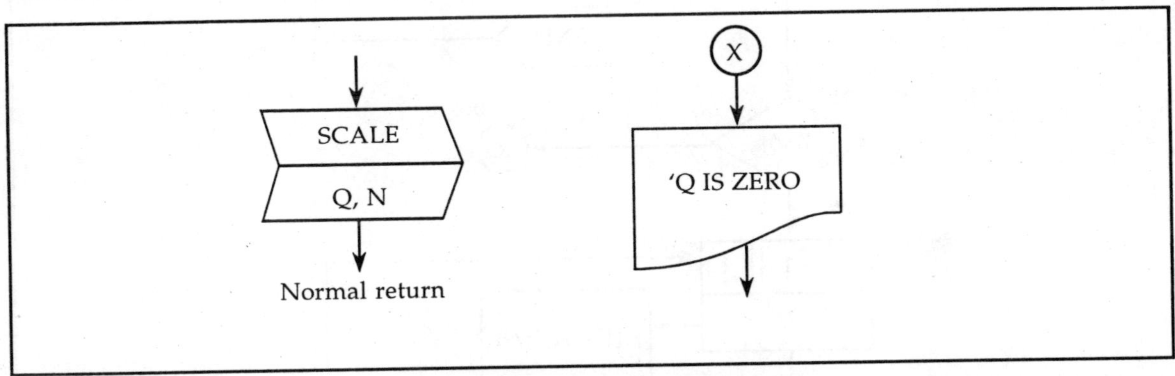

Fig. 25. Connector box for special return

In the example above, A and B are input parameters, so they can be given values by any expression when the subroutine is called. Thus the actual values of input parameters can be anything allowed for the right-hand side of an assignment statement, while the actual values of output parameters can be anything allowed for the left-hand side of an assignment statement.

A parameter can be both input and output. Suppose, for example, we need to sort the entries in a number of arrays into numerical order. We might then write a subroutine called SORT with parameters B (an array) and N (an integer). The subroutine is to sort the N elements B[1] to B[N] into order. Thus the array B is an input parameter, as is the integer N. The array B is also an output parameter. Note that a whole array can be passed as a parameter. It appears in the *call sequence* as the name of an array.

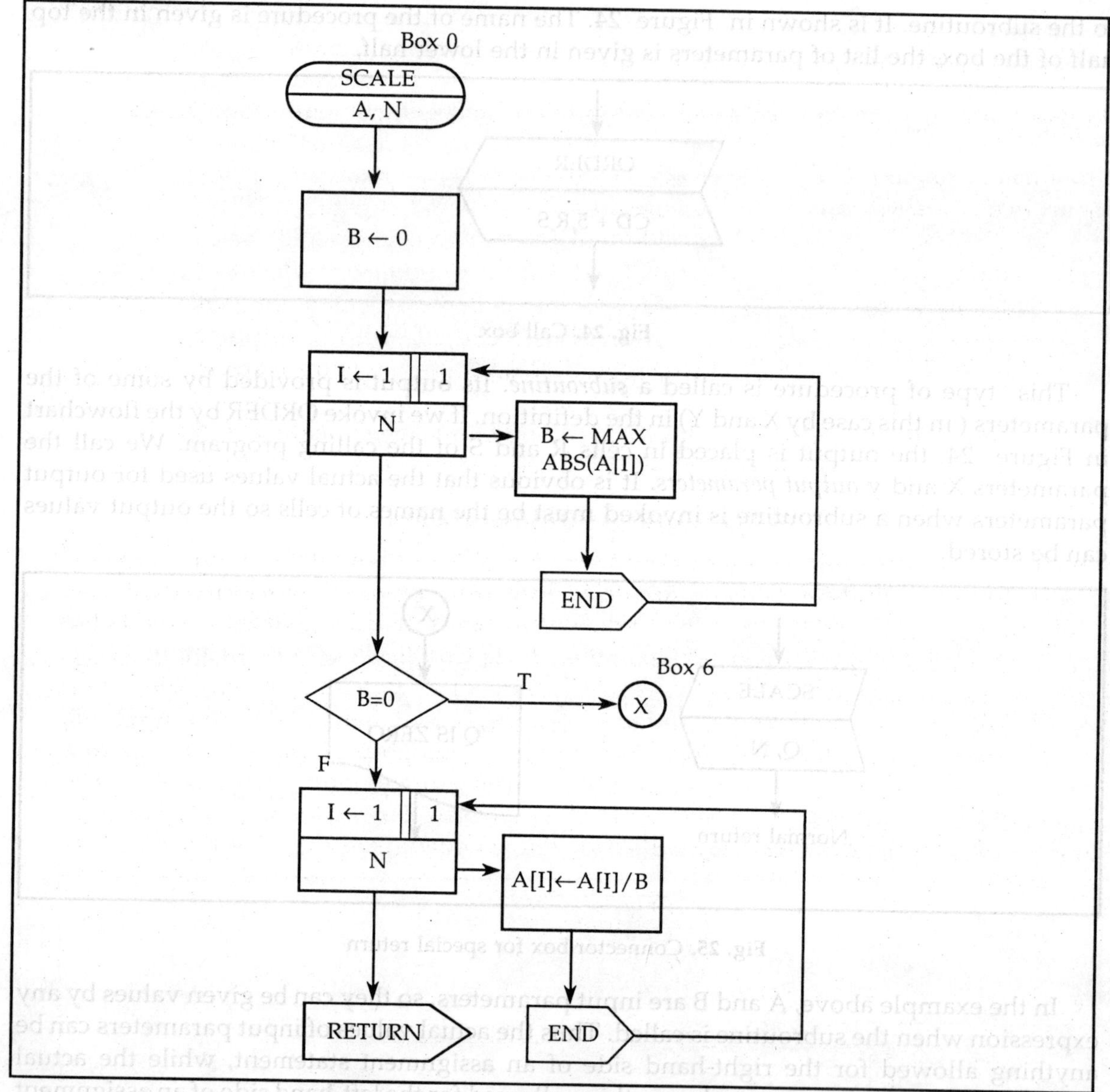

Fig. 26. Desired flowchart for Example 12.

When a procedure refers to an actual parameter value in the call sequence, it must know in what way it is represented. Thus, if the actual value of a parameter is an integer, the called program must use it an integer. If the parameter, name B (for a real) is used in a definition of a procedure, the calling program must supply a real as the actual parameter value. We will also require that if a parameter in the procedure definition is an array the actual value be an array.

Example 12 — Subroutine SCALE

We want to prepare a subroutine SCALE that will divide all N elements of a linear array by the element of largest magnitude, so that the resulting array has all elements in the range –1 to +1.

The solution is straightforward. We first find the value of the largest element in one loop, then divide by it in a second loop. If all elements are zero, however, the largest is zero. Since it is not possible to divide by zero, we want to take a special exit from the subroutine if this occurs. If the subroutine is invoked as shown. In Figure 25, we want to go to the connector labeled X if all elements are zero.

The flowchart for the subroutine is as shown in Figure 25. The connector in Box 6 is given the name of a connector in the main flowchart. If the case of all zeros occurs, the transfer to X will cause a special exit to Box X in the main flowchart of Figure 25 instead of the normal return to the next box.

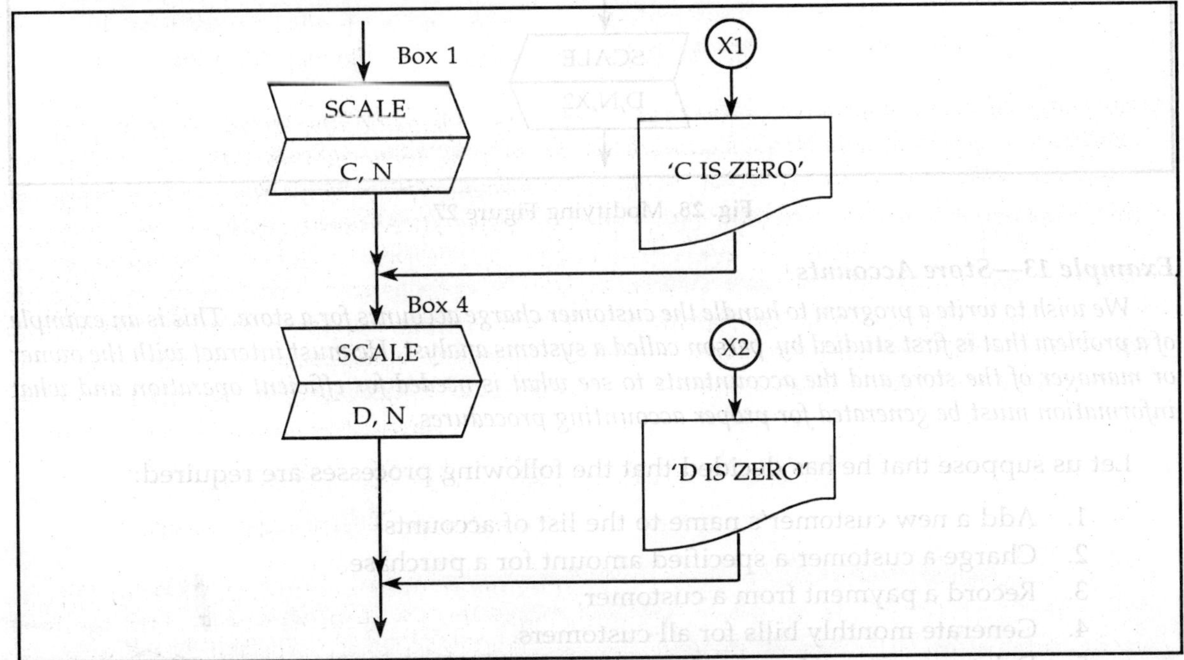

Fig. 27. Scaling the arrays C and D

If the subroutine is programmed as in Figure 25 an exit to X will occur if B = 0 no matter where it is called from.

Suppose we wish to scale the arrays C and D if possible, or print messages if either is not possible. That is, we would like to write the flowchart in Figure 27. We want to make a special exit to XI in the first case and X2 in the second. We do this by making X a parameter (called a *label parameter*) in Figure 26. Box 0 in that figure is changed to

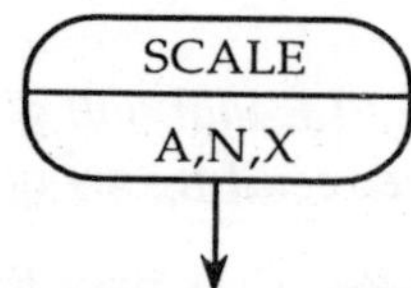

The X is a label because it is the name used in a connector box. Then Boxes 1 and 4 in Figure 27 can be changed to those in Figure 28. Needless to say, when labels are in the parameter list of the definition, the actual parameter values supplied must also be labels.

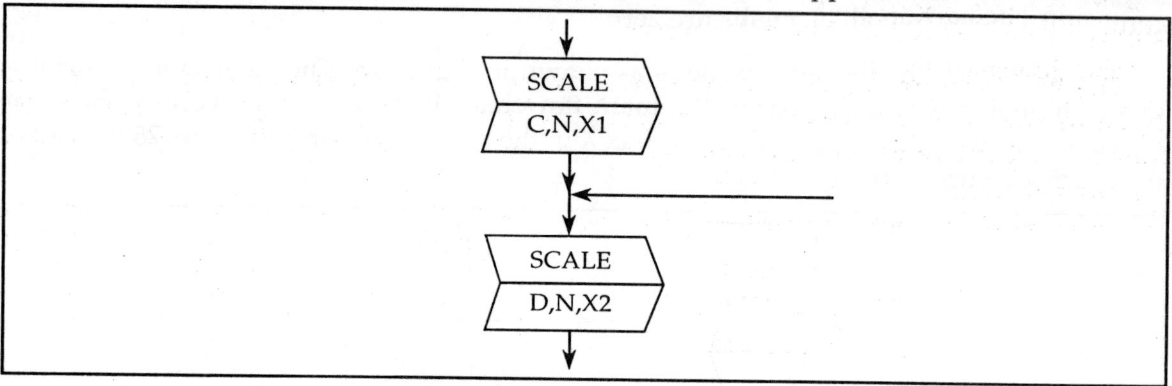

Fig. 28. Modifying Figure 27

Example 13—Store Accounts

We wish to write a program to handle the customer charge accounts for a store. This is an example of a problem that is first studied by person called a systems analyst. He must interact with the owner or manager of the store and the accountants to see what is needed for efficient operation and what information must be generated for proper accounting procedures.

Let us suppose that he has decided that the following processes are required:

1. Add a new customer's name to the list of accounts.
2. Charge a customer a specified amount for a purchase.
3. Record a payment from a customer.
4. Generate monthly bills for all customers.
5. Delete a customer's name from the list of accounts and generate a bill for him.

The input to the program is to be a set of cards. The first item on the card will be an integer 1 and 5, identifying the type of process as defined above. The second item will be the customer name except in case 4, when it will not be used. The third item will be the amount charged in case 2, the amount paid in case 3, and zero in all other cases. The fourth and final item will be the stock number of the item purchased in case 2 and zero in all other cases.

The computer must store a list of all individual purchases made so that an itemised bill can be generate. Therefore two teo-dimensional arrays will be used. AMOUNT [I, J] and ITEM[I, J] will contain the amount and the stock number of the Jth purchase by the Ith

customer, respectively. (Most programming languages require that the maximum size of arrays be known when the program is written, if you are going to implement this example on a computer, assume some numbers reasonable for the size of memory you have available.) Customer payments will also be recorded as a payment in AMOUNT. The corresponding position in ITEM should be a -1. The number of entries in AMOUNT and ITEM for customer I will be stored in N[I]. The outstanding balance for the Ith customer will be stored in BALANCE[I]. For example, if the tenth customer has made purchases of $10.13 for item 11 and $25. 11 for item 93, and paid $ 16.21 on his bill, his account information could read

BALANCE [10]	=	19. 63			
N[10]	=	3			
AMOUNT [10, 1]	=	10,13	ITEM[10, 1]	=	11
AMOUNT [10, 2]	=	16.21	ITEM[10, 2]	=	-1
AMOUNT [10, 3]	=	25.11	ITEM[10, 3]	=	93

The customer names will be kept in a linear array NAME of character strings. This array is to be kept in alphabetical order so that an alphabetical list of customers can be printed. This means that each time a new customer is to be added or removed from the list of accounts, many entries in the NAME array will have to be moved s well as the corresponding entries in the BALANCE, N, AMOUNT, and ITEM arrays. To avoid moving the latter we will add one more linear array called NCUST (customer number). When the first customer is added to the account list, his name is stored in Name[1] and his customer number, which is 1 as he is the first customer, is stored in NCUST[1], AMOUNT[1,J], ITEM[1,J], N[1], and BALANCE[1] contain his account information, if his name is SMITH and he charges $10.27 for item 5, his account would read

Name[1]=Smith, Ncust[1]=1,Balance[1]=10.27, N[1]=1.
Amount[1,1]=10.27, Item[1,1]=5

Now suppose a second customer named JONES is added. His name will go in NAME[1], pushing SMITH to NAME[2]. His customer number, 2, will go in NCUST[1], pushing the old value of NCUST[1], 1, to NCUST[2]. However, we need not move the information in the remaining arrays as we can use NCUST to give the index into the remaining arrays. Thus, if at any stage a customer's name is in NAME[J], we can access his balance by writing BALANCE[NCUST[J]].

Now we can outline the steps needed to perform each process.

1. Add a new customer's name to the list of accounts.

   Search through the list of names from the beginning until the fist larger name is found. If the name is present, print an error message. Move every entry in NAME and NCUST from this name down one place, and put the new name in the vacated spot. Assign the next available customer number to this customer. Set N and BALANCE entries to zero for this customer number.

Evidently we must also keep a record of the number of entries NN in the array NAME and the next available customer number NCN.

2. Charge a customer's account.

   Search for the name. Suppose it is NAME[J]. If it is not present, print an error message. Otherwise, let K = NCUST[J]. Increase N[K] by one, add the amount to BALANC[K], and store the amount and item number is AMOUNT [K,N,[K]] and ITEM [K,N[K]].

3. Record a payment.

   Handle as for a charge with item number equal to -1, but deduct the amount from the balance.

4. Generate a list of bills.

   Use a loop, generating one bill in each loop, listing the charges, payments, and balance. At this time the list of amounts and items should be cleared by setting N to be zero.

5. Delete a customer's name and generate a bill.

   Search for the customer's name. If it not present, print an error message. Otherwise, print a bill, then remove the name and move all later entries in NAME and NCUST up one.

A solution for a problem like this should use many subroutines. First, common areas of code should be identified and defined as subroutine. In this case we see that a search operation is used in four of the cases, and printing a bill is used in two of the cases. Therefore, we define two subroutines.

1.	Search—	parameters NM, NAME, NN, I, J meaning.
	NM	The name being sought
	NAME	The array to be searched
	NN	The number of entries in the array
	I	The index of the first entry in NAME greater than or equal to NM. Set I to NN + 1 if no entries satisfy this. (Output parameter)
	J	O if NM is not in NAME, 1 otherwise. (Output parameter)
2.	BILL-	parameters NM, K, N, BALANC, AMOUNT, ITEM, meaning:
	NM	Name of customer to be billed. K is the customer number. N, BALANC, AMOUNT, and ITEM are as defined above. The subroutine should also set N[K] to zero to clear the list of charges.

Secondly, we should define subroutines for various sections of the program so that relatively independent sections are in different subroutines. This makes for a better description of the program. In this case subroutines can be defined for each of the basic actions as follows:

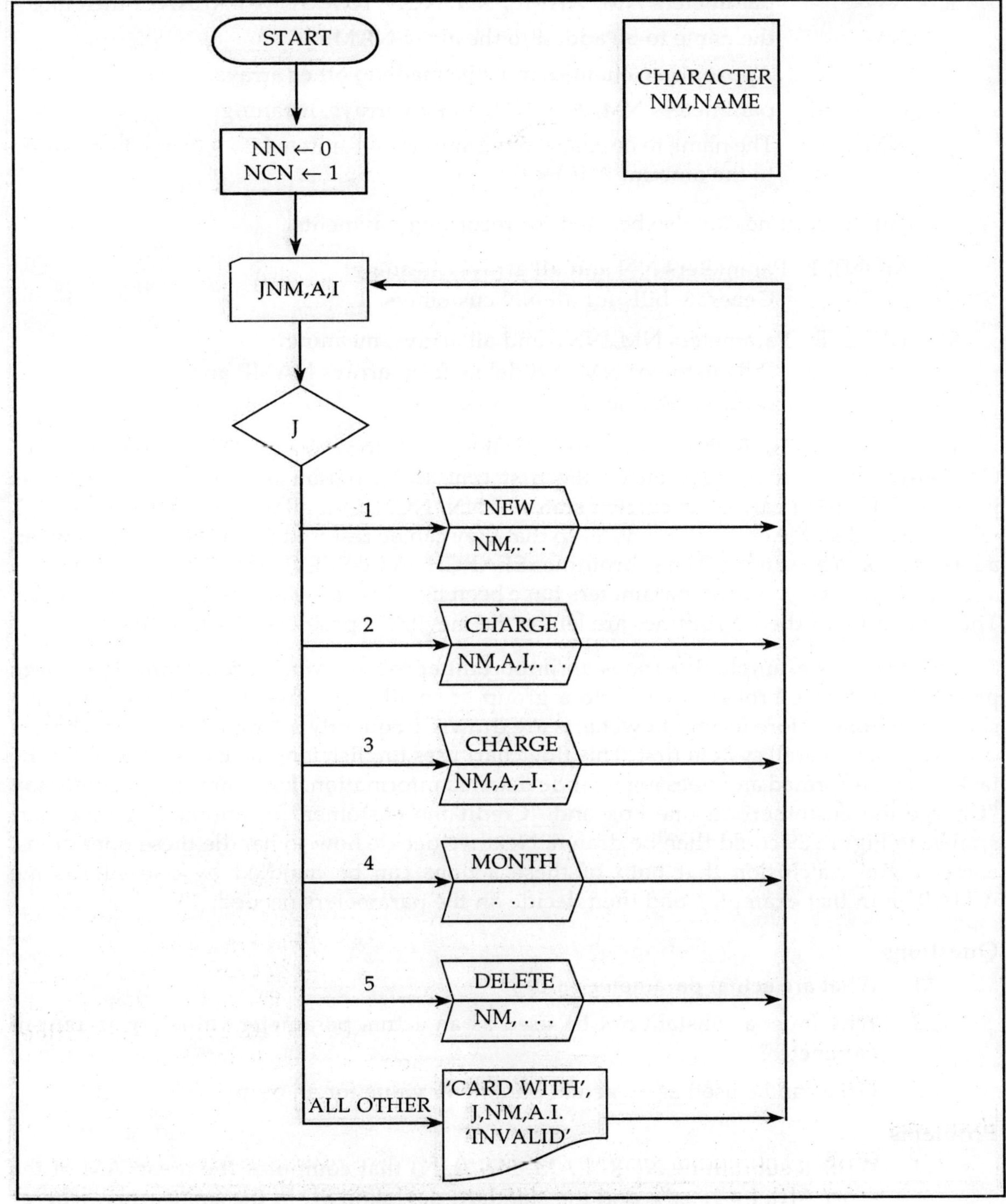

Fig. 29. Main program for Example 13

3. NW- parameters NM, NAME, NN, NCN, NCUST, N BALANC, meaning:
   NM the name to be added to the array NAME.
   Appropriate changes must be made to other arrays.
4. CHARGE- parameters NM, A, I, NN, and all arrays, meaning:
   NM The name to be charged the amount A for item I if $I \geq 0$ or to be credited to the amount A if $I < 0$.

This subroutine can also be used for recording payments.

5. MONTH - Parameters NN and all arrays, meaning:
   Generate bills for all NN customers.
6. DELETE - Parameters NM, NN, and all arrays, meaning:
   Bill customer NM and delete from arrays NAME and NCUST. Reduce NN by one.

The main program is shown in Figure 29. It sets NN to zero and NCN to one initially. Obviously, this is done only once—the first time the program is run. When a run has processed all input cards, the current states of NN, NCN, and all arrays have to be saved, usually on a disk file or similar device, so that they can be restored to the same values when a later run is to be started. The subroutines SEARCH and DELETE are shown in Figures 30 and 31, respectively. Not all parameters have been listed because of lack of available space. The remainder of the subroutines are left as the inevitable problems for the student.

The previous example illustrates an important approach to the programming of large problems: they are broken down into a group of small subroutines and functions. This should be done before formal flowcharts are drawn. frequently a "high-level" flowchart is drawn for the overall system first. This flowchart uses English language descriptions of the tasks to be performed and does not include detailed information. For example, we might say "Charge the customer" in one box and "Credit the customer" in another. A flowchart similar to Figure 29 could then be drawn. Next we decide how to handle these operations, come to the conclusion that both of these actions can be handled by one subroutine (CHARGE in that example), and then decide on the parameters needed.

Questions

*1. What are actual parameter values?

2. Why must a constant not be used as an actual parameter value for an output parameter?

3. What can be used as an actual parameter value for an output parameter?

Problems

*1. Write a subroutine NORM(AM, SD, A, N) that computes the mean AM of the array A[I], I = 1,.....N. and the standard deviation SD of the same array, where

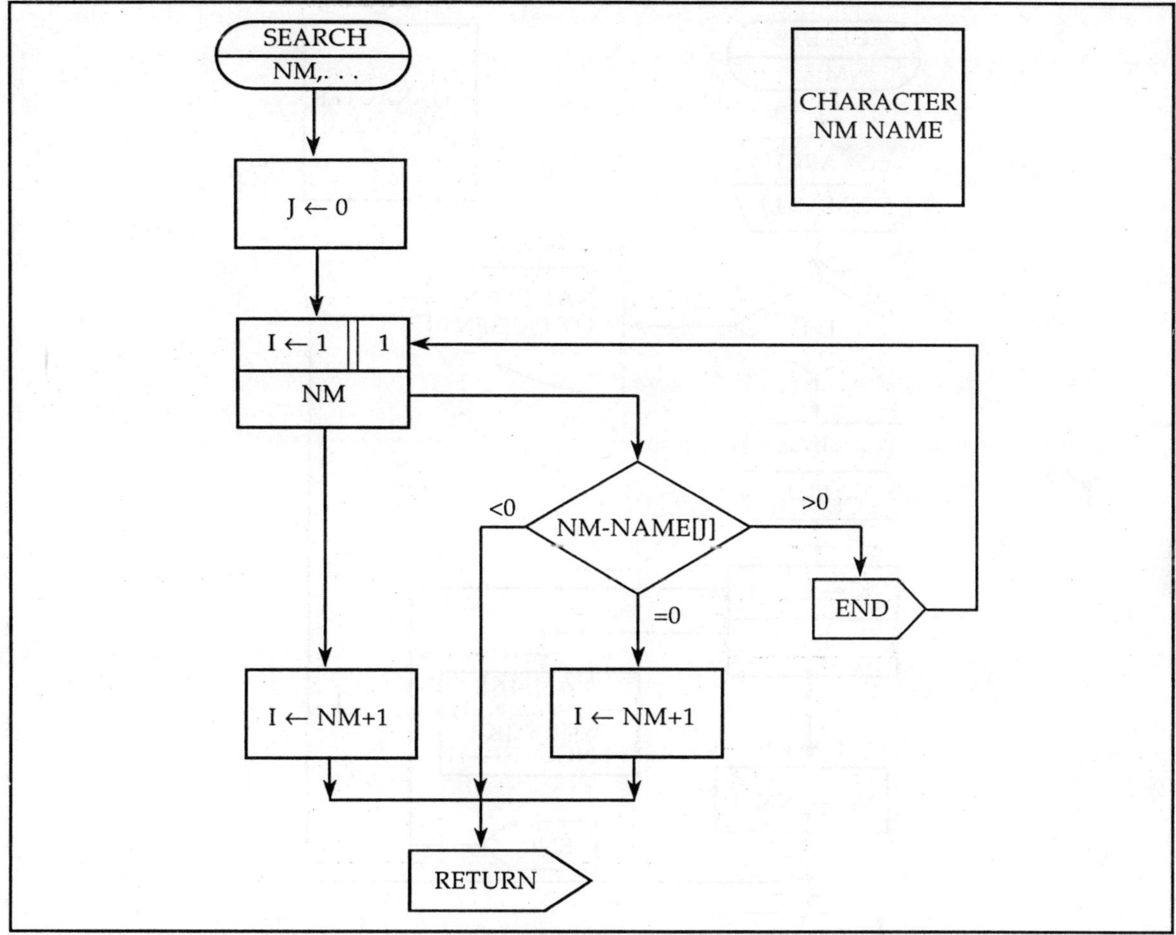

Fig. 30. Subroutine Search

$$AM = \frac{1}{N}\sum_{I=1}^{N} A[I]$$

$$SD = \sqrt{\frac{1}{N}\sum_{I=1}^{N}(A[1] - AM)^2}$$

2. Write a subroutine STNDRD(A, W, T, N, M) that has the following actions:

   The array A[I, J] contains the score on the Jth test for the Ith student. There are M tests and N students. Normalise the scores on each test to a mean of 0 and a standard deviation of 1.0 by first forming

$$AM = \frac{1}{N}\sum_{I-1}^{N} A[I, J]$$

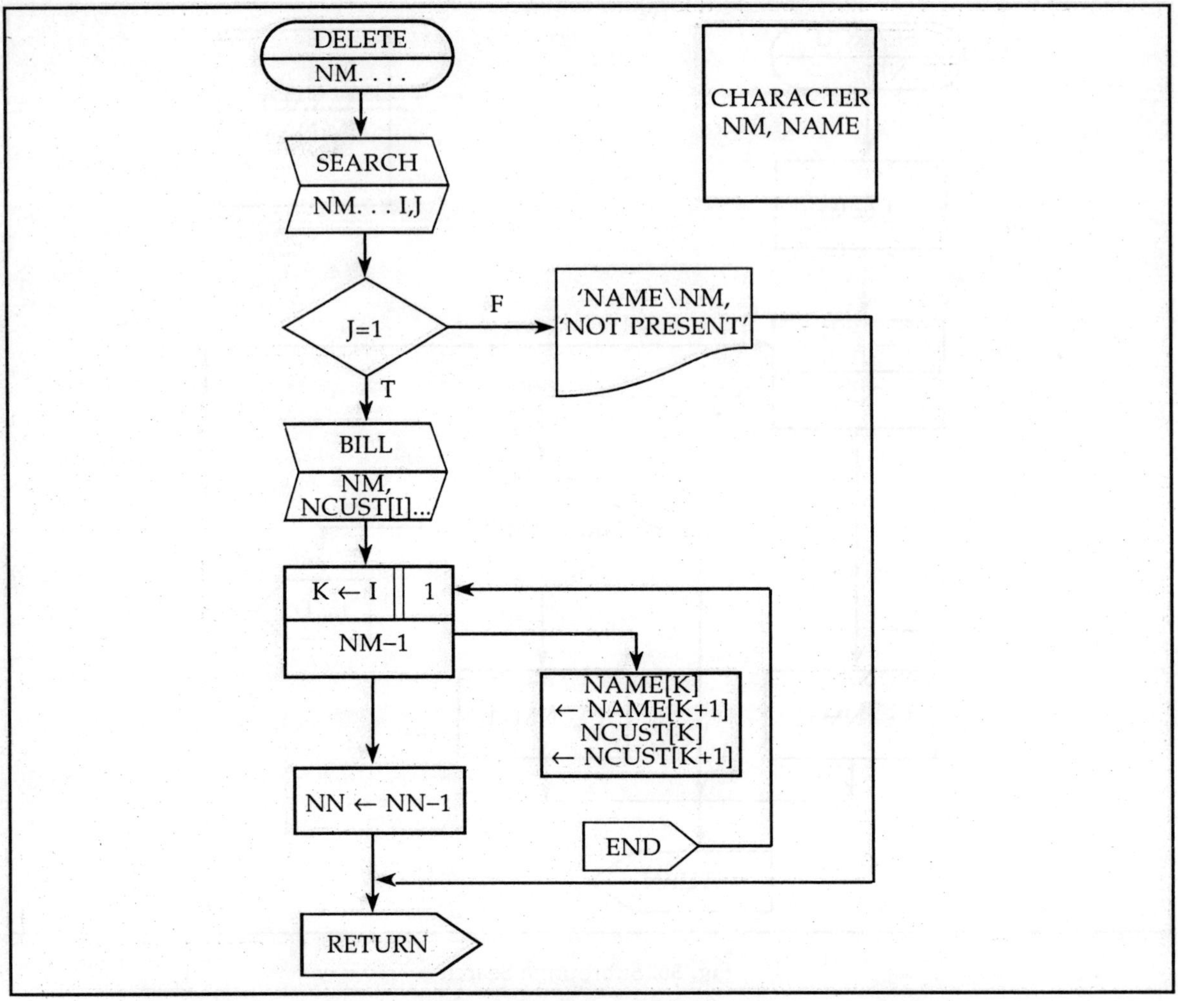

DELETE
NM. . . .
CHARACTER
NM, NAME
SEARCH
NM. . . I,J
J=1
F
'NAME\NM,
'NOT PRESENT'
T
BILL
NM,
NCUST[I]...
K ← I
1
NM–1
NAME[K]
← NAME[K+1]
NCUST[K]
← NCUST[K+1]
NN ← NN–1
END
RETURN

Fig. 31. Subroutine DELETE

and

$$SD = \sqrt{\frac{1}{N}\sum_{I=1}^{N}(A[1,J] - AM)^2}$$

and then forming

$$B[I,J] = \frac{A[1,J] - AM}{SD} \qquad 1 = 1 \;.....N$$

if SD ≠ 0, and B[I, J] if SD = 0

Repeat this for J = 1.....M.

Then form the weighted sum of the normalised scores and return the result in T, where

$$T[1] = \sum_{J=1}^{M} B[I,J] \times W[J]$$

3. Write the subroutines BILL, NEW, CHARGE, and MONTH required in Example 13.
*4. When a customer's name is removed by DELETE in Figure 31. the space that customer was using in the arrays BALANC, N. AMOUNT, and ITEM is not made available for use by customers added in the future. This means that as names are added and deleted, in size of these arrays (NCN) slowly increases, even though the total number of customers (NN) may never exceed some reasonable number. Can you think of a way of re-allocating customer numbers that are no longer in user, so that the array space can be reused?
5. Modify the subroutine SEARCH in Figure 30 so that it uses the binary search method (see Example 11.)

LOCAL AND GLOBAL, STATIC AND DYNAMIC STORAGE

When the CPU encounters a call on a procedure, it prepares information about the parameters and puts if in some memory calls. It then transfers to the code for the called procedure and executes that code. Both the calling and the called procedures will have their own data areas in memory and will be restricted to using that areas for their local variables. This is shown in Figure 32.

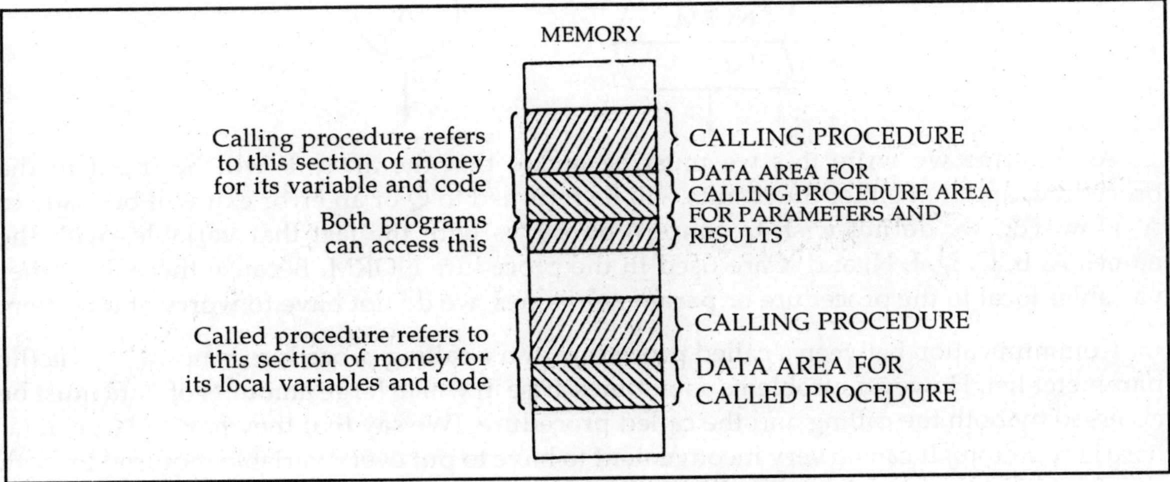

Fig. 32. Memory allocation for procedures

We have allowed two types of variables in a procedure - local variables totally interval to the procedure and parameters intended for passing input data between procedures. The restriction that prevents a procedure from accessing local variables associated with other procedures is one of convenience only; it is obvious that the machine language code for a procedure could use memory addresses referring to any part of memory. When a compiler translates a POL such as FORTRAN into machine language, it enforces this restriction by assigning different memory space to variables in each procedure so that they are different from variables of the same name in the other procedures.

Example 14—Normalisation of Scores

Suppose we have a one-dimensional array A that contains student scores on a test. We wish to find constants X and Y , where Y is positive, such that if we form

$$B[I] = (A[I] + X) \times Y$$

the smallest of the "normalised" scores B[I] will be 0 and the largest will be 100. The parameters to the subroutine should be A, B, and N (N is the number of scores.)

If the smallest of the A[I], I = 1,.....N is C, then we can take X to be - C. This makes A[I] + X zero when I is such that A[I] is minimum. If the largest element of A[I] is D, we can take Y to be 100/(D + X). Then (A[I] + X) × 100/(D + X) will be 100 when A[I] takes on the maximum value D. There is a problem if D + X is zero. This occurs if all of the A[I] are equal, in which case it is obvious that we cannot find an X and Y to accomplish the goal. For this case we must modify the problem statement and add an error exit to the parameter list. A flowchart for the solution is shown in Figure 33.

When we use this example, we may wish to write

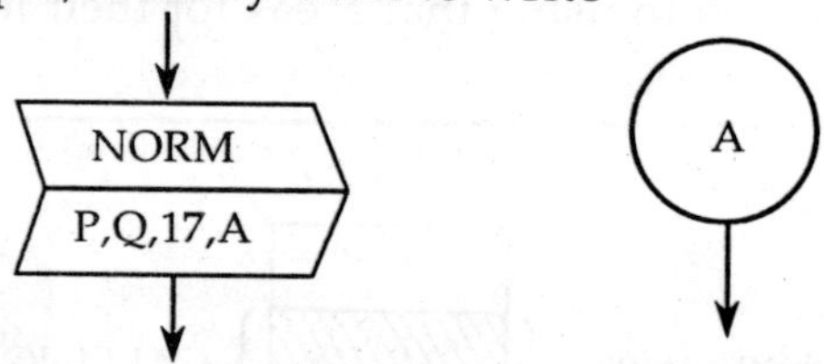

At the time we write this we must be aware that the array P will be input to the procedure, and that either the results will be returned to Q or an error exit will be made to A. However, we do not wish to concern ourselves with the fact that variables with the names A, B, C, D, I, N, and X are used in the procedure NORM. Because these are either variables local to the procedure or parameter names, we do not have to worry about them.

Communication between a called procedure and a calling procedure is normally via the parameter list. However, problems sometimes arise in which large amounts of data must be accessed by both the calling and the called procedure. (We say that they have a large data-base is common.) It can be very inconvenient to have to put every variable required by both procedures in the parameter list. We had to use very long parameter lists in Example 13. Therefore we use *global variables*. A variable that is global in a procedure is one that appears in the calling procedure. If, in Example 13, the variables NN and NCN and the arrays NAME, NCUST, BALANC, N, AMOUNT, and ITEM were global to all subroutines, it would not have been necessary to put them in the parameter lists.

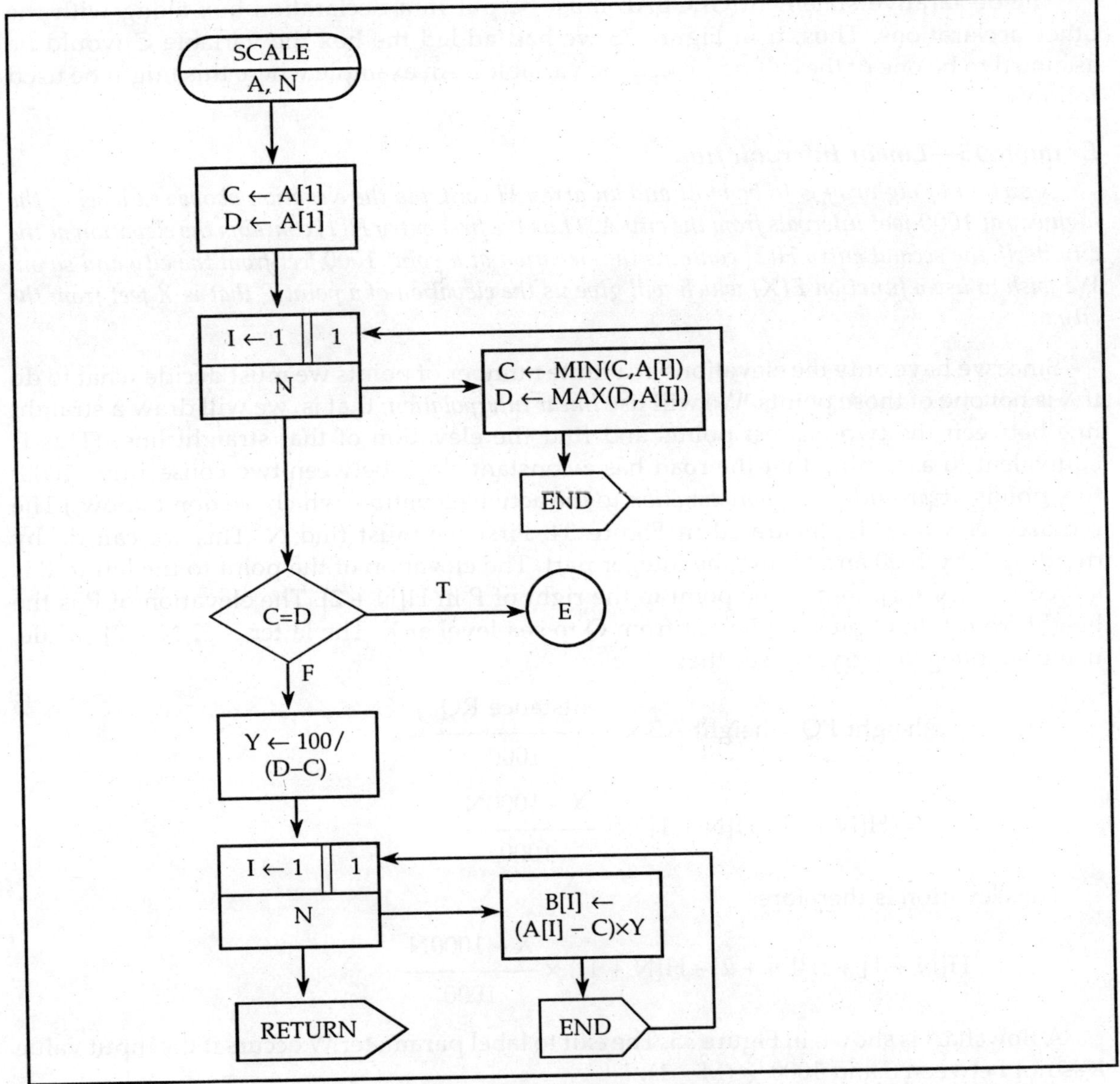

Fig. 33. Solution for Example 14

Global C

The declarative statement GLOBAL must be put in a declaration box along with the other declarations. Thus, if in Figure 33 we had added the box the variable C would be assumed to be one of the calling procedure variables. An example where this might be used follows.

Example 15—Linear Interpolation

A section of highway is to be built and an array H contains the elevation above sea level of the highway at 1000-foot intervals from the city A. Thus the first entry H[1] contains the elevation at the city itself, the second entry H[2] contains the elevation at a point 1000 feet from the city and so on. We wish to use a function E(X) which will give us the elevation of a point P that is X feet from the city.

Since we have only the elevations at a finite number of points we must decide what to do if X is not one of those points. We will use *linear interpolation;* that is, we will draw a straight line between the two nearest points and find the elevation of that straight line. (This is equivalent to assuming that the road has a constant slope between two consecutive 1000-foot points. It provides an *approximation* to the actual elevation, which we don't know.) The required elevation is illustrated in Figure 34. First we must find N. This we can do by dividing X by 1000 and taking the integer part. The elevation of the point to the left to P is stored in H[N + 1], that of the point to the right of P in H[N + 2]. The elevation of P is the height from P to Q plus the height from Q to sea level at X. The latter is H[N + 2], while, using simple geometry, we see that

$$\text{height PQ} = \text{height AB} \times \frac{\text{distance RQ}}{1000}$$

$$= (H[N + 2] - H[N + 1] \times \frac{X - 1000N}{1000}$$

The elevation is therefore

$$H[N + 1] + (H[N + 2] - H[N + 1]) \times \frac{X - 1000N}{1000}$$

A flowchart is shown in Figure 35. The exit to label parameter W occurs if the input value X is not between 0 and 1000 $\times$ (M – 1).

M is assumed to contain the number of elements in the array H. If X is less than zero, it refers to a point on the other side of the city; if it is greater then 1000(M – 1), it is off the end of the road we have prescribed. In neither case can we compute an elevation. Both H and M are global. They are not put in the parameter list because they refer to variables of he same name in the calling procedure. Global variables provide a more rapid and concise mechanism for communication between procedures than do parameters, because the passing of parameters requires time and memory space. However, parameters are more flexible. The function E defined by Figure 35 can operate only on the array H with M entries. If M and H had been

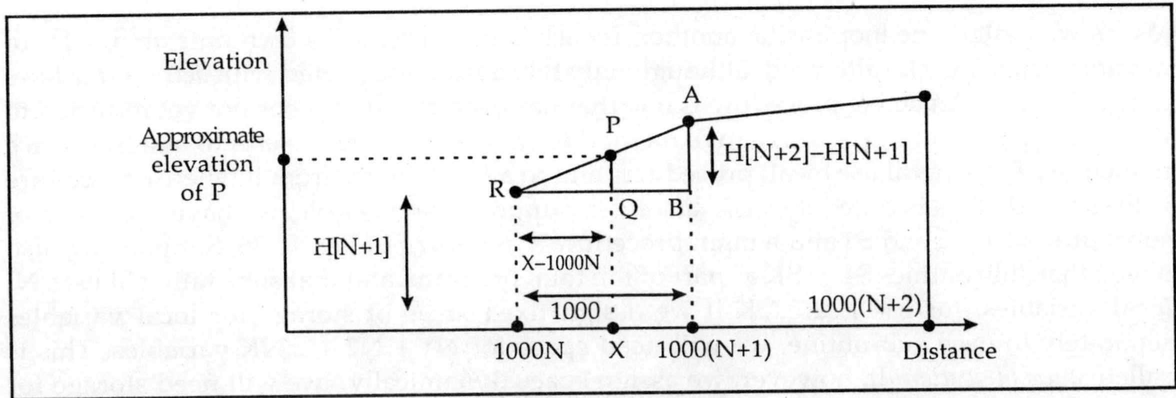

Fig 34. Liner interpolation

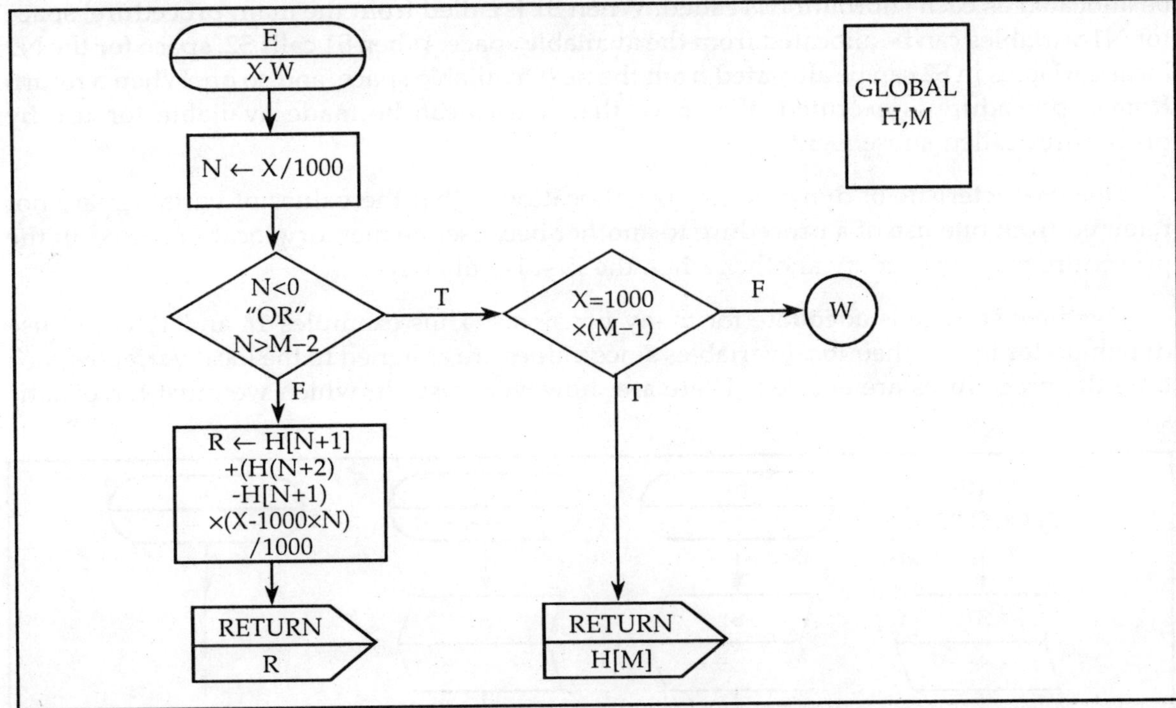

Fig. 35. Solution for Examples 15

put in the parameter list, it could have been used for liner interpolation in any table. If we had written a procedure to deal with similar arrays for many different roads, we would have preferred to use parameters rather than global variables.

Static and Dynamic Storage

We have stated that the local variables associated with a procedure are stored in an area of memory reserved for that procedure. Many procedures will be written for use in a typical problem. Some of the called procedures ill be the calling procedures of other procedures, just as we nested one loop inside another. If each procedure has its own data area, a lot of memory space may be allocated, although only those areas associated with *active procedures* may be in use. (An active procedure is one that has been called and has not yet returned to the calling procedure.) An alternative method for allocating data areas is to assign a space in memory for general use by all procedures and to allocate space from it when a procedure is first called. This is called *dynamic allocation*. Suppose, for example, we have the series of subroutines S1, S2 and S3 and a main procedure S as shown in Figure 36. Suppose we also have other subroutines S4, ... SK as part of the total program, and that subroutine SI uses NI local variables, for I = 1, 2, ...K if we assign fixed areas of storage for local variables separately to each subroutine, we will need space for N1 + N2 + ...NK variables. This is called *static allocation*. If, however, we assign space dynamically, we will need storage for only N1 + N2 + N3 variables at the time that subroutine S3 is being executed. This space can be allocated as each subroutine is called. When S1 is called from the main procedure, space for N1 variables can be allocated from the available space. When S1 calls S2, space for the N2 local variables in S2 can be allocated from the next available space, and so on. When a return from a procedure is executed, the space that it uses can be made available for use by procedures called subsequently.

One characteristic of dynamic storage allocation is that the values of variables are not retained from one use of a procedure to another because the memory locations used in the procedure may be used by another when the first is not active.

Dynamic storage is adequate for many problems. Thus examples 14 and 15 could use dynamic storage for their local variables since values are assigned to the local variables each time the procedures are entered. There are, however, cases in which we must have static storage.

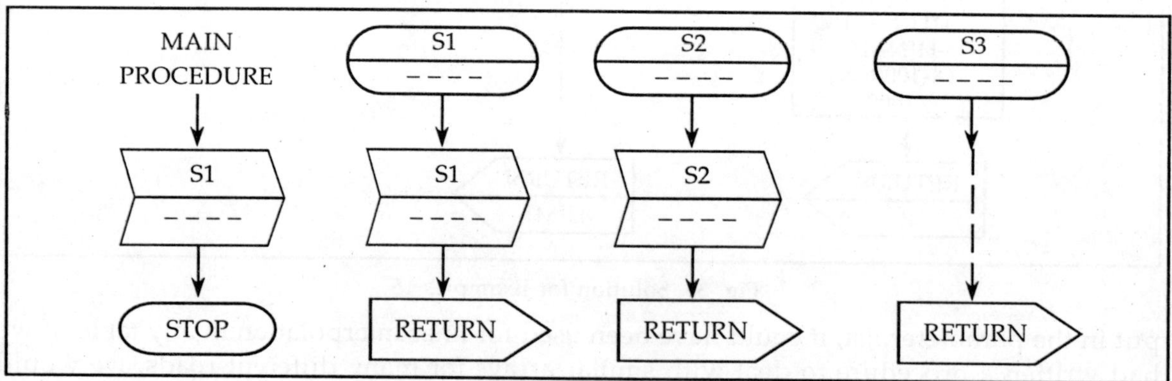

Fig. 36. Series subroutines and main procedure

Example 16—Page Layout

Suppose we are generating a long list of numbers and we wish to print these 5 per line 50 lines per page, with an integer at the start of each line in the sequence 1, 6, 11....etc., and a page number at the head of each page. It is often simpler to write a subroutine, say PRINT(X), which will accept the next number in the list (the parameter X) and put it in a position on the page. Every fifth call should cause this subroutine to print a line of the last 5 numbers. Every 50th line, a new page should be started and numbered.

The technique used is as follows: If this is the first call or the first call after the last line of the previous page was printed, a new page is started. A line count is then set to 1.

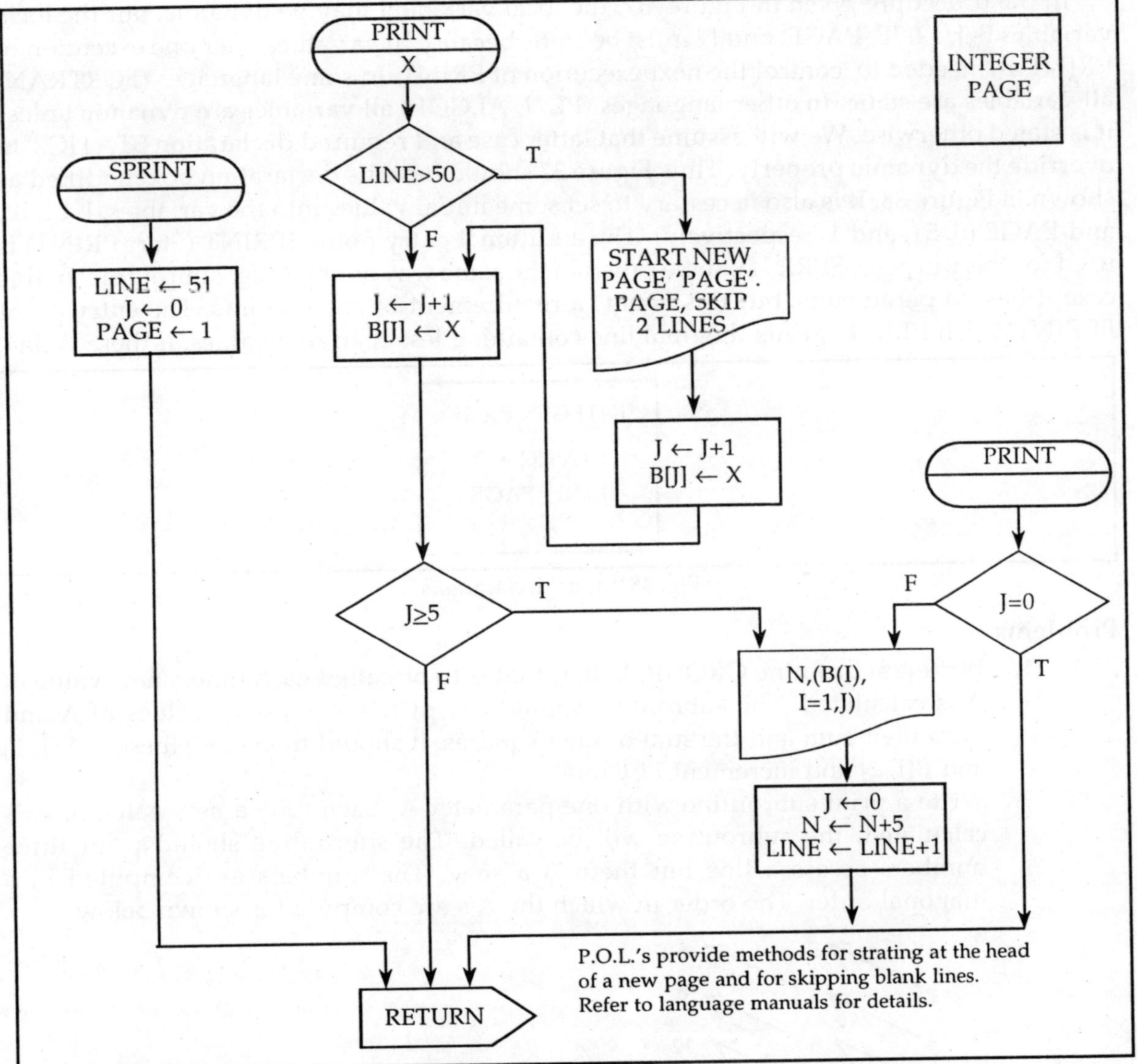

Fig. 37. Solution for Example 16

An array B[J], J =1,.....5 is used to save up to 5 numbers. The counter J is increased on each call until it reaches 5. Then a line is printed and J is reset to zero.

When a line is printed, the integer to be printed at the start of each line is incremented by 5. A line count is also increased by one. When it is greater than 50, a signal that we should start another page is given. When a new page is printed, the page count is increased by one.

A flowchart is shown in Figure 37. This subroutine contains two *entry points* besides PRINT. These will be discussed shortly.

In the procedure given in Figure 37, the local variable I may be dynamic, but the local variables B, J, LINE, PAGE, and N must be static because their values after one execution of PRINT are needed to control the next execution of PRINT. In some languages (FORTRAN) all variables are static. In other languages (PL/I, ALGOL) all variables are dynamic unless it is stated otherwise. We will assume that latter case and required declaration STATIC... to override the dynamic property. Thus Figure 37 should have its declaration box modified as shown in Figure 38. It is also necessary to set some initial values into the variables, J, LINE, and PAGE (0, 51, and 1, respectively). The additional entry point SPRINT (Start PRINT) is used for this purpose. SPRINT can be called in the same way as any other subroutine. In this case it has no parameters, but this is not a requirement of entry points. The entry point FPRINT(finish PRINT) prints the final line containing less than five values, if there is one.

Fig. 38. Static declarations

Problems

*1. Write a subroutine GROUP(A, B, I) that is to be called each time a new value of A is calculated. The subroutine should accept five successive values of A and form their sum and the sum of their squares. It should then store these in B[I, 1] and B[I, 2] and increment I by one.

2. Write a print subroutine with one parameter A. Each time a new value of A is calculated, the subroutine will be called. The subroutine should print three numbers across a line but there is a snag. The numbers are computed in a diagonal order. The order in which the A's are computed is shown below.

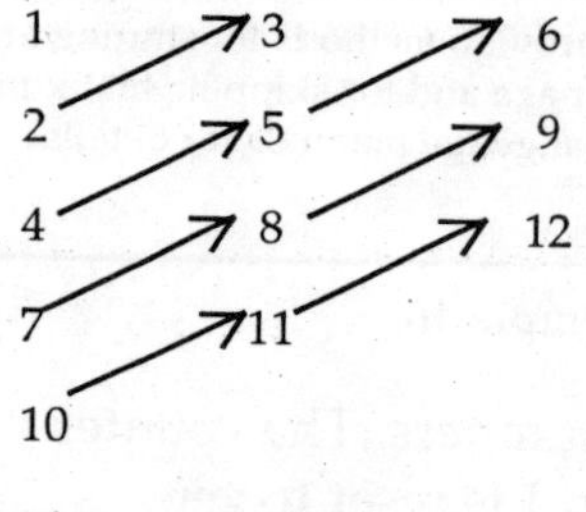

etc.

Therefore the partial contents of several lines must be saved.

3. Modify the solution to Example 16 so that the SPRINT entry point has parameters specifying the number of values to be printed on each line and the number of lines to be printed on each page.

Questions

*1. What are the advantages of local storage?
2. Why do we use global storage in some cases?
*3. What are the advantages of dynamic storage?
4. When do we need to use static storage?

ACCESS OF PARAMETERS

In earlier sections we gave a deliberately simplified idea of the way in which a calling procedure communicates parameter values with a called procedure. We implied that the called procedure could refer to the actual parameter values directly. In fact, there are several ways in which parameters are passed between procedures, and different POLs use different methods in this section we will discuss three basic techniques that can be used: *call by address, call by value,* and *call by name.* For simple usages there is no difference between the results of those three techniques. However, when a variable name appears as more than one actual parameter value or appears in an actual parameter value and is also global to the called procedure, the different techniques yield different results. In order for you to be able to determine the effect of any particular usage, we will discuss some of the details of implementation.

First we will examine both the types of parameters that can be used in a procedure and the kinds of actual parameter values that can be matched with them. Again each POL may allow more or less or these types. The restrictions we will develop here are logical restrictions, that is, ones that must to enforced to make sense out of the call and return. (Consult a language manual for a specific POL to see what additional restrictions are enforced.)

In the definition of a procedure its parameters are *dummy variables* because they stand for (or are placeholders for) constants, variables, or expressions that will be fed into the procedure when it is called. We classify the parameters by the way they are used in their procedure according to their structure, their type, and their access.

By *structure* we mean are the parameters single variables (that is, names of single cells in memory) or arrays?

By *type* we mean do the parameters refer to data consisting of integers, real numbers, labels, functions, or subroutines - or, of course, any of the other allowed data types in a given language, such as LOGICAL and COMPLEX?

By *access,* we mean are the parameter used as input to the procedure only, or output from the procedure (and possibly input as well)?

Every parameter must have one and only one of the attributes from each of the groups *structure, type,* and *access*. Thus a parameter could be a single real variable used as input only. Many of the possible combinations are disallowed in some languages. In FORTRAN, for example, labels, functions, and subroutines may be used as parameters only if they are single variables used for input. That is, the flowchart in Figure 39 is acceptable whereas the two in Figure 40 are not. In Figure 40a the label parameter X is an array. This is not permitted in FORTRAN (although it is acceptable in PL/I). In Figure 40b, the actual parameter value F in that call of procedure E2 is used as a function mane in the next box. In the subroutine E2, the corresponding parameter G is assigned the value SIN. We are thus trying to use a function name as an output parameter. This is neither permitted in FORTRAN not PL/I.

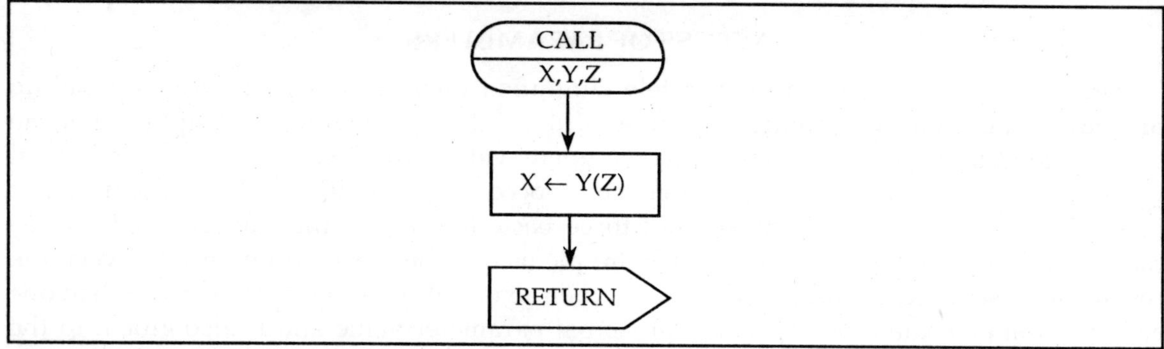

Fig. 39. Acceptable flowchart

Actual parameter values have *structure* and *type*. The permissible types of actual parameter values are exactly the same as the permissible types of parameters. In most languages, the type of the parameter and the type of the actual parameter must match. That is if the parameter is used as an integer, the actual parameter value must also be an integer. We can see why this restriction is desirable if we consider our hypothetical machine. Suppose we have a function F(I) that expects an integer value for the parameter I. If, in the calling program, we write F[1, 0], the actual parameter value 1.0 will be passed in the representation 05110000(= $=0.1 \times 10^1$) in our machine. The function will take this to be an integer, that is, the number +5110000.

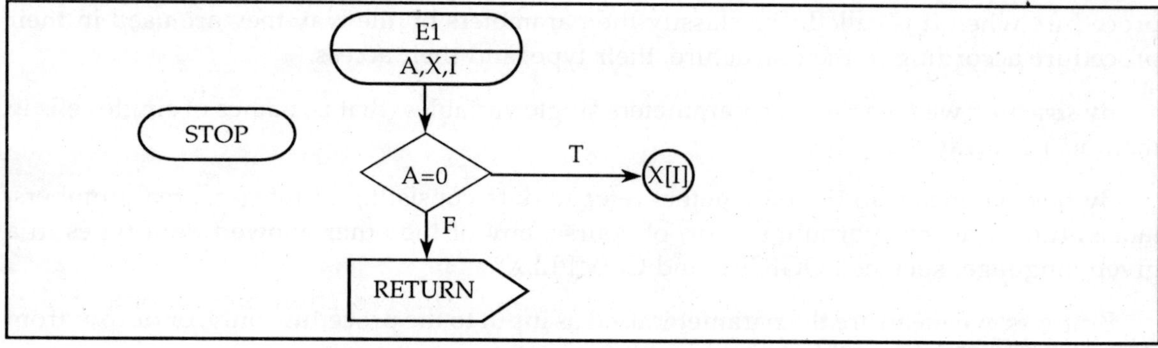

Fig. 40a. Use of label parameters unacceptable in Fortran (1)

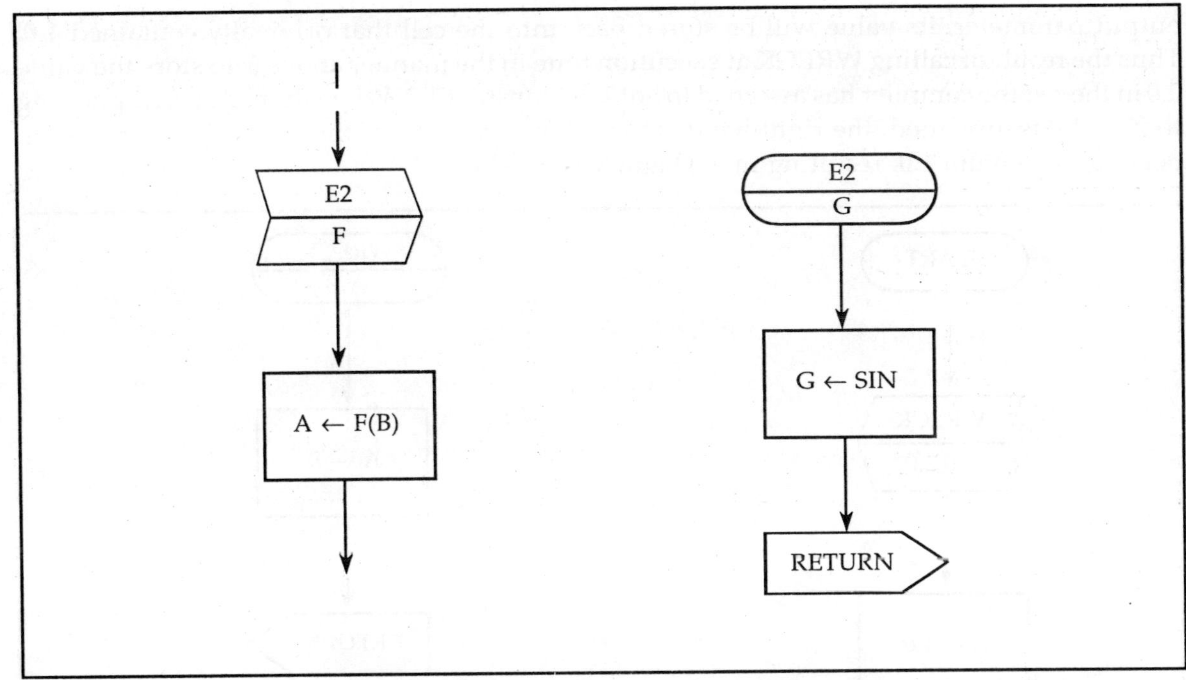

Fig. 40b. Use of label parameters unacceptable in Fortran (2)

The structure of actual parameter values includes, constants, expressions, single variables, array elements, and arrays. If a parameter is an array, then the corresponding actual parameter value must also be an array. This is evidently necessary because if the subroutine accesses the Ith element A[I] of the parameter A, the calling program must provide an array of cells corresponding to the array A. Many POLs will also restrict the parameter and the actual parameter value to be of the same dimension, that is, to have the same number of indices, each with the same range. [However, when we come to techniques for implementation, we will see that this restriction can often be sidestepped with useful results). If a parameter is a single variable, then the actual parameter value must have one of the first four types of structures. That is, it must represent a single entity rather than an array.

If a parameter is used for output, it is evident that the actual parameter value must represent a cell or set of cells in memory. That is, the first two types of actual parameter value structures (constants and expressions) may not be passed as output variables.

In many translators these restrictions are not checked. Hence the user can commit logical errors that lead to nonsensical execution time results. Consider the flowcharts in Figure 43. If the equivalent of this program were to be run under most FORTRAN systems the main program would cause the number 2.0 to be printed. This occurs because the main program is compiled with 1.0 and 2.0 in cells in its area of memory. When the subroutine WRECK is called it gets the value 2.0 for parameter B and stores it into parameter A. Since A is an output parameter, its value will be stored back into the cell that originally contained 1.0. Thus the result of calling WRECK at execution time in the manner above is to store the value 2.0 in the cell the compiler has assigned to hold the constant 1.0. When the code corresponding to Z — 1.0 is executed, the right-hand side will be copied from the cell the main program believes to contain 1.0. resulting in 2.0 being assigned to Z.

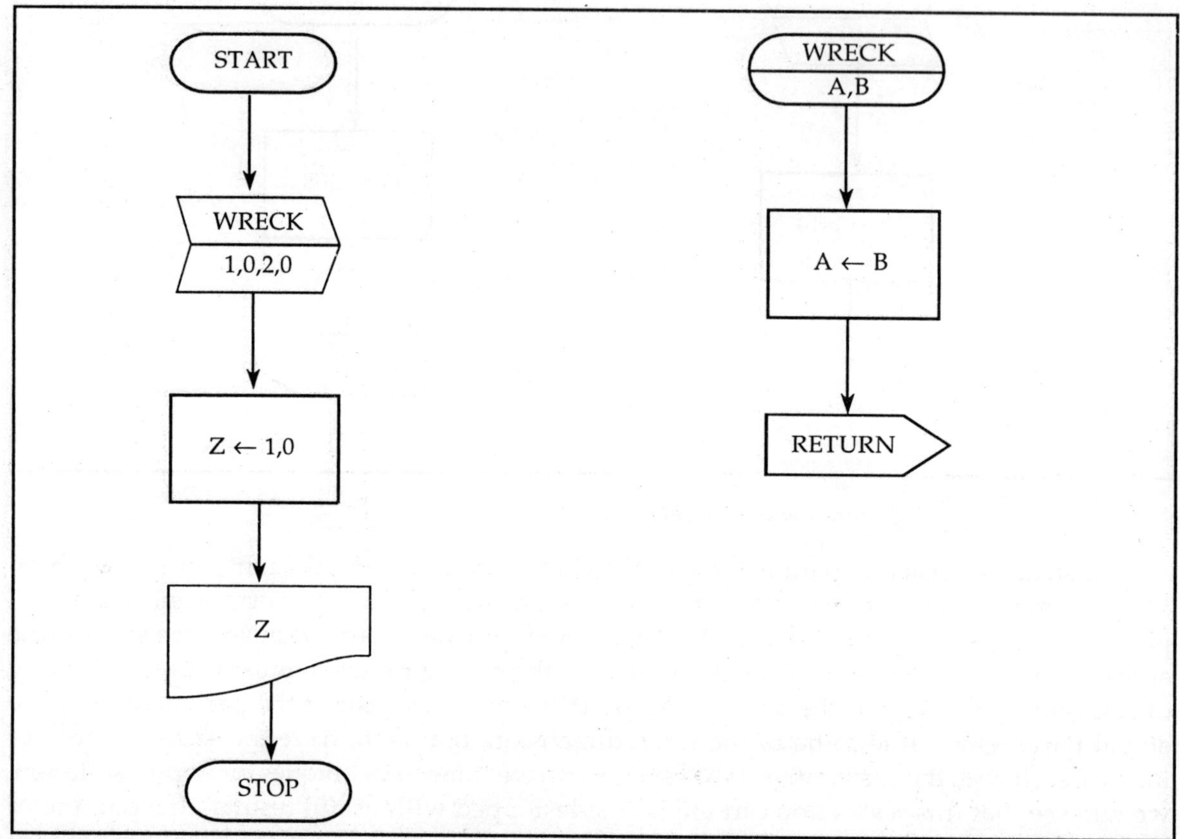

Fig. 41. Invalid use of parameters

Call by Address (Also Known as Call by Location)

The most common and one of the simplest forms of linking the actual parameter values to the parameters is by passing the address of the actual value from the calling program to the called program. The called program can then access actual values directly in the place they are stored and return results to these locations (in the case of output parameters).

The address usually passed is given in Table 3. If labels of procedure names are passed as actual parameter values, the address can be address of the location in memory where the labeled section of code or procedure starts. However, if label or procedure type variables are allowed, the address passed will have to be the address of a location containing the address of the start of the section of code or procedure. (Label variables are the names of cells in memory that contain the address of a labeled section of code.) Call by address is used for arrays in most FORTRAN compilers.

TABLE 3

Form of Address Passed as Parameter

Structure of Address Passed Actual Parameter	
Constant	Address of that constant in the calling program
Single Variable	Address of that variable in the calling program
Expression	Address of a temporary location Before the actual call; the calling program computes the actual parameter value and stores in this temporary location.
Array Element	Address of that element.
Array[a]	Address of the first element in the array

a. Some POLs pass the address of a "description" of the array used for the actual parameter. This description includes the address of the first element and the size of the array (number of indices, and range of each).

If an array is passed by passing the address of its first element, it is often permissible to pass the address of a single element in a larger array, even one with a different number of dimensions.

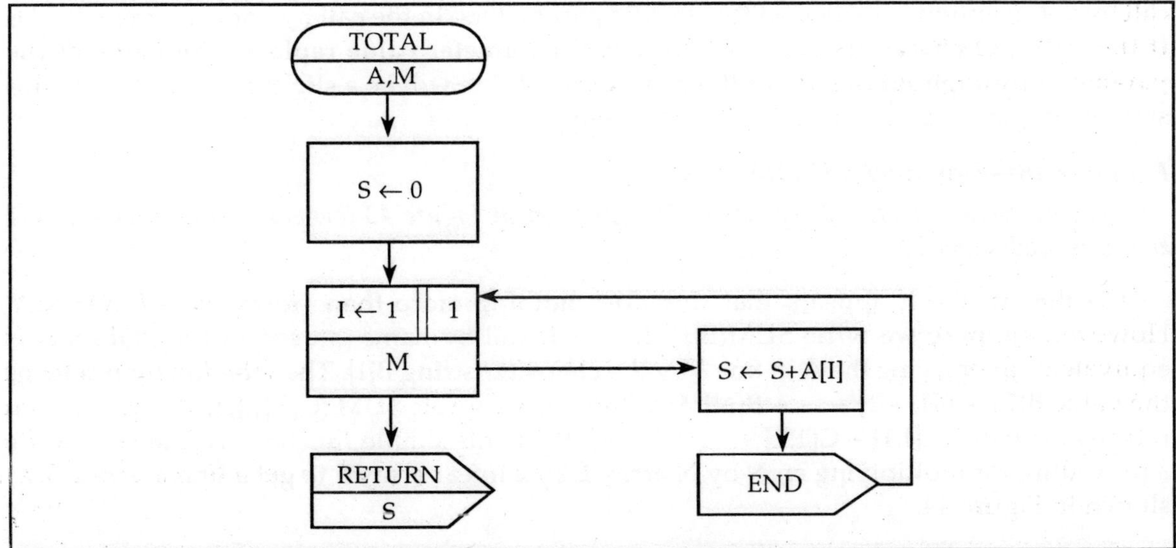

Fig. 42. Solution for Example 17

Example 17—Summing Columns of an Array

Suppose the array SCORE [I, J] contains the score of the Ith exam for the Jth student in the class. Suppose that arrays are stored by column, that is, element SCORE[I + 1, J] is one location beyond SCORE[I,J] in memory. We wish to find the total score of the Jth student; that is, we wish to form SCORE[1, J] + SCORE[2, J] + ...+SCORE[N, J]. The function shown in Figure 44 will accomplish this if call by address is used in the system and if the address of the first element of an array is passed when an array is used as an actual parameter value.

This function can be called by writing TOTAL[SCORE [1, J]N). The address of the element SCORE[1,J] is passed to the function that assumes this is the address of the first element of the array A. When it accesses the element A[I], the address of SCORE[1, J] plus I – 1 is computed. Since SCORE is stored by columns, this is the element SCORE[I, J].

Call by Value

When actual parameter values are *called* by *value*, the actual values are passed across to the procedure at the time of the call. Call by value requires that separate memory locations be provided by the called subprocedure for the values of the parameters during the execution of the subroutine. These locations must be loaded with the actual parameter values at the start of the procedure, and the values of output parameters must be copied back at the end. This is handles by the compiler. Call by value is an option in ALGOL and is standard for single values in many FORTRAN compilers. However, ALGOL does not copy the values back afterwards, so call by value parameters can only be used as input parameters in ALGOL procedures.

Call by Name

Call by name is the type of parameter linkage provided by an ALGOL compiler unless the call by value option is requested for specific parameters. In the call by name linkage. It is as **if the string of characters given as the actual parameter value replaces the name of the parameter throughout the use of the procedure.** (There will be a slight modification to this statement later.) Let us illustrate this by example.

Example 18—Summing a Vector

Suppose we are using call by name. The function in Figure 43 forms the sum of N – L + 1 elements, each named A.

On the surface it appears that this does nothing more than form (N – L +1) × A. However, suppose we write SUM(B[I], I,L,N). If call by name is used in the POL, this is equivalent to replacing the A in Box 3 by the character string B[I]. Then the function returns the value B[L] + B[L + 1] + ...+ B[N]. Similarly, if we wrote SUM (C[I,J],J,1,M) the function returns the value C[I,1] + C[1,2] + ...+C[I, M]. With this simple function we can then write a procedure for multiplying an N by N array E by a linear array F to get a linear array G, as shown in Figure 44.

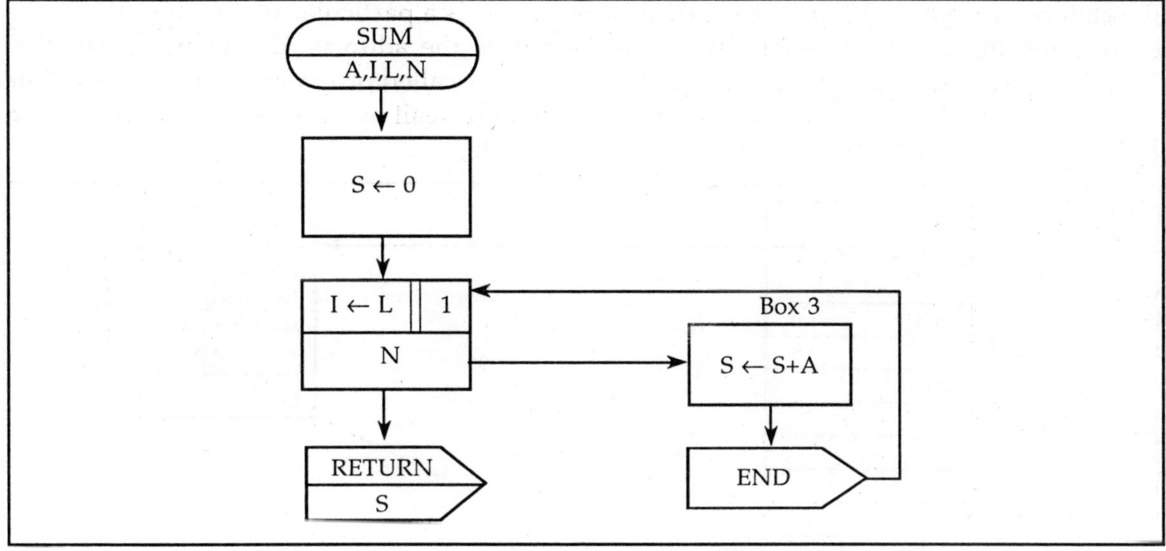

Fig. 43. Call by name example

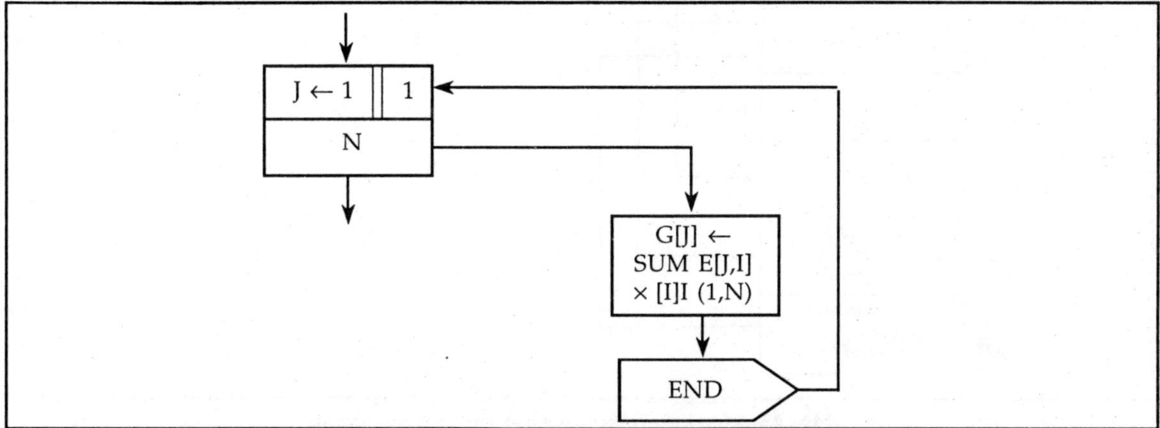

Fig. 44. Use of SUM procedure to form square array times linear array

Suppose we had written SUM(S[I], I,1,N). Then our rule states that Box 3 in Figure 43 contains S ← S + S[I]. This would apparently lead to an error, as the same name cannot represent both a single variable and an array. However, this is not a problem here; S in Figure 44 is a variable *local* to the procedure SUM. It bears no relation to any variables in the calling program, even if they have the same name. Thus Box 3 really says, in this case,

"S in procedure SUM ← S in procedure SUM + S[I] in calling procedure."

The results of using call by name can be determined most easily if the technique used in the computer is understood. The usual technique is for the calling procedure to pass an address of a *parameter subroutine* for each parameter. The parameter subroutines are part of the calling procedure. When the called procedure needs a particular parameter, it calls the corresponding parameter subroutine, which returns the address of a memory cell that contains the parameter. The address can be used by the called program to either access data or to return results. Thus in Example 18 above, with the call by SUM(A[J],J,1,M) we would have the arrangement in memory shown in Figure 45.

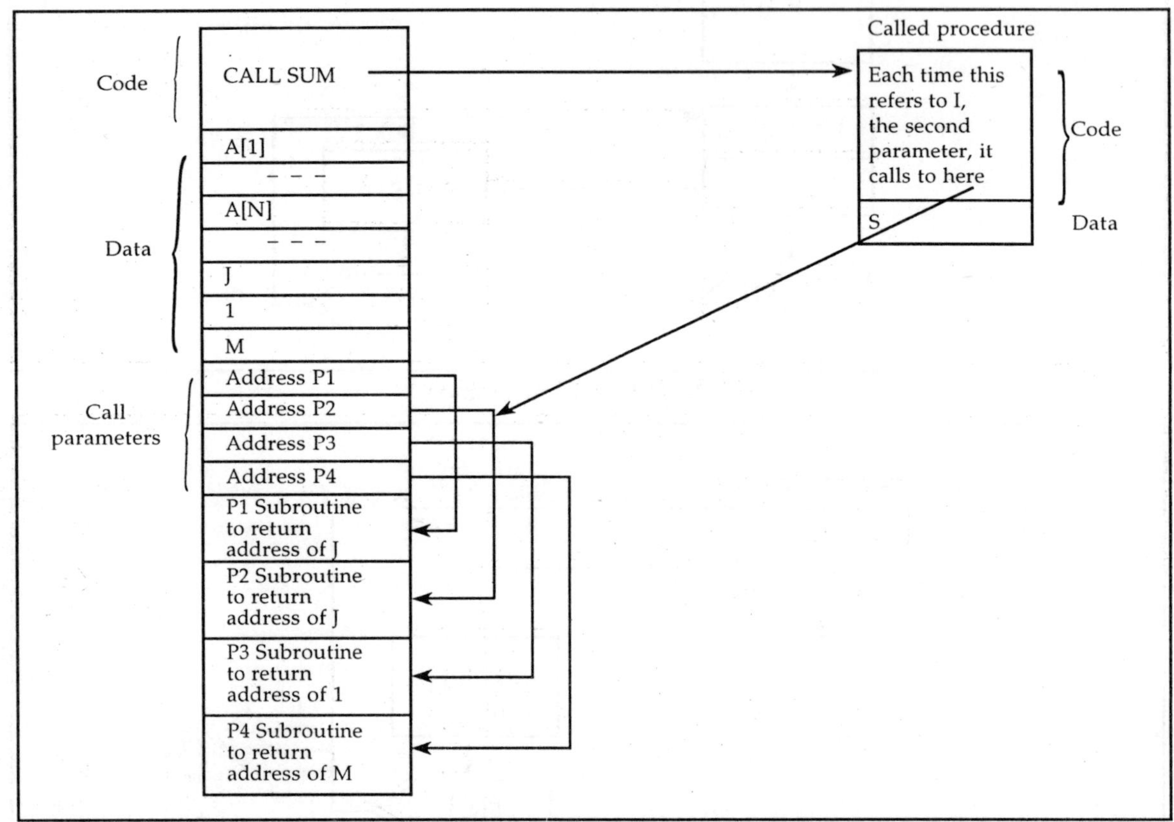

Fig. 45. Memory arrangement for call by name

When we understand this process we can answer the question "What happens if we call the function in Figure 46 by PROD(A[I] + B[I], I,1,N)?" It is not quite as if we had written A[I] + B[I] in place of A because that would have changed Box 3 to P ← P × A[I] + B[I]. Rather it is as if Box 3 read P ← P × (A[I] + B[I]). Each time that a parameter is needed in call by name, its actual value is recomputed. (This is necessary only if it is an expression or an array element indexed by a variable.)

Example 19—Differences Between Address, Value, and Name

We will illustrate the way in which the different techniques of parameter access can give different results. (This example is not supposed to do anything useful.) Consider the procedure in Figure 47. Suppose we use this by writing A ← R(B, B B+C). Suppose the initial values of B and C are 1.0 and 2.0, respectively.

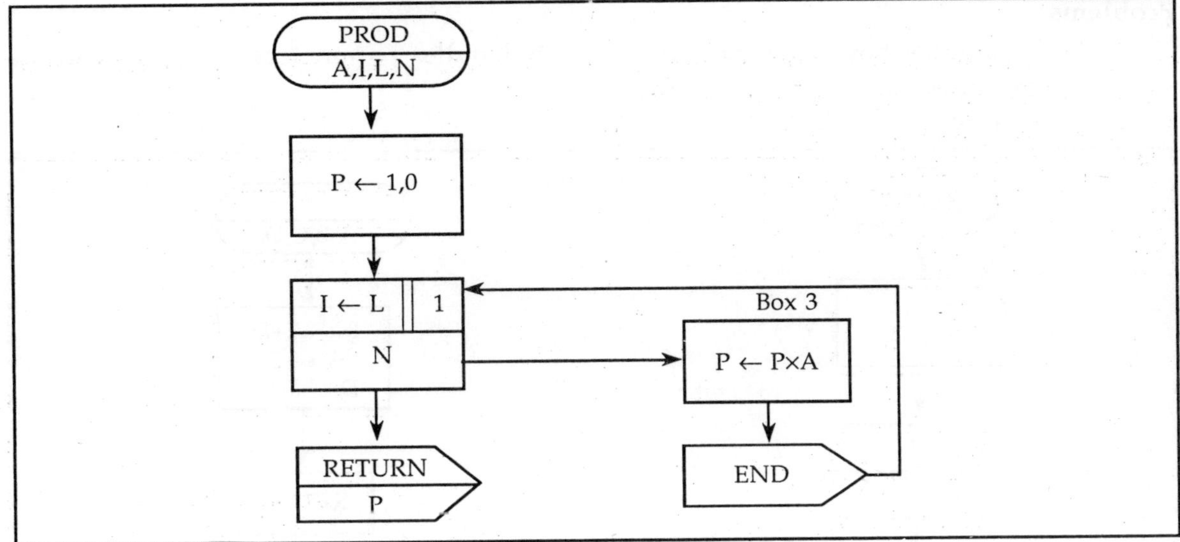

Fig. 46. The function PRCD

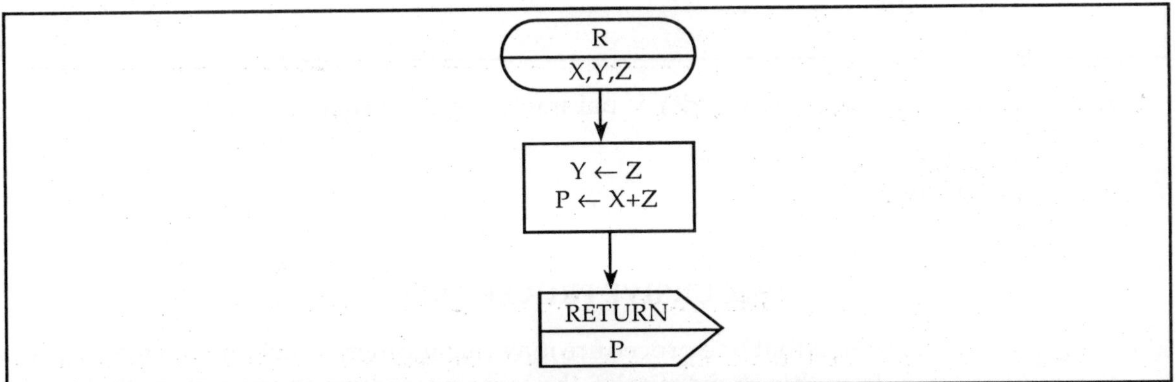

Fig. 47. Example 19

Consider first call by address. The calling procedure passes across the address of the actual parameter B for parameters X and Y and passes across the address of a location containing B + C; that is, 3.0 – for Z. Thus the function first stores the value 3.0 in cell B(Y←Z): then it stores the sum of B and 3.0 into the local cell P (P←X + Z). The result returned is therefore 6.0.

Now consider call by value. First cells X, Y and Z, local to the function, are assigned the values 1.0, 1.0, 3.0, respectively. Now the function stores 3.0 in Y(Y←Z) and 4.0 in P(P←X +Z). The result returned is 4.0.

Finally let us consider call by name. It is as if we performed the steps B←B←C followed by P←B + B + C. The effect of these is to store 3.0 in B and 8.0 in P. Thus the result 8.0 is returned.

Problems

1. Determine how your compiler actually handles parameters by trying various examples such as Example 19.
2. Consider

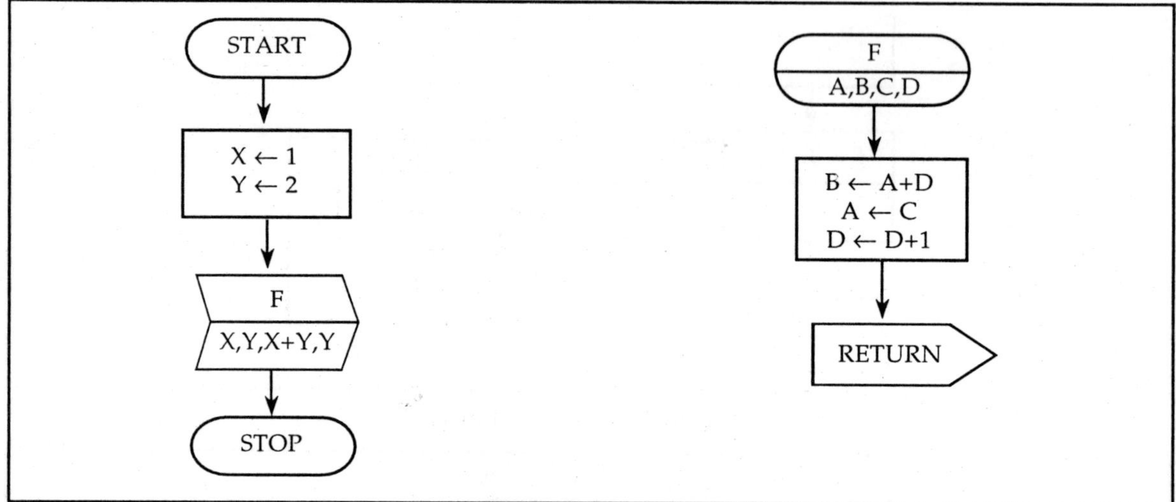

What are the final values of X and Y if parameters are handled

a. by value
b. by address
c. by name

RECURSIVE PROCEDURES

We have already mentioned that one procedure may call another, which in turn may call yet another, and so forth. If, in this chain of calls, the same procedure appears more than once-that is, if it has effectivewwwwwwwwwwwwsion by means of examples and then discuss some of the implications of recursive procedures.

Example 20—Binary Search

We previously discussed the binary search method in an ordered table and wrote straightforward procedures that implement it. We will not implement it by means of a recursive subroutine SEARCH with parameters B, A, L, M, and I. This subroutine should locate the variable B in the ordered table A[L], A[L + 1]....A[M] and return with I such that A[I] = B it a match is found, or return with I = 0 if no match is found. The reason for having the parameters L and M will be apparent below. If there are N entries A[1] to A[N] in the table, we expect the subroutine to be called initially with parameters B, A, 1, N, and I.

The basic technique of the binary search is to compare the searched item B with the middle entry A[(L + M)/2]. If there is a match, we have found the entry; otherwise we continue to search into either the first or the last part of the table. This is shown in Figure 50. (There is a serious error in this solution that will be pointed out later.)

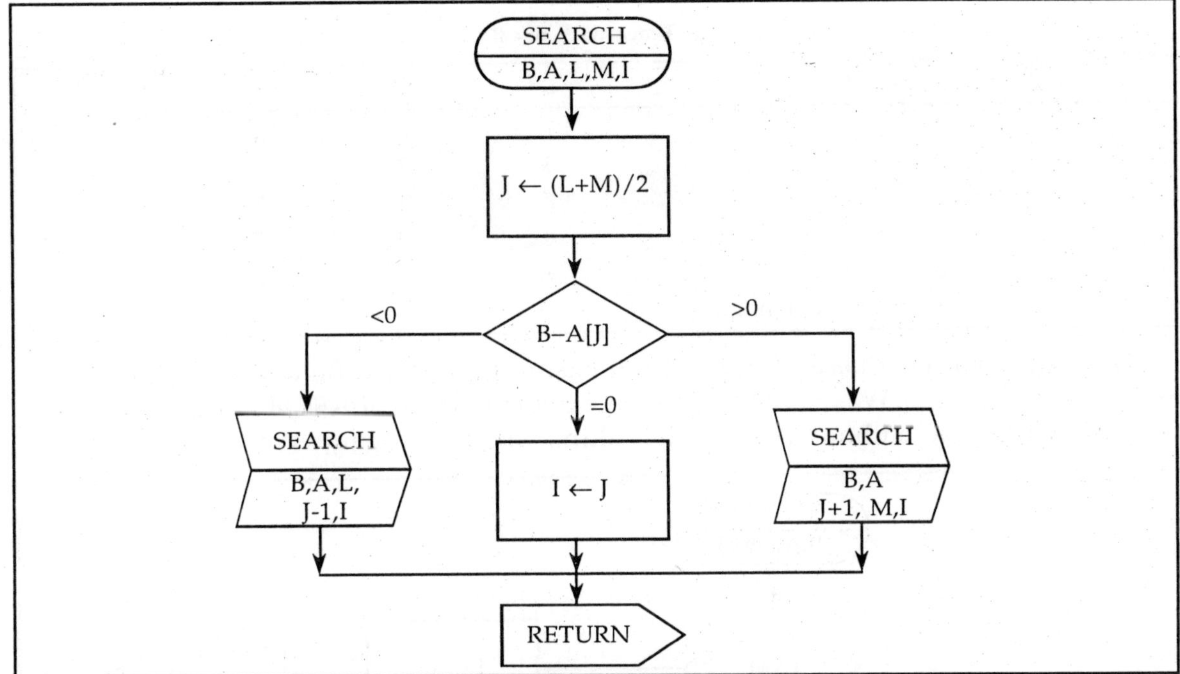

Fig. 48. Solution for Example 20

Figure 48 defines a recursive procedure. We can understand recursive procedures by imaging that many different copies of the procedure are available. The first call on the procedure transfers to the first copy. If that copy calls the same procedure, it transfers to the second copy. Each copy has storage for its own local variables. Similarly, if copy #2 calls the same procedure, it transfers to the third copy. A trace of the values of L, M, and J is shown in Table 4 for the case A[K] = K for $1 \leq K \leq 7$ if the initial call uses the parameters B, A, 1, 7, I, where B = 3. A match is found in the third call.

TABLE 4

Trace of Values A, M, and J

Call on Subroutine No.	L	M	J
1	1	7	4
2	1	3	2
3	3	3	3

Table 5 shows a trace for the same problem with B = 8. When we reach the call on subroutine #4 with parameter values 8 and 7 for L and M, respectively, subroutine #4 will compute J = (8 + 7)/2 = 7. Since B – A[7] is positive, yet another call on SEARCH is made with L and M equal to 8 and 7 again. We are now in an infinite loop.

TABLE 5

A Trace with B = 8

Call on Subroutine No.	L	M	J
1	1	7	4
2	5	7	6
3	7	7	7
4	8	7	7
5	8	7	7
(ad infinitum)			

The problem occurs because we did not ensure that only a finite number of calls on SEARCH are possible. We require that at some point a call on SEARCH must cause it to go to a RETURN box without recursively calling SEARCH again. We can take care of

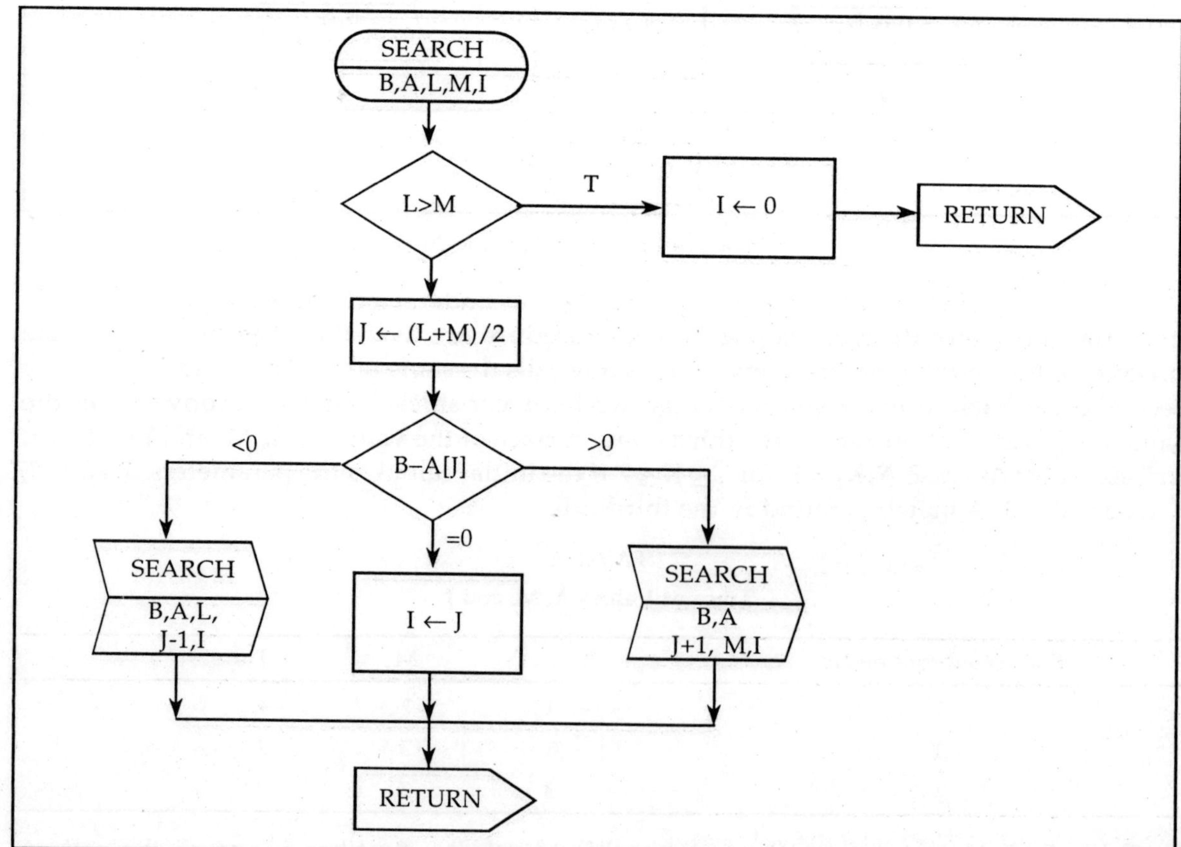

Fig. 49. Modified flowchart of Figure 48

the problem in this example by noting that if L > M, there are no entries in the table to be searched; hence B is not present. Therefore we modify flowchart 48 to that shown in Figure 49. If L > M, we set I = 0 and return immediately.

The major advantage of recursion is that it makes the statement of an algorithm more concise. The example above does not illustrate this adequately. By then we will have introduced more complex data structures. Recursion usually pays off more in non-numerical processing. The major disadvantage is one of lack of speed in some simple numerical problems. We will illustrate this with one of the common examples of recursion.

Example 21—Factorial by Recursion

We with to define a function FACT(N) whose value is N × (N -1) × (N – 2) × ......X 2 × 1 if N > 1, or 1 if N ≤ 1.

We note that FACT(N) = N × FACT(N – 1) if N > 1. Thus we can use the recursive procedure shown in Figure 50.

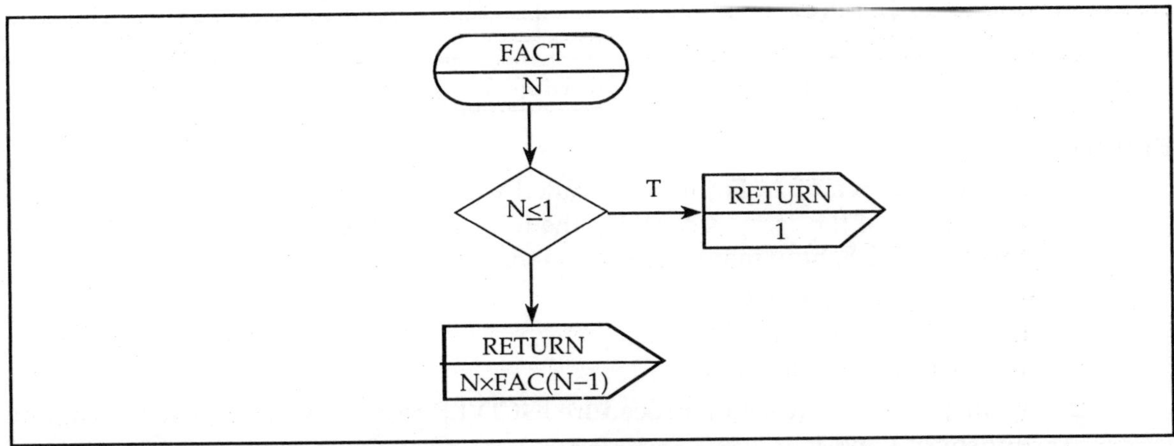

Fig. 50. Recursive procedure for factorial

The *iterative* method shown in Figure 51 leads to a more complex flowchart, but it will execute more rapidly on most systems. We can see this when we study the actual technique used for recursion. When the procedure in Figure 50 is first called, a section of available memory space is assigned for use in this invocation of the procedure. If the procedure calls itself, the next available section of memory space is assigned for use in the second level of invocation. These sections of memory correspond to storage in different copies in our analogy. Performing the call and assigning this memory usually take considerably more computer time than the time required to perform the overhead of the loop in Figure 51 hence the recursive approach is often slower. However, for non-numerical problems a nonrecursive approach is usually so much more complex that the small additional computer time is a good investment, since the procedure can be written and debugged more rapidly.

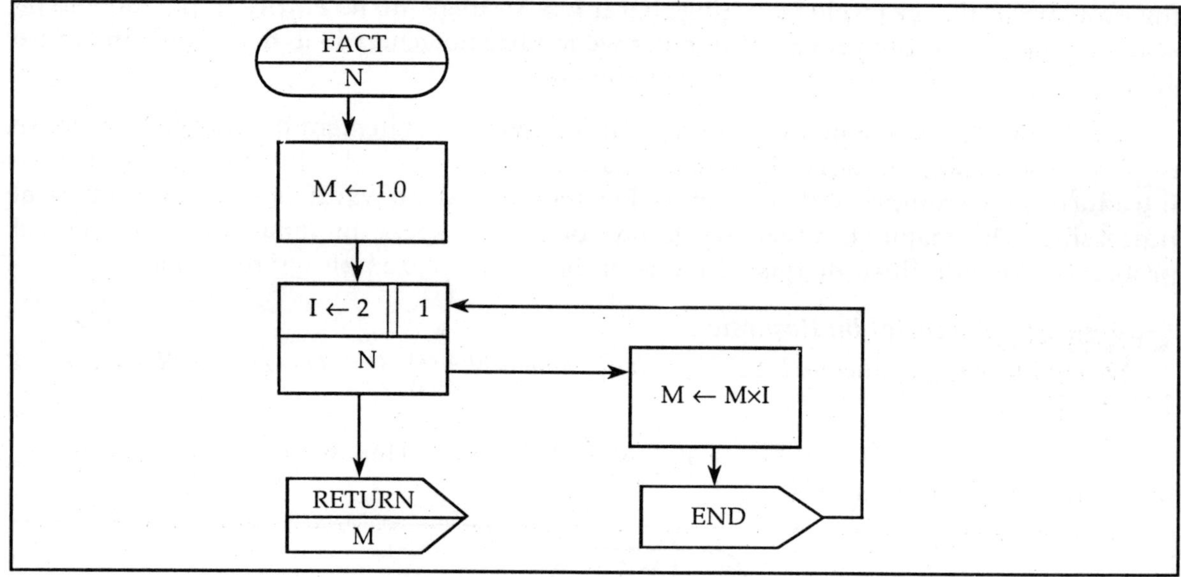

Fig. 51. Iterative procedure for factorial

Problems

1. If flowchart Search in Figure 49 is called with actual parameter values CONS X, 1, 10, I and of the array X contains the ten values -7.5, -5.2 -4.1, -1.7, 0.5, 1.2, 1,7, 1,9, 2.1 and 2.8, how many calls are made on SEARCH to locate CONS if:
   *a. CONS contains 0.5
   b. CONS contains 1.7
   c. CONS contains -8.3
2. Write a recursive function procedure IGCD(I,J) to evaluate the greatest common divisor of I and J.

18

Subprograms

What are Subprograms?

Memory space and computer time are always precious and we must write programs so that we make less demand on these valuables. Subprograms are useful techniques to achieve the above objective. Very often it happens that we may have to use some segments of a computer program which computes certain functional values repeatedly in several places in the same program. In such cases, it is advantageous to write separate program segments to evaluate such functions, give them some name and invoke them in the main program in as many places as required. Such program segments are called subprograms. There are two types of subprograms, namely, the system defined subprograms and the user defined subprograms. The library functions belong to the class of system defined subprograms. We have already said that the programs for several often repeated functions like sine, cosine etc. are made part of the language itself, so that the programmers are relieved of the burden of writing separate program segments for evaluating such functions. The programmer simply calls or invokes the function by using the code names given to those functions using the appropriate arguments and the call statement simply returns the value of that particular function. Apart from system defined functions, the programmer himself would like to define certain function and use them in his program at several places. The program segment for evaluating such functions are called subprograms and the different languages permit the use of different types of subprograms as we will see presently. The main difference between the system defined subprograms can be used by all the users in all their programs, whereas the user defined subprograms can be used only by that particular user and that too in the particular program where they are defined.

Subprograms in Basic

There are two types of user defined subprograms in BASIC in addition to the system defined library functions. The subprograms in BASIC are

1. DEF functions
2. Subroutines

DEF Functions

The DEF function otherwise called the user defined function is defined by a single statement The general form of the DEF function is

DEF function-name (arguments list) = expression

The keyword DEF tells the computer that the statement defines a user defined function. The function name can be as long as 31 characters, just like any variable name. The first two characters of the function name must be FN. The subsequent letters may be a combination of alphabets, numbers and decimal points subject to the condition that the total length does not exceed 31 characters. The function name is followed by the list of dummy arguments enclosed within parentheses. The dummy arguments are followed by the assignment operator (=). On the right side of the assignment operator the expression which is to be defined is given. The expression must contain the variables listed in the dummy arguments list. It can also contain variables which have been defined earlier but not included in the dummy arguments list. The general form of the DEF function is:

```
DEF FNA12(X)=X^3+4
DEF FNA34(X,Y,Z) = Y^2-4*X*Z
```

The user defined functions can be invoked by simply giving the name of the function with the dummy arguments being replaced by real or actual arguments. Suppose we want to evaluate the function FNA34 with A,B & C as real arguments one can write as:

```
S=FNA34(A,B,C)
```

In this case, B will replace Y, A will replace X and C will replace Z in the DEF functions. The expression on the r.h.s. of the DEF function will be evaluated and the computed value will be stored in the variable S. The DEF function can be invoked any number of times in the same program. More than one DEF function can be defined in the same program. All the DEF functions must be placed in the beginning of the program.

At the time of defining the function the arguments have no values and so they are called dummy, but when the function is invoked in the program the arguments must have values and so they are called real arguments. The main drawbacks of the DEF functions are that they can be defined only by one statement and they can return only one value. DEF functions can also be used to return string values. In that case the name of the function must contain the string variable name. For example, one can give the name FNA$ for a function which has to return strings. If more statements are required for computation and more values are to be returned to the program we have to make use of subroutines. Subroutines in BASIC are called GOSUB statements.

GOSUB Statements

The subroutines in BASIC are called GOSUB-RETURN statements. The general form of GOSUB-RETURN statements is

```
GOSUB line-number
...............
...............
line-number
...............
...............
...............
```

Return

Unlike a Function, a Subroutine is not given any name. The beginning of the subroutine is identified by the line number given after the word COSUB. The end of the subroutine is identified by the word RETURN. Consider the following program segment:

```
120 GOSUB 300
130 PRINT X,Y,Z
...............
...............
...............
300 X=A+B
...............
...............
...............
380 RETURN
```

When the statement 120 is encountered by the computer, the control is transferred to the statement number 300, which is the beginning of the subroutine. Then all the statements up to 380 will be executed. On sensing the word RETURN, the control will be transferred to the statement 130, which is next to the GOSUB statement. This means, that whenever a GOSUB is encountered the computer remembers the line number of the next immediate statement and comes back to that statement after executing the subroutine. The GOSUB statement looks somewhat like the GO TO statement, when you write GO TO 300 the control is transferred to the statement 300 just as the statement GOSUB 300. But in the former case the control never looks back and goes on executing the statements which follow 300 in sequence. In the latter case the control after executing all the statements starting from 300 up to the RETURN statement return back to the statement immediately following the GOSUB statement. Of course a subroutine must be invoked only by a GOSUB statement and not by the GOTO statement. Subroutines in BASIC form part of the program and they have no separate status as subroutines in FORTRAN. In BASIC the subroutines are compiled along with the program and not separately. A subroutine can be invoked as many times as required in the program. Consider the following program segment where a subroutine is invoked many times:

```
10 . . . . . . . . . . . .
40 GOSUB 1000
50 . . . . . . . . . . . .
. . . . . . . . . . . . . .
220 COSUB 1000
260 . . . . . . . . . . . .
440 GOSUB 1000
450 . . . . . . . . . . .
980 . . . . . . . . . . .
1000 . . . . . . . . . .
. . . . . . . . . . . . . .
. . . . . . . . . . . . . .
. . . . . . . . . . . . . .
1050 RETURN
9999 END
```

The computer starts executing the statements starting from 10. When the computer encounters the first GOSUB statement it stores the line number 50 to which it must return after executing the subroutine. When the computer encounters the same GOSUB statement for the second time it stores the number 260, to which it must return after executing the subroutine. When the computer encounters the same GOSUB statement for the third time it stores the value 450, to which it must return after executing the subroutine. After executing 450, it executes the statement 980. After executing 980, it tends to fall on the subroutine which starts from the statement 1000. This must be avoided since a subroutine must be invoked only by a GOSUB statement and the control must not fall on it by any other method. To prevent the control falling on the subroutine by accident, the statement immediately preceding the subroutine must be an unconditional transfer of control statement.

The important points to remember about subroutines are

1. Subroutines must be invoked or called only via GOSUB.
2. The last executable statement of every subroutine must be RETURN.
3. Subroutines may reference other subroutines.
4. Subroutines may reference system defined functions and user defined functions.
5. Remember that nested subroutines must have a strict hierarchical ordering. If a subroutine A references a subroutine B then B cannot reference A.
6. A subroutine can return any number of values to a program (In contrast to DEF functions which can return only one value.)
7. Subroutines are generally grouped at the end of the program just before the END statement.

Program for illustrating DEF Function Statement

Suppose you want to find the greater und the smaller on wo given numbers. We can define two DEF functions one for the greater number and another for the smaller number and write a program as shown in the figure 6.1.

```
10    REM program for illustrating DEF Function
20    DEF FNMAX(A,B) = (A + B + ABS(A-B))/2
30    DEF FNM1N(A,B) = (A + B - ABS(A-B))/2
40    INPUT "ENTER TWO NUMBERS A, B:"; A, B
50    MAX = FNMAX(A,B)
60    MIN = FNMIN(A,B)
70    PRINT "THE GREATER NUMBER IS:"; MAX
80    PRINT "THE SMALLER NUMBER IS:"; MIN
90    INPUT "ANY MORE TRIALS:";Y$
100   IF Y$ = "y" THEN 40
110   END
```

Fig. 1

The output will be as shown below:

```
ENTER TWO NUMBERS A, B: 24,78
THE GREATER NUMBER IS: 78
THE SMALLER NUMBER IS: 24
ANY MORE TRIALS: y
OK
```

Program for Illustrating the GOSUB Statement

Suppose you want to write a menu driven program, each item of the menu doing some job. For example one job may be to calculate the total allowances, another job may be to calculate the total deductions, another job may be to print the pay slip and so on. In the example program shown in the figure 2 we have used the GOSUB statement to print any one word/words based on our choice to be made from a menu. Now look at the program:

```
10    REM MENU DRIVEN PROGRAM FOR ILLUSTRATING THE USE OF GOSUB STATEMENT
20    PRINT "MENU OF CHOICES"
30    PRINT STRING$(40,CHR$(45))
40    PRINT "1.GOOD MORNING"
50    PRINT "2. WELL DONE"
```

```
60   PRINT "3. EXCELLENT"
70   PRINT "4. MARVELLOUS"
80   PRINT "5. END"
90   PRINT STRING$(40,CHR$(45)): PRINT
100  INPUT "ENTER YOUR CHOICE:"; CHOICE: PRINT
110  IF CHOICE = 5 THEN 500
120  ON CHOICE GOSUB 140,180,220,240
125  PRINT
130  GOTO 20
140  PRINT "GOOD MORNING"
150  RETURN
180  PRINT "WELL DONE"
190  RETURN
220  PRINT "EXCELLENT"
230  RETURN
240  PRINT "MARVELLOUS"
250  RETURN
500  PRINT "THIS IS THE END OF PROGRAM EXECUTION"
510  END
```

Fig. 2

The output will look as below.

```
MENU OF CHOICES
          * * * * * * * * * * * * * * * * * * * * * * * * * *
          1. GOOD MORNING
          2. WELL DONE
          3. EXCELLENT
          4. MARVELLOUS
          5. END
          * * * * * * * * * * * * * * * * * * * * * * * * * *
ENTER YOUR CHOICE: ? 1
GOOD MORNING
MENU OF CHOICES
          * * * * * * * * * * * * * * * * * * * * * * * * * *
```

1. GOOD MORNING
2. WELL DONE
3. EXCELLENT
4. MARVELLOUS
5. END

```
**************************
```

ENTER YOUR CHOICE: ? 5
THIS IS THE END OF PROGRAM EXECUTION
OK

There is one drawback in the GOSUB statement. You don't have dummy arguments as you have in the DEF Function. In some versions of BASIC the restrictions as regards the number of statements in the DEF function and the non-availability of dummy arguments in the GOSUB statement have been removed and this provision makes the development of program modules more comfortable.

COBOL CHARACTERS AND CONSTANTS

What is COBOL?

COBOL is a High Level Computer Language used for communicating with computers. It is a language for the machines, just as English is a language for the humans. It is a special purpose language used for programming business problems. The word COBOL is coined as an acronym for Common Business Oriented Language.

How Do We Start Learning COBOL?

Cobol is learnt just like any other spoken language. Every language has a character set and a grammar. So also has COBOL. We first start with the study of the character set. Then we learn the rules for coding COBOL Words, COBOL Constants, COBOL Opera tors, COBOL Expressions and COBOL Statements. Finally we learn to write programs for problems.

Plan of Study

We study the different topics in the following or order:

1. Character Set in COBOL
2. Rules for Coding Constants in COBOL
3. Rules for Coding Variables in COBOL
4. Rules for Coding Operators in COBOL
5. Rules for Coding Expressions in COBOL
6. Computation Statements in COBOL

7. Input and Output Statement in COBOL
8. Organisation of a COBOL Program
9. Control Statements in COBOL
10. Data Organisation in COBOL
11. File Operations in COBOL

Character Set in COBOL

There are three types of characters in every computer language, namely,

1. Alphabetic
2. Numeric and
3. Special

1.	Alphabets	:	*A, B, C, D, E, F, G, H, I, J, K, L, M, N, O, P, Q, R, S, T, U, V, W, X, Y, Z* (26)	
2.	Numbers	:	0, 1, 2, 3, 4, 5, 6, 7, 8, 9 (10)	
3.	Special	:	blank or space	
			+	plus
			-	minus or hyphen
			*	asterisk (multiplication symbol)
			/	slash (division symbol)
			=	assignment and equality symbol
			>	greater than
			<	less than
			.	period
			'	comma
			;	semicolon
			'	quote mark
			(	opening bracket
			)	closing bracket
			$	dollar sign

In all there are 51 characters used for coding purposes in COBOL.

What are Constants?

A constant is one whose value is given by itself. For example, when we say that the number 25 is a constant, we mean that the value of 25 is 25 itself. Constants can be either numeric or non-numeric. For example, the name of a person, say KRISHNAMURTHY is a non-numeric constant. Constants in COBOL arc called literals.

Data Types in COBOL

COBOL deals with three Data Types or Constants. They are:

1 Numeric
2. Alphabetic and
3. Alphanumeric

We will now study the rules for coding them one by one.

1. Rules for Coding Numbers or Numeric Literals

1. A Numeric Literal is coined by combining only numeric digits to a maximum length of 18 digits. The count does not include the decimal point and the sign.
2. A +ve or a -ve sign can be given preceding the first digit as well as the decimal point if any in the literal. An unsigned numeric literal is taken as +ve. If the numeric literal is -ve, it must be signed. Embedded blanks are not allowed anywhere in the literal.
3. A decimal point if present in the number shall not be the last character. The number 25 can be written either as 25.0 or simply as 25 (not as 25.). Numeric literals without a decimal point are treated as integers. Only one decimal point can be present in a numeric literal.
4. A literal shall not contain alphabets or any other special characters except in the +. - and (.) at the appropriate places.

Examples of Valid Numeric Literals

1. 23456
2. -34.56
3. -.5678
4. 34.0

Examples of Invalid Numeric Literals

1. 34+ (The sign shall not be at the end)
2. 24. (The decimal point shall not be the last character)
3. 34A6 (Alphabets shall not be present)
4. 23 56 (Embedded blanks shall not be present)
5. .-32 (The sign if present shall be the leftmost character)

2. *Rules for Coding Alphabetic Constants*

1. An alphabetic constant is coded by combining alphabets and spaces to a maximum length of 120 characters. The constant must have at least one alphabet.
2. The constant must be enclosed within single quotes.

Examples of Valid Alphabetic Constants

1. 'January'
2. 'accept'
3. 'basic pay'
4. 'a b'

Examples of Invalid Alphabetic Constants

1. 'abcd3' (Numbers are not allowed)
2. ' ' (There must be at least one alphabetic character)
3. abcd (The constant must be embedded within quotes)

3. *Rules for Coding Alphanumeric Constants*

1. An Alphanumeric Constant is coded by combining any valid COBOL character excepting the quote mark to a maximum length of 120 characters.
2. The constant shall be enclosed within quotes.

Examples of Valid Alphanumeric Constants

1. 'January'
2. ' '
3. '234'
4. 'asdf456'

It may be noted that pure blanks and pure numbers can also be coded as alphanumeric constants provided they are enclosed within quotes.

Figurative Constants

This is an additional facility in COBOL for the convenience of the programmer. Some constants are so frequently used, that reserved words are assigned to code them. They are referred to as Figurative Constants. The words SPACES, ZEROS ZEROES, LOW-VALUE, HIGH-VALUE are examples of Figurative Constants. We will see their use later when we write programs.

Summary

In this lesson we have seen the Character set used in COBOL and the rules for coding literals. In the next lesson we will see the rules for coding variables and how they are declared.

COBOL VARIABLES

What are Variables?

Variables are some symbols used for storing values or constants. Since the symbols can take different values at different times they are called variables as distinguished from constants. As far as the machine is concerned these symbols represent the addresses of the memory locations in the computer. These symbols can be manipulated as variables which we use in the conventional algebra.

Rules for Coding Variables

1. A variable is coined by combining alphabets, numbers and hyphens to a maximum length of 30 characters.
2. There shall be at least one alphabet in the name.
3. When the hyphen is used, it shall be only in the embedded positions. That is, a hyphen shall not be the last or the first character of a variable name. No two hyphens shall occur in succession.
4. Embedded blanks are not allowed.
5. Variable names shall not be reserved words.

Examples of Valid Variable Names

1. HOURLY-RATE
2. X
3. 2345A
4. BASICPAY

Examples of Invalid Variable Names

1.	2345	(There must beat least one alphabet)
2.	BASIC PAY	(Embedded blanks are not allowed)
3.	ABC+	(Special Characters are not allowed)
4.	ABC-	(The hyphen shall not be the last character)
5.	A - —BC	(No two hyphens shall appear in succession)
6.	READ	(Reserved Words shall not be used as variables)

Variable names are also called as identifiers or data names.

Importance of Descriptive Naming

The size of the data name up to 30 characters long enables the programmer to give meaningful names to data items. For example, the name DATE-OF-RECEIPT is more meaningful than the name D. In the conventional algebra we give single letter names lor variables. Such names are not meaningful. COBOL was specifically intended to be self-documenting, which means that by reading the program, one knows what data are used and what manipulations are done on the data. The problem with using cryptic names is that their meanings are forgotten by the programmer himself and never are understood by others, unless a list of definitions is given. The aim of a programmer must be to write a program which can be easily understood by all the readers.

Data Declaration Statements in Cobol

We said that variables are required to store constants. Since COBOL deals with three types of constants we require three types of variables. In COBOL, we code the different variables in the same way, but we make explicit declaration statements about the type of constant and the length of constant stored by each of the variables. It is only by looking at the declaration statements that one can identify the type of a COBOL variable.

Structured and Unstructured Data

There may be some data items which are grouped in a structure. For example, the data items like employee-number, employee-name, basic-pay, deductions etc. belonging to one person can be grouped together in a record. Such items are called structured data. Some data items may remain independent without forming part of any group. Such items are said to be unstructured data. The declarations for the structured data and the unstructured data are made in different formats. Presently we will deal with the unstructured data and later we will deal with the structured data. This sequence is only for the sake of simplicity.

Attributes of COBOL Data

Every COBOL data is described by three attributes. They are:

1. Level Number
2. Data Name and
3. PICTURE Clause

Hierarchical Structure of COBOL Data

COBOL data have a hierarchical structure just like the employees in an organisation have a hierarchical structure. The hierarchy of a COBOL data is denoted by a number called its level number. All independent data items have the same hierarchy and they are given the level number 77. Later we will see that the level numbers of structured data will vary.

Data Name

This attribute must be unique for every data item and we have already seen how the data names are coded.

PICTURE Clause for Numeric Data

The third attribute of the COBOL data is the PICTURE clause, which tells the type of data and the length of data. When the data is numeric it is indicated by coding each digit by the code 9. For example, a code given by 99999 or 9(5) can denote any 5 digit number, say 56789 or any number less than or equal to 5 digits. The highest number the code 99999 or 9(5) can denote is 99999.

PICTURE Clause for Alphabetic Data

When the data is alphabetic, it is indicated by coding each character by the code letter 'A.' For example, a code given by A AAAAA or A(6) can denote a string say, 'KRISHI.' If the string is longer, the number of code letters must be increased. Smaller strings can be denoted by longer codes, but longer strings cannot be represented by smaller codes.

PICTURE Clause for Alphanumeric Data

When the data is alphanumeric, it is indicated by coding each character by the code letter 'X.' For example, a code XXXXX or X(5) can denote a string 'abode' or '567' or ' 'or 'a b.'

The general form of the Data Declaration Statement is level-number data-name PICTURE string of 9's or A's or X's.

The word PICTURE is simply a code word. This can also be written as PIC.

Examples of Valid Data Declarations for Independent COBOL Data

1. 77 EMP-NUMBER PIC 9999.
2. 77 EMPLOYEE-NAME P1C X(15).
3. 77 DESIGNATION PIC A(10).

The first example tells that the data item EMP-NUMBER is an independent data item. It is a numeric data type of maximum length 4 digits.

The second example tells that the data item EMPLOYEE-NAME is an independent data of type alphanumeric with a maximum length of 15 characters.

The third example tells that the data item DESIGNATION is also an independent data of type alphabetic with a maximum length of 10 characters.

How to Represent Decimal Point and Sign in a Numeric Data?

A Numeric data item can have a decimal point and also a sign. There is a rule in COBOL which says that the actual symbols for the decimal point and the sign must not be put in the input data items. To overcome this difficulty, the COBOL framers have prescribed two code letters, V for the decimal point and S for the sign. These code letters are placed in the locations, where the actual symbols are to be present. Suppose one writes a declaration statement as

77 DEDUCTIONS PIC S999V99.

The above data declaration means that the data item DEDUCTIONS is an independent data item. The code letter S tells that the item is a signed one. The code letter V tells the position of the decimal point. The codes S and V are called the assumed sign and assumed decimal point respectively. These two code letters are not counted for the length of the data item in the fields described by them.

One can ask, how to input a negative data for an input variable into the computer. If you want to read an input data, say -23.5 for a variable X by the COBOL program, you have to key the data as -235 and give the data declaration statement as

77 X PIC S99V9 SIGN LEADING SEPARATE.

By writing like this, it is ensured that the sign is considered as a separate field.

COBOL Discipline

COBOL enforces lot of discipline in data organisation. Don't you think that by enforcing discipline in your office, better work can be turned out in a shorter lime. It is precisely for the same reason, COBOL enforces discipline in data organisation. Of course enforcing discipline requires more effort in program writing. The programmer has to spend more time in writing the discipline enforcing statements in a COBOL Program.

Reserved Words

Certain fixed words have been designated as reserved words, which have some specific meaning to the COBOL compiler. They cannot be used as programmer coined words. For example, the words like READ, WRITE, ACCEPT, DISPLAY etc., have some specific meaning to the compiler. There are about 300 reserved words in COBOL. A short list of the oft-repeated reserved words are given below. For a complete list, one must refer to the manual of the particular computer system used.

ACCEPT	ADD	ADDRESS	ADVANCING
AFTER	ASCENDING	ASSIGN	AUTHOR
BLANK	CALL	CLOSE	COBOL
CONSOLE	CURRENT-DATE	COMPUTATIONAL	COMPUTE
CORRESPONDING	CONFIGURATION	CONTROL	DATA
DATE-COMPILED	DATE-WRITTEN	DESCENDING	DISPLAY
DIVIDE	DIVISION	ELSE	ENVIRONMENT
EQUAL	EQUALS	ECEEDS	EXIT
FD	FILE	FILE-CONTROL	FILLER
GIVING	GREATER	INSTALLATION	IDENTIFICATION
INPUT	INPUT-OUTPUT	LINE	LINES
MEMORY	MOVE	MULTIPLY	NEGATIVE

NOT	NUMERIC	OBJECT-COMPUTER	OCCURS
OPEN	PERFORM	FUTURE	PIC
PLUS	PROGRAM-ID	RECORD	RENAMES
REDEFINES	REPORT	SEARCH	SECTION
SORT	SOURCE-COMPUTER	SPACE	SPACES
SPECIAL-NAMES	STOP	SUM	SUBSTRACT
THRU	UNEQUAL	UNTIL	USING
WORKING-STORAGE	WRITE	ZERO	ZEROS

Summary

In this lesson we have stated the rules for coding COBOL variables and we have also said that all COBOL data must be properly declared before they are used in the program. This is a sort of discipline enforced by COBOL. This discipline is conducive for better processing. In the next lesson we will study about the different types of operators used in COBOL.

COBOL OPERATORS AND EXPRESSIONS

What is an Operator?

An operator is a mechanism for manipulating data. There are three types of operators in COBOL. They are:

1. Arithmetic
2. Relational and
3. Logical

Arithmetic Operators

All computations with numeric data are done by arithmetic operators. Just as we have the arithmetic operators in algebra like +, -, x and /, we have different operators in COBOL. The algebraic form and the COBOL form of using the different operations are shown in the table below:

Operations	*Algebraic Form*	*COBOL Symbol*	*COBOL FORM*
Addition	a + b	+	A + B
Subtraction	a - b	-	A - B
Multiplication	a x b	*	A * B
Division	a / b	/	A / B
Exponentiation	a^b	**	A ** B

COBOL being a business programming language, people would prefer descriptive operator forms. COBOL provides mnemonic or descriptive operator forms for addition, subtraction, multiplication and division. They are ADD, SUBTRACT, MULTIPLY and DIVIDE. These forms are used only in statements and so we will consider these forms when we describe statements. Exponentiation operation has no corresponding nemonic or descriptive form.

What is an Expression?

An Expression is a means for computing a value. It may consist of a single variable or a single constant or a number of constants and variables connected by appropriate operators. COBOL-expressions can be Numeric, Alphabetic, Alphanumeric and Logical.

Rules lor Coding Arithmetic Expressions

1. Arithmetic expressions are coined by combining arithmetic variables and constants with arithmetic operators.
2. The arithmetic operators must be preceded and succeeded by at least one blank space. In fact all operators must be preceded and succeeded by at least one blank.
3. No two arithmetic operators shall appear in succession. If they occur, parentheses must be used to separate them. For example, A/-B must be coded as A/(-B).
4. When parentheses are used, the left parentheses must be preceded by at least one blank, but not followed by a blank. A right parentheses must not be preceded by a blank,.but must be followed by one blank.

Sequence or Hierarchy of Operators

When different arithmetical operators are used in an expression, one must know the order in which the various operators are performed. This is known as the hierarchy or priority of operators. The complete hierarchical rules for all the COBOL operators are as follows:

1. All Operations within parentheses.
2. Exponentiation Operator.
3. Multiplication and Division in the order in which they occur from left to right.
4. Addition and Subtraction Operators in the order in which they occur from left to right.
5. All relational operators have the same priority.
6. NOT Operator.
7. AND Operator.
8. OR Operator.

Nested Parentheses

When parentheses are used one inside the other, they are said to be nested. When parentheses are nested, the number of opening parentheses must be equal to the number of closing parentheses, otherwise the computer will give a syntax error. The various operations will be performed from the innermost to the outermost.

Relational Operators

There are six Relational Operators in COBOL. The coded forms and their meanings are shown below:

code		*meaning*
1.	=	equal to
2.	>	greater than
3.	<	less than
4.	NOT =	not equal to
5.	NOT >	not greater than
6.	NOT <	not less than

Logical Expressions

When two arithmetic entities are connected by relational operators, we get a new class of expressions called the logical expressions. When we write an expression, A > B, it has no numeric value. But it has a logical value, in that the expression may be true or false. The values TRUE and FALSE are called logical constant. Suppose A = 3 and B = 2, then the logical expression A > B is TRUE, but the logical expression A < B is FALSE. The following rules must be observed in forming logical expressions in COBOL:

1. The data types on the two sides of the relational operator must be the same. That is, a numeric can be compared only with numeric, alphabetic with alphabetic and alphanumeric with alphanumeric.
2. The two sides of the relational operators cannot be expressions, but only variables or constants.

The following are examples of Logical Expressions:

1. A = B
2. A > B
3. A < B
4. A NOT > C
5. A NOT < C
6. A NOT = C

It may be noted that once two arithmetical entities are connected by relational operators, the combination becomes logical and the combination can further be connected only with logical operators.

Logical Operators

There are three logical operators coded as NOT, AND & OR. Let us now consider the meanings of the logical operations.

Consider the following two logical statements:

1. December is the first month of a year.
2. January is the first month of a year.

We know that the first statement is FALSE and the second one is TRUE. Suppose we combine the two statements by AND and write as

December is the first month of a year AND January is the first month of a year.

This single statement which is obtained by combining one FALSE statement with one TRUE statement by the AND operator is FALSE. Suppose we combine the two statements by the OR operator and write as

December is the first month of a year OR January is the first month of a year.

This single statement which is obtained by combining one FALSE statement and one TRUE statement by the OR operator is TRUE.

We can now generalise and write that a combination of two logical statements connected by the AND operator will be TRUE only if both the individual statements are TRUE and FALSE if any one of them is FALSE or both of them are FALSE.

Again we write that a combination of two logical statements connected by the OR operator will be TRUE when both the individual statements are TRUE or if any one of them is TRUE and FALSE only when both of them are FALSE.

TRUTH Tables

The results of the three logical operations on logical entities can be represented in what are called TRUTH tables.

TRUTH Table for the AND & the OR Operators

Value of the logical entity A	*Value of the logical entity B*	*Value of A AND B*	*Value of AOR B*
TRUE	TRUE	TRUE	TRUE
TRUE	FALSE	FALSE	TRUE
FALSE	TRUE	FALSE	TRUE
FALSE	FALSE	FALSE	FALSE

TRUTH Table for the NOT Operator

Value of the Value entity A	*Value of the logical entity NOT A*
TRUE	FALSE
FALSE	TRUE

We have already given the rules for the priority of the different operators. Suppose we have an expression as follows:

A > B OR C NOT= D AND C = E AND NOT A = F

The priority of the different operations are shown below explicitly by putting parentheses.

A > B OR (C NOT= D AND (C = E AND (NOT A = F)))

Summary

In this lesson we have seen the different operators and the rules for coding COBOL expressions. Please remember that expressions are very important since they are the only means to get values or results to our problems. In the next lesson we will start studying about statements which form the basic building blocks of a COBOL Program.

COMPUTATION STATEMENTS

What are Statements?

Statements constitute the commands or the instructions to the computer coded in a computer language to do specific jobs like computing an expression, assigning values to variables, reading the data, printing the results, giving information to the computer about the program and the data, giving information to the readers etc. Statements which give information to the computer are called declaration statements and the statements which give information to the readers are called the comment statements. A statement in COBOL is the smallest meaningful unit to the computer, just as a sentence is the smallest meaningful unit to the humans in the spoken languages. There are different types of statements for giving instructions to do the different jobs as given below:

1. Compulation or the Assignment Statements
2. Input Statements
3. Output Statements
4. Control Statements
5. Declaration Statements
6. Comment Statements.

In this lesson we will study about the Compulation Statements.

COMPUTATION Statements

The Computation Statement is the most important statement in any computer language, since it is only this statement that gives the solution to our problems. The general form of the Computation Statement is:

```
                                (variable-2)
COMPUTE variable-1      =      (expression)
                                 (literal)
```

Note: In writing general forms in COBOL, the following conventions are adopted. Words in 'all caps' indicate that they are reserved words of the language. Words in small case indicate that they are programmer coined. If there are vertically stacked items inside braces, it means that one of the enclosed item has to be used at a time. The items given in square brackets are optional. The ellipsis (...) or three dots indicate that the preceding items can be repeated as many times as required.

In the above general form, the items on both side of the assignment symbol (=) are numeric. The above statement instructs the computer to compute the expression on the r.h.s. of the assignment symbol and assign the computed value to the variable on the l.h.s. The symbol (=) is called the assignment symbol or replacement symbol and it has a different meaning from the equality symbol used in algebra. If we write A = B in algebra, it means that A and B are equal. In COBOL it means that the value of B is assigned to A or the original value of A is replaced by the current value of B. Suppose we write the computation statement as

COMPUTE A = A + 1

We know that it is illegal to write A = A + 1 in algebra. In COBOL it is legal and it means, that the old value of A is replaced by A + 1. If the old value of A is 25, the new value of A will become 26.

Examples of Valid Computation Statements

1. COMPUTE AREA = Y
2. COMPUTE GROSS-PAY = BASIC-PAY + ALLOWANCES
3. COMPUTE VOLUME = 25

In the first example the r.h.s. is a single numeric variable. In the second example the r.h.s. is a numeric expression. In the third example the r.h.s. is a numeric literal. In all the above three cases the l.h.s. contains only an unsigned numeric variable.

Examples of Invalid Computation Statements

1. COMPUTE A + B = C + D (The l.h.s. cannot contain an expression)
2. COMPUTE -A = A + 34 (The variable on the l.h.s. shall not be signed)
3. COMPUTE 25 = A + B (The l.h.s shall not contain a constant, but only an unsigned variable)

4. X = X + Y (The reserved word COMPUTE is not present in the beginning of the computation statement and hence it is a syntax error)

Descriptive Forms of Computation Statements

In COBOL, there is another form of writing the computation statements using the descriptive forms of the arithmetic operations instead of the symbolic forms. These forms use the descriptive verbs ADD, SUBTRACT, DIVIDE and MULTIPLY. The exponentiation symbol has no corresponding verb.

ADD Statement

There are two forms of ADD Statement. They are:

1. ADD {literal-1}... TO (variable-2)
   [variable-1)
2. ADD (literal-1) {literal-2}... GIVING (variable-3)
   {variable-1} {variable-2}

In the first form, all the operands preceding the word TO are added together and the result is added to the item following the word TO and stored in that field. For example, if we write

ADD A, B, C, TO D

A, B and C are added together first. Then this total is added to D on the r.h.s. of the word TO and stored in the variable D itself. The old value of D is replaced by D+A+B+C. The above form of ADD statement is equivalent to the following COMPUTE statement.

COMPUTE D = D + A + B + C

In the second form, the operands preceding the word GIVING are all added together and the result is stored in the field succeeding the word GIVING.

Suppose one writes

ADD A, B, C GIVING D

A, B and C are added first. This total is stored in D. This is equivalent to the following COMPUTE statement.

COMPUTE D = A + B + C

Note: One must not write, ADDA to 5, since the receiving field or storing field is not a variable. But one can write ADD 5 to A. In this case 5 is added to the value in A and stored in A itself.

SUBTRACT Statement

There are two forms of SUBTRACT statement. They are:

```
1.  SUBTRACT   {literal-I}    ...   FROM    (variable-2)
               (variable-1)
2.  SUBTRACT   {literal-1}    ...   FROM    {literal-2]  GIVING (variable-3)
               {variable-1)                 {variable-2)
```

In the first form, all the operands before the word FROM are added together and the sum is subtracted from the operand succeeding the word FROM and stored in that operand itself. Suppose one writes

SUBTRACT A, B, C FROM D

A, B and C are added first. This sum is subtracted from D and the result is stored in D itself. This is equivalent to the following COMPUTE statement.

COMPUTE D = D - (A + B + C)

In the second form, all the operands before the word FROM are added together and the sum is subtracted from the variable immediately following the word FROM and this result is stored in the variable immediately following the word GIVING. Suppose one writes

SUBTRACT A, B, C FROM D GIVING E

A, B and C are added first. This sum is subtracted from D and the result is stored in E. This is equivalent to the following COMPUTE statement.

COMPUTE E = D - (A + B + C)

MULTIPLY Statement

There are two forms of MULTIPLY statement. They are:

```
1.  MULTIPLY   {literal-1 )    BY   variable-2
               {variable-1)
2.  MULTIPLY   (literal-I}     BY   (literal-2)  GIVING (variable-3)
               {variable-1)         {variable-2}
```

Suppose one writes, MULTIPLY A BY B

Then A is multiplied by B and the product is stored in B. This is equivalent to the following COMPUTE statement. COMPUTE B = A * B

Suppose one writes, MULTIPLY A BY B GIVING C. Then A is multiplied by B and the product is stored in C. This is equivalent to the following COMPUTE statement.

COMPUTE C = A * B

DIVIDE Statement

The DIVIDE statement is written in the following three forms:

1.	DIVIDE	[literal -1] (variable-1)	INTO	(variable-2)
2.	DIVIDE	[literal-1] (variable-I)	INTO	(literal-2) GIVING (variable-3) {variable-2}
3.	DIVIDE	(literal-1) {variable-1}	BY	{literal-2} GIVING (variable-3) {variable-2}

Suppose one writes, DIVIDE A INTO B. Then B is divided by A and the quotient is stored in B. This is equivalent to the following COMPUTE statement.

COMPUTE B = B / A

Suppose one writes, DIVIDE A INTO B GIVING C. Then B is divided by A and the quotient is stored in C. This is equivalent to the following COMPUTE statement.

COMPUTE C = B / A

Suppose one writes, DIVIDE A BY B GIVING C. Then A is divided By B and the quotient is stored in C. This is equivalent to the following COMPUTE statement.

COMPUTE C = A / B

ROUNDED and SIZE ERROR Options

The above two options can be given at the end of any form of computation statements. When the ROUNDED option is given, the least significant digit of the resulting value is rounded off to the nearest integer. When the SIZE ERROR option is given, the control will be transferred to any other para as required, if the final value after executing the ROUNDED option if any, exceeds the size of the receiving field. One can give the above two options as given below:

DIVIDE A BY B GIVING C ROUNDED ON SIZE ERROR GO TO ERR-PARA

A SIZE ERROR will will arise if the number of digit spaces alloted for the results is less than the computed result. For example, let the variable C be allotted 3 digit spaces to the lelt of the decimal point and 2 digit spaces to the right of the decimal point. Suppose the computed value of C is 2534.346. First the ROUNDED option is executed. The result becomes 2534.35. We find that a SIZE ERROR condition arises, since there are only 3 digit spaces to the left. The result will become 534.35. This situation is brought to the attention of the programmer by the SIZE ERROR option. When the SIZE ERROR condition occurs, the computer is asked to display the condition or take any other action appropriate to that condition by means of an imperative statement. It may be noted that the SIZE ERROR option will not cause the printing of the correct result.

The SIZE ERROR and the ROUNDED option can be used with COMPUTE statements as shown below:

COMPUTE C ROUNDED = A /B ON SIZE ERROR GO TO ERR-PARA

Let us now see the results obtained by doing the different forms of descriptive arithmetic operations. Let us assume that the values of A,B,C, D,E and Fare 5,6, 4, 3, 2 and 1 respectively. The following table shows the results after the execution of the different statements on the above data:

Operations	*A*	*B*	*C*	*D*	*E*	*F*
Values before each of the operations	5	6	4	3	2	1
Values after each operation						
ADD A TO B	5	11	4	3	2	1
ADD A, B TO C	5	6	15	3	2	1
ADD A, B, C GIVING D	5	6	4	15	2	1
SUBTRACT A FROM B	5	1	4	3	2	1
SUBTRACT A, B, C FROM D	5	6	4	-12	2	1
SUBTRACT A, B, C, D FROM F GIVING E	5	6	4	3	2	-16
MULTIPLY A BY B	5	30	4	3	2	1
MULTIPLY A BY B GIVING C	5	6	30	3	2	1
DIVIDE A INTO B	5	1.2	4	3	2	1
DIVIDE A INTO B GIVING C	5	6	1.2	3	2	1
DIVIDE A BY B GIVING C	5	6	.8333	3	2	1
DIVIDE 3 INTO B	5	2	4	3	2	1
ADD 5 TO B	5	11	4	3	2	1
MULTIPLY 4 BY C	5	6	16	3	2	1

Summary

In this lesson we have learnt about the most important statement, namely, the computation statement, which instructs the computer to compute the expression in a formula and store the result. In the next lesson we will see how we can input and output unstructured data in COBOL.

19

Development of Computer Programming Languages

LEARNING OBJCTIVES

After completing this chapter, you will be able to:

- Comprehend development of computer languages from the machine level to assembly level to high-level languages as well as their distinctive features.
- Understand the basic structure and features of high-level languages like COBOL and BASIC.
- Distinguish between Compilers, Assemblers and Interpreters.

OVERVIEW

Whatever be their make, CPU size or instruction format, all computers have two features in common: they perform specified activity by means of programs of instructions held within their memory and, the instructions, as held, are in the binary formats.

How then, do normal users, not oriented to binary formats, manage to convey their commands to the computers which can perform only at the binary level ?

The answer is: by means of artificially developed computer languages. A user writes instruction in accordance with the rules of these languages and enters them into the computer. Internally, the computer converts these instructions into signals which it can understand and then carries them out.

Over the years, the computer languages have passed through four generations of development (not to be confused with four generations of computers). Research is also progressing on the development of the fifth generation computer languages, to be styled as *natural languages.* The objective is that a user will simply type into a computer in a natural, language like Hindi, English or Russian, as to what he wants done, and the computer will carry out the required processing. The project is a part of developments under Artificial

Intelligence (A.I.). The respective characteristics of the first four generations of computer languages are as follows:

Machine Languages : The First Generation

The set of instructions (or programs) for the first computers were, in fact, written in the actual binary codes termed as machine (or absolute) codes. This coding process was extremely detailed, laborious and difficult to understand, more so because the instructions expressed in various strings of 0's and 1's were hard to distinguish one from the other or from data.

This would be better understood if we go over the situation faced by the early computers.

Supposing, there was a simple problem like :

$$A+B = C$$

Here, the instruction consisted of an *OPERATOR,* which specified the command to be carried out by the computer, viz. ADD, and of *OPERANDS* which identified the data (or *variables)* to be used, namely *A* and *B*.

To solve the problem, the Operator and the Operands had first to be loaded into the memory of the computer, which in those days was accomplished by means of punched cards.

It will be recalled that each memory location in a computer has to have a unique address. So, the Operator and the Operands had to be loaded in especially earmarked portions of the memory to avoid mix-ups. It will also be recalled that the contents of a memory location (composed of a number of bits) and the address of the memory location are two different entities; thus the memory location, say, 0391 need not contain the number 0391.

Now, the instruction in the case of this particular example is ADD. Each computer manufacturer had a unique code for carrying out a particular operation. To illustrate, one manufacturer employed the following codes.

Instruction	*Code (expressed in binary)*	*Equivalent in the Decimal System*
Add	00001	1
Subtract	00010	2
Multiply	00011	3
Divide	00100	4
	and so on.	

Supposing the contents of *A* had been loaded in location No. 5822, of *B* in location No. 5806 and the results of the addition (viz. *C*) were to be loaded in location 5814; the problem got expressed as follows in terms of binary

00001	101	101	011	1110	101	101	010	1110
(meaning) ADD		contents of location 5822 which is A (to)				contents of location 5806. which is B		
				101	101	011	0110	
				(to give) C to be located in location 5814				

The tediousness of instructing computers in this manner is obvious enough. The various numeric operation codes had no obvious relationship to their functions. Addresses of store locations used by the programmer had to be carefully noted and their numeric values used when the area was referred to. Again, the programmer had to keep a careful note of the numeric addresses of each program instruction so that the *branches* and *loops* (repetitive execution of instruction) could address the correct branch points. If the programmer was to make any alterations in this program, which altered the numeric address of any location (say, when inserting a new instruction between the existing instructions), all other references to the locations needed to be checked up and changed. This complexity and need for constant checking meant that a machine code program, particularly a long or complicated one, was difficult to write and was prone to many errors.

Assembly Languages: the Second Generation

The need for easing the process of program preparation led to the development of several **symbolic** programming languages commonly referred to as assembly languages.

The approaches to the development of these languages had two common features; one was **mnemonic coding** and the other **symbolic addressing.**

The machine languages had depended on number symbols for representing an operation code. For example, as mentioned earlier, in one machine language the symbol 1 stood for the operation ADD, 2 for SUBTRACT, and so on. The assembly language replaced them by easy-to-remember mnemonic symbols. The following samples (from a list of about 200 such codes in one of the assembly languages) illustrates.

Operation name	*Corresponding mnemonic symbol*
Input/Output	
Start I/O	S/O
Halt I/O	H/O
Arithmetic	
Add	A
Subtract	S
Multiply	M

Logic/Comparison	
Compare	C
Branch on condition	BC
Storage/RetrievallMovement	
Load	L
Load Register	LR
Store	ST
Move characters	MVC

Two repetitive, but essential tasks, in the programming process were assigning addresses in the processor memory to the data items to be processed and keeping track of addresses of the stored instructions. The approaches developed by the assembly languages in this regard were as follows. Instead of expressing an address in terms of its actual (or, absolute) location in the processor memory, data items were assigned symbols (or labels) as, for example OLDBAL for opening balance and NEWBAL for closing balance, say, in an inventory control application. When writing instructions (programs), the programmer referred to the data items by these symbols, rather than by a numbered address location in the memory. The task of assigning storage addresses was passed over to the computer (to be carried out with the help of assembly language software). This practice came to be referred to as *symbolic addressing*.

As regards assigning addresses to instructions and keeping a track thereof, the programmer now merely specified where the first instruction in the program was to be located in the processor memory. From that point onwards the computer (and the assembly language software) automatically stored all other instructions in the memory locations in a sequential order. Also, if at some stage, it was found necessary to insert another instruction in the program all the required adjustments were carried out by the computer itself, (unlike in the case of machine languages where such a burden fell on the programmer).

To illustrate programs.written in an assembly language, let us lake a simple inventory management problem like subtracting issues from the opening balance to arrive at the closing balance. It is assumed that the opening balance has been labelled as *OLDBAL*, issues have been labelled as ISSUES and closing balance as *NEWBAL*.

The associated program in one of the assembly language took the following format:

Instructions in Assembly language	**Explanatory Remarks**
L2, OLDBAL	This instruction loads the contents of the location labelled as OLDBAL into the accumulator (Register 2).

S2, ISSUES	This instruction subtracts issues from the contents of Register 2, giving the closing balance.
ST2, NEWBAL	This instruction stores the contents of Register 2 in the location labelled as NEWBAL, replacing whatever quantity was stored at that location.

The computations are complete.

Since a computer can understand only 1 and 0 signals, the computer vendors devised assembly language software (termed as *assemblers)* for the purpose of converting programs written in the assembly language (the source program) into machine-executable 1 and 0 signals (the object program). The actual conversion tasks were carried out by the computer itself.

It may be mentioned that with more experience the assembly languages also acquired quite a few refinements and sophistications. It was soon realised that many routines like initialisation, opening and closing files, reading records and creating files were in constant and repetitive use within programs and were common to most applications. In respect of such programming steps it was evidently possible to write short program segments to be included in any program which called for performing of these operations.

The procedure is as follows. An instruction, say, 'read a tape' is added to the symbolic system. When such an instruction is added, the Assembly system automatically inserts (assembles) the requisite detailed series of machine instructions in the machine language program. This instruction termed as *macro instruction,* or simply as *macro* is actually a *pseudo instruction* that is not translated into a machine instruction. Instead the macro instruction causes automatic insertion of machine language instruction. In other words, many machine language instructions — say, 20 or more — get assembled for macro. (Macro may be defined as involving large quantities). All the linkages are taken care of by the assembly program and the appropriate coding included in the machine language program.

In appraising the assembly languages it will be pertinent to mention that, while they did help in making a more effective use of the storage and other facilities of the computer, the programmer continued to remain saddled with the task of telling the computer quite explicitly as to what was to be done at each step with, typically, a separate instruction for each step to be performed. In other words, the programs written in these languages were, more or less, similar in concept to the machine code version, in as much as each instruction had a corresponding machine code equivalent (referred to as one-for-one correspondence).

The major vendors of assembly languages were:

Vendor		Assembly Language offered
IBM	:	AUTOCODER (used on IBM 1401 Systems)
ICL	:	PLAN (used on ICL 1900 Systems)
HONEYWELL	:	EASYCODE
CONTROL DATA	:	COMPASS
NCR	:	NEAT

Procedure-Oriented Language: The Third Generation

Largely developed/perfected during the 1960s, computer languages such as COBOL, BASIC, FORTRAN, C, and others are termed as procedural languages because of their orientation towards expressing the procedure or logic of solving general problems (as distinct from solving specific problems, accomplished by the Fourth Generation languages).

The Third Generation Languages are also referred to as *high level* language because a single, simple instruction written in these languages can specify a whole sequence of computer operations.

In contrast, the low-level assembly languages require the programmer to tell the computer explicitly what is to be done, with a separate instruction for each step, to be carried out.

A notable feature is that a program written in a high-level language can, generally, be understood by someone who is not conversant with the particular computer language. In the case of a commercial language like COBOL, the program resembles a highly artificial, but still recognisable, English. In the case of a scientific language like FORTRAN the resemblance is to mathematical notations.

To an extent, programs written in some of the high level languages are **portable,** that is, they can run on more than one kind of computer. However, there are also a few conflicting factors. To cite: a large number of, what could be called the *dialects* of the high level computer languages, have also emerged. This is because when a compiler is being written for a particular computer model, certain features of the language have to be modified or omitted having regard to the difficulty of translating them into the specific machine code. Thus while, in theory, a particular high-level language may be supported by several computer makes/models, in practice,differences may exist in makes/models in the matter of supporting certain sub-sets of the language.

Major languages in this category are:

COBOL. (**C**ommon **B**usiness-**O**riented **L**anguage). This language, widely used in business-type applications was developed in 1960 by an organisation called CODASYL (acronym for **C**onference on **D**ata **S**ystems **L**anguage), and has undergone quite a few significant revision since them.

This language calls for indepth training and extensive practice for attaining proficiency in it.

The Appendix to this chapter describes the general structure of this language supported by a practical exercise in COBOL programming.

BASIC (**B**eginner's **A**ll-purpose **S**ymbolic **I**nstruction **C**ode).

This language was developed in the USA by the Dartmouth College in 1963 and is very popular with Personal Computers. Contrary to the suggestion embedded in its name this language can be put to a good use by the beginners as well as by the expert programmers. It can also be used interactively, meaning that during the writing and running of the programs, the user and the computer can communicate with each other. It is suitable for use in time-sharing environments.

A description of the structure of this language, supported by an exercise in programming in BASIC, have been included in the Appendix to this chapter.

FORTRAN (**FOR**mula **TRAN**slation). This language has a scientific and mathematical orientation and is suitable for processing complex mathematical formulas and for solving engineering and scientific type problems.

C. Developed by Bell Telephone Laboratories, it is a general-purpose language which, of late, is becoming popular with Personal Computers. Its uses include writing of operating systems, compilers, database programs and certain types of scientific programs. The programs written in this language are highly portable and can run without any change on a number of makes/models of computers.

PASCAL It is a structured general purpose language, well suited for teaching programming techniques.

LISP A list processing language strictly meant for processing data presented in the form of a list.

GPSS **G**eneral **P**urpose **S**imulation **S**ystem).

This language is meant for modelling (simulating) other systems.

RPG (**R**eport **P**rogram **G**enerator). Introduced by IBM, this language is now available in version III. While using this language the user is required only to fill out certain special forms, which define the inputs, outputs and the records required to produce business-type reports, say, reports on accounts payable and accounts receivable. The user is not concerned with solution procedures; the RPG does the rest. For this reason some theorists prefer to categorise it as a *non-procedural language*. The use of RPG and other languages in this genre is somewhat limited.

As in the case of programs written in the assembly languages, programs written in the high-level languages (source programs), too, need to be translated into machine-executable format (object program). This task is accomplished by vendor-supplied language software termed as *compiler*. Like assemblers, compilers too are specific to each computer language supported by a particular make/model of computer.

There is yet another type of language software, termed as *interpreter*, which is used for translating programs written in a high-level language.

For understanding the functions and characteristics of an interpreter, it is first necessary to go over the nature of certain tasks carried out by the compiler software. These include:

- carrying out a **lexical scan** to eliminate redundancies in the source text;
- analysing the source statements to identify **syntax errors** (that is, errors arising from violation of the rules of the particular high-level language);
- performing an arithmetic scan to convert any arithmetic expression to a form suitable for computation;
- causing error messages to be printed or displayed, as required;
- listing the source code and the equivalent object code.

The programmer must correct all the errors thrown up by the compilation process and re-enter the corrected statements into the computer for re-compilation, until the computer has no errors to report.

The beginning programmers often get disheartened when carrying out the tasks involved in the analysis and correction of errors. An easier alternative to a compiler is the interpreter. Unlike compilers, which are supplied by the vendors only in the form of software stored on the operating system disk, the interpreter is usually hardwired into the computer circuitry, although some vendors also supply it in software form. The beginning programmer just loads the program written by him in the high-level language along with the data to be processed, onto the computer. If there is no error, the interpreter converts each instruction comprised in the program, individually, into the machine language and executes it immediately, before proceeding to the next program instruction. The translated instructions are not 'saved' and kept in the secondary storage, as is the case when a compiler is used.

The main advantage of an interpreter is that it eliminates the need for tedious compilation runs for correcting errors which often creep into the programs written by the beginners or when programs have to be modified to incorporate a few new features. The disadvantage is that in the execution of repetitive instructions (loops), say, in the preparation of a payroll of a large number of persons, the interpreter must re-translate each instruction into the machine language, every time it is encountered in the program. (This is not necessary in the case compilers as the instructions, after translation, remain, and can be used repetitively).

Obviously enough, the process of executing instructions by means of the interpreter is much, much slower compared to calling and using the stored object code.

However, in respect of languages like BASIC and PASCAL, which have an orientation towards teaching programming techniques, the vendors often supply both the compiler and the interpreter. The former is for use in production runs and the latter for teaching programming techniques.

In addition to assemblers, compilers and interpreters, it is also usual to classify two other categories of programs as sub-categories of language software. These are :

Librarian. This program enables a track being kept of the programs stored in the secondary storage devices.

Linkage Editor. This is a program that coordinates the output of language translators, for execution. It combines separately produced modules, resolves cross references among them, replaces, deletes and adds control sections and produces an executable load module, besides determining the amount of storage spare requirements.

Problem- oriented Languages: the Fourth Generation

Popularly referred to as 4GLs, the characteristics of these languages yet remain to be defined in clear-cut terms mainly because of differences in perception among their vendors. It is possible, however, to identify some of their common features.

They are not general-purpose languages like, COBOL or BASIC but have been designed to solve certain specific kinds of problems, particularly in the PC environments.

Besides being full-featured languages they also contain a complete set of *operators* (or commands), which can be easily learnt even by the beginners. They require the users merely to specify what the output should be without having to write the steps required for this purpose. Some of the well-known products in the 4GL category are:

Lotus 1-2-3. This package consists of three modules integrating spreadsheets, graphics and databases. The spreadsheets provide answers to WHAT-IF types of questions in the decision-making processes of managements.

dBase III PluS. This software package provides an integrated system for sorting, manipulating and retrieving data. It provides a complete set of database operators and may be used both interactively and in programs.

Interactive Financial Planning System. Drawing upon the existing MIS of the organisation, this package carries out the functions associated with Decision Support Systems (DSS) by providing answers to unstructured and unanticipated questions, needed by the top management in matters relating to financial planning.

Besides the afore-mentioned typical software packages, the 4GLs genre also includes the following.

Query Languages With simple commands some of these languages enable the end-users, who need not be programmers, to directly search the database of the organisation.

There are also languages which can be used only by data processing personnel for answering queries of the end-users. These languages have more detailed commands, can handle high volumes of data and are usually offered by the vendors of the complex DBMS packages already in use in the organisation.

Application GeneratorS. These packages comprise a number of preprogrammed modules to carry out some specific tasks, say, the calculation of MODVAT. The programmer merely has to specify his needs in a particular application. The *application generator,* thereafter, selects and runs the required module to meet the user requirements.

It will, however, be well to remember that 4GLs do not constitute a major replacement for the general-purpose, high-level languages of the Third Generation. The reason is that the 4GLs still continue to be non-standard and their control over output results leaves much to be desired. Also, they are weak as regards effective utilisation of available hardware resources. Bulk of programming, therefore, continues to be carried out in the Third Generation languages.

Since the 4GLs have strong PC-orientation, a more detailed discussion of the features of popular software packages in this category,' "Personal Computers and Computing."

APPENDIX A

OUTLINE OF COBOL AND BASIC LANGUAGES

While the respective fundamental of programming in COBOL and BASIC are vast subjects, requiring independent study and practice, it will, nonetheless, be useful to acquire some familiarity with the broad features of these languages.

It may be mentioned that all these languages are covered by the American National Standards Institute (ANSI) standards.

COBOL. The first version of this language, which appeared in 1960, has undergone quite a few revisions since then. The version in use at present was standardised in 1974.

The COBOL character set is composed of the 26 letters of the alphabet, the numerals 0 to 9 and 123 special characters. This language consists of :

- *names* to identify things
- *constants* (i.e. data which remains unchanged for each run), and literals (i.e. material which is to remain unchanged during compilation and will appear in the output in the same form as input by the programmer)
- *operators* that specify some action or relationship
- *key words* essential to the meaning of statements
- *expressions* consisting of names, constants, operators or key words

- *statements* containing a verb and an item to be acted on
- *sentences* composed of one or more statements properly punctuated.

A COBOL program is arranged in a standard coding format (Fig. 1) that facilitates writing and interpretation. The format has 80 columns (like an 80 column Hollerith Card). Each COBOL instruction is assigned a number, usually, 10, 20, 30 and so on. The instructions are so numbered because insertions can be readily made in the gaps. Certain rules need to be observed for writing the source statements in this format. Also, names may contain upto 30 characters and must not contain blanks. For this reason names very frequently contain one or more hyphens as this allows for the use of descriptive names without violation of rules, e.g. QTY-ON-HAND.

Another special requirement is that COBOL reserved words should not be used. These are the words which have a special significance for the compiler for generating appropriate machine instructions for the particular operation required. Examples are : SELECT, ASSIGN, FILE, ADD, REPORT. There are well over 200 COBOL reserved words.

COBOL programs are divided into four Divisions. The Divisions, in turn, consist of sections, paragraphs and entries.

The functions of these Divisions are outlined below with illustrations. (See program flowchart (Fig. 2) for a better understanding of the ensuing discussion).

The **Identification Division** is used to attach a unique identification such as program name, program number, program version, etc. to the program. Indeed, PROGRAM-ID entry is a must for every COBOL program.

Illustrative Entries

```
01000   IDENTIFICATION DIVISION
01010   PROGRAM-ID. STOK
01020   AUTHOR. R S VENKATESWARAN
01030*      REMARKS
01040*      SAMPLE COBOL PROGRAM
01050*      READS CARDS AND ADDS STOCK RECEIPTS TO QTY ON HAND
            BALANCE
01060*      SUBTRACTS STOCK ISSUES AND DEVELOPS A NEW ON HAND
            BALANCE.
```

The **Environment Division** has two sections :

COBOL CODING FORM

Program Name ....

Author ....

Page .... of ....

Seq. 1–6	I 7	Area A 8–11	Area B 12 … 20 … 30 … 40 … 50 … 60 … 70 72	Ident. 73–80

Fig. 1. A COBOL Coding Form

Seq.	I	Area A	Area B							Ident.
1 6	7	8 11	12	20	30	40	50	60	70 72	73 80

Fig. 1. A COBOL Coding Form

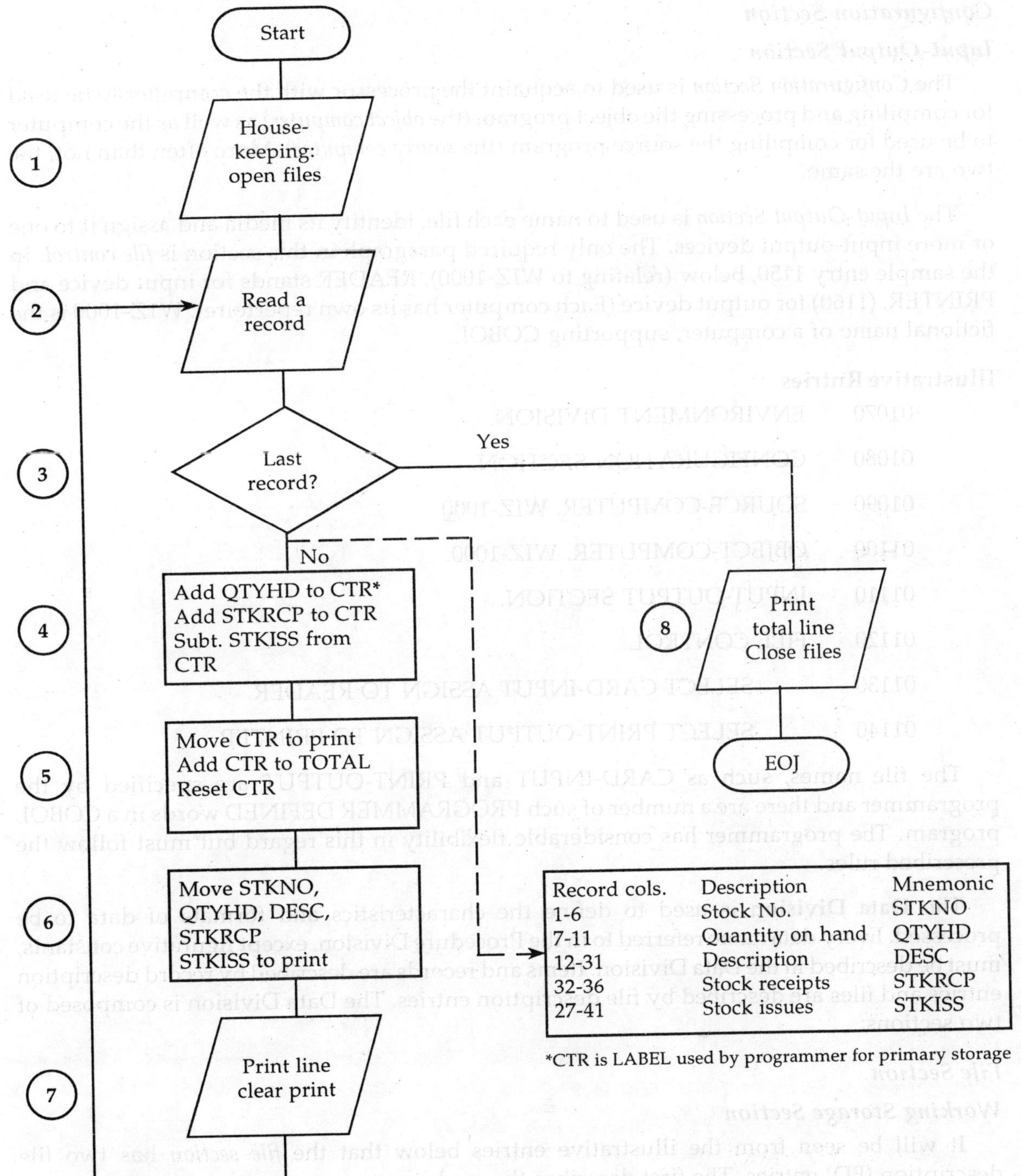

Record cols.	Description	Mnemonic
1-6	Stock No.	STKNO
7-11	Quantity on hand	QTYHD
12-31	Description	DESC
32-36	Stock receipts	STKRCP
27-41	Stock issues	STKISS

*CTR is LABEL used by programmer for primary storage

Fig. 2. Program Flowchart: Inventory Control Update

Configuration Section

Input-Output Section

The *Configuration Section* is used to acquaint the processor with the computer to be used for compiling and processing the object program (the *object computer)* as well as the computer to be used for compiling the source program (the *source computer)*. More often than not, the two are the same.

The *Input-Output Section* is used to name each file, identify its media and assign it to one or more input-output devices. The only required paragraph in this section is *file control.* In the sample entry 1150, below (relating to WIZ-1000), READER stands for input device and PRINTER, (1160) for output device (Each computer has its own repertoire). W1Z-1000 is the fictional name of a computer, supporting COBOL.

Illustrative Rntries

```
01070    ENVIRONMENT DIVISION.
01080    CONFIGURATION SECTION.
01090    SOURCE-COMPUTER. WIZ-1000.
01100    OBJECT-COMPUTER. WIZ-1000.
01110    INPUT-OUTPUT SECTION.
01120    FILE CONTROL.
01130        SELECT CARD-INPUT ASSIGN TO READER.
01140        SELECT PRINT-OUTPUT ASSIGN TO PRINTER.
```

The file names, such as CARD-INPUT and PRINT-OUTPUT are specified by the programmer and there are a number of such PROGRAMMER DEFINED words in a COBOL program. The programmer has considerable flexibility in this regard but must follow the prescribed rules.

The **Data Division** is used to define the characteristics and formats of data to be processed. Every data name referred to in the Procedure Division, except figurative constants, must be described in the Data Division. Items and records are described by record description entries and files are described by file description entries. The Data Division is composed of two sections:

File Section

Working Storage Section

It will be seen from the illustrative entries below that the *file section* has two file description (FD) entries. The first describes the card-input.

```
01150       DATA DIVISION.
01160       FILE SECTION.
01170       FD RECORD-INPUT.
```

The card-input file contains records identified as RECORD-IN. (See entries 1180 -1240 below). The record is sub-divided into its various fields such as STOCK-NUMBER and is described by a picture clause. The term *picture* is used to identify a coded description of data-item (field). For example, the picture clause X(6) describes STOCK-NUMBER as a six-position field containing alphanumeric data (PIC XXXXXX means the same thing). The picture (PIC) clause 9(5) identifies QTY-ON-HAND as a five-position field containing numeric data. Had the picture clause been A(5) it would have indicated that data consisted of a five digit alphabetic field.

The remainder of the RECORD-IN statements can be easily translated.

Illustrative entries

```
01180       01      RECORD-IN
01190               05 STOCK-NUMBER          PIC X(6).
01200               05 QTY-ON-HAND           PIC 9(5).
01210               05 DESCRIPTION           PIC X(20).
01220               05 STOCK-RECEIPTS        PIC 9(5).
01230               05 STOCK-ISSUES          PIC 9(5).
01240               05 FILLER                PIC X(39).
```

(FILLER is used to designate unused position of the record).

The following statements describe the printer file known as PRINT-OUTPUT, and its associated record identified by PRINT-LINE.

```
01250       FD      PRINT-OUTPUT
01260       01      PRINT-LINE PIC X(132)
```

Having given complete description of storage fields in the FILE SECTION of the DATA DIVISION, the next step is to provide for fields to store partial processing results for further computation, Leader data and the like. This is done in the WORKING-STORAGE SECTION. The following entries illustrate:

```
01270   WORK1NG-STORAGE SECTION.
01280   01    DETAIL-LINE.
01290         05 FILLE                    PIC X(34).
01300         05 PRT-STOCK-NUMBER         PIC X(06).
01310         05  FILLER                  PIC X(03).
01320         05 PRT-DESCRIPTION          PIC X(20)
```

```
          05 PRT-OPEN-BALANCE       PIC Z(05) 9.
          05 PRT-STOCK-RECEIPTS     PIC Z(10) 9.
          05  PRT-STOCK-ISSUES      PIC Z(09) 9.
          05 PRT-CLOS-BALANCE       PIC Z(08) 9.
          05  FILLER                PIC X(33).
      01  HEADER 1.
          02 FILLER                 PIC X(54) VALUE SPACES.
          02 FILLER                 PIC X(25) VALUE
          "***+ STOCK UPDATE REPORT ***"
          02 FILLER                 PIC X(53) VALUE SPACES.
      01  HEADER 2.
          02 FILLER                 PIC X(33) VALUE SPACES.
          02 FILLER'                PIC X(08) VALUE "STOCK NO"
          02 FILLER                 PIC X(06) VALUE SPACES.
          02 FILLER                 PIC X(ll) VALUE "DESCRIPTION".
          02 FILLER                 PIC X(05) VALUE SPACES.
          02 FILLER                 PIC X(07) VALUE "OPG BAL".
          02 FILLER                 PIC X(03) VALUE SPACES.
          02 FILLER                 PIC X(08) VALUE "RECEIPTS".
          02 FILLER                 PIC X(03) VALUE SPACES.
          02 FILLER                 PIC X(06) VALUE "ISSUES"
          02 FILLER                 PIC X(03) VALUE SPACES.
          02 FILLER                 PIC X(07) VALUE "CLC BAL".
          02 FILLER                 PIC X(32) VALUE SPACES.
```

The following two fields designated respectively as WORKING-COUNTER and TOTAL-COUNTER are also provided either at the beginning or at the end of the WORKING-STORAGE SECTION. They are identified and described as numeric fields and originally contain zeros.

```
      77   WORKING-COUNTER        PIC 9(6)    VALUES ZEROS
      77   TOTAL-COUNTER          PIC 9(7)    VALUE ZEROS.
```

A feature of COBOL is the ability to edit data on output to improve readability of listings. This is accomplished by means of COBOL editing symbols. One such symbol is letter Z indicating zero suppression. Thus the picture ZZ9 indicates that the leading zeros are to be suppressed for a quantity.

The **Procedure Division** is used to describe the internal processing that is to take place. All input -output operations, logical decisions, data movement, and computing operations must be defined in the Procedure Division.

Just as verbs in the English language designate action, so it is with COBOL verbs. Entries in the other divisions of COBOL source program describe/define things; the verbs specify the action, or procedures, to be carried out. Accordingly, the COBOL verbs form the basis of the Procedure Division.

The smallest unit of expression in this Division is the statement. Sentences, paragraphs and sections are the larger units of expression. A statement consists of a COBOL verb or the word IF or ON, followed by any appropriate operands (data-names, file-names, or literals) and other COBOL words that are necessary for the completion of the statement. There are four types of statements.

Statement	**Function**
Compiler directing	Directs the compiler to take certain actions at compilation time.
Imperative	Specifies unconditional actions to be taken by the object program.
Conditional	Contains a condition that is tested to determine which alternate path in the program flow is to be taken.
Note (Comment)	Makes it easier for the programmer to understand and follow the program. These statements are not included in the object program.

A sentence is a single statement or series of statements terminated by a period and followed by a space. Paragraphs consist of one or more sentences. A section is composed of one or more successive paragraphs and must begin with a section header.

Illustrative Entries

```
01580     PROCEDURE DIVISION.
01590     START-PROG.
01600          OPEN INPUT CARD-INPUT OUTPUT PRINT-OUTPUT.
01610          MOVE SPACES TO PRINT-LINE DETAIL-LINE.
01620          WRITE PRINT-LINE FROM HEADER 1 AFTER 2 LINES.
01630          MOVE ALL "*" TO PRINT-LINE WRITE PRINT-LINE AFTER 2 LINES.
01640          WRITE PRINT-LINE FROM HEADER AFTER 2 LINES.
01650          MOVE ALL "*" PRINT-LINE WRITE PRINT-LINE AFTER 12 LINES.
01660          MOVE SPACES TO PRINT-LINE.
```

Here there are no section headings and the first paragraph heading reads START-PROG. In this paragraph the input and output files are opened, and the PRINT-LINE is cleared of any data that may be there at the time the program is loaded.

The next paragraph, headed Read-A-Card is as follows:

```
01670    READ-A-CARD.
01680    READ CARD-INPUT AT END GO TO LAST-CARD.
```

The statement specifies: read-a-card, and when the last card has been read, to go (branch) to the LAST-CARD Paragraph.

The next three illustrative statements are :

```
01690    ADD QTY-ON-HAND TO WORKING-COUNTER.
01700    ADD STOCK-RECEIPTS TO WORKING-COUNTER
01710    SUBTRACT STOCK-ISSUES FROM WORKING-COUNTER
```

The instruct: Add quantity on hand to the storage area named WORKING-COUNTER, add stock receipts to WORKING-COUNTER and subtract stock issued from WORKING-COUNTER.

The next three statements are:

```
01720    MOVE WORKING-COUNTER TO PRT-CLG-BALANCE
01730    ADD WORKING-COUNTER TO TOTAL-COUNTER.
01740    MOVE ZEROS TO WORKING-COUNTER.
```

They instruct : Move the sum stored at WORKING-COUNTER to a storage field known as PRT-NEW-BALANCE and add the sum stored at WORKING-COUNTER to the storage field known as STORAGE-COUNTER. The last line says to clear the field storage field known as WORKING-COUNTER by moving zeros into that field.

The next two statements are:

```
01750    MOVE STOCK-NUMBER TO PRT-STOCK-NUMBER.
01760    MOVE STOCK-ISSUES TO PRT-STOCK-ISSUES.
01770    MOVE STOCK-RECEIPTS TO PRT-STOCK-RECEIPTS.
01780    MOVE QTY-ON-HAND TO PRT-OPEN-BALANCE.
01790    MOVE DESCRIPTION TO PRT-DESCRIPTION.
```

They cause indicative fields in the RECORD-IN file section to be moved to the PRINT-OUTPUT PRINT-LINE. It would be seen that the statement names shown here can be related to the names in the file section of the Data division.

The next three statements are:

```
01800    WRITE PRINT-LINE FROM DETAIL-LINE AFTER 2 LINES.
01810    MOVE SPACES TO PRINT-LINE DETAIL-LINE.
01820    GO TO READ-A-CARD.
```

They cause the paper to be spaced, a line to be printed, the print line to be cleared and the program to branch to the paragraph headed READ-A-CARD.

```
01830    LAST-CARD.
01840    CLOSE CARD-INPUT PRINT-OUTPUT.
01850    STOP RUN.
```

The LAST-CARD paragraph here is activated by a branch.operation that occurs after the last card has been read. This LAST-CARD paragraph says to move the literal TOTAL to the print line, move the data at TOTAL-COUNTER to the print line, space the paper, write the PRINT-LINE, close the CARD-INPUT and PRINT-OUTPUT files, and stop the job by returning control to the computer operating system.

In addition to the foregoing listings (given step-by-step for clearer under standing), the COBOL compiler may also produce a Data Division map showing each data-name and the storage address it represents, and the Procedure Division map showing machine language instructions and their storage addresses. These instructions are also referenced to their source statement in line number. In most cases several machine level instructions are generated for each source statement.

The foregoing COBOL program, when compiled and executed with data, will produce a 'Stock Update Report' in the following format:

***** Stock Update Report *****

Stock No.	*Description*	*OPG Bal*	*Receipts*	*Issues*	*CLG Bal*
11603	6MM Bars	100	50	25	125
12603	8MM Bars	88	20	53	55
13603	9MM Bars	226	114	362	8
14603	6MM Sheared Rods	50	10	50	10

Fig. 3. Stock Update Report

BASIC A program in BASIC consists of a group of statements, each of which is limited to one line and is numbered. Statements can be entered into the computer in any sequence, but the BASIC computer will place them in ascending order before executing the program.

The primary elements of a BASIC statement are *identifiers* and *operators.*

Identifiers represent values that may either be *constant* or *variable.* A *string of* characters, i.e. a sequence of letters of the alphabet, numbers or special characters, whose value cannot be changed throughout program execution are called *constants* and may be referenced through the use of a valid symbol. Values that vary during program execution are called *variables,* and must be represented by valid symbols. The program may refer to variable data only through the use of symbols, as the actual primary locations for each value (data item) are assigned by the BASIC compiler.

Operators specify mathematical operations to be performed or relational comparisons to be made. The symbols used are as follows:

Arithmetic Operator	**Relational Operator**
+ Addition - Subtraction /Division * Multiplication ** Exponentiation (and other symbols like =, <, ≥ etc.).	As in conventional mathematics

The portion of a statement to the right side of an equal sign specifies the value to be assigned to the variable on the left of the equal sign and is called an *expression.*

Some of the common BASIC statements are explained below :

Statement	**Function**
REM	It is a non-executable statement which enables the placement of *comment* in a program list to facilitate understanding. *Example* 10 REM THIS PROGRAM COMPUTES UNIT PRICE
READ	Specifies variables whose values are supplied by DATA statement *Example* 20 READ A, B1,C$, D *Note* In BASIC, where a variable name needs to be repeated, the same can be in the form of a **string.** This is achieved by ending the variable name with the sign $ as in C$.
DATA	Supplies values for variable in the READ statement. *Example* 30 Data 245, 99.99, "ABC 124", 50
INPUT	READ and DATA statements provide for entering data at the time when program is entered into the computer. When data is to be entered at the time of program execution, the values of the variables are entered by means of INPUT statements. *Example* 20 INPUT A, B, C, D
FILES	Another method of introducing data into the computer, at the time of execution, in respect of files that have been previously established and stored in the computer memory.

Example

10 FILES INPUT

DIM Specifies the maximum storing size (dimension) and causes storage spaces to be reserved for the storing variable.

LET Causes the value of expression to be assigned to one or more variables. The expression is evaluated at the correct values of the variables that appear in the expression.

Example

40 LET X = A + 6

GOTO Causes control to be unconditionally transferred to a specific statement.

Example

50 GOTO 10

IF-THEN Tests a relational expression ; if the relation is true, transfers control to the specified statement, if false, the next sequential statement is executed. IF is the statement used to conditionally alter the sequence of program execution.

Example

60 IF X = 1000 THEN 200

GOSUB/RETURN A sub-routine is referenced by means to a GOSUB statement. The execution of this statement causes transfer of control to subroutine. Control will then be transferred back to the statement following GOSUB when a RETURN statement is encountered within the subroutine. The RETURN statement causes control to be transferred back to the statement following the point of reference.

Example

```
120 GOSUB 300
130? "Z= ";Z
300 LET X = A + B
. . . . . . . . . . . . .
380 RETURN
```

When statement 120 (GOSUB) is encountered during the program execution, control is transferred to statement 300 and the sub-routine is executed. Upon reaching number 380 (RETURN), control is transferred back to statement 130, which is the first statement after GOSUB.

FOR Indicates a program *loop* upto and including a matching NEXT statement. FOR and NEXT statements must be paired.

Example

70 FOR N = A to B STEP 2

Here FOR N identifies the start of the loop and A is the variable that will be incremented by 2 until the loop has been executed enough times for the variables A to exceed the B variables. If STEP is omitted an increment of 1 will take place.

NEXT — Identifies the last statement of a FOR/NEXT loop. The NEXT variable must be the same as the simple arithmetic variable specified in the associated FOR statement.

Example

90 NEXT N

PRINT — Causes the values of the specified arithmetic and character expressions to be evaluated. Each expression or statement in the PRINT statement is separated from the following expression or constant by either a comma or a semicolon. PRINT contents must be enclosed in quotation marks and will be printed exactly as shown in the PRINT statement. A PRINT statement without any expressions or constants will cause a blank line on the report.

IMAGE — The IMAGE statement is used to specify a format to be used in PRINT USING statement. This statement consists of symbols that represent types of data written in the order and quantity in which the data is to be printed.

Example

100 USING DD, DD

(The symbol D here specifies numeric data).

PRINT USING — It is used to print output data according to a specified format in the IMAGE statement.

Example

150 PRINT USING 100; A

END — Indicates the end of program.

Example

220 END

A few sample programs in BASIC will further clarify:

The following program calculates the average of four numbers 11, 22, 33 and 44.

```
10    READ     A, B, C, D
20    DATA     11,22,33,44
30    LET      X = (A+B+C+D)/4
40    PRINT    X
50    END
```

The following is illustration of a program involving a loop.

```
10    LET      N = 1
20    IF IN    10 THEN 60
30    PRINT    N, N * 2
40    LET      N = N +1
50    GOTO     20
60    END
```

Here is an example of structuring a loop in a more concise manner :

```
10    N = 1    to 10
20    PRINT    N "SQUARED "; N ** 2
30    NEXT     N
40    END
```

It is to be noted that FOR statement (No 10) will cause repeated execution of the statement that follows, upto and including the matching NEXT statement.

Now follows a sample program entitled Inventory Control Update, followed by Inventory Control Report as generated by the program. (The flowchart, Fig. 2, used for explaining COBOL is relevant also in the case of this program, which illustrates most of the primary BASIC statements as well as fundamentals of programming).

```
10    REM      INVENTORY CONTROL UPDATE PROGRAM
20    REM      A$ = STOCK NUMBER, B -QUANTITY ON HAND,
               C$ = DESCRIPTION
30    REM      D=STOCK RECEIPTS, E=STOCK ISSUES, Y = TOTAL
40    PRINT    "INVENTORY CONTROL REPORT"
50    PRINT
60    PRINT    "STOCK      NUMBER      DESCRIPTION      QUANTITY"
70    PRINT    ".........  .........   .............    ............"
80    PRINT
90    LET      Y = 0
100   READ     A$, B, C$, D, E
110   IF       A$ = "0"THEN 20
120   LET      ..X = B + D = E
130   LET      Y = Y + X
140   PRINT    A$, C$, X
150   GOTO     100
160   DIM      A$(6), C$(20)
```

```
170    DATA    "11603", 100, "6MM ROUND BARS", 50,25
180    DATA    "12603", 88, "8MM ROUND BARS", 20,53
190    DATA    13603", 226, "9MM FLAT BARS", 144,362
200    DATA    "14603", 50, "6 MM SHEARED RODS", 10,50
210    DATA    "0",0, "0", 0,0
230    PRINT   "TOTAL"; Y
240    END
```

This program will produce the following report.

Inventory Control Report

Stock No.	*Description*	*Quantity*
11603	6MM ROUND BARS	125
12603	7 MM ROUND BARS	55
13603	9 MM FLAT BARS	8
14603	6 MM SHEARED RODS	10
	TOTAL	198

DONE

Fig. 4. Inventory Control Report

The functions of the various statements are explained below:

Statement No.	**Function**
10 - 40	Remarks statements used to identify the program and variables assigned to the data files.
50 - 80	Cause the report title and field headings to be printed. It is to be noted that the PRINT statements that have nothing following them (60 and 80) cause a blank line to appear in the Inventory Control Report.
90	Assigns the value of zero to the variable *Y*. This statement is required, as the first time that statement 130 is executed the variable Y to the right of the equal sign must have a value assigned to it. This is in accordance with the BASIC rule that all variables in an expression must be assigned a value.
100	A READ statement that assigns the DATA statement values to the specified variables. The first DATA statement fields will be assigned to the variables in the following manner :

A$= 123456

B = 100

SELF-TEST

1. True or False?

   (a) A processor that translates an assembly language program into machine language is called a compiler.

   (b) A set of instructions written by a programmer is referred to as the object program.

   (c) A set of program instructions as translated into machine language is referred to as the source program.

   (d) In multi-programming a CPU simultaneously executes instructions from two or more programs.

2. Which of the following languages will be most appropriate for each of the following applications.

(i)	Inventory processing and update	(a)	BASIC
(ii)	Simulation of inventory system	(b)	GPSS
(iii)	Time-sharing applications	(c)	COBOL
(iv)	Engineering stress analysis	(d)	FORTRAN

3. Put in proper sequence the steps required to translate a source program and carry out execution.

   (a) The data is read into the computer.

   (b) The set of instructions written by the programmer (source program) is read) into the computer.

   (c) The computer is read into the computer memory.

   (d) The compiler translates the source program into machine level language.

   (e) Execution commences.

4. True or false ?

   (a) An assembly language is a low-level language in which mnemonic symbols are used rather than binary based notation.

   (b) An assembly language program is easier to read and interpret than the one written in a high level language.

   (c) COBOL is a high level language designed to solve complex computational problems.

   (d) Macro instructions used in an assembly language program result in a sequence of instructions to be inserted into the user program.

5. Which Division of a COBOL program contains the Configuration Section and the Input-Output section?

(a) Identification Division
(b) Environment Division
(c) Data Direction
(d) Procedure Division

6. True or false ?
   (a) A BASIC program consists of a group of statements.
   (b) The two primary elements in a BASIC statement are identifiers and operators.
   (c) Identifiers consist only of constants, string of characters and numbers.
   (d) Identifiers consist only of variable string of characters, numbers, etc.
   (e) Operators specify mathematical symbols in respect of operations to be performed.
7. BASIC language is normally used in an on-line program development activity where:
   (a) Computational work is significant but files are relatively small.
   (b) The user is untrained in a common business-oriented language for programming.
   (c) The scientific and research needs are paramount.
   (d) The user has no access to a batch-oriented computer system having with the other language capabilities other than BASIC.
8. Match the following in the context of BASIC statements.

(i)	REM	(a)	Supplies value for variables in the READ statement.
(ii)	IF - THEN	(b)	Causes the value of expression to be assigned to one or more variables.
(iii)	GOTO	(c)	Specifies the maximum storing size and causes storage space reserved for storing variables.
(iv)	LET	(d)	causes control to be unconditionally transferred to a specific statement.
(v)	DATA	(e)	is an unexecutable statement.
(vi)	FILES	(f)	tests a relational expression.
(vii)	DIM	(g)	used as pair in a program loop.
(viii)	FOR/NEXT	(h)	one of the methods of introducing data into the computer.
(ix)	PRINT	(i)	causes the values of the specified arithmetic and character.
(x)	READ		expressions to be evaluated.
		(j)	specifies variables whose values are supplied by DATA statement.

9. In a BASIC program, the LET command is the command which:
   (a) Performs the input/output.
   (b) Provides the loop control.
   (c) Performs the arithmetic.
   (d) Determines the end-of-program condition.
10. What entry(ies) are mandatory in the Identification Division of a COBOL program?
    (a) Date, programmer name.
    (b) Program identification.
    (c) Source machine and object machine.
    (d) Programmer name and object machine.
11. Match the following:

(i)	RPG	(a)	a report generating language
(ii)	GPSS	(b)	a simulation language.
(iii)	CODASYL	(c)	an organisation for coordinating the development of COBOL.
(iv)	PASCAL	(d)	a general purpose structured language for teaching programming techniques.

12. A MACRO is:
    (a) A general purpose sub-routine, which can be used to cut programming by performing specific function with fixed parameters.
    (b) A general purpose routine which can be used to cut programming by performing a specific function with variable parameters.
    (c) A special purpose routine which can be used to perform a mathematical matrix manipulation.
    (d) A special purpose routine which is written by a COBOL programmer. Used for producing such programs as provide reports.
13. Match the following:

(i)	Lexical scan	(a)	Used for producing such programs as provide reports.
(ii)	Linkage editor		
(iii)	Generator	(b)	A function of the computer which enables elimination of redundancies and helps in producing condensed source programs.
		(c)	An output of the compiler in the form of object code for locating and inputting all the required modules, determining the total amount of space required by each module, etc.

4. Which of the following COBOL terms would be found only in the Procedure Division?
   (a) PICTURE (PIC)
   (b) VALUE
   (c) OPEN
   (d) SEQUENTIAL.

AN INTERLUDE

Processing an Application Program

It will be useful at this juncture to enter a computer room to gain an insight into the sequence of practical steps, as have to be undertaken, for processing a typical application program (say, payroll). The assumptions are that the program is entered through data entry machines, the data is held on magnetic tape/disk and that the output of the run is required to be printed on a line printer with a copy on magnetic disk.

ONE	*Operator places disk pack containing the program, in the disk drive.*
TWO	*By means of the console keyboard, the operator types in the instructions to the control unit to start.*
THREE	*The control unit activates the data entry file (spool file) and the program is read into the primary storage.*
FOUR	*Again, by means of the console keyboard, the operator tells the control unit in which disk pack the data can be found and which output units to use. The operator makes sure that there is adequate quantity of paper of the right sort in the line printer and that a magnetic tape has been loaded on a second tape deck to receive the output information.*
FIVE	*The control unit then activates the disk pack and the data is read into the primary storage.*
SIX	*The program is then carried out automatically with the control unit ensuring that each instruction is obeyed in the sequence laid down in the program. As the processing continues, there is a constant flow of both data and information between the arithmetic-unit and the storages both primary and backing. Data is read from the spool file and magnetic tape/disk packs; processed, and then written into the printer and the output magnetic tape/ disk.*
SEVEN	*When processing is complete, the control unit prints a message on the console and deactivates all the input and output devices.*
EIGHT	*The last instruction of any program is 'END' and the control unit sees that is carried out.*